Full Circle

Canada's First Nations

John L. Steckley
Humber College

Bryan D. Cummins
McMaster University

Prentice
Hall

Toronto

To my mother, Frances Anne (Cooper) Cummins,
who was always so supportive—B.C.

To my mother, Margaret Lawson Kerton, who long knew this day would come—J.S.

Canadian Cataloguing in Publication Data

Steckley, John, 1949–
    Full circle: Canada's First Nations

Includes bibliographical references and index.
ISBN 0-13-087830-8

1. Native peoples — Canada — History. I. Cummins, Bryan David, 1953– . II. Title.

E78.C2S686   2001   971'.00497   C00-931228-5

ISBN 0-13-087830-8

Vice President, Editorial Director: Michael Young
Editor-in-Chief: David Stover
Acquisitions Editor: Jessica Mosher
Signing Representative: Natalie Witkin
Marketing Manager: Judith Allen
Developmental Editor: Lise Creurer
Production Editor: Julia Hubble
Copy Editor: Reni Walker
Production Coordinator: Peggy Brown
Page Layout: Debbie Kumpf
Art Director: Mary Opper
Interior Design: Julia Hall
Cover Design: Amy Harnden
Cover Image: PhotoDisc

5   05 04 03

Printed and bound in Canada

Prentice Hall

Contents

Chapter 7: The Eastern Subarctic   68

Chapter 8: The Western Subarctic   77

Chapter 9: The Plains   91

Chapter 13: The Treaties   130

Chapter 14: The Golden Lake Algonquin and Algonquin Park: Missed by Treaty   141

Chapter 15: Fighting for Recognition: The Sheshatshit Innu and the Megaprojects   150

Chapter 16: The James Bay and Northern Quebec Agreement   159

PART 4: EFFECTS OF COLONIALISM   167
Chapter 17: Colonialism   167

Chapter 24: Native Governance   240

Chapter 25: Undoing the Past   249

Preface

Why call this book "*Full Circle*"? Primarily, we gave the book this name because the circle is a traditional image that is being used in many ways by Native people today to give more positive meaning to their individual lives, to their identity, and to their various cultures. *Full Circle* conjures drummers sitting in a circle, honouring the dancers who move around them with the heartbeat of their music. The title also suggests sentencing circles: medicine wheels used to apply a holistic approach to mental, physical, and spiritual health. Aside from these traditional connotations, this title is an apt metaphor that reflects the contemporary sense of Canada's First Nations coming full circle to a place they never completely lost but that many were kept from for several generations—a place of cultural strength.

Full Circle attempts to fill a void in the literature dealing with Canada's First Nations. Historically, these types of books focused primarily on either "traditional" or "contemporary" Natives, but rarely both. Representations of First Nations have often been frozen in the past or, on the other hand, denied appropriate cultural and historical context necessary to demonstrate Native issues most effectively. *Full Circle: Canada's First Nations* bridges this gap by examining both traditional and contemporary Native societies in Canada as distinct yet related systems that are perpetually in dialogue. Our approach recognizes that Native societies, like all societies, are dynamic.

In order to achieve the goals of this book, it was necessary to incorporate the complex cultural perspective—the "voice"—of the First Nations. We have therefore made great efforts to reflect this diversity through discussions of Native languages, oral traditions, writers, and individuals. We want readers to add Native words to their vocabulary and understanding, and to become familiar with Native people who have added and continue to add meaning to the lives of Canadians—Natives and non-Natives alike. Anything less would only repeat the silence of the past.

Of course, no one person (or two people in this case) or one introductory textbook on Native people can do much more than just begin to tell their stories. This is partially because of the complexity of the subject and, unfortunately, the enormity of ignorance existing in Canada about Native culture, history, and issues, despite centuries of contact between Natives and non-Natives.

In 1974, Shuswap political activist and writer George Manuel told a story that represents this ignorance. He spoke of a conversation he had had when he was working as a "boom man" for a lumber mill, the first time he had worked with non-Natives on what he termed "an equal footing." A worker with whom he had often sat and talked at coffee breaks said to him:

> "Can I ask you a question 'that's been on my mind for some time?"
> "Sure," I said.
> "Does Indians have feelings?" he asked.
> "Yes, Indians have feelings," I told him.
> "You know, my wife and I often talked about this, and since you're my friend I felt you wouldn't be offended if I asked you. We actually feel Indians is no different from dogs, no feelings at all for kinship." (Manuel and Posluns 1974:3)

Writing this book has decreased our own ignorance. We have learned how Native communities and media are effectively communicating much of what is missing from our society's understanding of Canada's First Nations. We have also discovered positive occurrences in Canada, such as the well-kept secret of how the policing of Native communities is increasingly being taken over by the people themselves. We hope this book helps enlighten readers to the diversity and vitality of Canada's First Nations.

Acknowledgments

Over the years, I have been fortunate in receiving the continued support of colleagues, especially Drs. Hermann Helmuth and John Topic of Trent University. More particularly, I am also forever grateful to Dr. Joseph So for his encouraging words: "Don't ever stop doing research and never stop publishing." I thank my colleague in Golden Lake, Kirby Whiteduck, for sharing his insights and expertise. I also thank my research assistant, Ms. Mithra Dubey, for always being prompt, diligent, and thorough; and Dave Lafleche, for his interest and enthusiasm. Lastly, my family has been an invaluable source of support. Pauline Lore and Frances Cummins—my late mother-in-law and mother, respectively—were always encouraging and are missed. A special thank-you goes to Tricia, who is always there.

Bryan Cummins

While many individuals helped with this work, the first thanks are reserved for my mother, Margaret Lawson Kerton, who always believed in me as a writer. Thanks also to my colleagues at Humber College, particularly Gina Antonacci, who helped us get started, and Wayson Choy, whose experience and reassuring confidence in my ability helped get the book finished. I thank my students for their genuine interest in the project (and not just to suck up to the teacher). My dog, Egwene, was a great help in knowing when I needed to write and when I needed to play border collie hockey. Lastly, I thank my wife, Angelika (Angie), whose support is never praised enough.

John Steckley

We would both like to acknowledge the contributions of Russ Blackbird, James Pardy, and Jim Silverstone, whose reviews provided great insight into shaping this text. We thank the following editorial team at Pearson Education Canada for their guidance: Nicole Lukach, the first person to believe in our vision, and Jessica Mosher, who helped us see it through; Lise Creurer, for her light hand on sensitive egos; Natalie Witkin, for signing us; Reni Walker, who had a whole new experience copy editing all the Native words; and, of course, Julia Hubble, the relief pitcher/editor who got us through the ninth inning.

ORAL
TRADITIONS

INTRODUCTION

Before Europeans came to their country, the aboriginal peoples of Canada recorded their laws and history and taught their lessons orally. They did not have or feel the need to write them down. Father Paul Ragueneau, a Jesuit missionary who lived among the Huron in the first half of the seventeenth century, wrote the following around 1646 on what he early learned about oral traditions:

> The elders of the country were assembled this winter for the election of a very celebrated Captain [i.e., leader or chief]. They are accustomed, on such occasions, to relate the stories which they have learned regarding their ancestors, even those most remote,—so that the young people, who are present and hear them, may preserve the memory thereof, and relate them in their turn, when they shall have become old. They do this in order thus to transmit to posterity the history and the annals of the country,—striving, by this means, to supply the lack of writing and of books, which they have not. They offer, to the person from whom they desire to hear something, a little bundle of straws a foot long, which serve them as counters for calculating the numbers, and for aiding the memory of those present,—distributing in various lots these same straws, according to the diversity of the things which they relate. (JR30:61)

In this chapter, we will be looking at a number of traditional Native stories. When you read the stories presented, it is good to keep in mind that they are only parts of much fuller stories, that they are translated from the more meaningful versions in their original languages,

1

that in being written they lose a lot because you don't get the tone and expression of the storyteller, nor the way he or she might act out parts of the story. You are getting a cheap imitation. Further, you will see in the stories a mixture of the sacred and the humorous almost simultaneously. Some of the jokes may not seem all that funny to you, but you must realize that humour requires a common context. Think about times that you have tried to explain a funny part of a movie or a television show to someone who did not see the movie or is not a regular watcher of the show. They probably didn't laugh like you did. Finally, keep in mind that one significant purpose of these stories is to teach and you (and the authors of this book) often do not have enough understanding to get the full benefits of what they have to teach.

TRUTH AND STORIES

All cultures respond to a human need to explain how it is that things are the way that they are. But we cannot completely know the answers. When we tell stories about the past, we can point our stories in the direction of truth as such makes sense to us, but there is no absolute truth that we can arrive at as a final destination. What happened is open to different interpretation and debate when we talk about what took place five minutes ago, let alone in centuries past. A definition of truth that works well in looking at history comes from Basil Johnston, an Anishinabe scholar who works for the Royal Ontario Museum in Toronto, in his article, "One Generation from Extinction" (Johnston 1991). He wrote that when an Anishinabe person says that someone is telling the truth, the person uses the term **w'daeb-awae**. This does not just mean that what that someone has said is true:

> It is at the same time a philosophical proposition that, in saying, a speaker casts his words and his voice only as far as his vocabulary and his perception will enable him. In so doing the tribe was denying that there was absolute truth; that the best a speaker could achieve and a listener expect was the highest degree of accuracy. Somehow that one expression "w'daeb-awae" set the limits of a single statement as well as setting limits on all speech. (Johnston 1991:12)

People who thus followed the rule of restricting what they say to what they actually knew would be respected by their listeners:

> Of that man or woman they would say "w'daeb-awae." Better still, people would want to hear the speaker again and by so doing bestow upon the speaker the opportunity to speak, for ultimately it is the people who confer the right of speech by their audience. In order to understand a people, you must try to see their truth. (ibid.)

CREE ORAL TRADITION: ÂTALOHKÂNA AND TIPÂCIMÔWINA

There are different types of stories, with different amounts of stress on what is important in terms of such factors as teaching, entertainment, and an attempt to get at what "actually happened." C. Douglas Ellis interpreted from listening to Cree Elders living by the west coast of James Bay that those people had two basic kinds of stories, expressed in Swampy Cree as **âtalohkâna** (usually translated as "legends") and **tipâcimôwina** (singular, tipâcimôwin; typically translated as stories, news, historical narratives, or personal experiences).

- twork.

BOX 1-1   Where Does the Name "Turtle Island" Come From?

Abr probe
nee.

Sacred Stories.

You might have heard people talking or writing about North America as "Turtle Island." That expression comes from an origin story shared by a good number of peoples. The story that is told below is one version held by the Wyandot people, descendants of the Petun and Huron, both Wendat, who had lived in southern Ontario until the 1650s. This version was told originally in Wyandot in 1912 by Catherine Johnson, who spoke Wyandot almost exclusively. Her translator was Mary Kelley.

When the story begins, there are two worlds. One, which is in the sky, is inhabited by a small number of people. The other, which is covered with water, is inhabited by animals:

uising work does.

> Several brothers and sisters were living together. The only meal they had every day consisted of a single basket of corn, the daily yield of their corn-patch.
>
> Tired of thus gathering the corn for every meal, the young woman thought to herself one day, "now, maybe, the easiest way is to cut the stalks [and gather the ears once and for all]." So she cut down the corn stalks and gathered them all. Her brothers, in their grief, spoke to her

and said, "You have spoilt everything and ruined our subsistence! You have wasted it all!" They dropped her through a hole into the ocean.

Wild geese were roaming about on the waters. Their leader exclaimed, "A body is falling from above. Let us all gather close together!" And the woman from above fell gently upon the backs of the Geese, as they were all assembled together. One of them spoke after a while and said, "We are getting tired. Let someone else now take our place." The Turtle, emerging from under the waters, said, "It is I, the next!" And the body of the woman fallen from above now rested upon the Turtle's back.

Then the Toad went [down] and came back with a mouthful of dirt. She gave the dirt to the woman fallen from above, saying, "Do this! Sprinkle it about at arm's length where you lie." The Toad meant her to sprinkle the [grains of] earth all around her. So the woman did; and the land grew around her. She rose and began to walk about the new land... . (Barbeau 1915)

We are all living on the top of the Turtle's shell now.

Âtalohkâna are stories that take place at a time when the world was changing into the world we know today. The main figures are cultural heroes, usually individuals who are tricksters such as **Weesakechahk** or **Chahkabesh**, animals who can readily talk to humans, or spirits who give advice to humans. The trickster figure has a number of different counterparts across Canada: Glooscap of the Mi'kmaq, Nanabush of the Ojibwa, N'api of the Blackfoot, and Coyote or Raven among the peoples of British Columbia.

Weesakechahk (from which is derived the English term "whisky jack," referring to a kind of jay) stories often have him trying to fool someone in an attempt to get food. In the end, he usually gets tricked himself. In the often-told story of the "Shut Eye Dance," he cons birds such as geese, loons, and ducks to dance a dance in which they keep their eyes shut. As they dance, he knocks them over the head. Eventually, one of the birds (a loon in one version) finds out what is happening and warns the others. The loon gets the flattened shape it has today for its efforts. Weesakechahk himself gets tricked in the end, as he puts the birds he can't eat head first into the sand, with their feet sticking out. The next morning he discovers that people have come and have stolen his birds, leaving only the feet, so he didn't earlier suspect a thing.

Chahkabesh is small, only 15 centimetres tall in some stories. He lives with his older sister and is very curious about things, which often gets him in trouble. As with all such figures, the world changes because of his adventures. In the last story of the Chahkabesh cycle of stories, he ignores his sister's warning not to look at the full moon, so it draws him in. We can see him there today.

Another kind of story that fits into this type is the **pâstâmowin** (plural, pâstâmowina), that is, speaking ill of sacred things, blasphemy that brings retribution (see Box 1.2). These stories are about what can happen if you break the rules by which a "good person" lives. In one such story, a man makes fun of someone else, ridiculing him for being bitten by a rabbit. He ends up dying by being bitten to death by rabbits.

The equivalent of the âtalohkâna among other peoples talk about a number of subjects, of which origins is a common theme. The following two are examples, one from the Peigan, and the other from the Dogrib.

Peigan Tradition: Old Man, the River, and the Origin of Death

N'api [Old Man] created the first Peigan woman and child out of clay. They walked down to the river where he told them who he was, and in a story both comical and sad, the following happened.

The woman asked N'api whether or not they would live forever. N'api replied saying that he had not ever thought about that before, and came up with a plan. He would take a piece of dried buffalo dung and throw it in the river. If it floated, when people die, they would come back to life after four days. But if it sank, they would die and not return to life. He threw the buffalo chip in the water, and it floated. However, the woman tried the same trick with a stone, saying:

BOX 1-2 **The Meaning of Pâstâmowin**

You can see something in the meaning of pâstâmowin by seeing how the root "pâstâ" is used in other words:

pâstâh: bring evil on s.o. [someone], cast an evil spell on s.o.

pâstâho: utter s.t. [something], which brings evil or bad luck on oneself

pâstâm: speak so as to bring evil on s.o.

pâstân: put pressure on s.o./s.t. to the point of cracking

pâstin: crack s.o./s.t. (e.g., an egg) while holding it

"No, I will throw this stone in the river; if it floats we will always live, if it sinks people must die, that they may always be sorry for each other." The woman threw the stone into the water, and it sank. "There," said Old Man, "you have chosen. There will be an end to them." (Sanders and Peek 1973:38)

Not long afterwards, the woman's child died. She cried a great deal, and said to N'api:

"Let us change this. The law that you first made, let that be a law." He said: "Not so. What is made law must be law. We will undo nothing that we have done. The child is dead, but it cannot be changed. People will have to die." (Sanders and Peek 1973:38)

The Origin Story of the Dogrib

The following is an English version of the story of the origin of the Dogrib, as was recorded by Petitot in 1891. Interestingly, the woman who marries the dog in this story is a Yellowknife.

[A] Tatsanottine [Yellowknife] woman. . . was dwelling with her two brothers N. of Great Slave lake. One day a strong and handsome stranger arrived, who, on the proposal of the brothers, took her for his wife. Waking in the middle of the wedding night she found her husband gone and heard an animal crunching bones at the fireplace. . . The same thing happened the next night. The bride and her brothers lighted torches, but found no animal. On the third night one of the brothers hurled a stone axe in the corner whence the noise of gnawing proceeded. A cry of agony was heard, and when a torch was lighted a great black dog was seen twitching in the death throes. As the human husband did not reappear, the brothers chased forth their sister because she had married a dog-man, a sorcerer, a Tlingit. She wandered into the treeless desert of Coppermine r, where in the course of time she brought forth a litter of puppies, which she kept hidden in a bag of reindeer skin. When they could run alone she was astonished to find on her return from hunting, prints of infants' feet in the ashes. Hiding one day, she saw the little dogs leap from the bag, becoming handsome children as soon as they reached the light. She ran and pulled the string of the bag, but not before three succeeded in jumping back in the dark hole. Two boys and two girls were kept forcibly in the daylight, and these became the progenitors of the Thlingchadinne [Dogrib]. (Hodge 1971:454)

Tipâcimôwin

The following is a tipâcimôwin called "How Ghost River got its name." Versions of this story are told on both sides of James Bay.

The Iroquois and the Cree were fighting each other. The Cree had a shaman who could predict when the Iroquois would arrive at a particular place:

So the People prepared. . . to lie in wait for the Iroquois for them to drift downstream. And they killed many then by doing this, having foreseen where they would lie in wait for them. They also took many as slaves.

And that is the reason why Ghost River is today called by that name, Ghost River. (Ellis 1995:177)

For historians, both Native and non-Native, a tipâcimôwin can be a tremendous source of information. Thanadelthur ("Marten Jumping" or "Shaking") was an eighteenth-century Chipewyan woman who escaped capture from the Cree. She was also instrumental in connecting her people with the fur trade, perhaps saving them from being totally defeated by

BOX 1-3   The Story of the Powerful Old Dogrib Man

The Dogrib became quite involved with the fur trade during the nineteenth century. A good indication of their attitude towards some of the traders working for the Hudson's Bay Company (H.B.C.) can be seen in the following tale told by **Vital Thomas**, a Dogrib storyteller, in 1966. It begins with a group of Dogrib travelling a long way to a post to ask for credit for much-needed supplies, only to be turned down by a stingy company clerk. Credit was often necessary for northern Natives to be able to trap, even to survive, and the H.B.C. often used it to create Native indebtedness. As the group returned home empty-handed, they came across a second group, who had among them a wise and spiritually powerful old man. He was asked to help them, and he agreed. The old Dogrib man started to sing "Hey hey, Pale Man! hey hey" and worked his arms down into the earth, about half the length of his arms. Then he said, "Here is the man we have been talking about" and hauled the H.B.C. clerk up out of the ground as far as his armpits:

> Then he began to rub his hands over the man's head as if he was pulling or cupping up water. All of a sudden he clapped his hands loudly and said, "Here it is! I got his mind right here in my hands!" And the Hudson's Bay man sank back through the earth. "He had gone home now without his mind. We got to hurry to get there. We got to do our trading fast and right back because I can't hold his mind very long." (Nabokov 1991:47-8)

the Cree. The written record of the time did not tell us her name, much of what she thought, and other important aspects of her story. Her story was preserved in oral tradition, however, and she became a hero to her people. In 1879, more than 150 years after she died, Chipewyan Alexis Enna-azè told her story to have it written down, filling in many of the gaps.

However, perhaps the most important role of a tipâcimôwin or any Native story lies in the fact that it teaches but does not lecture, allowing the listeners to learn from it what they can. This is well described by Mohawk writer Patricia Monture-Angus:

> The tradition of oral history as a method of sharing the lessons of life with children and young people...had the advantage that the Elders told us stories. They did not tell us what to do or how to do it or figure out the world for us—they told us a story about their experience, about their life or their grandfather's or grandmother's or auntie's or uncle's life. It is in this manner that Indian people are taught independence as well as respect because you have to do your own figuring for yourself. (Monture-Angus 1995:11)

The Great Law of Peace: An Iroquois Oral Tradition

A good example of an oral tradition and the benefits that such might hold to a people is what is known in Mohawk as **Gayanerengo:wa**, "it is a great good," known typically in English as the Great Law of Peace. This is a tradition that probably has lasted about 550 years.

While it is hard to put a precise date on it, most writers estimate its origin being from 1420 to 1550, while some say that it originated in 1451 and others 1536. This is because there is a reference in some versions of the story to an eclipse of the sun. There was such an eclipse in June of 1451 and in 1536.

A good insight into the period of time from which the Great Law of Peace came can be seen by looking at the archaeology of southern Ontario during this period, a good example of how archaeology and oral tradition can be used to reinforce each other (not an unusual thing). During this period, known as the Late Prehistoric by Ontario archaeologists, the population of southern Ontario peaked. Communities were clustering into what can be called tribal units. There is ample evidence of war. The pottery of the St. Lawrence Iroquoians, people who disappeared after Cartier encountered them in the 1530s, is found in six or seven of the easternmost Huron villages. Some villages were surrounded with multiple rows of palisades. Bones dug up from that period often show signs of violent death. It was within such a conflict-ridden social environment that the Great Law of Peace arose.

The following is a very basic outline of what the story is about. Keep in mind that the authors learned about what goes into this story primarily from written versions and have never heard the story told in an Iroquoian language. Their knowledge, therefore, can only be partial, far from complete.

Storyline

A woman and her adult daughter went to live on their own, apart from any community. They were worried about the warfare that surrounds them. The place where they lived is usually identified as being somewhere around the Bay of Quinte, at the eastern end of the northern shore of Lake Ontario. The nation that these two women belonged to varies according to source, but most people now believe that they were Wendat. To the daughter was born a boy called Deganawida, a name for which there is no translation, a name that no one since him can have. He is often referred to as the Peacemaker. His grandmother had a vision of the Creator in which the Creator expressed that her grandson would bring peace to his people.

When he was grown up to be a young man, he decided to share with the warring five Iroquoian tribes living to the south of him the vision of peace he had borne since childhood. He went first to the Mohawk. In a Mohawk community he was accepted by the peace chief, whom he named **Hiawatha** (sometimes translated as "He makes wampum"). Hiawatha spoke for him and helped to bring about the acceptance of the Peacemaker's vision, both with the Mohawk and with the others.

After the Mohawk accepted the vision, the two men went separately to speak with the neighbouring Oneida. Around that time, tragedy struck Hiawatha. His three daughters died. In mourning, he created strings of wooden beads that resembled shell-bead wampum. The Oneida invited him to their community using their copy of his wooden wampum. This is sometimes said to have been the origin of using wampum for this purpose. The Oneida were convinced that the Peacemaker's message was the path they should take.

The biggest obstacle to the Peacemaker's dreams came from the shaman/war leader of the Onondaga, named **Thadodaho**. This being the case, the Peacemaker arranged that the Onondaga, the middle of the five nations, were the last visited. There, Thadodaho was approached not only by the Peacemaker and Hiawatha, but by the four other nations who had accepted the vision. The Cayuga were convinced, followed by the Seneca, although the war leaders of the Seneca had not accepted the Peacemaker's message of peace.

The Peacemaker had to face some spiritual challenges along the way. For example, before he could make it to the major community of the Onondaga, he had to cross a lake. It is said that three times Thadodaho tried to use sorcery to create a storm on the lake, blowing back the Peacemaker's canoe. Three times the Peacemaker faced the challenge and calmed the waters of the lake.

At the eventual meeting of the five nations, the Peacemaker spelled out how the people would be brought together in one confederacy, or league. They would be divided into two moieties. One, referred to as the "fathers" (sometimes the older brothers), would be made up of the Mohawk, Seneca, and Onondaga. The other, referred to in council as the "sons" (less often as the younger brothers), would be made up of the Oneida and the Cayuga. The chiefs would sit in council with the "fathers" on one side of the fire and the "sons" at the other.

Issues would be resolved through consensus, as opposed to majority vote. When an issue was to be discussed, it would first be presented to the Mohawk chiefs. They talked about it and arrived at some kind of consensus. The Mohawk would pass on their consensus decision to the Seneca, who would then discuss the issue by themselves and try to arrive at a consensus, ideally one in support of what the Mohawk had decided. The two groups would then appoint a speaker to take this view "across the hearth or fire" to the Oneida, then the Cayuga, who would deal with it as the others did. If there were two different opinions coming from the Mohawk and the Seneca, the "sons" had to consider both. Finally, the "sons" would give their view, ideally a consensus, to the Mohawk, who would take it to the Onondaga. The Onondaga would ratify the agreement. If there was a split opinion, then the Onondaga were responsible for breaking the tie or for suggesting a new compromise to be discussed by the others.

The council of the confederacy thus formed was to be made up of 50 chiefs or sachems (an Algonquin word now in English). The distribution was that the Onondaga would have 14, the Cayuga 10, the Mohawk and the Oneida 9 each, and the Seneca 8. As there was no collective vote, this was more an honouring distribution than one that gave power to the nations that had the greatest numbers. The Onondaga were further honoured by being named the Firekeepers, meaning that they would host the meetings of the council. The Seneca war chiefs, who were finally convinced to accept the Peacemaker's vision, were honoured by being named the Doorkeepers, controlling access to the meetings of the council.

Also established through the Great Law of Peace was the Condolence Council, which used the invitation wampum first employed with Hiawatha. The Condolence Council is the most complex ceremony of the league, lasting anywhere from six to eight hours. Its purpose is to mourn a sachem's death and to "raise up" his successor.

The symbols of the confederacy were also established. Their collective name would be based on the noun root **nonhs**, meaning "house," combined either with the verb root **yonni**, meaning "to be extended, finished, whole," or the verb root **onni**, meaning "to make." The name would then be (in Seneca) **Hotinnonhysyonni**, "they are of the extended house," or **Hotinnonhson:ni:h**, "they build a house." At that same time, a great white pine tree of peace was planted, with weapons used to fight each other thrown at the roots, symbolizing that the five nations would not fight each other. Each nation also brought an arrow that would be part of a group bound together by sinew, to show that they were stronger together than they were apart.

BOX 1-4 The Gibson Manuscript

To get some sense of how long an oral tradition can be, consider the Gibson manuscript, the only complete written version of the Great Law of Peace recorded in one of the languages of the league. It was dictated by Chief John A. Gibson to the anthropologist Alexander A. Goldenweiser in 1912. Gibson was born in 1849. His mother was Seneca of the Turtle clan, so when he was of appropriate age, he received the Seneca sachem name of Skanyatai:yo? ("Handsome Lake"). His father was Onondaga, with the sachem name of Thadodaho. He was linguistically gifted. It is said that he was equally fluent in Cayuga and Onondaga, could speak Seneca, Oneida, and some Tuscarora, and sometimes performed rituals in Mohawk. His dictation of the Great Law of Peace, in Onondaga, took up 514 handwritten pages (with no translation). When it was finally published in 1995 with a translation, that part of the book took up 701 pages. Gibson died of a stroke at 63, just four months after completing his dictation of the manuscript.

GETTING IT RIGHT 1-1 The Song of Hiawatha

In 1855, Henry Wadsworth Longfellow wrote a famous poem called "The Song of Hiawatha." In that poem, Longfellow had Hiawatha as an Ojibwa hero, living "by the shores of Gitchi Gumme" (Ojibwe for "large lake," referring to Lake Superior), where "stood the wigwam" (Algonquian term for "house") of Nokomis (Ojibwe for "grandmother"). This is comparable to writing about a great German hero named Napoleon who lived in Berlin in the home of his Oma (German for "grandmother").

Native Individuals 1-1

Chahkabesh: A mythical figure, said to be only 15 centimetres tall, found in a number of traditional Cree stories.

John A. Gibson: A Seneca/Onondaga man whose recitation of the Great Law of Peace has helped to preserve that important oral document.

Hiawatha: Mohawk man who aided the Peacemaker in bringing the Great Law of Peace to his people.

Peacemaker: A man thought to be Huron/Wendat whose visions led to the development of the Great Law of Peace and thereby the Confederacy of the Iroquois.

Weesakechahk: A mythical figure, the culture hero/trickster in many Cree stories. ↳ 'Elder Brother'

KEY TERMS

âtalohkâna (Cree)

Gayanerengo:wa (Mohawk)

pâstâmowin (Cree)

tipâcimôwina (Cree)

CONTENT QUESTIONS

1. How did Basil Johnston define "truth"?
2. What is the origin of the name "Turtle Island"?
3. What is the Great Law of Peace?
4. How are âtalohkâna and tipâcimôwina different?
5. How did the Dogrib get their name?

 ## WEBLINKS

www.indigenous.bc.ca/v3/Vol3Ch6s2tos2.3.asp
The Royal Commission on Aboriginal Peoples Report includes a discussion of the importance of language and oral tradition for Natives in Canada. The complete RCAP Report, an excellent resource, recent and well-researched, is at <www.indigenous.bc.ca/rcap.htm >

www.civilization.ca/membrs/fph/storytel/indexeng.html
The Canadian Museum of Civilization's "Storytelling" exhibit—which you can visit in a virtual tour—surveys six examples of Native storytelling and the oral tradition.

www.ilhawaii.net/~stony/loreindx.html
Over 100 stories and legends of various North American Native groups have been compiled at the Native American Lore Index Page.

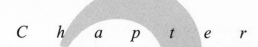

THE PEOPLING OF THE AMERICAS

INTRODUCTION

As we saw from the story of Turtle Island, and as we will see in the discussion of the Huron word "ondecha" in Chapter 3, "Connections to the Land," it is part of traditional beliefs for the people to say that they began life in the Americas, that they have been here "from time immemorial." It is similar to the set of beliefs set down in the book of Genesis in the Bible. Like Genesis, these stories are part of the covenant that the people hold with the spirit world, with the creator, guiding people who want to lead a good, spiritual life on the right path. You don't have to share the beliefs to know that the covenant must be respected.

While respecting the covenant and agreeing that Natives are the First Nations of the Americas by thousands of years, anthropologists do not agree with the notion of special creation of people in the Americas. What they believe begins with evolution. Scientific evidence demonstrates that from at least 4.4 million years ago to about 1 million years ago, all the hominids that were our ancestors (and their cousins) lived in Africa. At least about 900,000 years ago, the first hominids left Africa to travel east to China and Indonesia and, later, north into Europe. According to science, Natives could not have emerged first in the Americas; they had to get here from somewhere.

Long ago, anthropologists noticed that the aboriginal peoples of the Americas were similar in a number of ways to certain peoples living in Asia. Among the shared traits are straight black hair, relatively little facial or body hair, very infrequent baldness, brown skin, broad faces, and prominent cheekbones, which, some Native writers have said, came from leaning on their hands waiting for their treaty rights to be respected. Some Native groups also have the epicanthic eyefold identified as "looking oriental." Athapaskan-speaking peoples have been noted as sharing the so-called shovel-shaped incisors found among early humans and contemporary populations in Asia. Linguistically, the Athapaskans also have tones as part of their words, as is typical of languages on the Pacific Coast of Asia.

THE BERING STRAIT THEORY

How would they get to the Americas from Asia? Anthropologists look to the Ice Age and its effects on the Bering Strait that now separates Siberia from Alaska. The last Ice Age, referred to in North America as the Wisconsin, lasted, with some warming periods, between 75,000 and 10,000 years ago. During the colder periods of the Ice Age, a large amount of the world's moisture was locked up in the glaciers and ice sheets. Ocean levels dropped by more than 90 metres. The Bering Strait became a land bridge more than 1,600 kilometres wide known as Beringia. Large land mammals (mastodons, extra large bison, camels, and sloths) moved across the bridge and people followed them. The optimal time for entry was just before and just after the height of glaciation (24,000–22,000 B.C. and 10,000–8000 B.C.) when the climate was sufficiently cold for Beringia to be dry and warm enough to permit a large, ice-free corridor. It is generally accepted in the anthropological community that there were two corridors into the New World, the most frequently used being one that ran through central Alaska up the Yukon River valley. It then continued through the Mackenzie Valley in the Northwest Territories and south into the western provinces. There were huge continental glaciers on both sides: the Cordilleran centred over the Rocky Mountains while the Laurentide, about 2,900 metres thick at its maximum, centred over Hudson Bay.

The biggest question for anthropologists lies in how long ago Native people came to the Americas. The standard theory held that about 12,000 years ago people came across, and the aspect of their material culture that identified them to archaeologists was the **Clovis point**, named after the site in New Mexico where they were first discovered. Clovis points are spear points that are fluted or grooved, which aided in the killing of large mammals by making the blood flow more rapidly out of the wound. Clovis points have been found from roughly 11,600 to 10,200 years ago, situated across the Americas from Alaska all the way south to Tierra del Fuego at the southern tip of South America.

There are problems with confining the history of the Americas to only 12,000 years. It is difficult to imagine that people could have moved so rapidly from Alaska to Tierra del Fuego. There were people in northeastern Asia long before 12,000 years ago. Japan has at least one site dating back to 31,000 B.P. ("before the present"), for example. Slowly but surely, evidence is accumulating that points to human habitation prior to 12,000 B.P. The Monte Verde site in Brazil, which dates back at least to 12,500 and is accepted by virtually all anthropologists as valid, has established conclusively a pre-Clovis presence. And there are other, older sites that might gain the same level of acceptance with further research. These include the Meadowcroft Rockshelter in Pennsylvania, which would seem to be at least 15,000 years old, with some evidence suggesting an earlier layer that could go back as far as 19,000 years.

How long, then, have humans been in Canada? It is hard to say. One reason for this lies in the distinct possibility that the first peoples in Canada lived along the Pacific Coast. This makes sense since the coast is the closest part of Canada to Asia. It also makes sense when you consider languages. By far, the greatest variety of Native languages in Canada and the

United States exists on the West Coast. This suggests that people have been there longer than anywhere else. Why, then, aren't the oldest sites found there? It could be that the oldest sites are underwater. Living right along the coast is a good idea, because there is a great variety of foods there. However, when the Ice Age finally ended, the water level rose by at least 60 metres and the early coastal sites (if they existed) would have been covered in water.

KENNEWICK MAN AND THE BOAT PEOPLE

There is another theory, formerly rejected but now becoming popular in some anthropological circles, concerning how at least some early peoples got to the Americas. It suggests they travelled by boat. On July 28, 1996, two college students found some bones in Kennewick, Washington, by the shores of the Columbia River. They notified some anthropologists, who first thought the bones to be of a White settler, as the skull had a long head and a narrow and projecting face, as opposed to the more usual rounded head and wider and flatter face of aboriginal people. It wasn't very long before it was discovered that the skeleton was much older than initially thought, between 9,300 to 9,600 years old.

This individual, dubbed Kennewick Man (he was a man of some 45 to 50 years of age when he died), has touched off a number of controversies. One is the question of who "owns" the bones. The Native American Graves Protection Act and Repatriation Act of 1990 allows for ancestral remains connected with a particular people to be reburied. Five nations of the American Northwest Coast have pursued a court case to have the bones repatriated. Scientists see this as a unique opportunity to study early Native history. But, as Armand Minthorn, a religious leader of the Umatilla people, states, "We already know our history...It is passed on to us through our Elders and through our religious practices."

The other controversy lies in who this individual and other ancient skeletons like him found in the American West (e.g., the 9,400-year-old body wrapped in a mat at Spirit Cave, Nevada) and in South America (most notably the possibly 11,500-year-old "Luzia" found at Lapa Vermelha, Brazil) do and do not look like. In some ways (e.g., with the long heads), they look less like modern Native peoples and more like Austronesian-speaking peoples who have been in the island of Taiwan since at least 5,500 years ago and who travelled by boat to such far-flung places as Madagascar off the southeast coast of Africa, Samoa, Hawaii, Easter Island (not far from South America), and New Zealand. Could they have also travelled to the Americas? Kennewick Man similarly is said to resemble the Ainu. The Ainu are the indigenous people of Japan, living in that country and the islands immediately to the north of it for thousands of years before Japanese speakers moved in an estimated 2,000 years ago. They look different from the Japanese newcomers in a number of ways, including that they are relatively hairy. Natives of the Northwest Coast are known to have been hairier than Natives elsewhere in North America. Some Ainu customs are shared with Northwest Coast peoples, including making clothing out of bark (well processed with boiling and pounding), and having death songs. The boat trip may not have been all that difficult. The Japan Current has been known to take fishermen's net floats across the relatively narrow northern Pacific to the West Coast.

Much needs to be discovered and explained before the boat traveller theory for at least part of the peopling of the Americas can be considered to be proved.

EARLY PERIODS OF NATIVE HISTORY

In *A History of the Native People of Canada: Volume I (10,000–1,000 B.C.)*, one of the most influential archaeologists in Canada, J.V. Wright, Curator Emeritus of the Canadian Museum of Civilization, laid out what he felt were the first 9,000 years of Native history in Canada. As it represents, more or less, the orthodox archaeological view, it will be discussed as showing how archaeologists have set up these early periods.

What he sets up as Period I is 12,000 to 10,000 B.P. The material cultures of these times, known as Palaeo-Indian and Northwest Palaeo-Arctic, stretch across Canada with sites in the Yukon, the Prairies, Ontario, and Nova Scotia. The Northwest Palaeo-Arctic shares some features with what is called Dyuktai culture in Siberia, the latter dating back at least to 18,000 B.P. The shared features include wedge-shaped core tools (i.e., tools made out of the core of a rock, not the flakes that are broken off), microblades, bifacial knives (i.e., knives with a blade on both sides), and burins (stone tools for working with antler and bone).

Period II is set from 10,000 to 6,000 B.P., representing what is conventionally called the Early Archaic (10,000 to 8,000 B.P.) and Middle Archaic (8,000 to 6,000 B.P). It was a time when new weapons technology (e.g., including the "atlatl" or spear thrower) was applied to changing and localized environments, with less of the megafauna (i.e., big mammals) being hunted. People, in their material culture at least, began to change.

One important point should be made here. As archaeologists often say, the stone tools cannot talk. We cannot know what languages their makers spoke. At this stage, it is difficult to make firm connections between material cultural traditions that bear the names that archaeologists give them, and the peoples who live in Canada now. Human history shows that people don't usually stay in the same place for thousands of years. The people moved. Migrations are often spoken of in the traditional stories of the peoples. The Anishinabe people, for example, speak of moving west into Quebec, Ontario, and the Prairies from a place by the Atlantic.

By Wright's Period III (6,000 to 3,000 B.P.), more connections can be made. There is a good chance that the Middle Maritime culture of this period provided the ancestors for the Algonquian speakers of the Atlantic provinces and Quebec. Some have argued that the contemporary Middle Great Lakes-St. Lawrence culture may have been ancestral to at least some of the Iroquoian speakers of the contact period, although this connection is far from being proven. A much better case can be made for the Middle Shield culture becoming the Cree, Ojibwa, Innu, and possibly the Beothuk.

As we will see in Chapter 9, "The Plains," there was a great deal of disruption in that area after contact with the introduction of the horse and the gun, moving peoples in and out of the Prairie provinces. However, the Blackfoot and possibly some of the Siouan peoples may have at least, in part, their origins in the Middle Plains culture. The Middle Plateau culture has been linked with at least the Shuswap currently in the Plateau region. There seems to be more continuity in the Northwest Coast, with probably most of the current peoples descending from ancestors in the Early West Coast culture of this period, as can also be said for the Middle Northwest Interior culture and the Athapaskan speakers of the Western Subarctic. Although, as we will see in the Arctic section, there were technological innovations and migrations in the Arctic, the current Inuit have as their primary ancestors at least some of the groups forming the Early Palaeo-Eskimo culture.

HISTORY, PREHISTORY, AND THE MYTH OF THE "NEW COUNTRY"

Traditionally, non-Native historians made a distinction between "history" and "prehistory." History was a period of time recorded by writing and written about by historians trained in the analysis of written documents. Of course, this would be European writing for Canada. Prehistory was a period of time recorded through archaeology and through the oral traditions of the people. History books, then, tended to have short, cursory, introductory sections on prehistory, while the history was the focus. This is misleading. It creates the illusion, which the authors have heard, and no doubt the readers have heard as well, that this is a "new country." A similar illusion is created that Native people have only been on this land for "a few hundred years," an expression used more than a few times by politicians opposing Native peoples fighting for their rights, and even by judges, who have denied that Natives have rights. One of the authors has asked the following question of students taking Introduction to Anthropology and Canada's Native Peoples courses:

How long have Native people been on this land:

a) 500 years,

b) 500 to 1,000 years,

c) 1,000 to 5,000 years, or

d) more than 10,000 years?

It is no longer surprising to have students believing the second and even the first answer is right, when it is "d" that is correct. Before you read this chapter, which answer would you have given? As a short assignment, students have been asked to ask this question of five people, record their answers, and then record their response to the right answer. Many students have reported not only that relatively few of the people asked gave the right answer, but that some even defended, with heated arguments, the rightness of their wrong answer, sometimes claiming they read it somewhere.

Consider what would be the impression in the teaching of Canadian history if the distinction between prehistory and history were eliminated and there was an attempt to give an equal balance to all periods of history. If you live in Ontario, your history is at least 10,000 years long. How much of your history is Native history alone? The first Europeans came to Ontario a little less than 400 years ago. Do the math. At least 96% of your history is Native history before the coming of Europeans. Think of it like this: if there were an Ontario history textbook with ten chapters, each chapter depicting an equal percentage of history, then the first nine chapters would be Native history alone, as would be most of the tenth and final chapter. If you want to learn your history, you need to learn about Natives first, and for a long time.

KEY TERMS

clovis points
epicanthic eyefold
hominids

CONTENT QUESTIONS

1. What is the Bering Strait Theory?
2. Who is Kennewick Man?
3. Why can't we find some of the earliest sites on the West Coast?

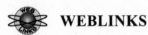 **WEBLINKS**

www.washington.edu/burkemuseum/kman/exhibit.htm
The Burke Museum of Natural History and Culture, in Seattle, maintains an online exhibit called "Kennewick Man on Trial."

www.canadianaboriginal.com/international/inter25.htm
The Canadian Aboriginal Web site <www.canadianaboriginal.com > reproduces a *New York Times* article on the Bering Strait Theory.

3

CONNECTIONS TO THE LAND

INTRODUCTION

It is hard to express in a few pages the Native connection with this land, a connection forged over thousands of years of living on this land. It can be seen, a bit, in talking about ancient sacred sites, such as the 40-ton Majorville Medicine Wheel in the Plains that dates back 5,000 years (see Chapter 5) or Mnjikaning, the 4,500-year-old fish weir that gave Toronto its name (see Box 3.1).

Months of the Year

The connection can also be seen, another small bit, in the terms the different peoples have for the months of the year, which are so much more connected with what is happening all around them than the terms that French and English speakers use. Take the following terms for two different months and you might see this:

April
Abenaki: Sugar Moon
Maliseet: Arrival of Spring Moon
Mi'kmaq: Egg-Laying (i.e., of waterfowl)
Ojibwe: Sucker Moon
Huron: Pickerel Come
Mohawk: Leaves Are Leaking a Little
Blackfoot: Frog Moon

BOX 3-1   Toronto: Poles in Water

Some 4,500 years ago, people wanting to catch fish in the fast-moving waters flowing between Lake Couchiching and Lake Simcoe in southern Ontario came up with a smart idea. They put cedar poles in the water to build a fish weir or trap, thereby fencing in the fish. Some of those poles are still in the water. The first name written down for this fish weir appeared in the Huron language in the 1600s. They referred to Lake Simcoe as **Ouentaronk**, "poles that cross." Later that century, the Mohawk moved into the area. The earliest rendition of their name for the lake was **Lac Tar8nteau**, "trees or poles in water," a name later written as "Toronto." By the end of that century, the Ojibwa, who had long known about the site and had visited it as allies of the Huron, moved into the area and took over the site. The name they gave to the fish weir and surrounding area is written today as Mnjikaning, "at the [fish] fence."

According to Ojibwa oral traditions, the fish weir site had significance beyond that of being merely a place where food could be obtained. It was a sacred place. According to one modern Ojibwa writer:

> People came great distances to spend time at this good place. They would help fix the Fish Fence. They came with their wounds and soreness looking for the healing powers of our medicine people. They came with their bad feelings looking for good therapy. Ceremonies were held often. More and more people came to spend some time at this good clean place. Lots of food. Lots of good talk about the future. It was a nice safe place to spend some time. People came from further away just to stay awhile. (Douglas n.d.:8)

Much of this sense was lost as the Ojibwa began to be inundated with non-Natives. The people who lived in the area were divided into several bands living separately from each other. The local Ojibwa community came to be known as Rama. Today, there is a strong move to protect the site and have it serve as a centre of revitalization of traditions and identity, a sacred place once more. The Rama community officially declared its name in 1993 to be Mnjikaning.

Moose Cree: Goose Moon
Tlingit: First Flowers Appear

August
Abenaki: Eating Moon
Maliseet: Feather Shedding Moon
Mi'kmaq: Young Birds Are Fledged
Ojibwe: Blackberry Moon
Huron: Corn Is Made
Mohawk: Time of Freshness, Newness
Blackfoot: When Choke Cherries Ripen
Moose Cree: (Geese) Flying Up Moon

Everything Gets Used: The Caribou

This link with the resources provided by the land can be observed in the descriptions of how completely Native groups used particular resources supplied by the land, such as the caribou and the bison. The following is taken from Part 2 on the culture area of the Arctic (Chapter 5, "The Arctic") in a discussion of the caribou (see also Chapter 9, "The Plains," regarding the bison):

> Caribou hair is hollow, trapping air, thus making it ideal for insulation, softness and lightness, ideal for clothing, footwear, tents, bedding, blankets, and bags. It has been calculated that fifty caribou were required to meet the needs of each person for a single year, with eight to eleven skins per person for clothing and twenty to thirty skins for tent coverings (Wright 1996:425).

E.S. Burch provides a good sense of the use of other parts of the caribou:

> Excellent thread can be made from their back sinew, and components of tools, weapons and utensils can be manufactured from their antlers and bones. People who consume all of the meat, viscera, stomach contents (rich in vitamin C), and fat of caribou are able to satisfy all of their nutritional requirements. If caribou are available in sufficient numbers at appropriate times of year, and if they are fully utilized, they can provide for the total subsistence requirements of a human population. (Burch 1995:129)

Ondech(r)a and Yandarachrio: The Huron Speak of the Country

The connection to the land can especially be seen in how the peoples themselves talk about or use the words that mean "country," "bush," or "land." Look at how the following two such Huron/Wendat nouns are used, as expressed in seventeenth- and eighteenth-century French-Huron dictionaries (Steckley 1993:18–21). We use these early recorded terms to demonstrate that this type of speaking is traditional to Natives, not some politically correct, New Age way of speaking.

The noun stem **-ondech(r)**- was the most often used word for "country." It is derived from a verb **-onde**- meaning "to have as one's country."[1] When used with the verb root **-ndionk**-, "to be skilled, able," it had the following meaning:

ondechandionk/to be able, capable on the land/

être bon piéton, être homme de voyage /to be a good pedestrian, traveller/ (Potier 1920:293)

The noun -ondech- did not just refer to the physical entity "country, earth," but also to the religious beliefs and practices of the Huron (collectively called **ondech(r)a**), as they were believed to have come out of the earth where they lived. In the following entry, using the verb root **-nde,ar**- meaning "to rise, raise," we see that a person could be referred to as being drawn out of the earth, the country when born:

atiaondechandera /she rose up, lifted up in the country/

c'est la qu'elle vint au monde /it is there where she came into the world. (Potier 1920:181)

In the following dictionary entry, the noun -ondech- is used with the verb root **-inde**- "to drag, draw" (literally meaning "dragged from the country") to mean something such as "since the beginning of time" when referring to the practice of carrying a corpse in a traditional burial ceremony:

on,8atondechinde on,8ahoarinnenha8i

/we draw, drag it from the country, we carry the corpse/

nous avons cette sorte de danse depuis le commencement, la naissance, l'origine de notre pais /we have had this kind of dance since the commencement, the birth, the origin of the country./ (Potier 1920:323)

Ondech(r)a also meant "country" in the political sense. Political leaders were sometimes referred to as Hennondecha ("they, country"). Part of the ceremony designed to bring about reconciliation when a Huron had killed another was referred to as **xondaie onsahondechari**, "this is that which rejoins the country."

The noun **-ndarach(r)-** is derived from the verb root -ndare-, "to dwell, exist" (Potier 1920:280). By itself, it was usually used to mean "dwelling, residence, habitation." The use of the expression "First Nation(s)" is new to the English language but is an old concept among Native people.

The seventeenth-century Huron used -ndarach(r)- in combination with the verb root -io-, meaning "to be large, good, great" to express the notion of a people being the original or first people in an area. This can be clearly seen in the following examples:

",andarachrio

être les maîtres habitans, les vrais, le/s/ naturels, les 1re habitants; les originaires par opposition a d'autres qui viennent ensuit se joindre a ces

"to be the master inhabitants, the true, the native, the first inhabitants; the natives in opposition to the others who came afterwards to join with these first ones" (Potier 1920:280)

Les sauvages sont les vrays et naturels habitants de ce pais

/The "savages" are the true and native inhabitants of this country/

on,8e n'on,8e daat endarachrio dex'ondechate

/humans who are humans are the very good, great ones in their dwelling place, this country/ (FH1693)

It should be noted that in the last entry, on,8e n'on,8e ("humans who are human") is a term used by speakers of Iroquoian languages to refer specifically to Iroquoian peoples and more generally to Natives as opposed to non-Natives.

KEY TERMS

yandarachrio (Huron)
-ondech- (Huron)
on,8e n'on,8e (Ongwehon:we; Huron)

CONTENT QUESTIONS

1. What does the word "Toronto" mean and what does that meaning refer to?
2. What is the significance of the Toronto site in terms of Native connection to the land?

3. In what ways can the caribou supply the needs of the people?

4. How are Native language names for months of the year different from those in English?

5. What do the noun stems **-ondech(r)-** and **-ndarach(r)-** mean and how are these meanings different from the nearest English equivalents?

 **WEBLINKS**

conbio.rice.edu/nae
The Web site known as "Native Americans and the Environment" is a good starting point for environmental issues, and under the "Internet" area of the Web site you can find an annotated list of other helpful Weblinks.

www.fnen.org
The Web site of the First Nations Environmental Network, a Canadian organization with a focus on environmental activism.

www.ankn.uaf.edu/iksgraph.html
The Alaska Native Knowledge Network's Web page on Indigenous Knowledge Systems provides information about traditional ecological knowledge and sustainable resource planning.

NATIVE
LANGUAGES

MISCONCEPTIONS ABOUT NATIVE LANGUAGES

For a long time in history books, in classrooms, and in people's minds, a good number of misconceptions have existed concerning Native languages. There are few areas that Canadians are more ignorant about. In the first part of this chapter, we will deal with three main misconceptions about Native languages.

Misconception 1: All Native Languages Are Related

Imagine you were a child looking up the following words in a dictionary:

chipmunk: n., small squirrel of N. Amer. [Indian name *achitamon*] (Morehead and Morehead 1972:78)

totem: n., tribal badge or emblem, usually an animal...[N. Amer. Ind., hereditary emblem] (385)

moccasin: n., Amer. Ind. soft shoe... [N. Amer. Ind.] (255)

skunk: n., small N. American animal like a weasel, which defends itself by emitting an evil-smelling fluid...[N. Amer. Ind. *segankw*] (352)

Reading this, and knowing no better, you would assume that "North American Indian" is a language. People frequently speak and write as if there were only one aboriginal language.

Individuals are said to be "speaking Indian." As we have just seen, dictionaries and books about place names tell us that some term is "an Indian word for" something. This would seem to be a smaller part of a larger stereotype that "all Indians are the same."

Imagine if a Blackfoot speaker wrote that "three" or "trois" is "European for" **nioókska**. Yet, as the terms for that number sound alike in almost all European languages, that statement is more true than to say that any word "is Indian for" anything. There is greater language variety in Native Canada than there is in Europe. As we will see, there are 11 aboriginal language families and isolates spoken in Canada, as opposed to only three native to Europe: Indo-European, which includes the vast majority of all European languages; Finno-Ugric, which includes Finnish, Hungarian, and very few other languages; and Basque, which stands alone.

Native Language Families

What do we mean by language family? A **language family** is a group of languages that have been demonstrated to be related. How is that relationship demonstrated? A variety of means is employed to analyze the association. Linguists look at commonalities in how words are constructed (**morphology**) and how they are put together into sentences (**syntax**). Iroquoian languages, for example, all have five different conjugations of verbs and nouns, based on the set of forms the pronominal prefixes take. Table 4.1 demonstrates how the Huron language works.

Linguists also look for cognates. **Cognates** are words, or roots of words, that sound similar, have similar meanings, and, ultimately, come from the same word. Table 4.2 shows the following cognate terms in Algonquian languages for "fish," and for specific fish, all believed to have originated from a single word for fish.

When a long list of cognates between two languages has been compiled, then it can be said that the two languages are related.

There are 11 aboriginal language families in Canada, ranging in size from large families encompassing many separate languages (e.g., Algonquian) to language isolates with no close relatives (e.g., Kutenai). The map of these language families shows a peculiar pattern.

TABLE 4-1	Five Huron Conjugations		
Conjugation	**Huron Term**	**Pronominal Prefix**	**English**
a- stem	skwatatiak	skw-	you (plural) talk
	ontatiak	on-	they (indefinite) talk
Consonant stem	skwahiaton	skwa-	you (pl.) write
	ehiaton	e-	they (indef.) write
e- stem	skwehieras	skw-	you (pl.) remember
	ayehieras	ay-	they (indef.) remember
Yen-/i- stem	skwentenrha	skw(en)-	you (pl.) have pity
	aitenrha	a(i)-	they (indef.) have pity
o- stem	tsoritha	ts-	you (pl.) season it
	ayoritha	ay-	they (indef.) season it

TABLE 4-2	Some Cognates in the Algonquian Language Family			
Language	**Root**	**Term for Fish**	**Terms for Specific Fish**	
East Cree	-name-	names	namekush	lake trout
			nameu	sturgeon
			namepii	white or red sucker
Ojibwe	-nme-		nmegos	lake trout, brown trout
			nme	sturgeon
			nmebin	sucker, carp
Abenaki	-nama-	namas	namagw	lake trout
Delaware	-name-	namées	————	————
Blackfoot	-mii-	mamii	sisákkoomii	dolly varden trout

Eskimoan goes right across the northern edge of the country. Apart from the Inuit in Labrador, the Atlantic provinces have only one language family: **Algonquian**. One more, **Iroquoian**, is added in Ontario and Quebec (except for the Inuit). In the Prairie provinces, there are three language families: Algonquian, **Siouan**, and **Athapaskan**. British Columbia breaks the mould. It has eight different language families, six of which exist in no other province (see Box 4.1).

BOX 4-1	Native Languages and Their Families

Language Family	Language	Location in Canada
Algonquian	Abenaki	Quebec
	Blackfoot	Alberta
	Cree	Quebec to Alberta
	Delaware	Ontario
	Innu	Quebec and Labrador
	Maliseet	New Brunswick
	Mi'kmaq	Atlantic Provinces and Quebec
	Ojibwe (Odawa, Algonquin, Saulteaux)	Quebec to British Columbia
	Potawatomi	Ontario
Athapaskan	Beaver	Alberta and British Columbia
	Carrier	British Columbia
	Chilcotin	British Columbia
	Chipewyan	Manitoba, Saskatchewan, Alberta, N.W.T.
	Dogrib	N.W.T.
	Han	Yukon
	Hare	N.W.T.
	Kaska	Yukon
	Gwich'in	Yukon
	Sarcee	Alberta
	Sekani	British Columbia

Language Family	Language	Location in Canada
	Slavey	N.W.T.
	Tagish	Yukon
	Tahltan	Yukon
	Tutchone	Yukon
Eskimo-Aleut	Inuktitut	Labrador, Nunavut, Quebec, Yukon, N.W.T.
Haida (isolate)	Haida	British Columbia
Iroquoian	Cayuga	Ontario
	Mohawk	Ontario, Quebec
	Oneida	Ontario
	Onondaga	Ontario
	Seneca	Ontario
	Tuscarora	Ontario
Kutenai (isolate)	Kutenai	British Columbia
Salishan	Bella Coola	British Columbia
	Comox	British Columbia
	Cowichan	British Columbia
	Halkomelem	British Columbia
	Lillooet	British Columbia
	Okanagan	British Columbia
	Pentlatch	British Columbia
	Sechelt	British Columbia
	Semiahmo	British Columbia
	Songish	British Columbia
	Squamish	British Columbia
	Straits	British Columbia
	Thompson	British Columbia
Siouan	Dakota	Manitoba and Saskatchewan
	Nakota	Manitoba and Saskatchewan
Tlingit (isolate)	Tlingit	British Columbia
Tsimshian	Southern Tsim	British Columbia
	Nass-Gitksan	British Columbia
Wakashan	Haisla	British Columbia
	Heiltsuk	British Columbia
	Kwakwala	British Columbia
	Nitinat/Nootka	British Columbia

Dialects

Not all the people who speak the same language can understand each other. Sometimes people speak dialects that are different enough to make comprehension difficult. A dialect is a variation of a language. Dialects might differ in pronunciation or might have different words for the same thing, or different meanings for the same word. Fred Wheatley, a respected teacher of Ojibwe, used to tell stories of how speakers of different dialects of Ojibwe would joke around with each other using dialect differences at logging camps. People asking someone to pass "that which spreads," meaning butter, would have knives given to them instead since the word for "butter" was also the word for "knife" in another dialect.

Cree has a good number of dialects, as it is spoken across Canada's north from Quebec to Alberta. One of the main distinguishing characteristics concerns a particular **phoneme**, or sound. Table 4.3 illustrates this. The word compared is the verb form "it is windy":

TABLE 4-3	Key Feature in Distinguishing Cree Dialects				
Plains Cree	**Woods Cree**	**Swampy Cree**	**Moose Cree**	**Attikamek**	**East Cree**
-y-	-th-	-n-	-l-	-r-	-y-
yotin	thotin	notin	lotin	rotin	yuutin

The distinction between dialect and language isn't just linguistic. There is a social or political element as well. The Innu are a separate people, so are considered to speak a separate language, but look at Table 4.4 to see how their language is more similar to East Cree than East Cree is to Swampy Cree.

TABLE 4-4	Similarities Between Separate Languages		
Innu (Montagnais)	**East Cree**	**Swampy Cree**	**English**
amishkw	amiskw	amisk	beaver
chiyaashkw	chiyaashkw	kiyaask	gull
chinosheew	chinushew	kinoseew	pike
ooteenaw	utenaaw	ooteenaw	village, town
nameekwosh	namekush	nameekos	lake trout

Misconception 2: There Are Only a Small Number of Words in Native Languages

A strong stereotype exists that states there can only be a few words in aboriginal languages. This stems originally from the fact that the early missionaries, explorers, and other early contact Europeans who first provided written descriptions of aboriginal languages often wrote of them in terms of what they didn't have. Many, for example, stated their first impression was that Native languages lacked "abstract terms." If they would have lived with the people and learned the languages in any depth, they would have discovered that such was not the case. However, later writers drew the information for commentary more from the earlier works, unthinkingly teaching modern readers a misconception. A classic case is of Father Francis X. Talbot, who, in his 1956 publication *Saint Among the Hurons: The Life of Jean de Brébeuf*, wrote that Brébeuf was "puzzled as to how he could express abstract and spiritual concepts. Their vocabulary was limited to specialized, concrete, material things that they knew through their senses" (Talbot 1956:74). This reflects Brébeuf's often cited first impressions of the Huron language. Brébeuf later learned much of the sophistication and potential for abstraction of the language. Unfortunately, he never wrote about that. His negative first impressions are what have survived into modern times.

Clearly, what Talbot should have said was that terms for abstract thoughts deeply rooted in French culture did not have ready equivalents in the language of a different culture that didn't have those concepts. The Huron didn't have terms for "heaven" and "hell," for example, because in their belief system they felt that each people, ideally, went to a community specific to them (e.g., the Huron went to their afterlife community while the Mohawk went to theirs). They didn't have a term for the single soul of Christian belief because they believed that we have two souls (see Box 4.2). The Huron who first learned French might have thought the French language was incomplete because it lacked terms for important concepts in their language. It must, for example, have been difficult for them initially to speak about corn in French (see below).

The misconception that we are dealing with here reflects the simple notion that many non-Natives find it difficult to imagine what terms in aboriginal languages would apply to. It reflects their ignorance of the huge world of possible meanings and of the great deal of knowledge held by traditional elders.

It is important to be able to know that there are meanings not well reflected in English or French, but represented by single words in aboriginal languages. One standard way of doing this is to show specialized vocabularies (e.g., the now famous infinite number of terms in Inuktitut for "snow" or "ice"). The Huron and other Iroquoians, for example, had corn as the staple of their diet. It should, therefore, not be surprising to discover that they had a number of terms relating to corn that have no equivalents in English or French. See Table 4.5 for a sampling of Huron terms for "corn."

Another way to counteract the notion that aboriginal languages contain a small vocabulary is to show something of the productive capacity of these languages. A brief illustration will demonstrate. Huron verb roots are the central building blocks around which the vast majority of words are constructed. The greater part of learning to speak, understand, read, or write Huron is understanding the morphology or structure of the verb. This is quite different from English or French, both of which are languages that, compared with many languages spoken around the world, have relatively small words with relatively few meaningful parts or **morphemes** (see discussion below).

In an eighteenth-century Huron dictionary, approximately a thousand verb roots were recorded. One way of getting a ballpark figure on how many words might be generated in this language would be to take one verb root, **-atey-** ("to burn"), and see how many words could be generated with it. A very conservative estimate of 7,669 was arrived at. If all verb roots are, on average, this productive, then there are theoretically more than seven-and-a-half million words in Huron. See Table 4.6 for some examples.

TABLE 4-5	Some Huron Words for "Corn"
oionkwenda	a small ear of corn
ondista	the stem of an ear of corn
oiontsenda	point of an ear of corn that is not covered with kernels
oia	a row of corn kernels
oiachia	the bran or inner part of the kernel
oechia	the skin of the kernel
onniona	germinated seed or kernel
awenienta	non-germinated seed or kernel

There are many more words for corn in Huron. We will never know all the terms, since the language is now extinct. Our only remaining sources of information are the dictionaries compiled by French Jesuit missionaries. They did not know much about corn, so could not have entered into a knowledgeable discussion in Huron on the subject.

TABLE 4-6	Words Generated from the Huron Verb Root -atey- ("to burn")
Huron Word	**English Translation**
uteyen	there is burning, a fire
teutende	there is not going to be fire
sateyaht	you (sing.) make fire
oteyannon	many things are burning
tewayateyasennik	fires don't start for me
esakwateyas	your shoes will burn
onteyatakwa	one makes fire with it (i.e., flint)
atayateyatandiha	come make me a fire!
atayateyatakwendiha	come make me a fire out of such material!
hoteyataskon	he frequently makes fires

Typically, modern dictionaries of aboriginal languages do not even come close to showing all the possible numbers of words that there are or could be. In the Delaware-English section of John O'Meara's recently published *Delaware-English/English-Delaware Dictionary*, there are more than 7,000 entries, the vast majority of them verb forms from which other words can be created. O'Meara gives, on average, about four or five words for each entry as a small, representative sample of what the root can create.

If you were to count all the Delaware words in that dictionary, you would get a number probably over 30,000. To see something of the productivity of Delaware, look at the following examples in Table 4.7, using the same noun root.

TABLE 4-7	Delaware Word Productivity: The Noun Root -aandpee- ("head")
English	**Delaware**
bang s.o.'s head against something	paakaandpéexumeew
be bare headed	mihtáandpeew
be red headed	maxkáandpeew
bump one's head	paakaandpexiin
crack one's head	pwahkaandpéexiin
forehead, top of head	laawáandpe
get hit on the head with a maul, have a bump on the head	mookkulaandpéexiin
have a swollen head	makwáandpeew
give s.o. a swollen head, hit s.o.	makwaandpéeheew
hit s.o. and give them a lump on the head	makwaandpehtéeheew
have a big head	xwáandpeew
have a bloody head	mohkwáandpeew
have a cracked head, have a cut on one's head	pasaandpéew
fall and....	pasaandpéexiin

TABLE 4-7 Delaware Word Productivity *(continued)*	
have one's head swell up	paasáandpeew
have a dirty head	niiskáandpeew
have a flat head	pàkáandpeew
have a flat head (of blow adders), have one's head go flat (when blowing)	pàkaandpéhleew
have a good head on one's shoulders	wuláandpeew
have a long head	kwunáandpeew
have a lump or bump on one's head	wchihkwáandpeew
have scabs on one's head	mukuyáandpeew
have one's head out in the open	mihtaandpéexiin
have one's head lying by the length of something (e.g., by a door)	sahkaandpéexiin
have one's head sticking out	saakáandpeew
lie with one's head sticking out,	
stick one's head out	saakaandpéexiin
have one's heads together (plural)	kchukaandpeexíinook
have s.t. tied around one's head	kulaandpeepíisuw
have s.t. wrapped around one's head	kpaandpeepíisuw
hit someone on the head	chàhwaandpéeheew
nod one's head	tàtamakohkwaandpéhleew
rub, pet someone on the head	siikwaandpéeneew
scratch one's head, have an itchy head	kshiipáandpeew
shake one's head	kwàkwtukohkwaandpéhleew

In his posthumously published dictionary of Western Abenaki, Gordon Day aptly says the following of this endangered language:

> No dictionary completely exhausts the resources of a language, and a dictionary of an Algonquian language must inevitably fail to exhaust its seemingly unlimited potential for word-making. In this edition I have only tried to make available a sizable sample from my own data. I hope it will be possible in a later edition to add more of this data and the vocabulary contained in the works of other writers and the notes of other field workers. (Day 1994:14)

His dictionary contained over 12,300 words.

Misconception 3: Native Languages Can't Be Used to Express "Modern" Life

All languages have equal structural capabilities to develop new terms. We discussed earlier how many terms the Huron had for corn. Yet, less than 2,000 years ago they didn't have corn. When they began to grow corn, their vocabulary adapted. Further, when they first came into contact with the French, they quickly developed a term for "gun" based on a word meaning "hollow tube" and a word for "metal" based on a noun root that referred to the hard skin of flint corn and to fish scales.

BOX 4-2	An Abstract Concept in Huron: The Dualic

The **dualic**, usually represented by -t(e)-, expresses "twoness." We find it used with a verb root that specifies a number, for example, -i- "to be two."

> **Tendi**: They two are two (the Huron number "2").

> **Teyiatontariye**: It is where a large body of water is two (i.e., Quebec).

Verb roots that express an obvious twoness (e.g., "to join," "to cut"), and those actions requiring two legs or two eyes also employed the dualic. However, it was also used more abstractly. The prefix is used with verbs that speak of uncertainty and of disturbances of the balanced order of life. Take the following for example:

> **Tehatoxwach**: He practises divination (i.e., possibly determining whether a disease is caused by a malevolent spirit or by a sorcerer).

> **Teoskendendakwan**: She is as pale as a ghost (i.e., from fear or disease).

The verb root **-ndawa-** means "to hunt." Adding the dualic prefix to the verb gives it a more sinister nature, as is expressed in the following:

> **Tehatendawaha**: He goes hunting for a long time without encountering other hunters or animals (e.g., is in a state of uncertainty).

There is often a sense of conflict that comes with the addition of the dualic to a verb, as can be seen by contrasting two forms of the same verb, one having the dualic:

> **Haonywandiyonkenni**: They surpass us in mind, are more intelligent than we are.

> **Tehaonywandiyonkenni**: They fool us, trick us, out-think us in a conflicting way.

The conflicting, uncertain nature of twoness can be related to three aspects of Huron society: souls, political structure, and culture heroes. First, the Huron believed that everyone had two souls: the mind and the heart. The former was associated with wisdom, peace, the thoughtful words of elders speaking in council. The latter was associated with strong emotions, such as sadness, anger, bravery and the desire for revenge. It was said that sometimes the heart was so powerful that it drove the rational mind out of a person. When the person calmed down, the mind returned. The potential for conflict between the two souls was always there. Second, the Huron divided political functions into those of war and those of peace, with separate leaders and meeting houses. The interests of each function could come into conflict with the other, the existence of both a stage for potentially destructive political uncertainty.

A spiritual parallel exists in the twin culture heroes who transformed the earth into the state in which we find it today. They worked at cross-purposes from the moment of their births. The first born would act to help the Huron who were to come, while the second born would negatively alter what his older brother had done. Eventually, the older brother killed his younger brother, leaving just one, and a state of peace.

Keep in mind here that the fact that English is the most prominent language internationally has nothing to do with the structure of English. It is not bigger because it is better. It is bigger because of the power and influence of the countries in which it is spoken. Its structural adaptability is no better than the structural adaptability of all Native languages. Think of how English speakers dealt with the definitive "modern" piece of technology, the computer, with terms for an animal (the "mouse"), old religious symbols ("icons"), and the product of a pre-Industrial Revolution manufacture ("web" from "weave"). In medicine, compare how the English language borrowed a Latin term for an animal (a crab) to refer to "cancer" with how the Cree used a term in their own language for another animal (the worm):

ê-mowikot manicôsa
"he/she has cancer"
[literally: "little worms eat him/her"]

manicôsa k'âyâwât omihkohk
"he/she has leukemia"
[literally: "he/she has little worms in his/her blood"].

(Wolfart and Ahenakew 1987:213)

The following "modern" terms in Ojibwe all stem from **-mzinaa-**, which refers to "making marks":

mzinaaksijgan = camera

mzinaakziged = to print, type, make out notices

mzinaatesing = to be a projected picture

mzinaatesjigan = movie projector

From a cognate term in Blackfoot, we get the following:

áísfínaakiohpi = television

iihtáísínaakio'p = camera

Before we complete this section, we need to discuss one of the structural differences between many Native languages and French and English: word length. Languages differ in how they form sentences. Some build relatively long words, typically verbs, and so have only a few words in a typical sentence. Other languages have relatively short words, so they have more words in a sentence (and word order tends to be seen as significant). Both sentences are roughly equal in length and equally complex or simple to learn how to form. It is only the boundary mechanisms that are different. For those languages with relatively long words, the boundaries are primarily between morphemes or word parts. For those languages with relatively short words, most of the boundaries are between words. The number of boundaries are about the same. Imagine you are a speaker of Mandarin and hear (not see) the following two sentences:

1. Ahayateyatakwendiheskwa.
2. He often used to go make fire for me out of such material.

Remember that we do not typically pause between words when we speak. To the Mandarin speaker, both sentences sound to be about the same length, the second being perhaps a little longer. However, to English speakers, the first sentence looks more

complicated when both sentences are written. There is a "visual prejudice" against it because the boundaries cannot be seen. Fewer visual clues are there. But say we break the
longer word down into constituent parts (i.e., morphemes), as demonstrated in Table 4.8
below:

TABLE 4-8	Huron Morphemes and Their Meanings	
Huron Morpheme	**Type of Morpheme**	**Meaning**
a-	translocative	motion away from the speaker
-hay-	pronominal prefix	"he" (as subject), "me" (as object)
-atey-	verb root	"to burn"
-at-	causative	causing something, "to make"
-akw-	instrumental	"out of such material"
-endi-	dative	"for"
-he-	dislocative	motion, intention, "go"
-s-	habitual	"often"
-kwa-	past	"used to"

Count up the morphemes: Huron has nine, English has fifteen (the word "used" has two
morphemes, "use" and "d"). The Huron sentence is simpler.

Most aboriginal languages employ the structural option exemplified by Huron in this example. One of the problems that those working on preserving aboriginal languages have to
deal with is the expectation (sometimes held by Native peoples themselves) that words
should be shorter. They have to overcome the visual prejudice that shorter words, but more
of them, is somehow "easier" to understand than fewer, longer words.

A QUESTION OF SURVIVAL

We have seen that the structure of Native languages allows for adaptability to modern life.
The big question that remains to be answered, however, is whether or not the languages
will survive to do that adapting. In 1982, linguist Michael Foster stated his belief that only
three Native languages would survive: Cree, Inuktitut, and Ojibwe. In the census of 1996,
only 11 of the 52 Native languages were reported as having more than a thousand speakers
(see Table 4.9).

However, the people are determined to preserve the languages. A solid core of Native language teachers is being developed across the country. There is not a language that is not
being recorded frantically and taught in some fashion. You could not say that 20 years ago.
There are success stories of minority languages around the world (e.g., Maori in New
Zealand and Welsh in the United Kingdom) that have not only survived but have increased
their population of speakers.

Innovative strategies are required. And it is very important that the next generation be involved. A disproportionate number of older people are among the speakers. However, information technology will be helpful on both counts. Northern communities, where the
languages are strongest, can and have overcome isolation with computers. Some languages
will become extinct, but the extinction of all these languages is not inevitable.

TABLE 4-9	Number of Speakers of Native Languages
Language	**Number of Speakers**
Cree	76,475
Inuktitut	26,840
Ojibwe	22,625
Innu	8,745
Mi'kmaq	6,720
Dakota	4,020
Blackfoot	3,450
South Slavey	2,425
Dogrib	2,030
Carrier	1,510
Chipewyan	1,305

BOX 4-3 The State of Native Languages: The Problems to Be Overcome

In 1995, a committee of elders and language resource people studied seven southern Shuswap communities with an eye to seeing the state of the Shuswap or Secwepemctsin language and figuring out what kind of programs the schools could offer to improve that state. They identified in fluent speakers people who could carry on and understand a conversation in Secwepemctsin for as long as the situation required, with vocabulary, grammar, and pronunciation that was acceptable to the elders. They found that one community had no fluent speakers, that only about 3.5% of people in the communities surveyed were fluent speakers, that virtually all fluent speakers were in their fifties or older, and that those who could speak the language often did not use it in the home, especially with the younger generations. These language problems are those that Native communities across Canada have to face. The Shuswap are confronting these problems with at least one immersion school and with university courses from beginner to advanced levels offered through the Secwepemc Cultural Education society acting in liaison with Simon Fraser University. Like other First Nations, they are considering introducing the language into daycare centres, with the help of the Elders. Time will tell whether this will be enough.

DIFFERENT EXPECTATIONS: NON-NATIVE

Apart from specific misconceptions, there are also problems flowing from the fact that non-Natives bring different expectations of languages with them when they think of aboriginal languages. The Indo-European language family is a large one, including a vast majority of the languages spoken in Europe. Languages with which most Canadians have at least some familiarity (English, French, Spanish, and Italian) are relatively closely related and have many similar features not shared as a package by languages belonging to other families. This leaves most Canadians with expectations about what languages "should be like," that draw from a narrow perspective of a fundamental sameness that, from the perspective of a speaker of an aboriginal language, reaches across the relatively superficial differences that exist between these languages.

Gender is a significant part of Indo-European languages in a number of different ways. In the Romance branch of this family, which includes French, Italian, Spanish, and Portuguese, among others, gender exists as an either/or category for nouns, affecting the articles and pronouns used with the nouns. English speakers in French classes are familiar with the difficulty of trying to figure out or remember the gender of a noun. Gender also appears in pronouns: "he" versus "she," "*il*" versus "*elle*." Inuktitut, and languages belonging to the Algonquian and Athapaskan families, do not make this distinction in their pronominal prefixes. Look at the following examples in Table 4.10.

Context will determine what gender you are talking about. I remember well a Cree from Waswanipi who, as a mature student and the mother of three children, told the story in class of returning as a child from residential school and listening to the grandmother tell a traditional story. The child interrupted the grandmother and asked "Are you talking about a man or a woman?" The grandmother just replied, "You have been with the White people too long."

How this language feature reflects the ways of thinking of the Ojibwe and their fellow Algonquians is open to discussion. In this case, we believe that this linguistic feature, built into the structure of the language itself, sheds light on traditional male-female relations in many First Nations cultures, where women were considered relatively equal with men (Brizinski 1993; Medicine 1983; Ezzo 1988; Ross 1996). This does not mean to imply that such relative equality did not exist among speakers of other language families, just that it finds expression in these cultures in this way.

DIFFERENT EXPECTATIONS: NATIVE

Hierarchy of Person

It is not enough to say what aboriginal languages are not, even when it is explaining how they do not fit into a stereotyped view, or how they do not fulfill the linguistic expectations of a French or English speaker. We should look, too, at what they do have, what monolingual speakers of aboriginal languages might expect, but find missing in English or French. We have chosen a few areas to give a small taste of what those expectations might be.

TABLE 4-10	The Gender of Pronominal Prefixes	
Language	**Word**	**Translation**
East Cree	Tikaashteneu	He/She inadvertently alerts him/her to his/her presence
Delaware	Ihalóhkeew	She/He used to work
West Abenaki	Bonasimek	One (i.e., she/he) puts or places, one is putting or placing
Blackfoot	Aaksittahsiinihkiwa	She/He will sing a victory song
Ojibwe	Niwaabamaa	I see her or him

We will begin with pronouns. Ojibwe has what is referred to as *hierarchy of person*, which reflects the very basic cultural value of *respect*. What this means is that the second person (i.e., "you"), always comes first in a word. In "**Niwaabamaa**," meaning "I see him/her," **-ni-** indicating the subject "I" goes first. It is different with the construction for "I see you," which is "**Giwaabaamin**." In this case, the prefix is **-gi-**, which is for the "you." The suffix **-min-** indicates that it is "I" that is doing the seeing. This hierarchy of person can also be seen in the distinction between first person plural (i.e., "we") forms. Algonquian languages distinguish between the "we" that includes the listener(s), called the first person inclusive, and the "we" that does not include the listener, called the first person exclusive. Take the example of the verb **-gindaas-**, "to read." Look at how the first and second person forms work in Table 4.11.

You can see that the inclusive form begins with "you" (i.e., with **-gdoo-**) and ends with "we" (i.e., with **-mi-**), while the exclusive form begins and ends with "we" (i.e., with **-ndoo-** and **-mi-**).

This is not just a linguistic feature, but one that reflects cultural preference as well, a cultural preference for considering the "you," the other(s). Consider this reflection by linguist Roger Spielmann. He observed this cultural preference virtually every day in Pikogan, part of the Algonquin First Nation, when people were making decisions. People he spoke with about decision making told him that they thought a lot about how what they were deciding would affect their families, extended families, their communities, and even their First Nation before making a major decision such as to go away to school or to take a job in another location—not the usual strategy of non-Natives. As Spielmann recounts:

> When making the decision to move away from the community to come to teach at the university...,the decision was made by my wife and myself. We really didn't take into account at all our...(...parents, grandparents and relatives), nor did we share the same sense of "community" as shared by the people at Pikogan. And we certainly didn't consider (or care) how our decision might affect our nation or our "people"! As a corollary to that, the Elders would regularly comment on how difficult it must be for my wife to live so far away from her parents (who live in British Columbia). It was so rare for someone from Pikogan to actually "move away" from their support systems of the extended family and community. (Spielmann 1998:46)

Animate and Inanimate in Algonquian Languages

Among speakers of Algonquian languages, an important expectation is the distinction of **animate** versus **inanimate**. It is just as all-encompassing as gender is in French and other Romance languages, affecting such key elements as noun plurals and the endings of verbs.

TABLE 4-11	First and Second Forms of Pronouns in Ojibwe			
Word	**Translation**	**Pronoun**	**Person**	
Ndoogindaas	I am reading	Ndoo-	first	
Gdoogindaas	You (sing.) are reading	Gdoo	second	
Ndoogindaasmi	We (excluding listeners) are reading	Ndoo- -mi	first	first (plural)
Gdoogiindaasmi	We (including listeners) are reading	Gdoo- -mi	second	first (plural)
Gdoogiindaasam	You (plural) are reading	Gdoo- -am	second	second (plural)

TABLE 4-12	Animate and Inanimate Nouns in East Cree		
Singular	**Meaning**	**Plural**	**Meaning**
Animate			
Es	sea shell (hinged)	esak	sea shells
Eskan	antler	eskanak	antlers
Inanimate			
Mishtikuut	wooden box	mishtikuuta	wooden boxes
Kaapaashtepaich	dryer	kaapaashtepaicha	dryers

In East Cree, for example, if the noun is animate, the plural ending is -**ak** (e.g., **awasis<u>ak</u>**, "children"), while inanimate plural nouns end with -**a** (e.g., **maskisin<u>a</u>**, "shoes"). Table 4.12 offers some examples of animate and inanimate nouns in East Cree.

As mentioned above, verb endings are affected as well. The following are examples of the distinction as reflected in intransitive verbs (i.e., those that do not take an object). Differences are underlined.

Milwasis<u>iw</u> awasis: S/he is good, child

Milwasi<u>n</u> maskisin: It is good, shoe

Chishiyaash<u>uu</u>: S/he sails fast in the water

Chishiyaash<u>tin</u>: It sails fast in the water

The same applies with transitive verbs (i.e., those that do take an object):

Niwapa<u>maw</u> awasis: I see him/her, child

Niwapa<u>hten</u> maskisin: I see it, shoe

Piskuchiwepin<u>ew</u>: S/he tosses him/her up into the air

Piskuchiwepin<u>am</u>: S/he tosses it up into the air

It is not as easy as it might first seem to figure out what is animate and what is inanimate. There are things deemed animate (and thus a "she/he" or a "him/her") that someone outside the culture and the language might not think of as "alive." Note, for example, the following animate terms in East Cree:

kaasiihkweusuup: hand soap

michihkun: a bone flesher made with bear bone

chishtuhchikanahchaapi: fiddle bow

Alternatively, some things an outsider might think of as "alive" might be deemed "inanimate"; for example, the following:

mihkwaapemikw: red-osier dogwood

paastinaahkwaan: club moss

wiihpaashkw: cow parsnip (Heracleum mazimum)

Some things vary. In East Cree, for example, "**ishkuteu**" is considered to be inanimate when it is referring to fire but animate when denoting a battery or a spark plug. And in some contexts and languages, a normally inanimate noun can be used with animate forms if it is considered alive (i.e., having a spirit) in the context of a story.

No two Algonquian languages have exactly the same set of animate and inanimate objects. Dialects of the same language sometimes differ. This should be expected. Each people has a unique history. However, there is still a great deal of agreement in Algonquian languages across Canada as to what is usually animate and what is usually inanimate. Observe the following sample of shared distinctions with Blackfoot, Ojibwe, and Delaware, each belonging to a different branch of the Algonquian family (see Table 4.13).

SYLLABIC WRITING

The history of syllabic writing in Canada is a tale of success. According to Olive Dickason, "by the nineteenth century and the early part of the twentieth century, the Cree had one of the highest literacy rates in the world" (Dickason 1992:241). The person credited with first putting the syllabic system together was an Englishman, James Evans (1801–1846). He came to Canada as a young man and became both a teacher and a preacher among the Anishinabe (Ojibwa) of southern Ontario. In 1840, Evans went out west of Norway House, by Lake Winnipeg, north of Winnipeg, to work with the Cree people there. His work developing a writing system is a good example of the collaboration of two different peoples. Evans had seen the Anishinabe, and later the Cree, use many symbols both in their art and in their communication between travellers along pathways and portages. It is possible that he had heard or even seen examples of the then well-publicized syllabic system developed by the Cherokee educator Sequoyah (c1770–1843), which had produced amazing literacy

TABLE 4-13 Agreement in Animate and Inanimate in Blackfoot, Ojibwe, and Delaware

English	Blackfoot	Ojibwe	Delaware
knees	animate	animate	animate
fingernails	animate	animate	animate
skin	animate	animate	animate
horns	animate	animate	animate
feathers	animate	animate	animate
sun	animate	animate	animate
moon	animate	animate	animate
stars	animate	animate	animate
ice	animate	animate	animate
kettles/pots	animate	animate	animate
bark	animate	animate	animate
leaves	inanimate	inanimate	inanimate
strawberries	inanimate	inanimate	inanimate
hair	inanimate	inanimate	inanimate
foot	inanimate	inanimate	inanimate

gains and a number of printed works by the 1820s. On the European side, he took some ideas from shorthand and from Greek.

In June 1841, he printed a book of Cree Christian hymns written in syllabics, reputedly the first book published in western Canada. The Cree took over from there, with catechists, trappers, and traders spreading the use of the system, and literacy, across the West. By 1889, John Maclean could say with some accuracy of the Cree that:

> The Indians of this confederacy, with very few exceptions, read and write these characters; and many of them, with no other teachers but the Indians around the camp-fires, have so grasped these principles that they can read with fluency the books printed in the syllabic system. (Maclean 1970:256)

From about 1851, many Christian works were written in syllabics in the Moose Cree dialect, causing it to be a liturgical or religious language for speakers of Ojibwe and other dialects of Cree. In the 1980s, linguist Lisa Philips Valentine studied a Severn Ojibwe-speaking community in northwestern Ontario. She found that the standard religious texts (i.e., their Bible, prayer and hymn books) of this very active Anglican parish were syllabic works written both in Moose and Plains Cree, something that contributed greatly to the high rate of syllabic literacy in the community.

Today, this syllabics system is used for every dialect of Cree and two dialects of Ojibwe (Severn, or Oji-Cree, and Saulteaux). Educational material for all grades covered by the Cree School Board of East James Bay in Quebec is produced in syllabics. Computer fonts containing syllabics are now readily available.

But this system is not confined just to Algonquian languages. Two additional Native language families have become involved. This includes the Athapaskan languages Chipewyan, Beaver, Slavey, and Carrier. In 1879, Reverend Edmond J. Peck, an Anglican missionary, altered the system to suit the different sounds of the Eastern Arctic dialects of Inuktitut (e.g., -v-, -g-, -ng-, and -q-), thus initiating a boom in Inuktitut religious material and literacy similar to that which had begun earlier among Algonquian speakers. When Nunavut came into official existence in 1999, this form of writing took on official status.

The Benefits of Using Syllabics

Understanding syllabics is easier than what the reader accustomed to the Roman alphabet systems of English or French might think. This is especially true for children, who early on perceive and comprehend syllables, and, without the biases of those having learned an alphabet first, seem to learn this system as quickly as they would an alphabet system. And they don't have to worry about problems familiar to English spellers such as a sound being represented by more than one symbol (e.g., the -f- sound being represented by -f-, -ph-, and -gh- in the English words "fine," "phone," and "enough"). Cree children taught literacy first in syllabics appear to be able to later transfer their literacy skills well into using an alphabet for learning English or French.

A syllabic system has the advantage of using fewer symbols in writing long words, cutting down somewhat on the visual prejudice of people accustomed to languages such as French and English that tend to have shorter words than do Cree, Ojibwe, and Inuktitut. Look at the following East Cree word written in syllabics and in Roman letters:

nanakwaanechishkuwew   = 20 letters

ᐊᐊ·ᛒᑐᒉᔲᐁ·ᐁ°   = 9 characters (plus three diacritics)

s/he wrinkled it by sitting on it

Further, the "identifiable Nativeness" of the syllabic system is a big plus. Native people were instrumental in its development and spread and it has formed a key part in Native literary traditions. Give students something that they can identify with and their performance in school improves.

Reading the Symbols

Basically, the system involves a given symbol representing a given consonant plus a vowel. The vowel that is being indicated differs according to which of four positions the symbol has been rotated to face. The position of -i- (pronounced -ee-) is always in opposition to that of -e- (pronounced -eh-), with -a- and -o- or -u- (in the case of East Cree) likewise opposites. The following examples using the -p- symbol will illustrate how this works. Like all examples to follow, they are from East Cree:

pe:	∨	petaapin	∨Ċ∧ᵃ	(it is daybreak)
pi:	∧	pisaaw	∧ ꜱ°	(it is a trench)
pa:	<	pataham	<C"◁ᴸ	(s/he misses hitting it)
pu:	>	puwaatam	>·◁Cᴸ	(s/he dreams of it)

A syllable final is a consonant that comes after a vowel and before another consonant or the end of a word. There are two different traditions as to how these are to be represented. The Eastern tradition involves smaller, raised versions of the consonant plus the -a- symbol, as can be seen in the following words:

| n: | ᵃ | eshkan | ▽ᵚᵇᵃ | (ice chisel) |
| na: | ᵃ | nanamichuu | ᵔᵔᴦⱼ | (s/he shivers with cold) |

In the Western tradition, special small symbols are employed. In the first word presented above, would be used. In both traditions, "ô" signifies a syllable final -h-. Both use a small raised circle (°) for a final -w-.

There are also diacritics, marks added to the basic symbols. One is a dot over the symbol, indicating that the vowel is long:

| taa: | Ċ | petaapin | ∨Ċ∧ᵃ | (it is daybreak) |

When a dot appears before a vowel in the Eastern and Western Catholic tradition (after the vowel in the Western tradition), that signifies that the consonant and vowel have a -w- between them:

| kwaa: | ·ᵇ | mihkwaaw | ᴦ"·ᵇ° | (it is red) |

KEY TERMS

cognates
dialect
hierarchy of person
language family
language isolate
morpheme
root

CONTENT QUESTIONS

1. What are three misconceptions about Native languages?

2. How many Native language families and isolates exist in Canada today?

3. How are Inuktitut and Algonquian and Athapaskan languages different from English and French in representing gender?

4. What is "hierarchy of person"?

5. What important distinction exists in Algonquian languages?

 WEBLINKS

www.sil.org/lla/cana.html
This Web site lists the Native languages of Canada, where they are spoken, and their numbers of speakers.

afn.ca/Programs/Languages/languages_homepage.htm
The leading Canadian political body for Native bands, the Assembly of First Nations, includes a link on its Web site to its report entitled "Languages: State of Emergency."

www.inac.gc.ca/pr/pub/orl/index_e.html
A report by a University of Toronto Professor of Anthropology, entitled "Oral Narratives and Aboriginal Pasts," commissioned by the federal government.

5

THE ARCTIC

PALAEO-ESKIMO (3000 B.C. TO 500 B.C.)

It began at least 5,000 years ago. People who were capable of making their home where no one else had lived, in the barren tundra and frozen coastlines of the North American Arctic, appeared on the East Coast of the Bering Strait in Alaska. Within about 200 years, they spread across the north, some even reaching Greenland, extending the Arctic human life-line nearly 5,000 kilometres east to west.

What did these first peoples have that enabled them to live in the Arctic? Their hunting arsenal was impressive. Asian-style, double-curved bows made out of several materials bound together, lances bristling with sharp-edged microblades, and perhaps spear-throwers to help them fling those weapons further. Probably from their Native neighbours on the East Coast, they learned to make and use harpoons that were armed with deadly detach-able heads that stuck into marine mammals. Flint microblades were used for cutting meats and skins, and burins with edges for carving antler and bone. The latter enabled them to make the small bone needles they used to stitch together with sinew thread the air-tight, tailored clothing necessary for keeping the cold out.

Their homes were tents, usually single-family dwellings. For cooking, they had stone-lined hearths or fireboxes in which they burned scavenged driftwood, twigs of dwarf willow, and fat-smeared bones of animals. Had they learned yet how to use the more plentiful oil rendered from animal fat to heat themselves? We don't know. Some stone lamps existed, but not until relatively late, and in small numbers. Perhaps they used skin or some other archaeologically invisible substance. Did they have boats at this time? It's not known for sure.

From 2500 to 1500 B.C., the Arctic climate warmed, creating more open water stretches to travel or hunt in than had existed before or that exist now. There is no direct evidence for their use of skin boats, but skin does not survive long to provide archaeological evidence. Still, one wonders how they could have crossed the Bering Strait without boats.

DORSET (1000 B.C. TO A.D. 1000) \Igloo

From 2000 to 1000 B.C., the Arctic became colder. Technological innovation met the challenge in the development of the Dorset cultural tradition, named after Cape Dorset on Baffin Island, where the first sites were found. They used more materials than before, including slate, which they ground into knives and projectile points. Robert McGhee estimated that the population within the core area of the northern parts of the Foxe Basin, Baffin Island, the islands in northern Hudson Bay, and both sides of the Hudson Strait grew from an earlier population of somewhere between 1,000 to 3,000 to between 2,000 to 5,000 at this time. Dorset innovative adaptations to colder weather include the familiar **igloos**, but also homes that were partially sunk into the ground, with sod walls and roofs made of skin. Oil-burning stone lamps, necessary for keeping both kinds of houses warm, also started to appear in large numbers at this time. Dorset people were better equipped than their predecessors for winter travel. They had sleds, with "shoes" or ivory plates protecting the runners of the sleds from rough ice. For walking on smooth ice, they had "creepers," pieces of ivory notched to form treads, acting like the spikes used today to climb telephone poles and mountains.

THULE (A.D. 1000 TO PRESENT) Kayak umiak

With a warming trend between A.D. 900 and 1200 that produced ice-free summers and milder winters, Thule tradition innovations increased the capacity to hunt sea mammals, particularly the massive bowhead whales. They developed **kayaks**, **umiaks** (skinboats eight to ten metres long that typically held twelve men), and harpoons with sealskin floats. When a seal, walrus, or whale was struck by such a harpoon, the float would wear the animal out and keep it from sinking. Land travel improved with the first clearly proven use of sled dogs. As a result, we find more permanent and larger communities, particularly in those areas where whale hunting was prominent.

What was the relationship between the Thule, who are directly connected with today's Inuit, and their Dorset predecessors? The Inuit have long told stories of the **Tunnit** or **Tunrit**, a gentle, seal-hunting people with whom they initially coexisted in peace, before they eventually fought. There is no evidence for the Thule killing off the Tunnit, so it is likely that the prevailing scenario was intermarriage and teaching of new skills. During the early 1920s, Knud Rasmussen, who was of mixed Danish-Inuit parentage, led a scientific expedition across the Arctic from Greenland to Alaska. An Inuk told him the following: "We counted the Tunrit a foreign people, yet they spoke our language, lived with us and had the same habits and customs as we had." (Wright 1996:444)   Tunnit

Inuit

Up until 1200, there was a great uniformity of Thule culture, something reflected today in the linguistic uniformity of **Inuktitut**, the language of the Inuit. This language is fundamentally the same from North Alaska, across the Canadian Arctic to Greenland. Fitting it into its broader context, Inuktitut belongs to the Eskimo-Aleut family, which has member languages (e.g., Yup'ik and Aleut) spoken on both sides of the Bering Strait, which separates North America from Asia. Some linguists have linked the **Eskimo-Aleut** family with the **Luorawetlan** family, found exclusively in northeastern Siberia. Others argue that long-term contact may have resulted in a borrowing that looks like genetic relation.

Estimates of Thule/Inuit pre-contact population in Canada range from about 22,000 to 35,000. The term "**Inuit**," which is a plural form meaning "people" (the singular is "**Inuk**," meaning "person"), has within the last 20 years replaced the more familiar "**Eskimo**." The latter term is based on an Algonquian root meaning "raw," said to relate to the Inuit practice of eating certain forms of meat and blubber raw.

Beginning from about 1200, and peaking from 1600 to 1850, the climate of the Arctic cooled, making up what is termed the Little Ice Age. During this period, the extent and duration of sea ice in the Arctic kept the bowhead whales in many areas from their summer feeding grounds. The Thule peoples were forced to move to different places and rely upon different animals reflecting local availability. This caused previous cultural uniformity to break up into a greater variety of cultural pieces.

In Canada, anthropologists have culturally subdivided the Inuit into eight groups, from west to east: the **Mackenzie Delta**, **Copper**, **Caribou**, **Netsilik** (Netsilingmiut), **Sadlermiut**, **Iglulik** (Iglulingmiut), **South Baffin Island**, and **Labrador and Quebec**. It should be stressed that, for the most part, this does not reflect any "tribal" distinction in terms of a people's sense of who they are. It is more a distinction imposed by outsiders, based on geography and on a few distinct traits. The Mackenzie Inuit took advantage of great numbers of beluga swimming up the Mackenzie River, herding them into shallow waters with their kayaks. One of their communities, Kittagazuit, a summer beluga camp, was occupied for centuries by up to 1,000 people, what McGhee rightly terms "the largest Inuit community between Bering Strait and Greenland" (McGhee 1978:116). Today, the Mackenzie Delta Inuit consider themselves distinct from other Inuit and call themselves **Inuvialuit**, "the real people." The Copper Inuit were primarily distinctive in using that metal for a good number of their tools. The Caribou Inuit relied more upon that animal, especially during the nineteenth century. Netsilik ("people of the seal") relied upon a variety of animals, but have long been particularly skilled, as their name suggests, at the seal hunt. Similarly, the Iglulik were more involved with pursuing walrus than were other Inuit ethnic groups.

They differed too in social features. The Copper Inuit traditionally were "rugged individualists." They stressed the nuclear family over the extended family, which others relied upon more. They were much more egalitarian than the Iglulingmiut, whose leaders' authority extended beyond the camp to include a whole band.

BOX 5-1	**Igloo: The Stereotypical Inuit Home**

Nothing is more familiar in the stereotype of the Inuit than the igloo or snow house. Not only do they not live in igloos today, and few have ever been in one, but traditionally the Inuit had a good variety of houses. These vary from summer tents to semisubterranean homes using such traditional building materials as whalebone, planks, and sod.

SOCIAL ORGANIZATION AND LEADERSHIP AMONG THE TRADITIONAL INUIT

For most Canadian Inuit groups, leadership existed in the form of an **isumataq** (or **ihumataq**), "one who thinks." He was usually an older man who held respected kinship status as father, older brother, or cousin, uncle, father-in-law, and/or grandfather with respect to those he led. But one did not gain that position purely on status. John Matthiasson describes the ideal attributes of an isumataq as follows:

> . . . a wise decision-maker, a good hunter, and an exemplar of Inuit values, and must have demonstrated all three qualities over time. He might be asked for advice on where men should hunt, or may decide when it was time for the band to separate. Although a skilled hunter, he would be sure to share his kills with members of his band and to loan his hunting equipment to other men when not using it himself. . . (Matthiasson 1992:91; see Burch 1995:128)

Matthiasson also pointed out that the band had the freedom to choose whether to ignore or to follow the isumataq's advice. They could even leave the band if they believed that the isumataq's advice was not sound. Outside of kinship, group identity existed at various levels, beginning with camps. While these were variable in size, the figures derived by anthropologist Marc Stevenson from a map drawn in 1839 by **Eenoolooapik**, a Baffin Island Inuit, are fairly typical (Stevenson 1997:62). The camps portrayed in that map ranged from about 33 to 51 in population. Winter hunting involved breathing-hole (**mauliqtuq**) sealing,

---

BOX 5-2   **Words in Inuktitut**

You will notice that a good number of Inuktitut words end with -k- or -q-. That is because those letters represent a sound that is used for a third person singular pronominal suffix: she, he, and it. Also, different dialects are distinguished by such features as the -h- in one dialect being an -s- in another (e.g., Netsilik "ihumataq" was Iglulik "isumataq").

angajuqqaq: An Inuktitut term for leader that implies the capacity to give orders to another.

igloo: Inuktitut term for any type of house.

i(s/h)umataq: "One who thinks"; Inuktitut term for a leader who suggests but does not give orders.

kayak: One-person skin boat invented by the Thule people.

maqtaak: The blubber from a marine mammal.

mauliqtuq: Breathing hole of a seal.

-miut: a suffix used to denote a group of people.

parka: English term derived from an Aleut word for Arctic head and neck covering.

tuktuk: Caribou.

Tun(n/r)it: A gentle, seal-hunting people in traditional Inuit stories, thought to be the Dorset people.

umiak: Large, seal-skin boat typically holding 12 people and could be over nine metres in length.

done in winter. To be done effectively, many hunters were needed since seals use many breathing holes, all of which needed to be watched. Traditionally, this might involve a camp of at least around 50. Beyond the camp were bands, signified by names ending in **-miut**. In Eenoolooapik's map there are three at the same level: the **Talirpingmiut**, the **Kingnaimiut**, and the **Kinguamiut**, numbering roughly 375, 211–257, and 434. Terms ending with -miut could also be used to refer to collections of bands, as can be seen in the name **Netsilingmiut**.

ARCTIC RESOURCES AND THE INUIT

Most often remarked upon in anthropological literature are the ways in which the Inuit adapted to life in a very difficult environment. What will be noted here are some of those resources and some of the uses made of them, both commercially and for subsistence.

Marine Mammals and Fish

The largest of the marine mammals was the bowhead whale, which can reach a weight of more than 40,000 kilograms. A successful hunt brought **maqtaak** (blubber) to eat, oil for lamps, and jaw and rib bones twice the height of a man to be used as the frames for houses made of stone and sod, or for sled runners. One whale could keep several families well supplied with food, dogfood, fuel, and building supplies for a year. The commercial hunting of these whales involved two parts of the whale. First, there was **baleen**, a flexible bone-like material growing in thin strips in the palates of certain species of whales used as strainers to trap tiny sea creatures for food. Nineteenth-century Euro-Americans used baleen for making the corsets that forced women's bodies into the thin-waisted hourglass shapes considered fashionable at the time. According to Keith Crowe (1974:104), the baleen from one whale could pay the cost of a year's voyage for a ship and its crew. Second, the blubber was rendered into oil that was burned as fuel and was used as lubrication for the machinery used in the fast-growing factories of the Industrial Revolution. The smaller beluga (500 to 1,000 kilograms) was also an important source of meat, maqtaak, and oil. It would be hunted commercially in great numbers by the Inuit during the twentieth century, up until 1963. The hide would be made into leather and the blubber rendered into the oil that would be used in cooking fats and for cosmetics.

Walrus were hunted for their skin, meat, bone, and oil but also for their tusks, which provided the ivory used in jewellery, sled shoes, ice creepers, fish spears, and a broad variety of tools generally. Their thick hide was useful for boots and for special outer winter pants that allowed the hunter to sit still on the ice while waiting to spear seals.

The most consistently hunted marine mammals for the Inuit were seals, namely the large (250 to 350 kilograms) bearded seal, harp seal, and smaller ringed seal (up to 80 kilograms). Seals provided fat for oil, meat, and, very significantly, waterproof skin, which was used for kayaks and umiaks, harpoon floats, summer coats and tents, and boots and beds. Initially, the commercial hunt for this animal was primarily for the oil, but during the twentieth century the seals were hunted more for the skins, particularly the "whitecoats" of the pups, once fashionable but no longer politically correct.

Fishing was important as well, especially for arctic char. Techniques included jigging, ice fishing, and constructing stone weirs that would direct the fish to where they could be speared. Scientists, wondering why the Inuit could eat so much animal fat and not die of heart attacks, learned that the fish oils they consumed were important in lowering cholesterol. The traditional Inuit have thus given modern medicine assistance in the fight against heart attacks.

Land Mammals

The most important land mammal was the caribou. Caribou hair is hollow, trapping air, thus making it ideal for insulation, softness and lightness, ideal for clothing, footwear, tents, bedding, blankets, and bags. It has been calculated that fifty caribou were required to meet the needs of each person for a single year, with eight to eleven skins per person for clothing and twenty to thirty skins for tent coverings (see Wright 1996:425). E.S. Burch provides a good sense of the use of other parts of the caribou:

> Excellent thread can be made from their back sinew, and components of tools, weapons and utensils can be manufactured from their antlers and bones. People who consume all of the meat, viscera, stomach contents (rich in vitamin C), and fat of caribou are able to satisfy all of their nutritional requirements. If caribou are available in sufficient numbers at appropriate times of year, and if they are fully utilized, they can provide for the **total** subsistence requirements of a human population. (Burch 1995:129)

The degree of usefulness of caribou changes with the seasons. While during the fall and early winter they have plenty of fat and their skins are in prime condition, during the spring and early summer their meat is very lean and therefore of limited nutritional value. The skins are thinner and have holes in them, courtesy of warble flies.

Like other important aspects of Inuit culture, **tuktuk** (caribou) are the subject of thousands of songs, a key component of Inuit culture. The following song comes from **Krilugok**, like many traditional Inuit, a songwriter and singer as well as a hunter:

> Tuktuk, tuktuk, caribou, caribou, come to me!
>
> I'll make boots with the skin of thy legs;
>
> Stay, stay with me, o creature of the land,
>
> Roamer of the valleys, wanderer of the mountains;
>
> Fear me not, and let me catch thee,
>
> Eyaya, eya, eya, eyaya, ya, ya. (de Coccola and King 1986:201)

Musk ox were also hunted not just for meat but as a multi-faceted resource. From their sweeping horns there was material for scrapers and for components in the composite bows. The fine underlying "wool" plus long-haired fur made their skins ideal for cold-resistant blankets, robes, and tents. The nineteenth century was deadly to these creatures, which were easy victims because they tend to stand and protect the herd rather than run. Inuit armed with guns and desperately needing food because of the vagaries of the whaling industry, and late nineteenth-century commercial hunters hunting musk ox for robes, drove the musk ox nearly to extinction.

The word "**parka**" entered the English language from Aleutian, a language related to that of the Inuit. This northern Native invention was carefully crafted with furs such as those of the wolverine, wolf, and dog that would not collect the moisture from human breath. The term "**husky**" comes from the word "Eskimo." These dogs, which might have accompanied people across the Bering Strait, were used both in hunting and to provide the dogpower necessary for the dogsled, a uniquely Arctic mode of transportation that varied in dogpower from two to more than fifteen. Polar bear fur was highly valued because of its resistance to cold water and because it was difficult to obtain. Fox fur, traditionally used, especially for a number of minor purposes, became quite valuable in commercial trapping.

INUIT PHYSICAL ADAPTATION *Hunters Response*

Inuit adaptation to the Arctic is physical as well as cultural. Heat retention has been facilitated by their longer torsos and shorter limbs and relatively few active sweat glands on their chests and backs. Inuit have proportionally larger sinuses than non-Inuit, allowing for the greater warming of air before its passage into the more sensitive lungs. Another crucial physical adaptation concerns Basal Metabolic Rate (BMR), the rate at which the body metabolizes nutritional intake. The Inuit have a higher-than-average BMR. When food is eaten, the rate at which it is metabolized and activated into energy is comparatively quick, making the Inuit better able to fight the cold.

Another adaptation is **Hunter's Response**, a phenomenon also shared by subarctic Native hunters. What is Hunter's Response? Imagine submerging your arm in near-freezing ice water for a while and then removing it from the water. For most people, it would take a long time for their arm's skin temperature to return to normal. With Hunter's Response, there is rapid readjustment to normal skin temperature as a greater-than-average amount of blood flows to the body's extremities.

POST CONTACT HISTORY

The first contact between Inuit and Europeans probably took place when the Vikings briefly settled on the northern tip of Newfoundland about 1,000 years ago. By the late 1400s, the Inuit first met European whalers. That contact reached epic proportions during the nineteenth century. Between 1820 and 1840, whalers on more than 1,300 British ships sailed by the north shore of Baffin Island, killing more than 13,000 whales. Commercial whaling peaked from 1868 to 1883 when American whalers plied their trade from Alaska to Hudson Bay.

Getting the Name Right 5-1

Eskimo: Derived from an Algonquian root meaning "raw" and said to refer to their practice of eating some blubber and meat raw.

husky: English term for an Arctic domesticated dog, derived from the word "Eskimo"; also used as a derogatory term for Inuit.

Inuit: Inuktitut term for "men," "people." Note that this is a plural term. As such, the word "Inuits" does not exist. The singular form is "Inuk."

Inuktitut: "Like an Inuk," the language of the Inuit.

Inuvialuit: The "real people," Mackenzie Delta term for themselves in distinction from other Inuit people.

There were good and bad ramifications of whaling for the Inuit. The British in the east and Americans in the west needed the skilled help of the Inuit, so some Inuit became prominent figures in the industry, first as members of whaleboat crews and later as owners of boats, including some respectable-size schooners. Cultural go-betweens often became traders, some eventually running their own trading posts or working as managers for the big company posts. Prominent hunters became successful leaders of communities of increased size, particularly in whaling centres such as Baffin Island. Such figures were known as **angajuqqaq**, leaders with more authority than the more egalitarian isumataq.

But there was a down side to commercial whaling: starvation and disease. In the winter of 1847–8, 20 of 160 at the Baffin Island community of Naujateling died of hunger "of whom several, horrible to relate, had gnawed the flesh from their own arms" (Stevenson 1997:75). In 1853–4, they lost about a third of their population to cholera. By 1883, it was a community of 20. There are many such stories.

The twentieth century started out badly for the Inuit. In 1899, three sailors from the Scottish ship *Active* landed on Sadliq (Southampton Island). During the next three years all but five of the Sadlermiut died of the diseases those men carried. The last survivor of that little-known group, which might have numbered around 200 at the time of contact, died in 1948. In 1919, a supply ship arrived at the Labrador Inuit community of Okak, bringing with it Spanish flu as well as the usual supplies. Only a handful survived, and Okak, founded as a mission community in 1776, ended.

From 1915 to 1925, the caribou population west of Hudson Bay suffered a sharp decline. The Caribou Inuit themselves would dwindle from 1,500 to 500 during that same period. Their separate existence would end after 1948, when, in addition to the overhunting of caribou by White southerners on northern projects, there came high enough levels of tuberculosis, influenza, and infantile paralysis that their homeland was put under quarantine for almost two years. During the 1950s, the survivors moved to the coast to join newly formed combined villages. Individuals of Caribou Inuit descent would become prominent in Inuit activism, both in the formation of the Inuit Tapirisat and in the push for Nunavut territory.

By the time the whaling industry collapsed early in the twentieth century, the number of whales had been severely reduced. Women's garments no longer contained whalebone stays. Petroleum was replacing whale oil as a lubricant and as fuel. In the 1920s, the commercial hunting of belugas and, more significantly, the trapping of Arctic fox would take its place. For a little over 10 years, the latter activity made some Inuit quite well off, particularly in the Mackenzie Delta and on Banks Island. Catholic missionary Father Frank Raymond de Coccola stated that, in 1938:

> A white fox pelt would trade for about $40. To an Eskimo this represented three boxes of twenty rifle shells in each box, or ten yards of calico for his wife's sewing or twenty five pounds of flour and a pound of tea or tallow to boot. (de Coccola and King 1986: 72)

As such, a trapper could get from $30 to $70 for one fur, making at least $9,000 during a good season, significantly more than the Canadian average annual income at that time.

But fox trapping was a risky business for the Inuit. Trapping fox took them away from where they could hunt their own food, making them dependent on expensive southern foods. Fox numbers rose and fell in cycles. During the 1930s and 1940s, the industry crashed when fashion changed, prices fell, and the fox were overtrapped. Inuit starved as a result.

In 1939, when Canada wanted to assert its territorial claims to the Arctic, the federal government decided to take official responsibility for the Inuit. In 1953, the negative side of

Native Individuals 5-1

Eenoolooapik (c1820–1847): A Baffin Island Inuk who was a guide and the first Inuk to be actively employed in the whaling industry.

Knud Rasmussen: A mixed Danish/Inuit who led an important scientific expedition across the Arctic from Greenland to Alaska during the early 1920s.

this relationship was made clear when the people of Inukjuak (Port Harrison) in Northern Quebec were forced to move some 3,200 kilometres north to uninhabited Ellesmere Island at Grise Fiord. Ottawa claimed that this was for the betterment of the people, as local natural resources were depleting and Ellesmere Island was untouched. A darker interpretation is that this forced move was made primarily to guarantee Canadian rights to that contested territory. Government officials did not seem to know or care that the resources available in the two areas were quite different, that Inuit adapted to life in one part of the Arctic weren't necessarily knowledgeable about surviving in another.

During the 1950s and 1960s, the Inuit were hard hit by tuberculosis. At that time, they had the highest rate of tuberculosis in the world (see chapter on colonialism).

In the census of 1991, 30,085 people claimed Inuit as their sole ethnic origin. Another 19,165 listed it as one of their origins, for a total of 49,250. In the 1996 census, 26,840 people claimed Inuktitut as at least one of their mother tongues.

Timeline 5-1

3000 B.C. to 500 B.C.: Palaeo-Eskimo Period.

1000 B.C. to A.D. 1000: Dorset Period.

A.D. 1000 to date: Thule Period.

A.D. 1200 to 1850: Little Ice Age.

1820 to 1840: Whalers on British ships kill more than 13,000 whales.

1999: Birth of Nunavut territory (see Chapter 25).

KEY TERMS

angajuqqaq (Inuktitut)
Hunter's Response
ice creepers
i(s/h)umataq (Inuktitut)
microblades
Tun(n/r)it (Inuktitut)
umiak (Inuktitut)

CONTENT QUESTIONS

1. What innovations are associated with the Dorset Period?
2. What innovations are associated with the Thule Period?
3. What was the probable impact of the Little Ice Age?
4. How are isumataq and angajuqqaq different?
5. What, for the Inuit, were the good and bad aspects of nineteenth-century whaling and twentieth-century arctic fox trapping?

 WEBLINKS

arcticcircle.uconn.edu
The Arctic Circle project provides extensive materials about northern Aboriginals.

www.innu.ca
The Inuit Nation's Web site features information about Inuit culture, land-rights issues, and more.

www.inac.gc.ca/pr/pub/indigen/ipsdca_e.html
You may also want to read a federal government report entitled "Indigenous Peoples and Sustainable Development in the Canadian Arctic."

THE EASTERN WOODLANDS

[handwritten annotations:]

large bodies
Hd.

Mi'Kmaq. (W). Abenaki.
1) Algonquians - Maliseet. Munsee (D)
2) Iroquoians. - Huron/Wendat.
- Mohawk.
- Oneida

OVERVIEW

The Eastern Woodlands in Canada encompasses two broad groups: Algonquians and Iroquoians. Most of the former speak languages that belong to the Eastern branch of the Algonquian family. In Canada, this includes Mi'kmaq, Maliseet, Western Abenaki, and Munsee (Delaware). Also in the area are the more southerly Central Algonquian peoples associated with the Ojibwa (e.g., the Mississauga, Potawatomi, Odawa, and Algonquin). The Iroquoians include the Huron and the Six Nations of the Iroquois.

Geographically, the Eastern Woodlands area is characterized by mixed deciduous and coniferous forests, providing a broad variety of wild plants and animals for the use of the people. The prominent presence of large bodies of water (i.e., the Atlantic, St. Lawrence River, and the Great Lakes) made fishing a significant enterprise traditionally among all of these people. In the south, corn-based agriculture (sometimes supplemented by beans and squash) provided most of the food.

Within the Eastern Woodlands, we find complex social structures extending beyond the band or local group. This includes clans (except for the Mi'kmaq and Maliseet), "chiefs," called "sagamores" in English for the Eastern Algonquians and "sachems" when referring to the Iroquois (both terms derived from an Eastern Algonquian term that was "saqmaw" in the Mi'kmaq language), and federated tribes or confederacies, the most notable being that of the Iroquois. Both clans and chiefs were determined matrilineally with the Iroquoians and the Delaware and patrilineally for the other Eastern Algonquians.

THE ALGONQUIANS

The Mi'kmaq

The story of the Mi'kmaq is one of a fight for survival. They live along the East Coast, but did not disappear, nor were forced west as were almost all fellow coastal peoples of the United States. In what Olive Dickason termed the "longest of all Amerindian conflicts in North America" (Dickason 1992:149), the Mi'kmaq fought against the British in defence of their land, something few Canadian Native groups did.

The term "**Mi'kmaq**" (sometimes Mi'kmaw), preferred by the people today to the older "Micmac," is said to be derived from a term for "allies." A more traditional name is "**Ilnu**," which, like the cognate "Innu" (see Chapter 7, "The Eastern Subarctic"), means "people." Their country stretches over Nova Scotia, New Brunswick, Prince Edward Island, the **Gaspé** (from Mi'kmaq "kaspe:k," meaning "outer ends") peninsula of **Quebec** (from a Mi'kmaq word meaning "it narrows"), and parts of Newfoundland. It is hard to determine Mi'kmaq numbers for the time of contact. When Father Pierre Biard estimated their population at just over 3,000 in 1616, they had suffered severe depopulation through roughly a century of European contact. They probably lost at least 50% to 66% of their people to European diseases. Add to that the fact that Biard was not aware of all of the Mi'kmaq communities and we get a pre-contact figure that was probably more than 10,000.

In 1610, Marc Lescarbot writes of how the Mi'kmaq made good use of different resources in their area throughout the year. In January (JR3:79–83), in small local groups of perhaps 30 to 40, they hunted seal, both for the meat and oil that they would keep in moose-bladder containers. In February and early March, they hunted a variety of animals, including beaver, otter, bear, moose, and **caribou** (a Mi'kmaq word meaning "one who scratches" as they scratch through the snow for food). It wasn't until the middle of March that great amounts of food were available as fish began to spawn, coming from the sea up the rivers and streams, at the mouths of which the Mi'kmaq set traps. First came the smelt, then the herring came near the end of April into early May. Also available at that time were salmon and sturgeon. One name for April was "Egg-Laying," as migrating waterfowl laid eggs in great numbers, which the Mi'kmaq then gathered. May was called "Young Seals" or "Get Herring."

In the summer, food was available in even greater abundance. As a result, the Mi'kmaq formed larger groups, numbering perhaps 200 to 300. From the sea they harvested oysters, clams, and lobsters. Using weirs and spears or bone hooks and lines, they fished for cod, plaice, and striped bass and speared porpoises and even small whales. As much as 90% of their food may have come from the sea (Miller 1995:349).

In the fall, they returned to smaller groups in order to pursue migrating birds, moose, and caribou. September was termed "Moose Calling" and October "Fat, tame animals." Especially sought were eel, which they boiled, roasted, or smoked for winter.

A key component of traditional Mi'kmaq social structure was the "**saqmaw**," a patrilineal position (i.e., reckoned on the father's side) typically inherited by the eldest son. A seventeenth-century Jesuit missionary described the duties of the saqmaw (which he writes as "sagamore") as follows, overemphasizing somewhat the power of the position. He stated that they provided:

> . . . dogs for the chase, canoes for transportation, provisions and reserves for bad weather and expeditions. The young people flatter him, hunt, and serve their apprenticeship under him, not being allowed to have anything before they are married, for then only can they have

a dog and a bag; that is, have something of their own, and do for themselves. Nevertheless they continue to live under the authority of the sagamore, and very often in his company; as also do several others who have no relations, or those who of their own free will place themselves under his protection and guidance, being themselves weak and without a following. Now all that the young men capture belongs to the Sagamore; but the married ones give him only a part, and if these leave him, as they often do for the sake of the chase and supplies, returning afterwards, they pay their dues and homage in skins and like gifts. (JR3:87–91)

Saqmaw leadership existed at various levels, from the small fall and winter groups, to the larger summer groups, to the district level, and, finally, to the "kji'saqmaw" or "great chief." Mi'kmaq country was divided into seven districts. The responsibilities of the district saqmaw included assigning hunting territories according to changing family grouping size and local resource conditions, meeting to decide issues of war and peace, conferring with saqmaw of lesser standing, and making sure that everyone had enough. Generosity was a prized value, which saw some district saqmaw giving away the best clothes and other possessions that they had (Miller 1995:354).

The Mi'kmaq were early involved with the fur trade and with Catholic missionaries, which drew them closer to the French than to the English. But the Mi'kmaq fought the English for their own reasons, coming into conflict at various times during the seventeenth and eighteenth centuries. The first "war" began in 1722, which led to a treaty in 1725 in which the Mi'kmaq exchanged their promise of peace for hunting and fishing rights. It was an uneasy peace.

The 1740s hit the Mi'kmaq hard. In 1746, typhus spread from the French fleet to the Mi'kmaq, killing an estimated 4,000, perhaps one third of their number in Nova Scotia. In July 1749, Colonel Edward Cornwallis led an English expedition of more than 2,400 English settlers to move into the east coast region of Nova Scotia, landing where the city of Halifax is today. The Mi'kmaq reacted by declaring war on the intruders on September 24. On October 2, Cornwallis responded by issuing a proclamation "to Annoy, distress or destroy the Savages commonly called Mic-macks, wherever they are found" (Upton 1979:52). A bounty of first £10 and later £50 was put on their heads, dead or alive. The conflict between the two lasted until November 1752, when the 1725 treaty was reaffirmed. This treaty was broken by English sailors who, for bounty money, killed and scalped six friendly Mi'kmaq who had helped them after they had been shipwrecked. Peace was re-established in 1762, but the situation became tense when the Americans sought Mi'kmaq aid in the American Revolution.

The aftermath of that war was deadly to the Mi'kmaq. After the fighting stopped in 1782, Loyalists from New York flooded Nova Scotia, tripling their population in one year to 42,000. This was particularly devastating to Mi'kmaq use of marine resources, as the settlers established communities along the coasts. Powerful as well was their impact on land animals, which can be seen in one statistic. In the winter of 1789, gangs of English poachers killed off a reported 9,000 moose and caribou in Cape Breton alone. During the next few years, there were reports of starvation among the Mi'kmaq.

The nineteenth century saw the rights of the Mi'kmaq constantly trampled. English squatters moved onto officially declared Mi'kmaq land, sometimes even taking over Mi'kmaq farms when the owners were away. The Mi'kmaq fought back through legal channels. **Andrew Meuse**, sagamore of the Bear River band, tried to fight the alcoholism that was being inflicted on his people by unscrupulous traders. His 1828 petition called for an end to the sale of alcohol to his people. The result was a law that left final action to the discretion of local magistrates. None of them acted to stop the trade.

The most famous Mi'kmaq petition came from sagamore **Paussamigh Pemmeenauweet** (**Louis Benjamin Peminout**), who sent these heartfelt words to Queen Victoria in 1840:

> I cannot cross the great lake to talk to you for my canoe is too small, and I am old and weak. I cannot look upon you for my eyes not see so far. You cannot hear my voice across the great waters. I therefore send this wampum and paper talk to tell the Queen I am in trouble. My people are in trouble. When I was young I had plenty: now I am old, poor and sickly too. My people are poor. No hunting grounds. No beaver. No otter. No nothing. Indians poor—poor for ever. No store. No chest. No clothes. All these woods once ours. Our fathers possessed them all. Now we cannot cut a tree to warm our wigwams in winter unless the white man please. (Upton 1979:89–90)

This petition initially made a great stir, but in the end little was done. The Mi'kmaq are still fighting for their survival, the most recent struggle being over their rights to fish (see case study). Today, there are more than 20,000 registered Mi'kmaq in Canada. The census of 1996 recorded that 6,720 people speak Mi'kmaq.

The Maliseet

The Maliseet live in seven small communities along their ancestral home by the St. John River in New Brunswick and Quebec. The name "**Maliseet**" (also spelled Malecite) is derived from a Mi'kmaq word, usually translated as "broken or lazy speakers," showing a Mi'kmaq bias concerning the slight differences between the two languages. The Maliseet today prefer to name themselves after the river, **Wolastoqewi**, "of the good (i.e., beautiful, navigable, and/or bountiful) river." The French first termed them "Etchemin" for reasons that are not yet clear.

Because they lived closer to the English of the United States than did the Mi'kmaq, the Maliseet were less inclined to raid the English and were quicker to come to agreement with them. The Maliseet were the main signatories of the 1713 Treaty of Portsmouth, New Hampshire, the first British treaty involving Canadian Natives. As Dickason states, this treaty, ". . . broke new ground by adding that Amerindians were not to be molested in the territories where they lived, and they were to enjoy 'free liberty for Hunting, Fishing and Fowling, and all other their Lawful Liberties & Privileges'" (Dickason 1992:178).

A locally well-known story tells us something about the poor treatment the Maliseet sometimes received in nineteenth-century New Brunswick. The story takes place around 1840. A young Maliseet man named **Pierre Lola** went to buy a ticket on the stagecoach from Fredericton to Woodstock, a distance of some 100 kilometres. He was refused because he was Native. Angry, he vowed to beat the stagecoach to its destination. They both started at eight o'clock in the morning. Lola led all the way through the rugged dirt roads, eventually winning the race by a narrow margin, a moral victory.

BOX 6-1	Placenames in Mi'kmaq

Anticosti (island): "forward land'"	**Quebec**: "it narrows"
Gaspé: "outer ends"	

In 1612, Father Pierre Biard reckoned there were fewer than 1,000 Etchemin. Today there are about 1,200 speakers of the Maliseet language in Canada, maybe 300 in the United States (Morrison and Wilson 1995:29).

The Western Abenaki

"**Abenaki**" is a general word of reference to different peoples living traditionally in what is now New England. It also refers to a confederacy that once linked the Mi'kmaq, Maliseet, Passamaquoddy, and Penobscot. The word is derived from **Aben-**, meaning "white or light," referring to morning and the east, and **-aki** (as in Milw<u>aukee</u>) meaning "earth" or "land" (Hodge 1971:1). Canadian <u>Abenaki</u> are mostly descendants of people who came from the river valley area of the Connecticut River, which covers parts of New Hampshire, Massachusetts, and Connecticut. Particularly important in the development of the Canadian communities were the **Sokoki**, whose name (Ozokwaki, pl. Ozokwakiak), means "the ones who broke up, broke away" (Day 1978:159), perhaps referring to an historic event when one Abenaki group departed from the others.

The Sokoki and the French first came into contact in the 1640s through the conflict the former had with the Montagnais and Algonquin allies of the French. Gradually, the Sokoki began to ally themselves with the French against their common Iroquois and English enemies. As they did so, they moved closer to French territory, coming down the St. François River to its mouth, across the St. Lawrence from Trois Rivières. A mission was established there in 1700. That community became known as Saint-François-de-Sales in French and Odanak in Abenaki. They would participate in virtually every French military move of the late seventeenth and eighteenth century, but would do so as allies with a sense of their own independence.

Their opposition to English incursion on their land can be seen in the following statement from **Jérôme Atecouando** ("Deer spirit-power"), a leader at Odanak. In 1752, he challenged the authority of the British to survey Abenaki lands without their permission, saying: "We forbid you very expressly to kill a single beaver or to take a single stick of wood on the lands we live on. If you want wood, we will sell it to you, but you shall not have it without our permission" (Dickason 1992:120).

Culturally, the Abenaki were similar to the Mi'kmaq and the Maliseet, but their more southerly residence resulted in some differences. They grew corn, beans, and squash and harvested the nuts of the butternut and chestnut trees. They were patrilineal, as were their northern cousins, but differed in having the more southerly traits of totemic clans (the turtle, bear, beaver, otter, and partridge at Odanak in 1736) and a clear distinction between peace and war leaders.

The precontact population of the Western Abenaki was at least 5,000; all Abenaki would probably more than double that. In 1991, the band rolls of Odanak and Wôlinak in Quebec added up to 1,613, with fewer than a quarter of the population actually living on the small reserves. In 1999, only one speaker of Abenaki remained in Canada, Cécile Wawanolet. She is working hard to preserve the language through her teaching.

The Delaware

At the time of first contact, the Delaware were located in the lands drained by the Delaware River, its tributaries, and the lower Hudson River. This put them in the area of what is now southeastern New York and Pennsylvania, New Jersey, and Delaware. At that time they were about 40 village bands, with a total population of at least 8,000 to 12,000. Linguistically, they formed three groups, the Munsee to the north and east, the northern Unami or Unalachtigo, and the southern Unami.

Delaware is not their name for themselves, but a word derived from the name of a Baron who was the governor of Virginia. They came to prefer **Lenape**, "real people," -**len**- meaning "ordinary, real, original" and -**ape**- meaning "man." Sometimes -**len**- is added again, giving the name **Lenni-Lenape**.

The Delaware were similar to the Iroquoians of the Eastern Woodlands. Corn was the staple of their subsistence, with deer the most important game animal. As with the Iroquoians, the lineages seem to have been determined matrilineally. One lineage supplied the chiefs of the village with a separation of war and peace chiefs as well. From at least 1750 on there is evidence for a three phratry system similar to that of the Iroquoians, with three groupings of clans labelled as Turtle, Turkey, and Wolf.

The Delaware were forced to move west. By the mid eighteenth century they were in Ohio. Today, Delaware living in the United States have their communities in Kansas, Wisconsin, and Oklahoma.

Some Munsee were influenced by Moravian missionaries to convert and form the Christian Delaware community of Gnadenhütten. Their leader was **Glickhican**, who had fought against the English but who became a Christian at about age 50 in 1769, baptised with the name Isaac in 1770. On April 13, 1773, he said:

> You appear to dread Glickhican, as formerly known to you. Yes, there was a time when I would have scorned to have been assailed in the manner you now meditate; but I am no more Glickhican, I am Isaac now, a believer in the true and living God, for whose sake I am willing to suffer anything—even death. (Curnoe 1996:36)

His statement was prophetic. On March 8, 1782, Isaac, his wife, 28 other men, 26 other women, and 34 children of the peaceful community of Gnadenhütten would be murdered by Pennsylvania militia who falsely accused them of siding with the British.

Some of the survivors of this massacre went to live by the Thames River in what is now southwestern Ontario, founding the village of Moraviantown in 1792. This community would prosper until October 5, 1813, when it was burned and looted by the American army after the defeat of the Native forces under the great Shawnee leader **Tecumseh** ("Across the Lake"). Tecumseh had been abandoned by the British forces under Major-General Henry Proctor.

Gradually, three Delaware communities developed in Ontario. These communities would be Moraviantown (or Moravian of the Thames), Munceytown (or Munceys of the Thames), and another group invited to live with the Six Nations by the Cayuga. Their language today is severely under threat. In the introduction to his excellent dictionary of Munsee Delaware, John O'Meara writes that:

> There may be no more than five or ten speakers of Ontario Delaware, as well as perhaps ten or fifteen individuals who understand Delaware to varying degrees. Most speakers known to me are in their seventies or eighties. (O'Meara 1996:vii)

THE IROQUOIANS

Iroquoian refers to a family of languages that at the time of contact were spoken along the eastern coast of the United States and into New York State. In Canada, speakers of these languages lived along the St. Lawrence and in southern Ontario. All of those languages

BOX 6-2	**Iroquoian Placenames**	
Word	**Language**	**Meaning**
Canada	St. Lawrence/Laurentian Iroquoians	village, community
Niagara	Neutral	neck
Ontario	Huron/Wendat	it is a large lake
Toronto	Mohawk	poles in water

spoken in Canada are now dead. This includes what is called **St. Lawrence** or **Laurentian Iroquoians**, which was spoken by the people or peoples that Jacques Cartier encountered along the St. Lawrence in the 1530s. Ironically, these people gave us the word "**Canada**," meaning "village" or "community." The irony continues in that another one of those languages, Huron, gave us the name "**Ontario**," meaning "large lake," for the province that was their ancestral home but is more their symbolic home now.

In addition to language, Iroquoians shared a corn-based agriculture making for relatively permanent communities with populations up to 2,500, a matrilineal clan system typically comprised of eight clans (the Mohawk and Oneida have only three), and political mechanisms linking tribes in alliances or federations. The best-known example of this is that of the Iroquois Confederacy.

The Huron/Wendat

When the French Jesuit missionaries came to live with the **Wendat** people they named **Huron** (see Box 6.6) during the 1630s, that people was a five-member confederacy numbering between 20,000 and 30,000: the **Hatinniawenten** ("they are of bear country" or Bear); the **Hatingeennonniahak** ("they made or used to make fishing net cords" or Cord); the **Arendayeronnon** ("people at the rock" or Rock); the **Ataronchronnon** ("people in the clay or swamp" or Bog); and the **Atahontayenrat** ("one has two white ears" or Deer).

To the west of them were the **Etionnontateronnon**, "people at the mountain," a grouping of at least two tribes. They were called the **Petun** by the French, as they were vital intermediaries through which the Huron obtained tobacco grown further south. The Petun might have numbered from somewhere between 6,200 to possibly as much as 10,000 during the 1620s. To the southwest of the Petun and Huron, from the western end of Lake Ontario to Niagara (a Neutral word meaning "neck") lived a related people that the French referred to as the **Neutral**, because that appeared to be their position with respect to the conflict between the Huron and the Iroquois.

During the 1640s, the Huron lost most of their battles against the Iroquois, who were raiding them to seek revenge, to boost their numbers depleted by disease and war, and to gain a better position in the European trade. By the 1650s, the Huron, Petun, and Neutral had been driven out of their home territory.

After the Dispersal: The Wendat Tribes Follow Different Paths

Their story did not end there, but followed three different plotlines. One led to joining the Iroquois. The Deer, along with the remnants of Neutral, joined the Seneca and formed a

BOX 6-3   Atsena's Speeches and the Division of the Huron

In 1653, **Atsena** ("Dish") made a promise to join the Mohawk. In May 1657, he was approached by a Mohawk delegation to Quebec and was asked to keep his promise. That night, the Huron decided to split their fates along three lines. The Bear would join the Mohawk. The Rock, who already had a number of their people living with that nation, reaffirmed an earlier promise to join the Onondaga. The Cord would stay. Atsena formally addressed the Mohawk representative with these words:

> My brother...it is decided; I am at your service. I cast myself, with my eyes shut, into your canoe, without knowing what I am doing. But, whatever may betide, I am resolved to die. Even if you would break my head as soon as we are out of range of the cannon here, it matters not; I am quite resolved. I do not wish my cousins of two other Nations to embark this time with me, in order that they may first see how you will behave toward me. (JR43: 193)

The leaders of the two other tribes expressed their sympathies for Atsena and the Bear. One of them, possibly the leader of the Cord, included with it three wampum belt presents and symbolic statements of concern:

> Take care...that my brother Atsena, who gives himself to you, does not fall into the mud in disembarking; here is a collar to make the earth firm where he will set foot on it. When he disembarks, do not allow him to sit on the bare ground; here is something wherewith to make a mat for him on which he may rest. And, that you may not laugh at the women and children when they weep at seeing themselves in a strange country, here is a handkerchief that I give you to wipe away their tears, and the sweat from their brows. (JR43: 193)

Atsena made a farewell speech to the French, of which the following is part:

> Take courage, Onontio ("Great Mountain," Huron name for French Governors),...take courage Ondesonk ("Hawk," Huron name for Father Simon Le Moyne), I leave you, it is true; but my heart does not leave you. I am going away, it is true; but I leave you my cousins, who are better than I am. And to show you that Quebec is ever my country, I leave you the large kettle, which we use in our greatest rejoicings. (JR43: 195)

Both the Mohawk and the Bear kept their promises. We hear no more of Atsena, but the Mohawk were to benefit from the addition of the Bear to their ranks. Joseph Brant is said to have had Huron ancestors on both sides of his family.

separate community in their territory. During the 1650s, the Huron, who had moved close to the French settlements, were faced with some tough choices. The Mohawk and the Onondaga were competing with each other to get the Huron to join with them. Both had lost many people to European disease and to war. The Huron saw the inability of the French to protect them, particularly in 1656 when the Mohawk successfully attacked the Huron community at Isle d'Orleans, half way across the St. Lawrence from Quebec.

BOX 6-4   The Homecoming

Late in August 1999, four groups of Wendat, coming from Lorette in Quebec, Michigan, Kansas, and Oklahoma returned home after 350 years. It was the first time the various groups had gotten together over that period of time. Their leaders worked together to come up with a declaration of the reformation of the Wendat Confederacy.

Their ancestors returned with them. In 1636, the Huron of the Bear tribe held a large Feast of the Dead. During this feast, more than 500 people who had died over the last 10 years or so were reburied together, in a powerful statement of the unity of the people: together as one in death as in life. In the mid twentieth century, these individuals were dug up by archaeologists interested in studying the Huron. A good number of scientific publications came from that study. At the homecoming of the Wendat peoples, the ancestors were returned to the ground.

The Huron that remained with the French moved into their current home community of Lorette or Wendake ("at the Wendat") near Quebec City in 1697. From 1685 to 1844, their head chief would bear the name of **Tsawenhohi** ("Vulture"), with a brief hiatus in the mid eighteenth century. A thriving community exists at Lorette today, contrary to the too commonly held belief that the Huron are "extinct."

The Formation of the Wyandot

A group of people, primarily Petun, but including some Huron and possibly some Neutral, came together in the 1650s to form a people who came to be known as the **Wyandot**, from a mispronunciation of "Wendat," a term the Huron and the Petun used to refer to themselves. Just as the Huron had the chief's name "Vulture," so the Wyandot had **Sastaretsi**. The Wyandot were led by a Sastaretsi from at least the 1650s until the nineteenth century. Their post dispersal history has been one of periodic movement to far-flung places, moving in the seventeenth century throughout the Great Lakes, settling in around Windsor/Detroit in 1701, and gradually extending to Ohio. In the nineteenth century, they were forced to move west, first to Kansas and then to Oklahoma. Communities of Wyandot now live in those last two named states.

THE IROQUOIS CONFEDERACY *Great Law of Peace.*

In the chapter on oral traditions in Part 1, we saw how the story of the formation of the people known usually as the Iroquois combines historical events and the principles by which an alliance was formed. The combination of the two is known as the Great Law of Peace (in Mohawk, **Gayanerengo:wa**, the Great Good). The resulting alliance or federation became known to the people by a name that means either "they build a house" or "they extend a house" (see Box 6.6). Sometimes the people refer to themselves as **Ongwehon:we**, which, loosely translated, means "humans who are human."

BOX 6-5   Outsider/Insider Names

Name	Source	Meaning
Iroquoians		
Huron	French	"people of rough hair" (because of their use of the "mohawk" haircut), an insult term in Europe
Wendat	Huron	?
Iroquois	Basque (?)	possibly from a verb meaning "to kill"
Hotinonhsyonni'		
or	Seneca version	"they extend a house"
Hotinonhson:ni:h		"they build a house"
Mohawk	Algonquian	"they eat animate things" (i.e., are cannibals)
Ganyen'geha:ga'	Mohawk	"people of Ganyen'ge', i.e., "At the Flint," once their principal village.
Oneida (from **Onenyode'a:ga:**)	Oneida	"people of the standing stone"
Onondaga (from **Ononda'ge:ga**)	Onondaga	"people of onon:da'ge" or "at the hill"
Cayuga (from **Gayohgho:non**)	Cayuga	"people of Oiogouen"
Seneca	?	?
Onondowa'ga:'	Seneca	"people of the large hill"
Tuscarora	Tuscarora	?
Algonquians		
Mi'kmaq	Algonquian	"allies"
Ilnu	Mi'kmaq	"people"
Delaware	English	named after a governor of Virginia
Lenni-Lenape	Munsee	"real people"
Abenaki	Abenaki	"land of the sunrise, east"
Maliseet	Mi'kmaq	"broken or lazy speakers"
Welastekwiyek	Maliseet	"good river people"

As discussed, the political system created involved 50 chiefs referred to in English as **sachems**. Each of the sachems was more or less hereditary, coming from the best qualified within a particular matrilineage that belonged to a particular clan. The holder of the position could lose his position if he were deemed to be acting for his own interests instead of those of his people. The woman who was the clan matron would divest him of the position, "dehorning" him as the expression goes.

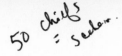

All leadership was not held by the sachems, however. There were also **Pine Tree chiefs**, people of ability, but not of a chiefly lineage, who rose to prominence because of what they had achieved.

The Mohawk

In the seventeenth century, the Mohawk had three principal communities of over 1,000 people, plus at least several other villages. Each of the three clans of the Mohawk, the Bear, the Turtle, and the Wolf could have dominated in each of the principal communities. Mohawk is not their traditional name for themselves (see Box 6.5). Their own name is **Ganyen'geha:ga'**, meaning "people of Ganyen'ge," the latter usually translated as "At the Flint," a term for what once was their principal village.

The easternmost member of the confederacy, the Mohawk were first to fight the French. First blood went to the newcomers. In 1609, Samuel de Champlain decided to strengthen the French connection with their new allies, the Montagnais, Algonquin, and Huron, by joining in a raid on the Mohawk. These Native nations had helped the French. Military assistance had been requested in return. In July, attacking deep in Mohawk country, the combined forces, bolstered by the surprising effects of the French guns, killed 50 Mohawk warriors and took 10 to 12 prisoners.

Thus began a smouldering antagonism that would flare up periodically through the seventeenth century, to be revived in nationalistic French history texts of the nineteenth and early twentieth centuries, and then again by ethnocentric elements in the Quebec media in the 1990s.

Three mission communities were formed in Canada. In the 1660s, French Jesuits founded **Caughnawaga** ("At the Rapids"), near Montreal. By 1673 there were possibly more Mohawks there than in the more independent villages in New York. From Caughnawaga came **Kateri Tekakwitha**, a Mohawk/Algonquin who died young but, after her death, became a heroine to Native and French Christians of New France through miraculous cures that were attributed to her spiritual intercession. She was beatified in 1980, one step away from becoming the first Native saint. Today, her name is borne by a Native-Catholic movement.

Sometime around the mid eighteenth century, at the borderline between Ontario, Quebec, and New York, the mission community of St. Regis or **Akwesasne** ("Where the Partridge Drums") was formed from part of the Caughnawaga community.

Early in the eighteenth century the Christian Mohawk community of **Oka** (Algonquin, "walleye" or "pickerel") or **Kanehsatake** (Mohawk, probably "there is plenty of sand"), was founded by Sulpician missionaries, again in the Montreal area. The French king promised the land to the Mohawk. However, unknown to the Mohawk at the time, the powerful Sulpicians pulled some strings so that the land was given to them instead. For more than two centuries the Mohawk unsuccessfully appealed to French and British governments for basic rights to the land. They were even denied the right to cut firewood without Sulpician permission. Some Mohawk left for Ontario to form **Wahta** ("Maple") in 1881, in part because of the tension with the controlling Sulpicians, in part because the government made an offer better on paper than it would prove to be in land. The Sulpicians bowed out early in the twentieth century, leaving the powder keg that would explode in Oka in 1990.

During the American Revolution, a Mohawk named **Thayendanega** ("He sets two sticks," i.e., signifying bets, side by side) or **Joseph Brant**, a Pine Tree Chief, rose to prominence. He also set side by side his loyalties to the British and to the Mohawk. While he respected the British and their religion, siding with them militarily and translating the gospel of St. Mark and the Book of Common Prayer into Mohawk, he also pushed for pan-Indian unity and demanded of the British that they be true and faithful allies. At the end of the American Revolution, Thayendanega addressed General Haldimand requesting that the Native nations that had put their lives at risk in their ancestral homeland by their allegiance to the British not be abandoned by them. He addressed Haldimand as "Brother" and said that he had been sent on behalf of all the Native allies of the King:

> . . . to know whether they are included in this treaty with the Americans as faithful allies should be, or not? and whether those lands which the great being above has pointed out for our ancestors & their descendants, and placed them there from the beginning, and where the bones of our forefathers are laid is secured to them? or whether the blood of their grand-children is to be mingled with their bones, thro' the means of our allies for whom we have often so freely bled? (Kelsay 1984:43)

In part as a response to these demands, land was purchased from the Mississauga in southwestern Ontario to be set aside for the Iroquois and those who wanted to come north with them. In 1785, that community had 464 Mohawk, 381 Cayuga, 245 Onondaga, 231 Delaware, 162 Oneida, 129 Tuscarora, 78 Seneca, 74 of the Siouan group, Tutelo, and the rest in smaller numbers of both Siouans and Algonquians. From some of the land later lost by the people, the city of Brantford in Ontario, named after Joseph Brant, was formed.

At the same time, another group of Mohawks, following **John Deserontyon**, founded a community by the Bay of Quinte, at the eastern end of Lake Ontario. It is generally known today as Tyendinaga, after Joseph Brant's Mohawk name.

Today, there are reputedly 2,000 speakers in Canada, making it the strongest Iroquoian language in this country, with another 1,000 in the United States.

The Oneida

Traditional western neighbours of the Mohawk, speaking a closely related language, are the Oneida. The name comes from **Onenyode'a:ga**, "people of the standing stone," referring both to the name of their principal historical village and to a particular rock said to always be near its location. A stone returned to the Oneida community in New York in 1974 is said to have been the original one.

The Oneida were smaller in number than the other Iroquois nations, with only one major community. This being the case, they had to replenish losses from war and disease from other peoples. In the Jesuit Relations of the mid 1640s it was reported (JR27:297 and JR28:281) that Mohawk men had joined to make up for warrior losses resulting from their fighting with the Huron and Algonquin. Early in the eighteenth century, the Oneida generously gave the Tuscarora land on which to settle and invited various Eastern Algonquian groups to join them in the 1780s.

Originally neutral in the American Revolution, owing to the influence of Presbyterian minister Samuel Kirkland and the wishes of the young warriors, who acted against the sachems in this matter, most Oneida sided with the Americans. Some even participated in the 1779 American attacks against Onondaga, Cayuga, and Seneca communities. They would discover that such loyalty would not be rewarded. While the federal government made promises of land, these were nullified by New York's efforts to divest them of that land. Most of them were forced to leave the state that they defended, the majority going west to

Wisconsin. Some headed for Canada, as members of the Six Nations community. Four hundred and ten others purchased land near London, Ontario, and from 1840 to 1845 moved into a separate settlement.

Today, there are approximately 200 speakers of Oneida in Canada and fewer than 50 in the United States.

The Onondaga

The name "Onondaga" comes from **Ononda'ge:ga**, "people of onon:da'ge," or "at the hill," their principal community, one of two reported during the seventeenth century. The Onondaga are also called the "Name Bearers" and "Fire-Keepers" in council, showing their significance in the confederacy. Today, between Six Nations in Canada and their community in New York, there are fewer than 100 speakers of Onondaga.

The Cayuga

The Cayuga had three principal villages during the seventeenth century, one of which gave them their name, **Gayohgho:non**, "people of Oiogouen." The meaning of the village name is unclear. Today, they have no community of their own. They live with the Seneca in New York and Oklahoma, with the Oneida in Wisconsin, and with the others of the Six Nations in Ontario. Currently, Cayuga is the second-strongest Iroquoian language in Canada, with 360 speakers here and 10 in the United States.

The Seneca

The Seneca were the largest Iroquois nation during the seventeenth century, with two main communities, one east, one west, each having various satellite villages. In 1665, the French were calculating the warrior strength of their Iroquois enemies. The Seneca were recorded as having 1,200, the Mohawk between 300 and 400, the Cayuga and Onondaga 300, and the Oneida 140 (Tooker 1978a:421). Warriors of this period generally made up between 25% and 35% of the population. They had their numbers enhanced by a community in their country made up of the Deer tribe of the Huron, the Neutral, Susquehannock, and others who were Seneca by adoption.

The term "Seneca" is somewhat mysterious, used in different versions during the seventeenth century to refer to various Iroquois groups. No meaning is known. Their traditional term for themselves is **Onondowa'ga'**, "people of the large hill." Perhaps at some point that referred to a physical feature near a significant community. They are referred to as Doorkeepers in council, as they were the westernmost nation.

Despite having villages attacked in 1779 by the Americans, most of the Seneca decided to stay in New York, having the fewest numbers of the confederacy going to Six Nations. But New York became a hard place to live in the years following the revolution. The Seneca were hard hit by alcoholism and other nasty effects of social disruption. But with the problem also came an answer. On June 15, 1799, a Seneca bearing the sachem name of **Sganyadai:yo**, "Handsome or Beautiful Lake" (1735–1815), but who had done little to that point to add distinction to that name, had a vision, the first of three that would follow over the next year. The visions provided the **Gaiwi:yoh**, or "good message," which combined condemnation of

BOX 6-6   Native Words

Akwesasne: "Where the Partridge Drums," Mohawk community located at the connecting points of New York, Ontario, and Quebec.

Arendayeronnon: "People at the rock," the Rock tribe of the Huron.

Atahontayenrat: "One has two white ears," the Deer tribe of the Huron.

Ataronchronnon: "People in the clay or swamp," the Bog tribe of the Huron.

Caughnawaga: "At the Rapids," a Mohawk community near Montreal.

Etionnontateronnon: "People at the mountain," the Petun or Tobacco nation.

Gaiwi:yoh: "It is a good, great, or beautiful matter," the name for the teachings that sprang from the visions of Handsome Lake.

Gayanerengo:wa: "It is a great good," the Great Law of Peace, the combination (Mohawk) history and set of teachings that brought the Iroquois together.

Hatingeennonniahak: "They used to make fishing net cords," the Cord tribe of the Huron.

Hatinniawenten: "They are of bear country," the Bear tribe of the Huron.

Kanehsatake: The name for the Mohawk community associated with Oka.

Oka: An Algonquin word meaning "walleye" or "pickerel."

Ongwehon:we: Loosely translated means "humans who are human," and refers to members of the Iroquois Confederacy.

Onontio: "It is a large hill," a translation of Governor Montmagny's name, subsequently the Iroquoian name for all governors of New France.

sachem: Derived from an Eastern Algonquian word for leader (see saqmaw) and used to refer to the 50 chiefly titles of the Iroquois.

saqmaw: Mi'kmaq word for leader; cognates have entered English as "sachem" and "sagamore."

Sokoki: From Ozokwaki (pl. Ozokwak-iak), "the ones who broke up, broke away," the main group making up the Abenaki of Canada.

Wahta: "Maple," name for Mohawk community near Georgian Bay.

alcohol, witchcraft, love medicine, abortion, adultery, and other social ills, with the promotion of traditional songs, dances, prayers, and European methods of farming and formal education.

Handsome Lake spread his message across Iroquois country until his death in 1815. But it did not die with him. Others codified what they had heard so that there developed a strong oral tradition of the words of Handsome Lake, known as the Longhouse Religion. That tradition is still strong today.

The Tuscarora

The Tuscarora took a hard road to Canada. At the time of first contact there were several thousand Tuscarora living in Virginia and North Carolina. During the seventeenth and early

Native Individuals 6-1

Jérôme Atecouando ("Deer Spirit Power"): An eighteenth-century Abenaki leader at Odanak.

Atsena ("Dish"): The chief of the Atinniawenten or Bear tribe of the Huron, who in 1657 led his people in joining the Mohawk.

John Deserontyon: An eighteenth-century Mohawk who led a group of his people to live in a community at the eastern end of Lake Ontario.

Glickhacan: A Munsee leader killed at Gnadenhütten in 1782.

Pierre Lola: A nineteenth-century Maliseet known for a legendary race he won against a stagecoach.

Andrew Meuse: A nineteenth-century Mi'kmaq saqmaw of the Bear River band.

Paussamigh Pemmeenauweet (Louis Benjamin Peminout): A Mi'kmaq saqmaw who sent a petition to Queen Victoria in 1840.

Sastaretsi: The name of the traditional chief of the Wyandot.

Sganyadai:yo ("Handsome or Beautiful Lake"): A Seneca sachem whose visions led to the development of the Gaiwi:oh, or Good Message.

Kateri Tekakwitha ("She Moves Things"): A seventeenth-century Mohawk/Algonquin who is one step away from becoming the first Native saint.

Tecumseh ("Across the Lake"): A Shawnee leader who led Native troops from a number of nations on the British side during the War of 1812.

Thayendanega ("He sets two sticks side by side") or Joseph Brant: A Mohawk who, during the American Revolution, led his people in fighting on the side of the British and later in their forced migration to southwestern Ontario.

Tsawenhohi ("Vulture"): The name of the traditional chief of the Huron of Lorette for almost every year from 1685 to 1844.

Cécile Wawanolet: The last speaker of Abenaki at Odanak.

eighteenth centuries, they had land taken from them and legal agreements to respect their territory were violated by incoming settlers and their governments. For years, the Tuscarora protested peacefully, to no avail. Finally, in 1711, they reached their breaking point and attacked a settler community full force, beginning what is known as the Tuscarora War. For the next two years, battles raged, until late March 1713, when they were soundly defeated. Several hundred Tuscarora were killed and 400 more were sold into slavery.

The survivors looked north for a safe refuge. The Oneida invited them to live in their territory, sponsoring them in 1722–3 to join the confederacy as the sixth nation. By 1771, they numbered about 1,000. During the American Revolution, some followed the Oneida in siding with the Americans, while others took the opposite position. One hundred and twenty-nine ended up going to the Six Nations reserve, where they number today around 800.

Timeline 6-1

2500 B.C.: First construction of the Mnjikaning fish weir.

1450s: Possible date for the formation of the Iroquois Confederacy.

1650s: The dispersal of the Wendat peoples (Huron and Petun).

1700: The establishment of the Abenaki mission at Odanak.

1713: The Maliseet sign a treaty with the English.

1722–3: The Tuscarora are asked to join the Iroquois Confederacy.

1725: First treaty between the Mi'kmaq and the English.

1746: Around 4,000 Mi'kmaq die from typhus spread from the French fleet.

1752: Second treaty between the Mi'kmaq and the English.

1782: About 90 Delaware of Gnadenhütten are killed.

1785: The formation of the Six Nations community in southwestern Ontario.

1799: Seneca Handsome Lake's first vision.

1924: Six Nations forced to have elected rather than hereditary government.

1990: The conflict at Oka.

1999: The homecoming of the Wendat.

Tuscarora today is the most threatened of the languages of the Iroquois. In the 1980s it was claimed that there were seven speakers in Canada and only forty in New York in the United States. There are fewer speakers today.

There is no agreement as to what the name "Tuscarora" (expressed in the twentieth century as Skaru:ren') (Rudes 1987:267) actually means.

KEY TERMS

Gaiwi:yoh (Seneca)
sachem
saqmaw (Mi'kmaq)
matrilineal
patrilineal
Pine Tree chiefs
weir

CONTENT QUESTIONS

1. What two linguistic groups belong to the Eastern Woodlands culture area and what nations does each include?
2. Where were the three different paths taken by the Wendat tribes?

3. How were the Delaware culturally similar to the Eastern Iroquoians?
4. What is the difference between "Iroquois" and "Iroquoian"?
5. What situation initially set into play the context for the Oka crisis?

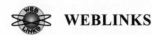 **WEBLINKS**

www.axess.com/mohawk/index.htm
A good list of links on the Iroquois and Mohawk is presented at Kahon:wes's Mohawk and Iroquois Index.

collections.ic.gc.ca/heirloom_series/volume2/volume2.htm
For detailed yet readable accounts of Mi 'kmaq ways of life (click on "Chapter 1"); on the St. Lawrence Lowlands Iroquoians and Algonquians (click on "Chapter 2"); or on the Woodland Natives ("Chapter 3").

www.dickshovel.com/aben.html
Deals with Abenaki history.

www.mikmaq.net/english/index.html
Deals with the Mi'kmaq.

www.oneida-nation.net/
Deals with Oneida history and the history of the Iroquois generally.

www.woodland-centre.on.ca/mm.html
The Woodland Cultural Centre presents information about various Ontario Natives.

THE EASTERN
SUBARCTIC

- Cree
- Montagnais
- Naskapi
- Ojibue.
- Attikamek
Beothuk.

OVERVIEW

The Western and Eastern Subarctic regions are physically dominated by the Canadian Shield. This means, first of all, that there is a lot of hard rock scraped bare by glaciers. Scattered throughout are glacially dumped sands, clays, and gravels, resulting in the type of northern swampland known as **muskeg** (originally a Cree word), rivers and lakes. Combined with the long winters and short summers, the Subarctic might seem a harsh place to live, but it provides ideal habitat for a number of animal species that supplied a good living for the people. These include caribou in the north, **moose** ("muus" in East Cree) further south, beaver, muskrat, and hare. Birds are also in abundance, including grouse, migrating water-fowl such as Canada and snow geese, and a variety of ducks. Also plentiful are fish such as trout, whitefish, sturgeon, burbot, and pike.

A few features separate the Eastern Subarctic from its western counterpart. First, the area has a shorter period of occupation. The first significant occupation in the Subarctic began in the west with the "Shield culture" archaeological complex (Wright 1996:261) about 8,000 years ago, gradually moving east as the glaciers melted away. Not until between about 5,000 and 4,000 years ago did Shield culture make its way to the Hudson Bay Lowlands of Ontario and Quebec and to Labrador.

Second, the languages spoken in the Eastern Subarctic are **Algonquian**, rather than Athapaskan. The languages and associated peoples typically assigned to the Eastern Subarctic are **Cree**, **Montagnais**, **Naskapi**, **Ojibwe**, **Attikamek**, and **Beothuk** (who died off in

BOX 7-1	**Moose Cree Terms for Months**

Names for months reflect events and situations that are important to the people at that time. What do these terms teach you about what was important to the Moose Cree?

Month	Moose Cree Meaning
January	Great Scattering About Moon
February	Old Moon
March	Eagle Moon
April	Goose Moon
May	Frog Moon
June	Sprouting Moon
July	(Goose) Moulting Moon
August	(Geese) Flying Up Moon
September	Snow Goose Moon
October	(Geese) Flying Off Moon
November	Freeze Up Moon
December	Scattering About Little Moon

Newfoundland by 1829). This appears as more diversity than actually exists. Montagnais, Naskapi, and Attikamek are dialects of Cree. Ojibwe is a near relative of Cree. The linguistic closeness can be seen in Box 7.2.

Third, the Algonquians of the Eastern Subarctic have a much longer period of contact with Europeans than did the Dene of the Western Subarctic. The Montagnais, Naskapi, and Beothuk encountered whalers, fishermen, and explorers from at least the 1500s onwards. The Montagnais and the easternmost of the Ojibwa dealt with the French during the 1600s, while the Cree by the shores of Hudson Bay and James Bay connected with the Hudson's Bay Company and the fur trade from 1670.

BOX 7-2	**Similarities Between Eastern Subarctic Algonquian Languages**

Montagnais	East Cree	Swampy Cree	Ojibwe	English
amishkw	amiskw	amisk	amikk	beaver
chiyaashkw	chiyaashkw	kiyaask	kayaashk	gull
chinosheew	chinushew	kinoseew	kinooshe	pike
ooteenaw	utenaaw	ooteenaw	ooteenaw	village, town
nameekwosh	namekush	nameekos	nameekoss	lake trout

GETTING IT RIGHT 1-1 **Algonquin vs. Algonquian**

It is very confusing to have the almost identical terms "Algonquin" (or "Algonkin") and "Algonquian" (or "Algonkian"') refer to two different groups. Perhaps it is useful to remember that the smallest word ("Algonquin") has the smallest scope of reference (i.e., to a single people) while the largest word ("Algonquian") has the largest scope of reference (i.e., to a language family).

THE CREE

The name "Cree" is not their own term for themselves. First written as "**Kiristinon**" in 1640 (JR18:229), it comes from a French version of part of an Ojibwe name for a Cree band living south of James Bay. English writers shortened that to a word they could more readily pronounce. Prior to contact, the home of the Cree centred around James Bay and the southern part of Hudson Bay, as well as the area of the rivers that flow into those bays. Their numbers at that time have been estimated as between 15,000 and 20,000. After contact, this homeland extended both north and west, largely on account of the fur trade. Today, the Cree are the largest and most widespread Native society in Canada, living from northern Quebec to northern Alberta. In the 1996 census, 76,475 people listed Cree as one of their mother tongues, the greatest number for any Native language.

One way of subdividing the groups of Cree is by dialect. Outside the Eastern Subarctic there are the **Plains Cree** of the three Prairie provinces. Within the Eastern Subarctic there are the **Swampy Cree** of the western James Bay and Hudson Bay drainage systems. Along with the Plains Cree, they make up most of the Cree speakers. Then there are the **Woods Cree** of northern Manitoba and Saskatchewan, the **Moose Cree** (southern end of James Bay), **Attikamek** (southcentral Quebec), and the **East Cree** (east of James Bay and Hudson Bay).

Too much can be read into dialect groups. They were not separate "tribes" with one leader or a linked council of leaders. Traditionally, the Cree were organized into smaller units, with informal leadership based on respect, wisdom, and suggestion.

BOX 7-4 **Five Cree Words You Know**

Saskatoon: from a Cree word meaning "big, wood berry," referring to the Saskatoon or service berry, an important resource for Prairie people.

Saskatchewan: from a Cree word meaning "it flows fast," referring to the Saskatchewan River.

moose: from a Cree word meaning "moose."

muskeg: from a Cree word meaning "swamp."

Winnipeg: from a Cree word referring to salty, silty, or muddy water, a term for Lake Winnipeg.

BOX 7-5	The Cree in Politics

Over the last 30 years, Cree leaders have had a strong impact on the Canadian political scene. Three of those leaders, with books for learning about their lives are:

Billy Diamond:
Chief: The Fearless Vision of Billy Diamond, by Roy MacGregor, Toronto: Penguin Books, 1989

Elijah Harper:
Elijah: No Ordinary Hero, by Pauline Comeau, Vancouver: Douglas & McIntyre, 1993

Ovide Mercredi:
In the Rapids: Navigating the Future of First Nations, by Ovide Mercredi and Mary Ellen Turpel, Toronto: Penguin Books, 1993

Beyond the nuclear family, two groups were important: the hunting group and the "macroband." The hunting group, sometimes called the "microband," was made up of several linked families, consisting of 10 to 20 people in total. Hunting groups would space themselves out according to the availability of resources in the area, often being anywhere from 15 to 80 kilometres away from their neighbouring group. The kinship pattern is what is termed "bilateral," meaning that both the mother's and the father's families were of equal importance. This made for greater flexibility in forming the hunting group than if one side were considered more important than the other. The hunting group would be together from late August until early June of the next year.

From late spring through the summer, a number of these hunting groups would get together to form macrobands of perhaps 75 to 150 people, possibly more in some instances. While the "food" reason for getting together was usually to fish at places where large numbers of fish could be found, this time together served social needs as well. It was a time to share information, to renew old acquaintances, and to pursue romance.

THE INNU: MONTAGNAIS AND NASKAPI

The population of the **Innu** (Montagnais and Naskapi) at the time of early contact is difficult to determine. The French encountered only some of their bands and disease early struck the southernmost Innu quite hard. Estimates of their number vary from 4,000 to 10,000, with the latter figure probably being closer to an accurate reckoning. Today, they have a population of over 12,000.

Montagnais

The **Montagnais** ("people of the mountain") received that name in French first from Samuel de Champlain. The term refers to the hilly country in which some of the bands lived. Their own name for themselves comes from a word (**Ilnu** for the southern Montagnais, **Innu** for the eastern Montagnais) meaning "human being, person." They differ from the Naskapi in

BOX 7-6   The Endurance of the Montagnais

Jesuit Father Paul Le Jeune, one of the most ethnocentric of missionaries in New France, said little that was positive about Native culture. Still, he admired the way that the Montagnais would patiently endure hardship: "[they] surpass us to such an extent, in this respect, that we ought to be ashamed" (JR6:233). When he agreed to winter with the Montagnais in 1633–4, they let him know that he would have to be strong to endure the occasional hardships of their lives. They warned him that:

> We shall be sometimes two days, sometimes three, without eating, for lack of food; take courage Chihiné, let thy soul be strong to endure suffering and hardship; keep thyself from being sad, otherwise thou wilt be sick; see how we do not cease to laugh, although we have little to eat. (JR6: 233)

several ways. They speak a different dialect. They live further south, with almost all of their communities existing along or near the north shore of the Gulf of St. Lawrence to the southern portion of the Quebec–Labrador peninsula. This means that they have a greater variety of wildlife upon which to draw, not being as dependent as the Naskapi on herds of caribou. This also means that they have a longer history of contact with Euro-Canadians, involving a longer and more intense participation in the fur trade. This contact has been almost exclusively with the French, while the Naskapi have dealt more with the English; therefore, currently, the Montagnais are more likely to speak French while the Naskapi are more likely to speak English.

Naskapi

Naskapi is a name that first appeared in the Jesuit Relation of 1643 as "Ouachkapiouek" (JR24:154). There is no definitive translation for this word. It seems, however, that negative connotations have become associated with the name (see Speck 1977:241), most likely coming from missionaries and traders who thought them "less civilized" than the Montagnais. The Naskapi, supplied with most of their needs by the caribou, tended to keep themselves apart from the products and influence of these non-Natives. During the nineteenth century, frustrated fur traders pressed the reluctant Naskapi to bring in furs. One trader, Donald Henderson, refused ammunition to the Innu living near his post in the 1840s, with the intent of forcing them to bring in furs. Being then dependent on guns for their hunting, they starved, with more than 100 deaths being reported (Wadden 1996:31).

   Their term for themselves is **Mushuau-Innu**, "barren ground people," so used because of their association with the homeland of the barrens caribou upon which they live. The herd they hunt today is the world's largest wild caribou herd, numbering more than half a million animals. Because of their reliance on the caribou, the Mushuau Innu were traditionally quite nomadic, following the travelling of the caribou. Innu elder **Maniaten**, a woman who had grown up when the caribou hunt was still relatively free from outsider influence, told Marie Wadden, author of the award-winning book *Nitassinan*, that in the fall her family used to go first from Uashat (Sept-Îles) to Schefferville, 490 kilometres, then sometimes to Kuujjuasq (Fort Chimo) by Ungava Bay, 370 kilometres, then to **Utshimassit** (Davis Inlet), 500 kilometres, then finally 300 kilometres to Michikamau Lake. Maniaten spoke of how hard those trips were:

> We carried our canoes, supplies, and even put the children on our backs. Many times the babies would cry and Mother would stop, unload what she was carrying and breastfeed the child. The older children walked behind because they were slow. Mother would keep encouraging the children; she would say, "Keep it up, we're getting closer to the next lake." When we got to a lake or river we'd pile everything back in the canoe and paddle off. (Wadden 1996:48–9)

Naskapi nomadism has been a strike against them politically. Missionaries and government officials have negatively referred to such land use as "primitive." In the courts, it has typically been treated as "non-use" of the land. But, in some senses, we should consider how many of us are nomads, too. I travel 20 kilometres to work each day, for a total of 200 kilometres a week. That means that in one semester alone (16 weeks), my "nomadism" takes me 3,200 kilometres, nearly twice the distance travelled by Maniaten's family. The serious point to be made here is that nomadism can be an effective, long-term use of the land and should not be dismissed as ineffective or outmoded. The Naskapi lead a good life with their nomadism, the most efficient use for their country ever devised.

THE OJIBWA/ANISHINABE

The name "**Ojibwa**" (sometimes spelled Ojibway in Canada, Chippewa in the United States, or Ojibwe when referring to the language) was originally recorded in 1667 as "Outchibouec," the name of a band living near what is now Sault Ste. Marie. The usual reference in the literature is to this term being a reference to the "puckering up" of their moccasins. The term that almost all groups of the Ojibwa use to refer to themselves is some form of **(A)nish(i)nabe** (plural ending, -k). Prior to contact with Europeans, this word was probably used primarily to refer to "human beings." After contact it came to refer to "Natives," particularly those of a shared linguistic and cultural heritage.

During the seventeenth century, there were a number of bands living near the north shores of Georgian Bay and Lake Superior. These would be similar in nature, perhaps larger in size than the Cree macrobands. Three of those names survived: Mississauga, Saulteaux, and Ojibwa. The first later came to refer to the mixture of Georgian Bay bands who fought their way south during the last two decades of the seventeenth century to settle into southern

---

BOX 7-7 **Five Words You Know in Ojibwe**

chipmunk: from an Ojibwe word referring to squirrels.

woodchuck: from an Ojibwe word referring to the woodchuck.

totem: from an Ojibwe word referring to clan.

Mississauga: from an Ojibwe word meaning "large river mouth."

pecan: from an Ojibwe word meaning "nut."

Ontario. Saulteaux (pronounced "so-toe") is now used to refer to the combined bands that moved out west into the Prairies with the fur trade and with the European push into Ojibwa country. They will be discussed in Chapter 9.

Two closely related people should be mentioned here, as they speak dialects of Ojibwe and are generally considered part of the Ojibwa. At the time of first contact, the **Odawa** or **Ottawa** lived on Manitoulin Island (where they still live today) and the Bruce Peninsula. Since that time, they have been associated with the history of Oklahoma and Michigan, an association reflected in the fact that General Motors in Detroit named a car after a great Odawa leader, **Pontiac**.

The **Algonquin** (or **Algonkin**), whose name is said to be derived from the Maliseet word "elakomkwik," meaning "they are relatives or allies," at the time of contact lived along the Ottawa River and by the rivers that feed into it. Currently, they live in eastern Ontario and western Quebec.

One further group should be mentioned, the Potawatomi. Their language is very close to that of Ojibwa. During the first half of the nineteenth century, they were forced across the border into southwest Ontario and were taken in by Mississauga bands in the area.

Some key differences exist between the Cree and the Ojibwa. The Ojibwa were patrilineal, reckoning kinship primarily along the father's side. Clans, unknown to the Cree, interwove throughout Ojibwa country. The word "**totem**" itself comes from the Ojibwa word for clan. The following is a contemporary interpretation of the nature of this tradition coming from Edward Benton-Banai, a respected Elder within the Midewewin, an organization involved with the revival of Ojibwa traditions. After identifying the seven original clans, he stated that each clan had a specific function to play for the people:

Crane and Loon Clans = chieftainship, leadership

Fish Clan = settling disputes, meditation, philosophy

Bear Clan = protecting the community, medicinal plants

Marten Clan = warriors, war strategists

Deer Clan = poets

Bird Clan = spiritual leaders (Benton-Banai 1988:75–7)

THE ATTIKAMEK

The Attikamek (also spelled Atikamekw) are difficult to track historically. Most books about Natives in Canada fail to mention them or only refer to them as existing in the seventeenth century. Since that time, in part because they were forced to move several times, much of their story has only sketchily been told. They also have a name problem. The name **Attikamek** (literally "caribou fish," signifying the whitefish), first appeared in 1635, referring to a group numbering about 550. From 1692 until 1972, they were generally called "Têtes de Boule" ("Roundheads"), not a complimentary name. That year, the people declared that they preferred "Attikamek." Today they live in three communities in south-central Quebec, east of the Algonquin, south of the Cree, and west of the Montagnais, the people to whom they are most similar and most closely tied. They number slightly less than 4,000.

BOX 7-8 — Judith Kawiasiketcht: Attikamek Medicine Woman

Judith Kawiasiketcht ("She dries meat") was born on May 10, 1916. She was married at 15 and bore 18 children. Over the many years of her life, she learned the traditional medicines of her people. Her knowledge of plants would impress any botanist. Her son is apprenticing with her to learn those ways—not an easy process, as the following words from his mother show:

The first time I sent him to look for a medicinal plant for a woman who was sick, he returned with the wrong plant...So I told him to go back to the bush and bring me a sample of all the species of pine he saw. That's what he did and I showed him the one I needed. Then, he went back and found the right one. Now he knows. When I ask him to go find a plant, he brings me exactly the one I want.

Native Individuals 7-1

Edward Benton-Banai: An Ojibwa Midewewin Elder.

Judith Kawiasiketcht: An Attikamek Elder and medicine woman.

Maniaten: A woman who is a Sheshatshit Innu Elder.

Pontiac (c1720–1769): A Detroit area Odawa war chief who, during the period from 1762–1764, was a leading figure in a pan-Indian resistance.

Timeline 7-1

1500s: First European contact with the Montagnais, Naskapi, and Beothuk.

1635: First recording of the term "Attikamek."

1640: First recording of the word "Kiristinon" to refer to the Cree.

1643: First recording of the word "Naskapi."

1667: First recording of the word "Outchibouec" to refer to the Ojibwa.

1670: Establishment of the Hudson's Bay Company in Cree territory.

1762–1764: The pan-Indian resistance movement typically associated with Pontiac, the Odawa leader.

1950s: Development of the iron mines in Innu country.

1972: The Attikamek reclaim their traditional name.

KEY TERMS

Algon(qu/k)ian
(A)nishinabe (Ojibwe)
totem (Ojibwe)
bilateral

CONTENT QUESTIONS

1. In what three ways is the Eastern Subarctic culture area different from the Western Subarctic?

2. What peoples are typically associated with the Eastern Subarctic?

3. How many different dialects of Cree are spoken across Canada?

4. Distinguish between the hunting group (microband) and the macroband.

5. How is the traditional sociopolitical structure of the Ojibwa different from that of the Cree?

 WEBLINKS

arcticcircle.uconn.edu/HistoryCulture/Cree
An excellent starting point for learning more about the Cree of Northern Quebec.

www.geocities.com/Athens/Acropolis/5579/ojibwa.html
For an introductory article on the Ojibwa, you may want to read Kevin Callahan's piece.

www.innu.ca
The Innu home page.

C h a p t e r

8

THE WESTERN SUBARCTIC

Handwritten notes:
- Chipewyan.
- Yellow Knife.
- Dogrib.   - Mountain.
- Hare
- Slavey
- Sahtú

OVERVIEW

The Western Subarctic cultural area encompasses an area of short summers and long winters. It is a bare, glacially swept land with streaks of rivers and depressions of lakes and swamps. In the north are treeless barrens and "small sticks" coniferous forests of black spruce and slender deciduous gatherings of willow, birch, and poplar in the south. Despite how harsh this sounds, the Western Subarctic is rich in animal life, primarily with vast herds of caribou and an abundance of fish such as pickerel, char, and whitefish.

With the exception of the northern Cree, who moved into the area over the last few centuries, Western Subarctic peoples speak Athapaskan languages. The speakers of this family of languages live in Alaska, the Yukon, the Northwest Territories, and the northern part of the Prairie provinces in the north, and in the southwestern part of the United States with the Apache and the Navaho, people who had once lived in Canada. The word **"Atha(b/p)aska"** comes from a Woods Cree word translated as "'(where) there are plants one after the other'" (Gillespie 1981:168) or "'there are reeds here and there'" (Smith 1981:269), referring to the lake of that name.

The Athapaskan-speaking peoples to be discussed in this chapter are the Chipewyan, Yellowknife, Dogrib, Hare, Slavey, Sahtú, Mountain, Gwich'in, Hän, Upper Tanana, Tutchone, Tahltan, Tagish, Kaska, Beaver, and Sekani.

BOX 8-1	Dene

One characteristic shared by all Athapaskan-speaking people (north and south) is the use of the term "Dene," meaning "man, person, or Indian." Four of the First Nations discussed in this chapter have a version of the word in their name. These include:

Thlingcha-dinneh, "Dog side people" = Dogrib

K'ashogotine, "Big willow people" = Hare

Dené Thá = Slavey

Dunne-za = Beaver

Chipewyan

The Chipewyan were at contact and are now the largest and most widespread of the Western Subarctic First Nations. The Chipewyan's population at that time would have been at least 3,500 to 4,000. Now there are more than 5,000. Their name was derived from a Cree word, **"Chipwayanewok,"** meaning "Pointed Skins," first recorded in 1776. This is generally said to refer to the way the fronts and backs of their traditional poncho-like robes dangled down in points.

The Chipewyan are typically termed in the literature as being "edge of the forest" people, living primarily in the transitional area between the barrens and the boreal forest. In the woods was their main threat, the **Ena** ("Enemy"), known to English-speakers as the Cree. Their early eighteenth-century battles made such an impact on them that 200 years later stories were still told of heroes. One story told of the woman **Thanadelthur** (Marten Shakes) (see Chapter 1, "Oral Traditions"), who connected them with the fur trade and with a supply of guns, while other stories told of heroes such as **Dza-ghal-iaze** ("Lower Leg Trembles Little"), who led them to victories against the Cree. Today, there are several First Nations communities where Cree and Chipewyan live together without the biases of the past.

By the middle of the eighteenth century, the Chipewyan had established a relatively independent position in the trade. Much to the disappointment of the English traders, they traded almost exclusively for necessities and not the fancy, expensive frills. In the 1740s, James Isham characterized them as unusual in that they preferred "[d]ressing very plaine; using their former Custom's, Seldom trading [for] any finery for Such usses But what they traffick for is Chiefly necessary's for Life, such as powdr, shott Guns &c" (Abel 1993:61).

Chipewyan who became involved in the trade were more often middlemen than trappers, sometimes making profits that frustrated both their European and Native partners. In 1771, for example, they were recorded as charging their fellow Dene sixty marten skins for a brass kettle weighing about a kilogram, roughly ten times what they had paid for it at the post at Churchill.

But contact with the trade also brought them into contact with European diseases, primarily smallpox. According to explorer/trader Samuel Hearne, smallpox killed up to about 90% of the Chipewyan in 1781. While he was probably speaking only about the eastern bands of the Chipewyan, the effects on the whole group still would have been devastating.

They recovered well and today Chipewyan communities are thriving in the northern part of all three prairie provinces as well as in the Northwest Territories.

| BOX 8-2 | **Chipewyan Artist Alex Janvier** |

Chipewyan **Alex Janvier** is an artist. His most famous work is a "Morning Star," which he painted on the domed ceiling of the Museum of Civilization's River Gallery in Hull, Quebec. He painted it in 1993, supported by specially rigged scaffolding some 27 metres off of the ground. As a young man, his art was primarily a vehicle for the expression of his anger. He would sign his paintings with the number 287, his government-imposed treaty number. Now, his attitude has changed:

> I don't want to let Canadians off the hook for our shitty history, but we can't always be talking about what's wrong—that just creates despair. . . I used to be angry and blame government for failing us. But we've got to start showing some progress so young people don't feel so helpless about the future. (Wallace 1999)

Yellowknife

The Yellowknife were named after the copper that they used, not only for knives but also for awls, lance tips, axe heads, arrowheads, ice chisels, beads, bracelets, needles, necklaces, and even dishes. They were once a small, independent group who tried to establish a middle-man role in the fur trade similar to that of their culturally close but more powerful neighbours, the Chipewyan. Some minor battles ensued (see next section on the Dogrib). By the twentieth century, the descendants of the Yellowknife have identified with and have been incorporated into the Chipewyan First Nation.

Dogrib

The name of this people was first written in 1678 as "Alim8spigoiak," Moose Cree for "dog side." In 1829, Sir John Franklin recorded their name in their own language as "**Thlingcha-dinneh**," "Dog side people." The name comes from a traditional Dene story. The Cree term seems originally to have referred generally to the Dene, as did the English translation, but it gradually became permanently attached to the Dogrib (see Chapter 1, "Oral Traditions").

The traditional territory of the Dogrib is between the two largest bodies of water in the Northwest Territories, Great Slave Lake and Great Bear Lake. To the west, their neighbours are the Hare to the north and the Slavey to the south. Linguistically they are just as close. As late as the 1970s, Dogrib Elders could still understand those languages, but with some difficulty. To the east were the Yellowknife, who entered into deadly conflict with the Dogrib. There had traditionally been some problems between the two people, but the disruption caused by the fur trade upped the stakes of their conflict.

The intensified battle between Dogrib and Yellowknife began during the 1780s but became particularly violent during the 1820s. Stories about the fighting differ, but it seems that the Yellowknife, with their earlier contact with the fur trade, were the primary aggressors, led by the indomitable **Akaitcho**. The kidnapping of women, a common element in traditional Dene stories, is prominent in the telling of the story of the struggle. A Dogrib leader, **Kanoobaw**, complained in 1824 that:

> We suffered our Wives, our Daughters and our Mothers to be taken from us, with their Children. Our Furs also, this we considered of little importance, they were only skins of Animals, but even our Nets upon which our existence depended, were likewise taken from us, and frequently our Axes, Guns or whatever was most useful or necessary to our Maintenance. (Abel 1993:91)

One reason given for the intensification of the fighting was that a Yellowknife, Tausigouai, who had allegedly killed three Dogrib women whom he had kidnapped, had had his throat slit by a fourth kidnapped woman, who feared for her life.

Although there was killing on both sides, it seems that the Dogrib fared the worst until 1823. During that year, the Dogrib achieved their first significant victory, wiping out the encampment led by a Yellowknife named Longlegs. Thirty-four Yellowknife died.

Peace came about a few years later, largely through the oratorical force and spiritual strength of **Edzo**, who grew into a legendary figure in the history of the Dogrib. Stories differ as to how he brought about peace between his people and the Yellowknife. According to Kerry Abel, ". . . there is agreement that Edzo's sister had married a man named Kaw-tay-whee who was living with Akaitcho's band, and through this connection a lasting peace was arranged" (Abel 1993:95).

The peace that Edzo brought about lasted and his name lives on in Dogrib stories, and in the community name "Rae-Edzo."

In the twentieth century, Dogrib leaders have been prominent in the fight for Native self-government. In 1969, **James Wah-Shee** became the first president of the influential Indian Brotherhood of the Northwest Territories. In 1971, the Dogrib became the first among the Dene to run their own school, naming it Chief **Jimmy Bruneau** Elementary School after a leader who led the fight in the middle of the century to maintain traplines in their own terms, not as dictated by the federal government. **George Erasmus** was president of the politically innovative "Dene Nation" from 1976–1983, eventually becoming the Chief of the Assembly of First Nations from 1985–1991. He was awarded the Order of Canada in 1987.

The precontact population of the Dogrib was probably something over 1,200 but that number was reduced, primarily by disease, to around 750 by the 1930s. During the last few generations the number of Dogrib has slowly been growing, reaching 1,700 by 1970 and extending beyond 1,900 by 1986. In the 1996 census, Statistics Canada listed the number of speakers at 2,030, second among Dene languages.

Hare

The Hare live north and northwest of Great Bear Lake, along the Mackenzie River to the west. Half of their traditional territory is north of the Arctic Circle. At first contact, they probably numbered between 700 and 800. Today their population is over 1,000. The Hare were first recorded as being the "Peaux de Lièvre" ("hare skins") by the French during the late eighteenth century. During the nineteenth century, they were typically referred to by some version of the Athapaskan term used by Sir John Franklin in 1824, **Kawchodinneh** (literally meaning "hare-big-people"), signifying "Arctic Hare people." Their main contemporary term for themselves is **K'ashogotine** (literally meaning "willow-big-people [of]"), signifying "Big willow people." It is so close to the other term that it is possible it started as a pun or a shaman's disguised term.

The name "Hare" stems from the people's practice of using hare skins cut in long spiralling strips, from which were woven capes, shirts, blankets, even tents, and from their

| BOX 8-3 | **Frank T'Seleie's Speech** |

Oratorical skills have long been prized among the Hare. One good example comes from a speech made by **Frank T'Seleie**, chief at Fort Good Hope during the Mackenzie Valley Pipeline Inquiry.

On August 5, 1975, addressing the president of a gas company wanting to put a pipeline through the country of his people, he said:

. . . there is a life and death struggle going on between us, between you and me. Somehow in your carpeted boardrooms, in your panelled office, you are plotting to take away from me the very centre of my existence. You are stealing my soul. Deep in the glass and concrete of your world you are stealing my soul, my spirit. By scheming to torture my land you are torturing me. By plotting to invade my land you are invading me. If you ever dig a trench through my land, you are cutting through me. . . . (Watkins 1977:16)

general dependence on hares for food. This would have made for a precarious existence as the population of the snowshoe hare, their main source of food, crashed every seven to ten years. In the more northerly barrens area there were caribou and musk ox in the willow, poplar, and birch forested areas near the Mackenzie River and Great Bear Lake, moose, and fish such as whitefish and trout in the Mackenzie River and Great Bear Lake. However, there were still times during the nineteenth century (and as recently as 1920) that these resources could not compensate for the loss of the hares, and some people died of starvation.

The Hare language is close to that of their neighbours, the Slavey and Dogrib to the south. Elders midway through the twentieth century found their language mutually intelligible with Slavey and Sahtú Dene. The Hare were unusual among the Dene in that they (as did the Gwich'in) got along with their Inuit neighbours to the north.

Fort Good Hope, by the Mackenzie River, was where a Northwest Company (later Hudson's Bay Company) post was formed in 1806; this would later become the largest Hare community. The fur trade would also have an occasionally lethal effect. In 1825–6, it brought killing disease to the Hare. In 1835 and in 1841, some Hare died fighting with Métis traders.

They would have other bouts with disease during the twentieth century. In 1928, death came with cholera and influenza. In the 1930s, tuberculosis hit epidemic proportions. By the early 1960s, when the disease had been brought under control, more than half of the Hare adults had been hospitalized at some time.

Slave(y) or Dené Thá

The Slave(y) received that name because of an historic situation. The Cree who lived east and south of them had obtained weapons in the fur trade by the eighteenth century. This gave the Cree a weapons advantage over the Slavey, who were not so armed. The Slavey were driven further west towards the Mackenzie River from their traditional homes by Great Slave Lake, their namesake. The word "slave" is a somewhat misleading English translation of the Cree word "**Awokanak**," which refers typically to a domesticated animal. While for a period of time Slavey were captured as prisoners by the Cree, and some were adopted into that people, it would be overstating the case to call them slaves. By the nineteenth century, the Slavey were part of the trade and were able to act independently, much to the chagrin of Chipewyan neighbours who wished to control their access to trade goods. The name **Dené Thá** is now often used by the people to refer to themselves.

Living by the Mackenzie River, their diet consisted predominantly of fish, traditionally caught with nets made of twisted willow bark or with lines made out of the same material with hooks made of bone, antler, wood, or birds' claws. As many as 200 people would gather together in a temporary community to catch fish. The Slavey also have long been involved in hunting, enticing moose with birchbark moose callers and by rubbing antlers on branches during mating season.

At the time of first contact, there were perhaps only about 1,250 Slavey, but their numbers have grown so that in the census of 1996, speakers of one of the major dialects of their language, South Slavey (the other being North Slavey), numbered 2,425, first among Athapaskan languages. North Slavey has fewer than 200 speakers.

Sahtú or Bear Lake Dene

A newly established, but nonetheless important, Dene group in the Western Subarctic is the **Sahtú** ("Bear Lake") **Dene**, a mixture of Slavey, Dogrib, and Hare who came together during the fur trade to form a distinct group. They are named after Great Bear Lake, where their home territory is located. Something of the toughness of traditional Sahtú Dene life can be seen in the words of George Blondin, describing a time in the 1940s when he was 19. He had just returned from trapping and taking his furs in with some friends. He was ready to go trapping again, but the others couldn't go. It was January, the coldest, darkest month of the year. What would he do?

> My own father, Edward, had an idea. "Go and get your traps," he said, "and trap for lynx at Turíli." Turíli was at the other end of Sahtú, about 320 kilometres from where I had last been trapping. I would have to travel 640 kilometres to pick up my traps.
>
> People thought I was too young to travel alone. But my father said, "I've taught him enough. He can look after himself. If something happens to him, it's his own fault." (Blondin 1996:256)

In 1994, along with the Métis, they signed an agreement that gave them title to 41,437 square kilometres, $75 million in long-term compensation, and a share in resource royalties.

Mountain

There exist unclear historical references to the "Mountain" Dene, which have them inhabiting the Mackenzie Mountains that straddle the Yukon and Northwest Territories border, territory associated today with the Hare and the Slavey. The modern survey literature of the area regularly makes reference to them and puts their name on maps, but does not say who they are or point out exactly where their communities might have been.

Gwich'in

The **Gwich'in** (sometimes written as "Kutchin") were early known in written history by an uncomplimentary name. "Loucheux," a word derived from the French word "louche," means "squint-eyed." Their own name for themselves, Gwich'in, means "People." With a designation of location, it can be used to refer to a specific group. For example, members of the Old Crow[1] band are known as Vuntut Gwich'in, "people of the lakes," referring to their annual muskrat hunt from April to June in an area where there are many small lakes.

Traditional Gwich'in territory, which includes much of the interior of the Yukon, is divided by rivers, primarily the Yukon and Mackenzie rivers. The word "Yukon" itself is thought to be derived from a Gwich'in word referring to the Yukon River, with the probable meaning of "great" or "white river." The main traditional source of food and supplies for the Gwich'in is caribou. At the time of first contact, they are believed to have numbered about 3,000, roughly a thousand more than now, in nine or ten regional bands in the Yukon, the Northwest Territories, and Alaska.

The Gwich'in lived the furthest north of any Dene people, bordering on the land of the Inuit. Thus it comes as no surprise that they shared aspects of their material culture: fishing spears with a strong double hook; composite bows made from three pieces of wood joined together, reinforced by twisted sinew; and sleds with runners, rather than the toboggans of most northern Dene people.

Being situated in the western part of the region, they also came under the influence of people of the Northwest Coast, having three ranked clans, and a more hierarchical social structure than most of their Dene neighbours.

The Gwich'in language is most closely related to that of the Hän and of the Tutchone (North and South), so much so that a number of written works refer to the other peoples as speaking Gwich'in. They have a long, written tradition for the area, their language first being written in the 1860s in a script developed by Anglican missionary Robert McDonald. It was used in the transcription of the Bible, the Book of Common Prayer, and hymns in Gwich'in, and is well known by many middle aged and older Gwich'in today. Since the 1970s, in schools such as the Chief Zzeh Gittlit School at Old Crow, a more modern alphabet has been used to teach children the language of their ancestors. Charlie Peter Charlie is a major source of information on Gwich'in language and traditional culture. In 1988, at 69 years of age, he was awarded the Order of Canada for his work.

The Gwich'in have a distinct sense of being a people separate from other Dene nations. This might be a reason why, in 1991, they came to an agreement, separate from the others, with the federal government. The agreement reduced their land to 22,332 square kilometres (with subsurface rights to only 93 square kilometres), for a promised $75 million over 15 years. The Gwich'in showed the nature of their priorities when one of the first planned uses of that money was to set up the Tl'oondik Healing Camp.

Hän

The Hän speak a language close to that of the Gwich'in and of the Upper Tanana, which is not surprising since they lived on what is now the Yukon and Alaska border, between the other two peoples. Speakers of the language are called "**Hän Hwëch'in**" (the latter term cognate with Gwich'in), meaning "people of the river." The river referred to is the Yukon. Older people fluent in the language can read Robert McDonald's Christian literature in Gwich'in from the nineteenth century.

There were probably about a thousand Hän when gold was discovered in the middle of their territory in 1898. Within a year there were about 25,000 newcomers in Dawson City and the Hän were compelled to move to the Moosehide reserve, three kilometres down river from that town. By 1932, after being hit by the newcomer-borne diseases of smallpox, flu, typhus, and mumps, that community had diminished to 56. The people managed to survive and the community's population grew to the approximately 400 of today. Their language has had a tougher time of it, especially since 1957 when the federal government suspended services to Moosehide, forcing people to move to Dawson. Says **Archie Roberts**, Hän Elder and language teacher:

> Everyone spoke Hän in the village in them days. We used to have our own Indian constable and Indian court. But after we moved into Dawson all that stopped. You heard less and less of the language as the Elders died off. (Wright 1988)

That was over 10 years ago. Today there are about 20 speakers left, most of them living in the community of Eagle in Alaska, but the language is being taught to children and adults alike in Dawson.

Upper Tanana

The territory of the Upper Tanana is centred around the river of the same name, which flows into the Yukon River in Alaska. The people, who speak a language close to that of the Gwich'in and Hän, live in one Yukon community, Beaver Creek, and in three communities in Alaska, where they have been actively involved with Alaskan Native politics. They are sometimes referred to as Nabesna.

Tutchone

The Tutchone have long been associated with the area of the southern Yukon. Elders still tell stories of a volcanic eruption that occurred within their territory some 7,000 years ago. The people's name, short for **Tutchun tah kutchin**, means "wooded country people." It is difficult to determine how many Tutchone there were at the time of first contact during the nineteenth century, but a typical estimate is around a thousand, similar to their numbers today.

The area traditionally provided a diverse lifestyle based on a number of different resources: wood bison (until a few hundred years ago), caribou, mountain sheep, mountain goat, moose, muskrat, beaver, and salmon. Copper was also an important resource that the Tutchone would heat up, dip in cold water, and then hammer to make tools.

Prior to contact, they were involved with a significant trade with the Chilkat Tlingit, exchanging the products of their hunting (hides, fur, and clothing) for products of the sea (walrus ivory, seal fat, the oil of the eulachon fish, dried clams, and shells), expanding to include European trade goods in the 1790s. A trading post was established in their territory, named Fort Selkirk by the Hudson's Bay Company agent Robert Campbell in 1848. This fort was overtaken in 1852 by the Tlingit, asserting their rights to control local trade, but is today an historic site. The name "Campbell" lived on among the local Tutchone.

Linguists have only recently come to recognize that Tutchone is really two different but closely related languages, Northern Tutchone and Southern Tutchone (the people, of course, have known this for a long time). Northern Tutchone was first recorded in the 1890s by an Anglican missionary, but it wasn't until the 1970s that Southern Tutchone was written in a systematic way. This was achieved by a member of the First Nation, **Daniel Tlen**, who first began this life mission upon the death of his grandmother while he was living in Toronto:

I realized then that no-one had done anything with Native languages. So I went to the faculty of linguistics at Victoria, and told them I was a Southern Tutchone speaker who wanted to work on my language. It took me about ten years to get my degree, studying part time and working in between. It was probably the hardest thing I've ever done.... (Wright 1988)

Tahltan

The Tahltan live in the interior of British Columbia, close enough to the mountains that they have been considered to be Plateau peoples by some writers. The spiritual and material centre of their traditional world is the Stikine River, which traditionally supplied them with a trade route and an abundance of at least five different types of salmon. Situated as they are on the upper reaches of this river, which flows to the ocean, they have long been in close contact with Northwest Coast peoples, especially the Tlingit, their long-term trading partners. This shows in their sharing such cultural traits as social status, the potlatch, and the matrilineal moieties of Raven and Wolf. Their language was said to have between 100 and 1,000 speakers in 1982.

Tagish

BOX 8-4   **Tagish: The Tale of an Elder**

Like most people in her community in her time, Angela Sydney was both **Tagish** and **Tlingit**, having a name in both languages and a parent of each heritage (i.e., Tagish father and Tlingit mother), but her primary identity was Tagish. The name "Tagish" is an English transcription of a Tlingit mispronunciation of a Tagish community's self-designation: **ta:gizi**. It means "it [spring ice] is breaking up." Since the time of their first entry into written history during the last quarter of the nineteenth century, the Tagish have never numbered much more than a hundred.

During the nineteenth century, the Tlingit controlled the Tagish trade with the Pacific coast. At the same time, the two peoples intermarried to a great extent. The linguistic effect of the trade dominance and of the intermarriage was such that in 1887 a geologist named Dawson wrote of them as being Tlingit speakers with Dene culture.

The Tlingit trade control ended in 1896, with the discovery of gold by Skookum Jim, Angela Sydney's uncle. The resultant Yukon Gold Rush of 1896–8 swamped Tagish country with a sudden influx of between 30,000 and 40,000 prospectors and other outsiders.

Angela Sydney was born in 1902. What did it mean to be a Tagish woman then? It meant learning how to snare hare for food and how to trap, prepare, and sew the pelts of fox, mink, muskrat, and weasel. As Angela Sydney said:

All women worked on skins, those days: women trapped around while men hunted. Then they made fur—when a woman fixes skin, then it belongs to her and she can trade it. (Cruikshank 1992:84)

At 14, Angela Sydney was married to a Tlingit man who was twice her age and was chosen by her parents. It was a common practice. Her mother had done

continued

continued

the same thing. The following year, she gave birth to the first of her seven children, four of whom were to die young through German measles.

She spoke Tlingit to her children because her husband didn't speak Tagish. She also would come to speak Tlingit to her grandchildren and great-grandchildren, but was recorded as saying, regretfully, that "I wish they spoke Tagish, too, so they could understand me better."

The Tagish were matrilineal, reckoning descent along the female line of two matriclans, each of which belonged to a separate moiety or spiritual/ceremonial half of society. Angela Sydney was Beaver clan of the Crow moiety. Clan property was both material and non-material, possessing territories but also names, songs, stories, and curing knowledge. Both Angela Sydney's Tagish and Tlingit names were inherited from the stepmother of her mother. It was the usual practice for a child to inherit all of the names of an adult. Her Tagish name was **Ch'oonehte' Ma**, meaning "Mother of Deadfall." Deadfall was the name of a dog. Both Angela and her grandmother had a dog with that name. Her Tlingit name was **Stoow**.

Angela Sydney was fated to become a particularly important culture bearer. Her mother became blind when her daughter was very young, so Angela spent a great deal of time helping her with her work and listening to the stories passed down through generations of mothers and daughters.

In 1912 and 1914, she had the good fortune to experience the last two potlatches in the area. The potlatch was the Pacific Coast's most important religious ceremony, made illegal by the federal government in 1884 (see Religion, Colonialism), eight years before Angela was born. These potlatches made such a lasting impression on the teenage Angela that, as an old woman, she was able to present and explain one of the sacred potlatch songs that told a story about how a woman raised a woodworm as her own child, until it got so big that her family felt they had to kill it because of how big it was getting (Cruikshank 1992:94–7). In 1984, she held a potlatch that marked her putting up gravestones for her brothers and sisters who died during an epidemic in 1898.

In her early years, too, Angela Sydney heard and spoke the Tagish language:

> Mom and Dad spoke Tagish lots of times, to each other, and my mother said when I was really small I used to talk like that too. But as soon as we [Angela and her sisters and brothers] got a little older—four or five years old—we started talking Tlingit. (Cruikshank 1992:69; addition, authors)

It is fortunate for the Tagish, and for the rest of us who can learn from the unique knowledge and vision of life contained in the Tagish language, that Angela Sydney was so gifted with linguistic ability. We see this gift manifested in a number of ways. Not only was she able to retain a working knowledge of Tagish long after Tlingit and English became the tongues of her day-to-day speech, but also, when she was in her eighties, she could speak five of the seven Yukon Native languages: Tagish, Tlingit, Tahltan, Southern Tutchone, and Kaska.

It was estimated in 1982 that there were five speakers of Tagish left. This was probably an optimistic estimation.

continued

Angela Sydney seems to have been the only Native speaker working to preserve the language. According to linguist John Ritter, "[w]ithout her, we would not have a record of the Tagish language, heritage and (linguistic) genealogy [i.e., the relationships of that language to others]" (Fisher 1986: addition, authors). For some 30 years she worked with linguists recording the language and other aspects of her cultural heritage as much as possible. In 1977, along with two other women, she put out a booklet of stories

entitled *My Stories Are My Wealth*. Within a few years she published the following: *Tagish Tlaagu/Tagish Stories*, *Haa Shagoon*, and *Placenames of the Tagish Region, Southern Yukon*.

In 1986 she received the Order of Canada, the first Yukon Native woman to do so. She died at 89. Her legacy is best summarized in her own words:

> I have no money to leave to my grandchildren. . . My stories are my wealth. (Cruikshank 1992:36)

Kaska

These people appear in the literature with two different names: Nahani and Kaska. We are using Kaska here, as it reflects the usage of the people themselves.

The western location of the Kaska people, in northern British Columbia and southern Yukon, gave them close contact with Tlingit traders. Not surprisingly, then, they shared a significant number of cultural traits with the Northwest Coast nations. These traits include matrilineally determined moieties (Wolf and Crow) and potlatching.

The Kaska language has several dialects, each influenced by whoever their neighbours were: Tagish, Tahltan, or Sekani. The Kaska's small numbers, perhaps 1,500 at the time of first contact and a few hundred speakers today in a population of well over a thousand (the legacy of repression of Kaska in residential schools) and the lack of written materials in the language have made preservation of the language a difficult job, but one that the people feel is necessary. A good sense of this is captured in the words of Kaska Chief Hammond Dick in 1988:

> During our annual general assembly we translated everything to the Elders and to the public. It was tedious but people realized the importance. When you've been brought up to be ashamed of your own language, it helps to see it given respect that way. (Wright 1988)

In 1998, the Kaska of the Liard First Nation were the first Yukon people to sign a tripartite agreement on policing with the Yukon and federal governments. Because of this agreement, this community of some 800 people would get four aboriginal police officers stationed at the local R.C.M.P. detachment. As part of this agreement, the community formed a committee that would influence decisions on such key justice issues as restorative justice issues involving pre-charge diversion, bail, and sentencing. While this might not seem like a big deal to non-Natives who have no understanding of the problems of First Nations' justice (see Chapter 24), the importance of this agreement was underlined by Chief Ann Bayne:

> This agreement is a significant step for our First Nation towards self-government. . . It will recognize and respect our laws and traditions and ensure our community attains and maintains control of our destiny and that of future generations. (Solicitor General, www.sgc.gc.ca/ Releases/e19980709.htm)

Dunne-za or Beaver

In northwestern Alberta and northeastern British Columbia live the **Dunne-za** or Beaver. Their territory, stretching between the Rocky Mountains to the west and Lake Athabaska to the east, and dominated by the Peace River, is a varied one. It consists of rich prairie lands, along with muskeg, forest, and mountainous terrain. That has enabled the people to draw upon a variety of resources, with one author claiming 46 different mammal species[2], the most significant of which are moose, bison, and caribou. In order to take advantage of such diverse species, the Beaver historically had to move often from place to place, travelling as far as 400 kilometres during the course of a year. Hunters were said to have the capacity to kill particular animals because they had sought out the animal spiritually and learned from its "**muyine**" ("song"), a word used to refer to spiritual power or to a person's medicine bundle. Robin Ridington describes this spiritual relationship as follows:

> In order for a hunt to be successfully completed, the animal had to have previously given itself to the hunter in a dream. Both animal and hunter were supposed to have been known to one another before their physical meeting in the hunt itself. Animals were believed to be pleased by the hunter's respect for their bodies[3] and to notice his generosity in distributing the meat. Hunters sought to develop an ability to think like game animals in order to predict their behaviour. They were trained to interpret the environment from an animal's perspective. The hunter's understanding of an animal's thought process was believed to be mirrored by the animal's understanding of how humans fulfilled obligations incurred in the hunt. (Ridington 1982:161)

The Beaver language is very close to that of the Sekani, the Kaska, and the Slavey, close enough to be at or near to mutual intelligibility. Although the Beaver used to be connected with the Sarcee before the latter linked their fate to the Blackfoot Confederacy, their time apart has had a linguistic toll.

The people refer to themselves as "Dunne-za," usually translated as "real people." The Beaver appellation seems to have come from the Chipewyan word for the Peace River, once written as **Tsa des**, meaning "beaver river." The northern Plains Cree called them **amiskiwiyiniw**, meaning "beaver person."

By about 1760, the Beaver had been driven out of the eastern part of their traditional territory by the Cree, who were armed with guns obtained in the fur trade. The Beaver allied with the Slavey to fend off the intruders. When the Cree and the Beaver agreed in the early 1780s not to fight for a while, the peace they achieved was memorialized in the name now held by the main river in Beaver territory: the Peace River. Fighting, however, resumed from the 1790s into the 1820s.

At the time of first contact, the Beaver probably numbered around a thousand, somewhat less than their current population.

Sekani

The word "**Sekani**" means "People of [on] the Rocks," referring to the Rocky Mountains. They seem to have been part of the Beaver First Nation, who were driven west into the mountains, where they took on this new name. Not surprisingly, their language is very close to Beaver and, to a lesser extent, to Sarcee. It is difficult to know how many Sekani there were at the time of contact, but they probably numbered at least 500.

Native Individuals 8-1

Akaitcho: Nineteenth-century Yellow-knife leader.

Dza-ghal-iaze ("Lower leg trembles little"): Legendary eighteenth-century Chipewyan leader.

Edzo: A Dogrib leader who brought peace between his people and the Yellowknife during the 1820s.

George Erasmus: Dogrib who was the Chief of the Assembly of First Nations, 1985–1991.

Alex Janvier: Modern Chipewyan artist.

Angela Sydney: Last speaker of Tagish.

Thanadelthur: Eighteenth-century Chipewyan woman who was instrumental in connecting her people with the fur trade.

Daniel Tlen: A Southern Tutchone linguist.

James Wah-Shee: Dogrib, first president of the Indian Brotherhood of the Northwest Territories.

Their territory, including the river valleys of the Parsnip and Findlay Rivers, the plateau and mountain regions of northern British Columbia, while not particularly rich in resources, at least offered a diversity that could be accessed at different times of the year. This would traditionally include buffalo, moose, caribou, bear, porcupine, beaver, woodchuck, deer, mountain goat, and mountain sheep. Diamond Jenness, who studied the people in 1924, referred to their feeling disdain for fishing as only to be done when absolutely necessary.

The small numbers of the Sekani, probably only around a thousand during the nineteenth century, have historically and presently put them in the position of having to establish good relationships with their Native neighbours. Today, one community, Fort Ware, is affiliated with the Kaska Tribal Council and other Sekani are connected with the Carrier-Sekani Tribal Council.

Timeline 8-1

1781: Smallpox kills a reputed 90% of the Chipewyan.

1780s: Peace is established between the Beaver and the Cree, giving Peace River its name.

1820s: Dogrib Edzo brings peace between his people and the Yellowknife.

1860s: Gwich'in language first written down.

1896–8: Gold rush in the Yukon.

1930s: Tuberculosis hits epidemic proportions among the Hare.

1986: Tagish woman, Angela Sydney, receives Order of Canada.

1988: Gwich'in Charlie Peter Charlie receives Order of Canada.

1985–1991: Dogrib George Erasmus chief of the Assembly of First Nations.

ENDNOTES

1. The English name "Old Crow" comes from the name of a nineteenth-century Gwich'in leader, Te Trhim Gevtik ("Walking Crow").

2. This includes moose, wood bison, beaver, muskrat, marten, red fox, black-footed ferret, raccoon, weasel, rabbit, deer, caribou, hare, black bear, grizzly bear, and porcupine, to name just a few.

3. As with other Native cultures, this included treating the bones with respect (e.g., not throwing them to the dogs or into the fire) and addressing the animal respectfully after death.

KEY TERMS

Atha(b/p)aska(n) (Cree)
Awokanak (Cree)
Dene
moiety
muyine' (Beaver)

CONTENT QUESTIONS

1. To what language family do all the languages of the peoples of the Western Subarctic belong?
2. Which of the people have a word for "people" as part of their name?
3. Why was one of these groups called "Slave(y)"?
4. Why are there no more speakers of Tagish?
5. How did Peace River get its name?

 WEBLINKS

arcticcircle.uconn.edu/ANWR/anwrgwichin.html
An article on the Gwich'in of Alaska and Canada.

www.ssimicro.com/providence/band.htm
The fairly small Web site of the Fort Providence Dene band.

www.friendshipcentres.com
The Northwest Territories Council of Friendship Centres.

http://yukoncollege.yk.ca/language/YNLCinfo
This site discusses the Yukon Native Language Centre and the languages spoken in the Yukon.

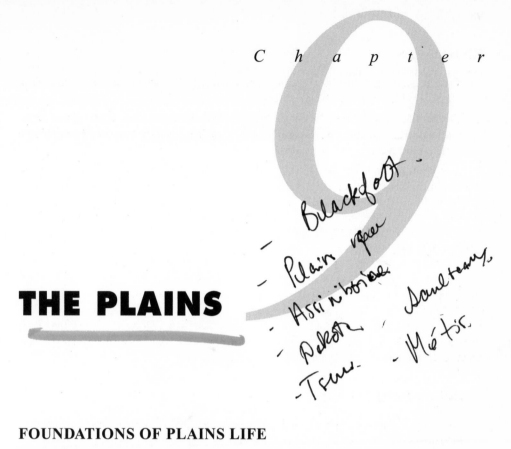

C h a p t e r

THE PLAINS

(handwritten margin notes:)
- Blackfoot
- Plains ?
- Assiniboine
- Dakota
- Tsuu
- Saulteaux,
- Métis.

FOUNDATIONS OF PLAINS LIFE

Archaeologists record people living in the Canadian Plains area (i.e., most of Alberta and Saskatchewan and part of Manitoba) at about 11,500 years ago. The grasslands and bison that we associate with the Plains came shortly afterwards, about 11,000 years ago.

The Buffalo

Buffalo (technically bison) provided for almost all the needs of Plains life. The first need was food. The Blackfoot refer to buffalo meat as **nitapiksisako**, meaning "real meat." This

<table>
<tr><td colspan="2">BOX 9-1   How Much of
Plains History Is Native?</td></tr>
<tr><td>If Natives began living on the Plains 11,500 years ago, and Europeans first saw the Canadian Plains less than 300 years ago, this means that more than 97% of Plains history is Native history alone.</td><td>Imagine a textbook with ten chapters, with each chapter portraying an equal part of that history. The first nine chapters would be devoted to Native history, as would more than 70% of the final chapter.</td></tr>
</table>

included not only fresh meat but also **pemmican**, buffalo jerky made by pulverizing thin strips of dried, lean buffalo meat, adding to it crushed, dried **saskatoon** (service) berries, and hot fat produced by boiling the marrow of the bones. It supplied important food in the winter when fresh meat was not readily available. It would later become a major component involved with the fur trade, serving as "fuel" for canoeing travellers.

But the buffalo didn't just give the people food. Their summer-slain skins provided lodge covers and bags for holding household goods. Their winter hides provided overcoats, mittens, caps, and warm moccasins. The thick hide on the buffalo's neck was used for making shields and strips of untanned rawhide were used for binding cords for knives, clubs, and other tools (Friesen 1997:97).

Human society was constructed around its relationship to the buffalo. The traditional Plains band of 25 to 100 reflected the number of people necessary to drive buffalo. Warrior societies were developed primarily to police the hunt so no one would spook the buffalo herd.

Ingenious hunting methods were developed. Earliest was the **buffalo cliff drive** or **jump**. At sites such as the 3,000-year-old Head-Smashed-In-Buffalo-Jump (now a park) in southern Alberta, buffalo were driven through carefully created lanes, then over a cliff.

The **buffalo pound** evolved once bows and arrows entered the Plains, around A.D. 250. Compared to spears, these weapons were more efficient and safer for the hunter in killing large numbers of buffalo. The work involved was complex. If a natural site like a canyon was not available, a corral was constructed. This consisted of

> . . . a walled enclosure, generally circular in shape, ranging from 10 to 75 metres in diameter. Extending from the entrance in a "v" shape were two wings of spaced stations made of piles of rocks, wood, or dried buffalo chips. . . These lines stretched out for several kilometres and the open mouth of the "v" was almost two kilometres in width. The pound itself was hidden from the view of the bison as they ran towards it, following the lines of the "v," which grew ever narrower, and then it was too late. (Friesen 1997:101)

During the nineteenth century, Euro-Americans slaughtered buffalo by the tens of thousands, often just for the hides, leaving the flesh to rot. In 1876, the Blackfoot leader **Crowfoot** said, "We all see that the day is coming when the buffalo will all be killed, and we shall have nothing more to live on. . . then you will come into our camp and see the poor Blackfoot starving" (Dempsey 1972:89). By the 1880s, the large buffalo herds were no more. Only a few hundred buffalo remained.

Spiritual Foundations of Plains Culture

One key aspect of the spiritual life of Plains culture is the **iniskim**, or "buffalo stone." The practice of using these stones, usually fossils bearing a spiral shell, goes back thousands of years. The story of the first iniskim tells of a woman trying to find food during a time of famine. An iniskim spoke to her, teaching her the prayers and ceremonies necessary to bring buffalo to the people. Blackfoot children wore iniskim in necklaces; warriors had iniskim woven into their hair; shamans carried iniskim in medicine bundles; the dead were buried with iniskim.

For thousands of years, **medicine wheels** have been part of spiritual life in the Canadian Plains. These stone structures typically are centred around a cairn or pile of stones on top of a prominent hill. Stone "spokes" radiate outwards. Individual medicine wheels often had long histories of use. The Majorville Medicine Wheel, constructed of about 40 tons of rock, dates to around 5000 B.P. and was still the focus of religious activity when Europeans first came to the Plains. At the centre is a cairn of field stones and soil 9 metres in diameter and 1.6 metres high. Surrounding it is an oval ring some 29 metres by 26 metres, connected with 26 to 28 boulder spokes.

The **Okan** (Blackfoot: "ceremonial pole"), or Sun Dance, was the main ceremony of the Plains people. It was initiated, sponsored, and presided over by a woman:

> The decision to hold a Sun Dance was made by a pure woman—i.e., a virgin or faithful wife—who had a male relative in danger of losing his life. A husband might be ill or a son may not have returned from a raid. The woman made a public vow that if the person's life was spared, she would sponsor a Sun Dance. Then, if her prayer was answered, she began preparations for the summer festival. (Dempsey 1995:392)

Sometimes, as a spiritual offering, young men inserted leather thongs through their chest or back muscles, attaching the other end either to a pole or to a buffalo skull. Then they would dance until the thongs ripped free. This was one reason given in 1895 when the federal government banned the Sun Dance. The following is a response by an anonymous Blackfoot:

> We know that there is nothing injurious to our people in the Sun-dance. . . It has been our custom, during many years, to assemble once every summer for this festival. . . We fast and pray, that we may be able to lead good lives and to act more kindly towards each other.

> I do not understand why the white men desire to put an end to our religious ceremonials. What harm can they do our people? If they deprive us of our religion, we will have nothing left, for we know of no other that can take its place. (Nabokov 1991:225)

The ban was lifted in 1951 when the Indian Act was changed.

Innovations That Changed Plains Life

The Plains have long been an area of dynamism. Several times in Plains history innovations have swept across the grasslands, changing people's lives, sometimes bringing new people to the area. When Europeans came to the Canadian Plains, six First Nations lived there, of which only one had lived in the area from before the seventeenth century.

Prior to Contact

Around 8,000 years ago, an invention developed earlier in the southeastern U.S. transformed Plains culture. The **atlatl**, or spear-thrower, was a device held in the hand into which the non-pointed end of the spear was placed. This meant that the spear could be thrown with greater force and accuracy, rather like adding length to a person's arm.

Over the next few thousand years, other innovations enhanced Plains life. Dogs were domesticated and trained to transport loads by carrying bundles and pulling **travois**, devices made from poles. Second, the people learned how to render the marrow of bones into fat by boiling cracked bones in water containers heated by placing hot rocks inside. This enabled them to make pemmican, a Plains staple.

The Horse: Changing the Human Face of the Canadian Plains

The horse had a huge impact on Plains culture. People could travel further, more often, and carry more things with them. Homes and bands became larger. It changed the buffalo hunt through the development of the dramatic and potentially deadly "**surround**" of buffalo by racing riders. It became a standard of wealth. Some acquired more horses than they could possibly ever use, between 50 and 300. **Sackomaph**, a Peigan chief, is reported to have had between 4,000 and 5,000 horses, 150 of which were sacrificed at his death. It also created strife between peoples. The fastest way of obtaining horses was to steal them, which became a test of young manhood. The human map of the Plains would also change. Those with horses had a huge military advantage over those who did not.

Horses were newcomers to the Plains, as can be seen in the names Plains peoples gave them:

Blackfoot: **ponokamita**, "elk dog"

Plains Cree: **misstutim**, "large dog"

Lakota Sioux: **sungkawakan**, "special or sacred dog"

The trail of the horse to the Plains began in New Mexico around the turn of the seventeenth century when the Spanish established horse ranches, employing Natives and working them hard. The Apache took the horses and took off, quickly becoming some of the best riders in the world. Horses gradually moved north, sometimes ridden by peoples looking to expand their territory. The **Shoshoni**, around 1700, rode onto the southern edges of the Canadian Plains, threatening the Blackfoot. Over the next few decades the Blackfoot, Sarsi, Assiniboine, and Cree joined together to fight hard to fend them off, a difficult task since the Shoshoni had greater access to horses. The tide was turned when the Blackfoot acquired both horses and guns.

CANADIAN PLAINS NATIONS IN THE NINETEENTH AND TWENTIETH CENTURIES

There are seven nations that live in the Canadian Plains today, speakers of languages of three different language families.

Blackfoot

The Blackfoot speak a Western Algonquian language. Connections with Central or Eastern Algonquian languages can be seen in Box 9.2.

Nineteenth-century artist George Catlin referred to the Blackfoot as "the most powerful tribe of Indians on the continent." Three tribes make up the Blackfoot nation: **Siksika**, **Kainai**, and **Peigan**. In 1823 it was estimated that there were 4,200 Siksika, 2,800 Kainai, and 4,200 Peigan. Current figures have 15,000 Piegan in the U.S. and 8,000 Kainai, 5,000 Siksika, and 2,500 Peigan in Canada.

Historically, these three tribes shared language and customs, intermarried, and were military allies. Their collective name in their own language can be **Sakoyitapix** ("prairie people"), **Apikunipuyi** ("speakers of the same language"), or **Nitsitapix** ("real or true people"), a term also used to refer to Natives generally (Franz and Russell 1995:135).

The word "siksika" means "black foot." The name is derived from an individual in the origin story who walked over the ashes of a prairie fire, making his moccasins black in the process. The English collective name of the allied tribes, "Blackfoot" ("Blackfeet" in the United States), reflects the fact that White traders established first contact with Siksika and does not indicate any special status of that group over the other two.

BOX 9-2	Blackfoot Connections with Algonquian Languages			

Blackfoot	Ojibwe	Delaware	English	Word Form
k-	msko-	maxkii-	red	prefix
aapi	waab-	waapii	white	prefix
owaa	waawaan	wahwal	egg	inanimate noun
naamoo	aamoo	aamweew	bee	animate noun

"**Kainai**" means "many chiefs." In the origin story, when the black-footed traveller walked into the Kainai village, he asked who the chief was. Many claimed to be. This nation's English name, **Blood**, comes from a name given to them by the Cree, a reference to their practice of sometimes covering their clothes with red ochre.

"**Peigan**" ("Piegan" in the U.S.) is derived from "**Apikuni**," variously translated as "scabby robes" or "poorly dressed robes." The black-footed traveller called them that in the origin story because their women had scraped the buffalo skins poorly, leaving pieces of meat and fur.

Traditional Blackfoot social organization began with a **tipi**, which would house a single household, including a husband, wife, or wives, and children. The next level of social organization was the band, built usually on the extended family. This "microband" could number from 25 to over 100. Optimum size related to such practical considerations as the number of people necessary to hunt buffalo and the amount of grass available for the band's horses. Households might shift membership in the bands according to kinship alliances, friendships, agreement or disagreement with band leadership, and the hunting and raiding success of the band. They would camp together during the winter usually for defensive purposes only a short distance from other such bands. Like the buffalo they hunted, they would amalgamate into larger groupings of 100 to 200 households during the summer.

Bands had names based on incidents or on distinctive features of individual band members, often with a humorous twist. The following are names taken from a recently published Blackfoot dictionary: Bulrushes or Cattail, Many Ghosts, Hairy Nose, Never Laughs, White Chest, Padded Saddle, White Robe, Never Lonesome, and Gopher Eater. Names could also change with new incidents. For example, "the Followers of the Buffalo" became "Camps in a Bunch" once they had settled on a reserve.

Bands would have peace chiefs and war chiefs. There was no formal chief beyond that level. When bands got together, the most respected leader might be appointed as the head for that particular context. That went for both war and peace leaders. When the Kainai got together during the middle of the nineteenth century, **Mekaisto**, or **Red Crow**, would tend to be chosen to lead. If the collection of bands faced danger, **White Calf** would be put in charge.

Important to traditional Blackfoot life were age-graded Warrior or All Comrades societies. A boy would join such a society in his early teens. After about five years, those in his group would purchase the emblems and rights of the society one step older than they, in return selling the emblems and rights to those one step younger. Those in the age ranges of 20 to 25 and 25 to 30 were most often used to police a camp, especially during the buffalo hunt. Not all men moved up. Some stayed with younger men, a sign that they were not as effective or successful as their peers.

Women were, and are, major players in Blackfoot society. The Blackfoot have a term, **ninauposkitzipxpe**, which means "manly hearted woman," referring to a type of woman well described in the following passage from Oscar Lewis in 1941:

> About a third of elderly (sixty years or older) North Piegan women in 1939, and a few younger women, were considered manly hearted. . . Such women own property, were good managers and usually effective workers, were forthright and assertive in public, in their homes, and as sexual partners, and were active in religious rituals. They were called "manly-hearted" because boldness, aggressiveness, and a drive to amass property and social power are held to be ideal traits for men. . . [T]he manly-hearted woman is admired as well as feared by both men and women. (Kehoe 1995:115)

Plains Cree

The Plains Cree are known in their own language as **Mamihkiyiniwak** ("Downstream People"). They were relatively new to the Plains, formerly living in parkland and woodland areas. By at least the seventeenth century they began to move in. As they became involved with the fur trade, they moved deeper into the grasslands.

Much has been written about the conflict between Plains Cree and Blackfoot during the nineteenth century. Less stressed is the equally long alliance and trade relationship that previously existed. According to **Saukamappee**, the linking began as a call for help. It was 1722. The Peigan, hard hit by Shoshoni incursions into their land, sent out messengers to ask for assistance. Two arrived at Saukamappee's camp and 20 Cree joined the fight. No one won the battle, but the connection was made.

In 1732, the Cree and Assiniboine again joined the Blackfoot against the Shoshoni. This time the Cree and Assiniboine had with them 10 guns. According to Saukamappee's account of the battle, "Our shots caused consternation and dismay along their whole line. The battle had begun about Noon, and the sun was not yet half down, when we perceived some of them had crawled away from their shields, and were taking to flight" (Milloy 1988:8). The Cree then began to supply guns in trade with the Blackfoot.

This positive relationship ended, in part, because the Cree found horses hard to come by through trade. An easier way to obtain horses was raiding. A particular target for the Cree from at least the 1790s was the **A'ani** ("White Clay People") of southcentral Saskatchewan, better known by the insulting term Gros Ventre ("Big Belly"). This put the Blackfoot in a difficult position. The A'ani were their main link to the horse market in the south. They then had an alternative source for guns: the trading posts of Edmonton House and Rocky Mountain House, set up in their territory in 1795 and 1799 respectively. In 1806, the Blackfoot chose sides; they attacked the Cree. Battles were fought off and on from that time until their last major conflict in 1870. The A'ani were forced to retreat to the United States.

The Plains Cree flourished in the Plains, their numbers growing from an estimated 4,900 in 1809 to around 12,500 by 1860. Their numbers and military reputation caused them to be feared by federal officials of a newly formed Canada expanding into the west. Fear led to blame concerning the Riel Rebellion of 1885. But the vast majority of the Plains Cree remained loyal to the Queen, in whose name their treaties had been signed. They put their trust in peaceful processes, despite the fact that the federal government was confining them to small reserves and starving the people by not delivering on oral and written promises made in the treaties. Particularly prominent in both the peaceful process and in the falsely assigned blame was **Mistahimaskwa** ("Big Bear"). He risked his life trying to maintain peace but was put in prison for not being able to control young men frustrated with how the Plains Cree were being treated.

Assiniboine

The word "**Assiniboine**" is derived from a Cree term meaning "those who cook with stones," giving them their English name, "Stonies." This refers to the Assiniboine method of cooking in which a hole lined with rawhide was filled with water. Heated rocks were then placed inside to cook meat and vegetables in a stew or soup. Today, the Assiniboine prefer to be referred to as Nakota (also spelled Nakoda), which is cognate with the word "Dakota."

The Siouan-speaking Assiniboine were relative newcomers to the Plains. They moved onto the Plains during the latter half of the seventeenth and early eighteenth centuries, almost totally abandoning their woodland territories north of Lake Superior and the parklands of southern Manitoba and northern Minnesota.

The connection between Cree and Assiniboine was very close. Many in both societies could speak each other's unrelated language. They fought side by side against the Dakota and Blackfoot. The Blackfoot called the Assiniboine **Niitsisinaa**, "original Cree" (Franz and Russell 1995:135).

Dakota

Almost all the literature on the Canadian Plains, and about Native people in Canada generally, ignores the very real presence of the Siouan-speaking Dakota in Manitoba and Saskatchewan. Yet, today, Dakota speakers outnumber speakers of Assiniboine. They very quietly moved north into the area during the nineteenth century, becoming closely linked with the Saulteaux.

Tsuu T'ina (Sarcee/Sarsi)

Also relative newcomers to the Plains are the **Tsuu T'ina** ("earth people" or "many people"), an Athapaskan-speaking people. Until recently they were usually known as **Sarcee**, a Blackfoot term with a number of different translations. During the eighteenth century, they

---

BOX 9-3   **Why Object to Being Called "Sioux"?**

Why did the Sioux change their name? Imagine if you were called by the name used to refer to you by neighbours who don't like you. Sioux is an abbreviated English version of a French adaptation of the word "Nadouessioux," meaning "little snakes"—an insulting term that

Ojibwe speakers used to refer to people who didn't speak an Algonquian language. Dakota has long been a term used by the people themselves. Sioux was a name imposed by English-speaking people. You will see similar stories throughout this book.

split from the people known as the **Tsatine** ("Beaver people") or **Dunne-za** ("real people") who live in the Northwest Territories, just south of Great Slave Lake. They are linked linguistically with peoples who had moved south through central British Columbia over a thousand years before, eventually ending up in the American Southwest. These travellers are the Apache and the Navajo.

During the latter part of the eighteenth century, they linked their military fate with the Blackfoot, as part of the Blackfoot Confederacy. Even though their numbers were relatively small, estimated as 840 in 1809, they were not to be discounted as a fighting force, and did help drive back the Shoshoni. Around 1800, Alexander Henry wrote:

> These people have a reputation of being the bravest tribe in all the plains, who dare to face ten times their own numbers, and of this I have convincing proof during my residence in the country. (Friesen 1997:127, citing Hungry Wolf and Hungry Wolf)

Disease hit the Tsuu T'ina hard during the nineteenth century, reducing the numbers of their single community to 160. Today, their numbers have risen to about 1,200 but their language is severely threatened, with only about 10 speakers left.

Saulteaux

Also entering the Plains during the eighteenth century was the branch of the Anishinabe, known usually as **Saulteaux**. They received this name because many of their ancestors came from the area of the "sault," or "rapids," of Sault Ste. Marie, where Lake Huron and Lake Superior meet. They often refer to themselves as **Bungee**, a term derived from an Ojibwe word meaning "few, little, a little."

As a Plains people, the Saulteaux usually allied themselves with the Plains Cree during the battles of the eighteenth and nineteenth centuries, fighting alongside the Plains Cree and the Assiniboine against the Sioux during the late eighteenth century and with the Cree against the Blackfoot in the 1860s.

The Saulteaux had the smallest number of any Plains people at that time, with their population being estimated as 336 in 1809. Today their communities are found in Manitoba, Saskatchewan, and British Columbia.

Métis

The story of the Métis in Canada is one of a unique people. Genetically and culturally, their formation represents a mixture of European (primarily French) and Native (primarily Cree). Their language, **Michif**, is one of the clearest examples of that fact, being partially French (mostly the nouns) and partially Cree (mostly the verbs).

The Métis came into being during the eighteenth century, when the fur trade was extending west into the Prairies. The French voyageurs who manned the big canoes made personal connections with Natives in the area—very personal when it came to Plains Cree women. The marriages between the two (whether or not they were sanctified by the Catholic church) were practical for both cultures. Their children learned from each people.

From the Native culture they learned how to hunt buffalo and how to prepare pemmican, the staple food for the fur trade. European culture taught them how to farm and how to build and use the big ox-driven carts they utilized to carry large loads of pemmican from the hunt to their homes.

By the beginning of the nineteenth century, there were several thousand Métis, most of them around the area of present-day southern Manitoba.

The Métis developed a sense of nationhood not only from their distinct culture but from battles they won. One of the "enemies" that they fought was the Hudson's Bay Company. This organization had been given most of what is now Canada in 1670 by King Charles II, who had little idea of what he was giving away so freely: a monopoly of trade on the lands drained by the waters that flow into Hudson Bay.

In 1811, Lord Selkirk, a leading official in the Hudson's Bay Company, arranged for settlers to be brought to what is now the Winnipeg area. The settlers got along with the Métis, whose land they were sharing, but the governor of this new colony made enemies with the Métis by declaring that they should not be providing pemmican for the trade, as the trade was an H.B.C. monopoly. This conflict came to a head in 1816 when Governor Semple and about 25 of his men challenged the leader of the Métis, Cuthbert Grant (c.1793–1854) and a slightly smaller group of his people. When the smoke cleared, the governor and his men were dead, as was only one of the Métis. A song was composed to celebrate this victory (unfortunately referred to as the Seven Oaks "massacre" in many history textbooks). The people started calling themselves the "New Nation" and the song became their national anthem.

For several generations the Métis had worked for the Northwest Company, a rival of the H.B.C. based in Montreal. In 1821, the H.B.C. absorbed its competitor and could truly be said to hold a monopoly after that date. But the Métis continued to challenge the company. This came to a head in 1849 when a Métis named **Pierre-Guillaume Sayer**, among others, was charged with trafficking in furs. Despite the fact that he was charged, he was let go once the trial was over. This perhaps reflected the fact that a good number of armed Métis were waiting outside the courtroom.

The Métis inherited the political alliances and enemies of their Cree mothers, grandmothers, and great-grandmothers. They fought alongside the Assiniboine and Saulteaux, and fought against the Dakota Sioux and the Blackfoot. In 1851, a group of Métis met and defeated a much larger force of Sioux at the Battle of Grand Coteau, another victory for the New Nation.

This sense of self came under severe threat during the 1860s. In 1867, the year of Canadian Confederation, the new country began negotiating with the H.B.C. for a massive transfer of land. People moving out to the West at that time included in their numbers "Canada Firsters," who arrogantly declared to the Métis that the future in the West belonged to them and not the "half breeds." The antagonism was exacerbated by the presence of outsiders surveying land held by the Métis for generations. In 1869, the Métis took action. A 25-year-old, college-educated man named **Louis Riel** emerged as their leader. They formed a provisional government and blocked the entry of the Canadian governor at the U.S–Canada border. Their government had the support of most people but made the unfortunate mistake of imprisoning, and eventually executing, an especially obnoxious White, Protestant, Ontarian by the name of Thomas Scott, an action that would have dire consequences for Louis Riel.

In 1870, most of the proposals put forward by the provisional Métis government were put into legal place by the Manitoba Act. The Métis had their rights to the land recognized through legal papers known as "scrip." Riel's status became an unusual one. He was officially exiled by the federal government but time and again he was elected to parliament by the people of Manitoba, both Métis and non-Métis alike.

Native Individuals 9-1

Cuthbert Grant: Métis leader who won the Battle of Seven Oaks in 1816.

Mekaisto ("Red Crow"): Great nineteenth-century Blackfoot leader.

Mistahimaskwa ("Big Bear"): A nineteenth-century Plains Cree leader who fought for a good treaty for his people and who was wrongfully imprisoned for the actions of others during the Second Riel Rebellion.

Louis Riel: College-educated Métis who was chosen to lead his people in two rebellions against mistreatment by the federal government.

Sackomaph: A nineteenth-century Peigan chief reported to have had many horses.

Saukamappee: An eighteenth-century Plains Cree from whom we have learned much about his people and their relationship to the Blackfoot.

In the Manitoba of 1871, there were 9,800 Métis, 5,270 of whom were French-speaking (the rest spoke English). In the same area there were only 1,600 Whites, and a greater number, undetermined, of Cree. That was to change with the westward migration of settlers. With them came land speculators and government officials who were not above working out scams to cheat the Métis of their scrip. The laws relating to scrip changed 11 times over 12 years and most Métis ended up moving west into what is now Saskatchewan and Alberta.

In the 1880s, the Métis found themselves in a similar situation to that which they had faced earlier in Manitoba. They again called upon Louis Riel, then living peacefully in Montana, to lead them in what would become known as the Second Riel Rebellion. They would lose this time, thanks to the technology used against them (i.e., the new railroad, steamboats, and the precursor to machine guns) and due to Riel's reluctance to fight. He would be hanged in 1885, largely because of his authorization of the execution of Thomas Scott years earlier.

Throughout the twentieth century, the Métis were still in an uncertain political position. Some, in Alberta, live in what are termed "colonies," developed during the 1930s. They have been fighting for royalties for the oil and gas extracted from their land. Other Métis organizations suffer from the lack of definition of who is and isn't Métis and from a lack of federal recognition of their status. In the 1981 census, 98,255 Canadians identified themselves as Métis, while in 1991 75,150 claimed Métis origin, with 137,500 others saying they were Métis and something else.

According to a recent court decision, the definition of Métis is someone who:

1. has some ancestral family connection (not necessarily genetic),

2. identifies himself or herself as Métis, and

3. is accepted by the Métis community or a locally organized community branch, chapter, or council of a Métis association or organization with which that person wishes to be associated. (Plainspeak 2000:4)

Timeline 9-1

9500 B.C.: First archaeologically documented arrival of people on the Plains.

9000 B.C.: Arrival of buffalo and grasslands on the Plains.

6000 B.C.: Introduction of the atlatl, or spear-thrower, to the Plains.

3000 B.C.: First construction of the Majorville Medicine Wheel.

1000 B.C.: Creation of Head-Smashed-In-Buffalo-Jump.

A.D. 250: Bows and arrows come to the Plains.

1700: Horses appear on the Canadian Plains.

1722: The Plains Cree and Blackfoot join forces against the Shoshoni.

1790s: The Gros Ventre are driven out of the Canadian Plains.

1816: The Métis defeat Governor Semple at the Battle of Seven Oaks.

1849: Métis trader Pierre Guillaume Sayer is released at the end of his trial.

1851: The Métis defeat the Sioux at the Battle of Grand Coteau.

1869–70: First Riel Rebellion.

1880s: Large buffalo herds are no more.

1885: Second Riel Rebellion.

1895: The Sun Dance is made illegal.

1951: Ban on Sun Dance is lifted.

KEY TERMS

atlatl (Nahuatl)

iniskim (Blackfoot)

Ninauposkitzipxpe (Blackfoot)

Nitapiksisako (Blackfoot)

CONTENT QUESTIONS

1. What did buffalo provide for the Plains people?
2. What is the Sun Dance?
3. How did the horse change Plains life?
4. Identify the three language families spoken in the Canadian Plains.
5. What are Warrior Societies?

 ## WEBLINKS

www.metisresourcecentre.mb.ca
One of many Web sites with information about the Métis, this is the home page for the Métis Resource Centre.

collections.ic.gc.ca/heirloom_series/volume2/volume2.htm
A good introductory article on the Plains Natives appears at Chapter 3 of the Canada Heirlooms Series (Volume 2). Click on "Chapter 3."

THE PLATEAU

OVERVIEW

The Plateau (often earlier referred to as the Cordillera) is a diverse region—physically, linguistically, and culturally. The people live in areas of plateaus, mountains, and river valleys, which supply them with valued resources such as salmon (particularly in the lower river regions), black-tailed deer, elk, beaver, marmot, mountain goat, and important roots such as the camas and the bitterroot. Linguistically, there are three different groups: Athapaskan, Salishan, and Kootenayan—the same amount of linguistic variation that you would find in the eastern six provinces of Canada.

THE ATHAPASKANS

Carrier

The name "Carrier" is derived from the Sekani term **aghelhne,** meaning "the ones who pack." This referred to a funeral ritual in which a widow gathered and carried with her (for three years) the cremated remains of her spouse. A more generally preferred name in most Carrier communities, for them and for their language, is Dakelh, from **uda ukelha** ("people who travel by water in the morning," which has a general reference as "Natives"). Different names appear for distinct groups within the Carrier. The northern Carrier of Moricetown and Hagwilget refer to themselves as **Wet'suwet'en**. The people from the Babine Lake area are sometimes called **Ned'ut'en**. Similar to the peoples of the Northwest Coast, the Carrier

---

BOX 10-1   **Justa:**
When Electricity Came to Tachie

Justa became band manager for the Carrier community of Tachie in the early 1970s when he was around 30. His community did without those things that most other Canadians took for granted at that time: running water, a sewage system, televisions, telephones, even electricity. This meant that they had to use coal oil lamps for light and clothes had to be washed by hand. This is a short commentary on the coming of electricity to Tachie.

When electrical power came to Tachie in 1972, the people were glad to get rid of their lamps and lanterns and other devices that used gas or coal oil. Justa drove around the community with a truck to collect all the things that the people were tossing out. Justa's father refused to throw away the lamps that he had, saying:

> "You know that what you've got is not going to last forever. Someday it will break down and then where will we be for lights?" Nobody paid any attention to him. What the heck, they thought, we've got power and we'll never need these old lamps again! Of course, Dad was right—the first big storm dropped trees on the power lines and suddenly the village was in darkness again. I kept some of the newer lamps that had been thrown away and when there was this first power outage, I had a light shining out of my windows; it was almost the only light in Tachie.
> (Moran 1996:308)

(and their fellow Athapaskan-speaking Chilcotin) had social divisions that have been termed "nobles," "commoners," and "slaves." It should be noted that these European terms exaggerate the social distance between the different divisions and don't allow for the social mobility that did exist between groups.

The Carrier were the predominant Native group in the Plateau that the Northwest Company encountered when it established a network of inland posts in 1805. The Carrier established their own powerful trade networks, particularly through one leader, named **Kwah** (meaning "chief, leader"; c.1755–1850). One famous incident happened that included Kwah and James Douglas, who would later become governor of the colony. In 1823, two Carrier killed two White men. One of the Carrier was quietly killed under mysterious circumstances and the other had evaded the Hudson's Bay Company (which had taken over the N.W.C. in 1821) until 1828, when he was killed either by Douglas or by someone connected with Douglas. This could have led to an escalated conflict between the Carrier and Whites, but the situation was defused. There are two traditions of interpretation of why trouble didn't happen. Non-Native writers have long claimed that it was Douglas's diplomacy and strength that defused the situation in a confrontation with Kwah. Pageants or reenactments have been staged where his Métis wife, Amelia, was considered to have a key role. However, Carrier oral tradition suggests that Kwah refrained from retaliation for his own reasons, probably under the influence of his two grandsons, then young men.

In 1996, 1,510 people reported themselves as speaking Carrier (both Southern and Northern dialects), making it the leading B.C. Native language in terms of numbers.

BOX 10-2   Wet'suwet'en Salmon Conservation

At the time of first contact, the Wet'suwet'en enjoyed a rich salmon fishery on the Bulkley River, a tributary of the Skeena River. Their preferred method of fishing was using weirs and other traps. These methods enabled them to practise sound conservation as they were selective; that is, they made it relatively easy for the people to select how many and what age fish they would catch and how many they should let go, thus ensuring that the numbers stayed at a healthy level. However, beginning in the early 1900s, federal fisheries officers claimed that inland fishing such as was practised by the Wet'suwet'en took too many fish. Perhaps it would be more accurate to say that their perception was that such fishing took too many fish away from the more highly regarded (by the government) non-Native enterprises that harvested many more salmon. The Wet'suwet'en fish weirs persisted until the mid 1930s, when fishways were installed. While these helped the salmon swim upstream, they also destroyed the weirs. The Wet'suwet'en had to use other fishing methods, such as gill netting, jigging, and gaffing, which weren't as selective as the weirs and the traps.

During the 1990s, conservation became very important as the stocks of salmon became depleted. Two conservation measures taken by the Wet'suwet'en show how they acted to preserve the salmon. One of these measures was banning jigging for salmon. This practice involved using a short pole with a heavy line and sinker and a large three-pronged hook. The idea was to snag the fish as they went past. There was a high loss rate (17%, according to a Wet'suwet'en Fisheries study) using this method, which included injuring but not immediately killing the fish that got away. The Wet'suwet'en Hereditary Chiefs banned the practice, beginning in 1994, and the ban was enforced by the Wet'suwet'en Rangers. They were successful. Had the ban been set and enforced by the Department of Fisheries and Oceans, it might not have achieved such a high level of success.

Wet'suwet'en fisherman **Adam Gagnon** observed that, when the river was low during August, the fishways were too low for the salmon to swim upriver. He and a few others dip-netted 200 salmon a day for three weeks, releasing the fish at the upper end of the fishways. During the winter, he built a diversion system that diverted enough water so the fishways would be higher during the low period. His work is one reason why the local stocks of pink and sockeye salmon increased the next year.

There is still going to be a struggle to preserve this language, however, in a story that is familiar in many Native communities. Fluent speakers in most Carrier communities are 40 or over. Younger adults raising small children do not or cannot speak Dakelh and, therefore, very few children are still being raised in the language. The fight will be to turn this around.

Chilcotin

Their name, traditionally written as Chilcotin, but often now as Tsilhqot'in, means "young-man's river people." Their precontact numbers vary in estimation from 1,500 to 2,500, not far off of their numbers today. In 1982 it was reported that there were 1,200 speakers out of a population of 1,800, but studies have pointed to a severe decline in the number of speakers of Tsilhqot'in since then. Today, they live on a few reserves on their own and in at least one mixed in with the Carrier. They are best known historically for an incident that was destructive to their people and that still lives on in the memories of the people's Elders. This incident is known by the somewhat exaggerated name of the Chilcotin War.

The Chilcotin War

Although a fur trade post had earlier been established and ultimately abandoned in their country, the Chilcotin had been fundamentally untouched by European society until 1862, when they were hit hard by both the Gold Rush and smallpox. They were then powerfully affected by two White men, with disastrous results. One was Joseph Trutch. His deep-seated racial prejudice can be seen in the following quote from 1850: "I think they are ugliest & laziest creatures I ever saw, & we sho[ul]d as soon think of being afraid of our dogs as of them." He arrived in British Columbia in 1859 and worked for five years as a surveyor and engineer. In 1864 he was made the Chief Commissioner of Lands and Works. His land policies still have a negative impact on aboriginal land claims in British Columbia. He could not "'see why they should either retain these lands to the prejudice of the general [i.e., White] interest of the Colony, or be allowed to make a market of them either to the Government or to Individuals.'" Making "a market of them" was the legally prescribed act of making treaties, something that took place that century in every province west of Quebec. The Chilcotin rightly felt that the official attitude in the young colony was to take their land with no recompense. This feeling was exacerbated when Alfred Waddington began to construct a road through the heart of Chilcotin territory in 1863. The road crew hired Chilcotin to work for them. They were treated poorly, promissory notes were issued instead of pay, and the people had little food.

In the spring of 1864, a road crew foreman named Brewster accused half-starved Chilcotin workers of stealing flour. He took down their names and issued a prediction that they would die of smallpox. To the Chilcotin, that probably sounded like a threat, like he would deliberately spread the disease. On April 29, three Chilcotin went to the man who operated a ferry on the Homathko River and asked him to share food with them. In their culture, if someone had food it was shared with those who did not. The ferryman apparently refused. He was killed and food was taken.

The three Chilcotin went to the road crew that night, talking with 16 Chilcotin who worked with 12 White men. They were fairly easily persuaded to attack the White men. Their food situation and the White move on their land were probably the main factors in their decision. They killed nine of the road crew and three escaped. Further down the road was the hated Brewster and three others. They were soon killed.

The Chilcotin met up with a respected older leader of their people, Telloot (sometimes Taloot or Tellot), and their number grew to about 30. They later killed a White settler who, like Brewster, had apparently threatened them with smallpox and had earlier driven them off of a traditional campsite, claiming it as his own.

When the newspapers in the capital of Victoria found out about these incidents their reports were predictably one-sided and they called for vengeance. The editor of the *British Colonist* said that White colonists should not rest until "every member of that rascally murderous tribe is suspended to the trees of their own forests." Governor Seymour organized two parties to go to Chilcotin country. A man called Cox led one group of about 50 men,

BOX 10-3	British Columbia Placenames from Plateau Peoples

Name	Nation	Meaning
Chilcotin	Chilcotin	young man's river people
Kamloops	Shuswap	meeting of the waters
Okanagan	Okanagan	head of the river
Kootenay	Ktunaxa	people of the dense forest or brush

mostly Americans, in the area to bring back gold. A Chilcotin leader referred to as Chief Alexis, who had not been involved with the action, was sent to Seymour to bring a message from the two leaders of the uprising, Telloot and Klatsassin. Those two men offered to cease hostilities and give themselves up. According to the Chilcotin, Cox said that he would guarantee the Chilcotin's safety if they came peacefully to a meeting arranged for August 11. Telloot, Klatsassin, and six others accompanied Chief Alexis in good faith. Cox apparently broke his word, surrounded them, and commanded them to lay down their weapons and surrender. Telloot is reputed to have smashed his rifle against a tree, declaring "King George men [i.e., the British] are all great liars."

Two were freed with no charges laid and one escaped. Five were convicted: Telloot, Klatsassin, his 18-year-old son, and two others. The judge, Chief Justice Matthew Baillie Begbie, was not without sympathy for their cause, saying "[t]he treatment of the Indians, employed in packing, received at the hands of Brewster and his party was at once calculated to arouse their cupidity [desire for goods] and provoke their vengeance." However, in September they were hanged in front of an audience of about 200. All told, 20 White men had been killed, but the death toll for the Chilcotin was not recorded. If it had been, it might have included those Chilcotin who died of starvation in the winter of 1864–5, driven out of their homeland by the disruption of the time. The road they had fought to stop ended up only stretching for 64 kilometres. Waddington had a mountain named after him.

It is important to discuss this issue because, for the Chilcotin, the affair is still very much alive. In 1993, B.C. Attorney-General Colin Gabelmann apologized to the Chilcotin for the executions of the five men, calling the hangings a tragedy.

KOOTENAYAN

Ktunaxa or Kutenai

The people call themselves "Ktunaxa," which is sometimes translated as "people of the dense forest or brush." The English name "Kutenai" (also spelled "Kootenay") is said to have come from the Blackfoot pronunciation of their name.

While the people have been in the mountains for thousands of years, their territory used to extend east into the Prairies, about half way across what is now Alberta. Their traditional culture incorporated such Plains features as a military/police group (e.g., the Crazy Dogs Society) and the Sun Dance. The more powerful Blackfoot drove the Ktunaxa out of the Prairies by the middle of the nineteenth century.

Their language is unique, related to no other, but with fewer than 200 speakers and a writing system that came into existence only 25 years ago, it is under threat of extinction. However, the people are fighting for its survival. Elders present the language in the Ktunaxa daycare centres and the people have developed learning modules in the language for at least grades 4 and 6.

Traditionally, the people were divided into two separate bands, called in English the Upper Kutenai and Lower Kutenai (based on their position on the Columbia and Kutenai rivers). Now, under the Ktunaxa-Kinbasket Tribal Council, there are seven bands, or First Nations. Five are located in Canada—the St. Mary's or A'Qam, the Lower Kootenay or Yaqan nukiy ("the people where the rock is standing"), Tobacco Plains or ?akin'kuntlasnuqtli? ("people of the place of the flying head"), Columbia Lake or Akisq'nuk ("two bodies of water"), and Shuswap (where Shuswap is spoken)—and two are located in northern Idaho and northwestern Montana. They number around 2,000 today, probably slightly more than their population at first contact.

INTERIOR SALISH

The Salish ("people") live both in the Plateau region (where anthropologists have termed them "Interior Salish") and on the Northwest Coast (where they have been termed "Coast Salish").

BOX 10-4	**Turning Things Around at the St. Eugene Mission**

In 1873, the Oblate Fathers of the Roman Catholic Church founded the St. Eugene Mission. In 1910, buildings were constructed to form the first residential school in the area. The school ran for about 60 years, acting as an agent of assimilation to children from the Ktunaxa, Okanagan, Shuswap, and Blackfoot First Nations. It was a place where Native culture was attacked.

In 1970, the residential school was closed. Four years later, the five Canadian First Nations of the Ktunaxa Tribal Council were awarded joint ownership of the 346 acres of land and the run-down but substantial buildings that stood there. Twenty years later, restoration work was set in motion in earnest, with an aim to develop a resort. With funding from the Department of Indian Affairs and Northern Develop-ment for planning, setup, and employee training costs, it is expected to bring both employment and tourism dollars to both Native and non-Native communities in the area.

While most of the development is centred on the standard resort features of hotel (with 119 guest rooms), 18-hole golf course, recreation centre, and meeting/convention facilities, the Ktunaxa intend to add unique features that will promote their culture. This will include a tipi camp, a cultural interpretation centre, and a centre for selling the distinctive crafts of the Ktunaxa. These latter features caused Elder Ann Mary Joseph to remark that ". . . since it was within the St. Eugene Mission school that the culture of the Kootenay Indian was taken away, it should be within that building that it is returned."

Anthropologists typically group the Interior Salish into five different divisions, typically including the Shuswap, Okanagan, Lillooet, Thompson, and Lake, but the latter has disappeared as a group in Canada, moving to the United States.

Shuswap or Secwepemc

The Shuswap or Secwepemc (as they prefer to be called) are Salish speakers who live in southcentral British Columbia in 17 bands. They were hit hard by the smallpox epidemic of 1862 but still numbered about 7,200 late in the nineteenth century, a figure not too different from their population today. There are fewer than 500 speakers of Secwepemc.

The Shuswap have long been prominently involved with Native politics on provincial, national, and international levels. Along with the Chilcotin, they formed the British Columbia Interior Confederacy in 1945 and were the main driving force behind the North American Indian Brotherhood. A leading figure in that involvement was **George Manuel**, who was first president of the largely B.C.-centred North American Indian Brotherhood, then the National Indian Brotherhood (precursor to the Assembly of First Nations) from its beginning in 1970 to 1976, and finally the World Council of Indigenous People, an international organization launched at Port Alberni, B.C.

Okanagan

The name Okanagan comes from a word meaning "head of the river," referring to the highest point to which salmon could ascend. The people live both in northern Washington and in southcentral British Columbia, with a combined population of over 3,000 but fewer than 500 fluent speakers of their language, Nsilxcin. There are two main ways in which the people are promoting their language today. In the Okanagan First Nation community, they have developed a daycare centre at which an Elders' group, the Okanagan Language and Cultural Society, and a local theatre group are adapting children's games and stories to incorporate the Okanagan language. They also have an educational institution, the E'nowkin Centre in Penticton, at which courses in speaking, reading, and writing Nsilxcin are taught.

Lillooet

The Lillooet or Lil'wat ("Wild Onion") speak a language that has two dialects, Upper and Lower St'at'imc. In Mount Currie, their largest community (over 1,200), they were one of

---

BOX 10-5   Getting to Your Roots

Two roots, the camas and the bitterroot, have long been important resources for Plateau people. In Nsilxcin, bitterroot is called **spitlem**. April was called **Spitlemtem** (i.e., bitterroot month) because it was gathered by women in upland areas in April and May, the first fresh food of the spring. The First Roots Ceremony is an important traditional spring ceremony for the Okanagan people, celebrating the gift of new food and highlighting another year's passage from winter into spring.

the first bands in Canada (beginning in 1975) to successfully run an in-community teacher training program, in connection with Simon Fraser University. Together, the students who were training to be teachers and the university staff developed a program that not only successfully graduated fully qualified teachers but also brought their language into modern times with an accurate writing system, rigorous language curriculum, and a dictionary. Initially, the children they taught were somewhat resistant to the language lessons, thinking (like many non-Natives) that they were irrelevant to their future careers and lives. However, through extension of the language material into social studies and science classes, the students began to realize the interconnection of identity (through language and culture) and a career in the "modern" world. The education of the children in the language is necessary to its survival, as there are fewer than 300 fluent speakers.

Thompson/Nicola/Ntlakyapamuk

The people sometimes labelled as Thompson and Nicola (or just one of the two), or sometimes Ntlakyapamuk, are speakers of a language currently written as Nle7kepmxcin (as taught through the Nicola Institute of Technology).

One reason for this labelling confusion is that these people have had a long tradition of working together in common initiatives, crossing the ethnic borders that might be placed upon them by outsiders. In 1879, a large number of these people and some of their neighbours gathered together at Lytton to come up with solutions to the problems of adapting to the newcomers. According to Robin Fisher, they

> . . . agreed on a set of regulations designed to foster the education of their children, to improve sanitary and medical facilities in the village, to subdivide arable land on an individual basis, to reduce the number of non-working days, to abolish the potlatch, and to levy fines for drunkenness and gambling. (Fisher 1977:179)

They elected a Nicola head chief and a council of 13 to administer these important ordinances. The local Indian reserve commissioner, Gilbert Sproat, wrote to Ottawa saying that the Lytton meeting demonstrated "the laudable desire of the Indians to make efforts, at their own cost principally, to improve the physical condition and the minds of their children and to train themselves for citizenship" (Fisher 1977:179).

The settlers were horrified by any thought of a confederation of Natives (who still outnumbered the settlers). The editor of an influential newspaper, the *Victoria Daily Standard*, referred to the meeting and its developments as "in every way objectionable," and expressed his concern that the people might try to "obtain some privilege or concession antagonistic

Native Individuals 10-1

Adam Gagnon: Wet'suwet'en fisherman whose conservation measures have helped the salmon.

Kwah ("leader, chief"; c1755–1850): An important historical Carrier chief.

George Manuel: A Shuswap politician who became the president of the National Indian Brotherhood.

Timeline 10-1

1828: Confrontation between Kwah and James Douglas.

1862: Gold rush in the interior of British Columbia.

1862: Epidemic of smallpox strikes the interior of British Columbia.

1864: Joseph Trutch made the Chief Commissioner of Lands and Works.

1864: Chilcotin War.

1880: Aboriginals constitute a majority of the recorded population of British Columbia of 49,459.

1891: Aboriginals considered to constitute less than one third of the population of 98,173.

to white interests." His influence, plus settler letters to Ottawa, plus the opposition to Native political initiatives by the Indian superintendent in Victoria and the department responsible for "Indian Affairs" in Ottawa quashed this move for self-government. Sproat was bullied out of his job the next year and was replaced by Peter O'Reilly, brother-in-law of the hated Joseph Trutch and a man with a track record of imposing reserves on the people that ignored such concerns as burial grounds and fields the people had been planting and grazing their cattle on for years.

KEY TERMS

bitterroot

camas

CONTENT QUESTIONS

1. What three language groups exist in the Plateau?
2. Identify two salmon conservation measures initiated by the Wet'suwet'en (Carrier).
3. Which of the Plateau languages has no known related languages?
4. Why did the Chilcotin War take place?
5. Why was the group that gathered at Lytton in 1879 unable to achieve its goals?

 WEBLINKS

www.cyberlink.bc.ca/kktc/   Deals with the Ktunaxa or Kootenay.

www.schoolmet.ca/aboriginal/enowkin/   Deals with the En'owkin Centre, where the Okanagan people teach their language, Nsilxcin, and other aspects of their culture.

www.secwepemc.org/secwho.html   Web site for the Secwepemc Cultural Education Sociey.

http://vaughan.fac.unbc.ca/bc_aboriginal/wet/comgmt.html   Web site for the Wet'suwet'en fishery.

C h a p t e r

THE
NORTHWEST
COAST

OVERVIEW

The Northwest Coast is unique. There are more superlatives that can be used for this cultural area than any other. One is that the people drew from the richest natural resources in Canada. The sea provided well for the people, with whales, several varieties of seals, porpoises, sea lions, sea otter, five main species of salmon (sockeye, coho, chinook, chum, and pink), halibut, herring cod, oolichan or candle fish (so named because of all the oil they contained), clams, mussels, crabs, eggs from sea birds, and seaweed. And then there are the trees. The spectacular woods in British Columbia helped the Northwest Coast people become the most spectacular woodworkers, building totem poles, houses up to 42 metres long made out of massive poles and long planks, impressive cedar war canoes up to 13 metres (possibly 20 metres) that could carry 60 people, and square boxes made out of one piece of flat wood steamed so that it would be pliable enough to bend. Not surprisingly, with these rich resources and with the people's careful management of the resources, we find that the Northwest Coast had the densest population, at least 50,000 people along a fairly narrow 2,000-kilometre-long stretch of coastline in British Columbia. Villages lasted longer than anywhere else, some showing continuous occupation for as many as 4,000 years. Imagine a Canadian town being 4,000 years old! The societies had the greatest degree of stratification, with powerful chiefs that existed nowhere else in Native Canada, nobility, commoners, and even prisoners who constituted a servant/slave class (although with more rights and respect than was ever afforded to African slaves brought to the Americas).

The Northwest Coast also has the greatest variety of languages in Canada, more than what exists in all of Europe. There are the language isolates of Tlingit, Haida, and Tsimshian, along with the language families of Salish and Wakashan—five of the eleven aboriginal language varieties found in Canada.

A key feature of Northwest Coast cultures, one that has slowly come to affect decisions in their land claims, is that they have arguably the clearest defined notion of property in Native Canada. What is meant here is that families or lineages had clearly demarked ownership of rights to hunt, fish, pick berries, or harvest other materials from a geographically defined territory. In a number of ways it is closer to European notions of "ownership of land" than what existed in the rest of Native Canada. They have had a long, hard fight, however, to demonstrate that to anthropologically ignorant judges.

One more traditional feature should be mentioned here. Kinship was determined matrilineally among the Tlingit, Haida, and Tsimshian to the north, with two major organizations (typically identified as the Raven and the Eagle or Wolf), known by anthropologists as moieties, being the main social divisions.

TLINGIT

The Tlingit ("people"), whose traditional homeland stretched over some 640 kilometres of coastline, are the northernmost of the Northwest Coast peoples and, at one time, might also have been the most numerous. It has been estimated that in the eighteenth century they numbered as many as 15,000. They were also a powerful people, successful as raiders to the south and as traders into the interior of Alaska, British Columbia, and the Yukon. As traders into the interior, they held a virtual monopoly on goods from the sea and the cedar bark and wild mountain goat wool blend blankets that came to be named after one of the Tlingit groups, the Chilkat. Their trade grew stronger with early European contact, as both Russians and British saw the practicality of having Tlingit middlemen. This contact also had the inevitable negative side, as smallpox diminished Tlingit numbers first in 1775 and then, more seriously, in the great epidemic of 1835–40, which some writers claim killed off half of the people. The Gold Rush in 1895, with the influx of so many outsiders, finally broke the back of the Tlingit trade.

While the Tlingit language has a similar grammar to neighbouring Athapaskan languages, the two do not share vocabulary to any significant extent. This is a good argument for the position that Tlingit is a language isolate. The close contact between Tlingit and Athapaskan peoples, including a significant amount of intermarriage, not only produced grammatical similarity but also made the cultures very similar, too.

The majority of Tlingit live along the Alaskan panhandle, the narrow southern coastline of that state. There are three groups in Canada that are identified as Tlingit: the Taku River Tlingit of Atlin, British Columbia, and the Teslin Tlingit and the Carcross-Tagish First Nation, both in the Yukon. All three are descended from coastal Tlingit who moved up the Taku River and who married extensively with Athapaskans living in the interior. Despite the political difficulties of having the land they claim divided by the non-Tlingit borders of Alaska, British Columbia, and the Yukon, all three groups have been able to reach advanced stages of the treaty process. The Tlingit connection with the land to which they are asserting their rights was well expressed in 1915 by Chief Taku Jack to the Royal Commission for Indian Affairs for British Columbia:

Atlin means big lake, and that is the place where we used to stay. That is the reason I used to think that the whites were not going to give me any trouble because they call us after this lake. They call us Atlin Indians because they know I belong to this country. (http://eaoluco-web.eao.gs.gov.bc.ca/project/mining/tulsequa)

HAIDA

The Haida, whose name (actually Xa'ida) means "people," are strongly connected with the islands known in English as the Queen Charlotte Islands but in Haida as "Haida Gwaii." As is typical of Northwest Coast peoples, the sea and the forests provided well for them, with the sea providing them with fur seals, sea otters, and sea lions in particular.

The Haida numbered over 8,000 at the time of first contact, near the end of the eighteenth century, but with smallpox and the other negative effects of dealing with the newcomers, they diminished to about 500 by 1915. They once had 14 communities but were compelled to relocate into two: Massett and Skidegate. The villages they were forced to abandon now stand as sacred places and efforts are being made to preserve the totem poles and buildings that still remain. Today there are about 2,500 Haida, both in Canada and in the panhandle of Alaska. Their language, called Xaadas, is generally considered to be a language isolate (although a few scholars have tried to connect it with the Dene languages). It has about 350 speakers, most of them in Canada.

The Haida have long offered resistance to outsider control. This tradition featured such leaders as **Koyah** ("Raven," ?–1791 (?)) who resisted English attempts at controlling the fur trade by attacking ships with his war canoes, to **Reverend Peter Kelly** (1885–1966), who fought for aboriginal rights in British Columbia through the Allied Tribes of British Columbia (formed in 1916), to **Bill Wilson**, who continued that fight in modern times. The tradition continues today with **Guujaaw**, recently elected president of the Haida Nation, who is putting through a lawsuit to the British Columbia Supreme Court to get recognition of Haida rights to Haida Gwaii.

BOX 11-1   **Families or Houses of the Haida**

Traditional social divisions of the Haida begins with two moieties, Raven and Eagle, which break down into clans, which could be divided into houses or families. The following are names of some of these houses:

House	Meaning
Naalgus-haida	"dark house people"
Nakalas-hadai	"clay house people"
Nakalnas-hadai	"empty house people"
Nakedduts-hadai	"people of the house that went away discouraged"
Nayuuns-haidagai	"great house people"
Nasagas-haidagai	"rotten house people"

What do you think **-na-** means in these words?

BOX 11-2   Bill Reid (1920–1998)

Bill Reid is a controversial Haida artist who combined two worlds to draw attention to Haida art and land claims, in the process making himself rich and famous. His father was White and his mother was Haida. As with many mixed Native heritage Canadians, his Native ancestry was hidden from him. He was raised in Victoria. It wasn't until he was a teenager that he learned of his Haida background. A powerful moment in Bill Reid's life came when he was 23, during his first trip to Haida Gwaii where he met his grandfather, Charles Gladstone, a stone carver of argillite and an engraver in silver. Gladstone had inherited the tools and probably had been taught by his uncle, noted Haida sculptor Charles Edenshaw, whose work can be seen in museums and in books around the world. Both would be indirect mentors of Bill Reid.

Reid got a job working as a CBC radio announcer in Toronto in 1948. There he learned both European-tradition skills and Haida designs. He studied jewellery-making part-time at what is now Ryerson University and apprenticed at the Platinum Art Company. He also spent hours studying a Haida totem pole that was kept at the Royal Ontario Museum. That totem pole gave him his first significant insights into the patterns of Haida art.

He returned to Vancouver in 1951 where, between hours working for the CBC, he practised his art in a basement workshop. He began to focus, through museum visits and books, on the works of his great-great-uncle Charles Edenshaw—the hundreds of pieces of gold and silver jewellery his ancestor had created.

Reid next became involved, through the Department of Anthropology at the University of British Columbia, with the salvage and restoration of rotting Haida totem poles and houses. When he received his first big contract in 1958, he quit the CBC to dedicate himself to this project, now an outdoor exhibit at the U.B.C. Museum of Anthropology. From the 1960s to the 1970s, he became well known for creating beautiful jewellery and small, wooden carvings using Haida designs.

His major fame, however, came about in a controversial way. He contracted Parkinson's disease, a neurological disorder that made it increasingly difficult for him to use the fine motor skills necessary for carving. But during the 1980s, his previous works and his ability to deal with non-Native media enabled him to acquire lucrative contracts that he could not refuse. In 1982, the Dogfish Transformation Pendant, a gold necklace based on a boxwood carving he had made earlier, sold for $100,000. Jim Hart, a young Haida artist who worked for him, did much of the work. Increasingly, through the 1980s and early 1990s, Haida artists such as Hart, Guujaaw, Sharon Hitchcock, and Don Yeomans, Kwakiutl painter Ben Houstie (who painted drums for Reid that fetched up to $20,000), and local White artists such as George Rammell, worked on Reid's art. Famous pieces were only designed and supervised by Reid, with a great deal of creative and manual input from others. These include such works of art as "Lootas," a 15-metre war canoe displayed at Vancouver's world fair, Expo 86; "The Spirit of Haida Gwaii," a five-ton bronze sculpture based on a small, black argillite "spirit canoe" he studied at a museum, which was purchased for $1.5 million in 1991 for the Canadian Embassy in Washington; and, a copy, "The Jade Canoe," purchased by the Vancouver airport for $3 million (the highest price ever paid for a Canadian work of art).

Reid's position among the Haida is complicated. He is respected for popularizing Haida art and for his consistent and effective public support of Haida land claims. However, he is criticized by some of the people for overstating his role in the preservation of traditional Haida art forms, for sometimes exploiting and not properly crediting the input of other Haida artists in "his" works, and for using non-Native artists in the making of "Native art."

TSIMSHIAN

The different Tsimshian peoples are named after the two rivers that centre their traditional territory: the Tsimshian ("people [inside] of the Skeena River) and Gitxsan (earlier spelt Gitksan, "Skeena River people") after the more southerly of the rivers, and the Nisga'a after the more northerly, the Nass River. The Gitxsan and the Nisga'a can be considered as speaking dialects of a language, while the Tsimshian speak a dialect different enough to be considered a related language. Most scholars consider Tsimshian to be a language isolate, while some consider it a distant branch of the Penutian family.

It has been estimated that the Tsimshian had a population of between 6,000 and 10,000 at the time of first contact and number more than 8,000 now. They are culturally similar to the Tlingit and the Haida but differ in having four main social divisions, or phratries (Eagle, Raven, Wolf, and Killer Whale), rather than the two moieties of the Haida.

WAKASHAN

The name Wakashan is said to be derived from a word, "waukash," meaning "good," that Captain James Cook heard and assumed was the name of a people living by Nootka Sound. Wakashan peoples were traditionally similar socially to their northern neighbours in that the structure of their society was hierarchical, with leaders that were heads of powerful houses owned by leading lineages. They were different from the northerners, however, in that their society was not divided into two moieties. There were at least 10,000 Wakashan-speaking people during the early nineteenth century.

The people are divided linguistically into two groups: Northern and Southern Wakashan. The Northern Wakashan include the **Haisla**, who live just south of the Tsimshian and are associated with the community of Kitimat; the **Heiltsuk**, who are particularly associated with the community of Bella Bella; and the **Kwakiutl** (a name that applied properly to only one community) or, more correctly **Kwakwaka'wakw**, by far the most numerous, powerful, and most often academically discussed group.

The Southern Wakashan include the single community people of the **Nitinat**, and the more numerous **Nootka** or **Nuu'chah'nulth** ("All along the mountains"). The latter name is the name that the people use, while the word Nootka, assigned to them by English speakers, is said to come from the time in 1778 when the people met with Captain Cook. According to the story, he asked them what sound they were at (now called Nootka Sound) and they interpreted him as asking directions concerning Vancouver Island, and said "notka," meaning "circle around."

One distinctive traditional trait of the Nuu'chah'nulth is that they hunted whales, including humpbacks, which could reach 15 metres in length, and grey whales, which could reach nearly 14 metres. That was one reason why they had to build especially large canoes (i.e.,

---

GETTING IT RIGHT 11-1 | **Haida and Haisla**

The names "Haida" and "Haisla" look quite similar. The authors have read several pieces in which the better-known name "Haida" has been used instead of the lesser-known "Haisla" (see Friesen 1997:177).

BOX 11-3   Carla Robinson

Carla Robinson, the evening anchor for CBC Newsworld, is part Haisla and part Heiltsuk. She was born and spent most of her childhood in her father's Haisla community of Kitimat, but also lived for a while in her mother's Heiltsuk community of Bella Bella. She was first inspired to be a journalist when she was 14. She saw a Native television reporter and felt that she could also get such a job. At 16 she got a job as a reporter at the *Northern Sentinel Press* (circulation approximately 25,000), where she first achieved some prominence for writing front-page articles on the death and subsequent memorial feast for Nisga'a hereditary Chief James Gosnell.

Since then, she has worked her way up the journalistic ladder, writing for Native print media such as *Aboriginal Voices* and *Dreamspeaker*, working as a mainstream media reporter for CBC's "Midday" in British Columbia, as a reporter and producer for CBC's Native current affairs series, and "All My Relations" (which had about 350,000 listeners after the first show) before she landed the job at CBC Newsworld.

Carla has commented on her career and the role of employment equity in her success. When she was asked about being a "token Indian" at the CBC, she replied:

> Like others, perhaps because I am Native I have managed to get a few jobs. If it was not for employment equity, I would more than likely not be given half the chances I have had. However, some people have had similar appointments and have not taken advantage of the opportunities available. . . Unless we get a few Native people in there, we will continue to appear to exist on charity and tokenism. But employment equity is not charity nor is it tokenism, it is necessary and important to address the historic disadvantages we face as Native people. (*Aboriginal Voices*)

boats approximating the size of the animals they hunted), which other peoples were eager to obtain through trade. Typical of this hierarchical people, only the chief had the right to hunt whales, and he would go through an elaborate eight-month ritual before the hunt. Beginning in November, he would walk into the cold Pacific Ocean and rub his skin with nettles until he bled. The ceremonial name of the great Nuu'chah'nulth leader, Maquina, was **Tsaxhw'sip**, meaning "harpooner."

COAST SALISH

The Coast Salish are divided into a number of separate groups, most prominently the **Stó:lo** Nation (formerly often referred to as the Cowichan), which encompasses 19 bands, the Squamish, Sechelt, Songish (Lkungen), Nuxalk (Bella Coola), and Comox. It has been estimated that at the time of contact they had as many as 32,000 people and were reduced to as few as 4,120 in 1915.

The meaning of the word Stó:lo is "river [people]," the river in question being the Fraser River of southern British Columbia, beside which many of the Stó:lo live. Estimates of their population prior to contact vary, with 10,000 being the minimum figure. Being so

BOX 11-4   **Maquina (fl1786–1825): A Man of Extreme Numbers**

Maquina ("moon" or "possessor of pebbles") was a powerful Nuu'chah'nulth chief that we know a lot about because of John Jewitt. In 1815, Jewitt published an account of his three years living as a captive with Maquina. Of course, this account has the biases of an outsider, but it is a good source for numbers. Maquina is a good extreme example of Northwest Coast hierarchical society (rather like how kings Louis XIV and Henry VIII are good extreme examples of European monarchies). Keep in mind, however, that Nuu'chah'nulth society, even in Maquina's day, did not have the poverty or starvation of European monarchies. Also keep in mind that one reason that Maquina's numbers were as high as they were is that he and his people were going through a "sudden riches" period due to the fur trade. Here are his numbers:

Number of wives:	9 (at one time)
Number of "slaves":	50
Number of people living in his house:	100
Size of his house:	
Dimensions:	45 metres long
	11 to 12 metres wide
	4.2 metres high
Ridge Pole:	30 metres long x 2.5 metres in circumference
Planks:	3 metres long x 1.2 to 1.5 metres wide
Size of his canoe:	14 metres (hollowed out pine)

Native Individuals 11-1

Maquin(n)a: A powerful Nootka leader of the late eighteenth and early nineteenth century.

Bill Reid: A prominent twentieth-century Haida artist.

Carla Robinson: A Haisla/Heiltsuk anchorwoman for CBC Newsworld.

close to the centres (e.g., Vancouver and New Westminster) that the settlers moved to in large numbers, they were hard hit by the effects of European colonization. In 1782, for example, it has been estimated that about 62% died of smallpox.

The language of these people is Halq'eméylem (or Halkomelem), which has three dialects: Upriver, with such communities as Chehalis and Chilliwack; Downriver, with such communities as Musqueam and Coquitlam; and Island, the most populated, with communities with such well-known names as Cowichan and Nanaimo ("named people"). Among the most notable achievements of the Stó:lo today is the curriculum they have developed for both their own schools and the non-Native schools in the urban areas that are near to the people. Their educational Web site, put together by the Stó:lo Curriculum Consortium, is a model that other Native (and non-Native) peoples could learn a lot from (see reference at the end of the chapter). Innovative education initiatives of the Stó:lo also include Chemainus Native College and Malaspina University College.

KEY TERMS

hierarchical
notka
oolichan
phratries

CONTENT QUESTIONS

1. Why were the peoples of the Northwest Coast able to have stratified societies and long-term houses and communities?
2. What is the longest period of continuous occupation of a Northwest Coast community?
3. How many language isolates and families are found in the Northwest Coast?
4. What are the main social divisions of the Tlingit, Haida, and Tsimshian?
5. At the time of contact, which was the largest in number of the Northwest Coast peoples?

 WEBLINKS

http://209.1.224.11/Athens/9479/haida.html#nis
This site deals with the Haida languages and Hiada Gwaii, their homeland.

www.aboriginalvoices.com/1999/06-03/robinson.html
An article on Carla Robinson.

www.mala.bc.ca
Malaspina University College and its programs concerning the local Native groups.

www.hallman.org/indian/history.html
Bruce Hallman's excellent resource documents the history of Natives on the Pacific Coast of North America, including first-person accounts of contact between Natives and European settlers.

home.istar.ca/%7Ebthom
This site, by Brian Thom, is an excellent source for Coast Salish information.

www.bcfn.org/bcfn/firstnationbands.htm
A list of Native bands in British Columbia.

collections.ic.gc.ca/heirloom_series/volume2/volume2.htm
The Canada Heirlooms Series, in "Chapter 8" of its series, presents an article entitled "The Monumental Cultures of the Northwest Coast Peoples."

THE ROYAL PROCLAMATION AND THE INDIAN ACT

THE ROYAL PROCLAMATION OF 1763

The Royal Proclamation of 1763 has been referred to as the Natives' Magna Carta. In 1763, King George III, following the Treaty of Paris, which concluded the Seven Years War with France, issued his Royal Proclamation. This dealt with a number of issues, including those pertaining to Natives. It stated that any lands within the territorial confines of the new governments (which included present-day Quebec, Florida, West Florida, and Granada) that had not been ceded by the Indians ". . . are reserved to them, or any of them as their Hunting Grounds."

The reason cited for this was:

> whereas it is just and reasonable, and essential to our Interest, and the Security of our Colonies that the Several Nations or Tribes of Indians with who We are connected, and who live under our Protection, should not be molested or disturbed. . . .

Also, the proclamation dealt with land *not* within the limits of the new government. It reserved ". . . for the use of said Indians, all Land Territories not included within the limits of our Said . . . governments, or within the Limits of the Territory granted to the Hudson's Bay Company."

Regarding that last point, in 1670, the Hudson's Bay Company, a business run by English traders, received its charter from the British Crown. Charles II gave the company monopoly of trade in the lands drained by the waters that flow into Hudson Bay. It was given the rights to land as well, calling it Rupert's Land after the prince who helped set up the company.

No one at the time had any idea of the size of what had been given to the company. In essence, it amounted to most of Quebec, a good piece of Ontario, all of Manitoba and Saskatchewan, and a major part of Alberta.

In order to prevent fraud, the proclamation provided a way in which lands could be acquired for settlement. Indian lands "shall be purchased only for Us, in our Name, at some public Meeting of Assembly of the said Indians." This implied that all lands that had not been surrendered by the Indians to the Crown belonged to the Indians. It reserved all unsettled land for the use of the Indians as their hunting grounds. It provided that lands required for settlement had to be bought from the Indians and could only be bought by the Crown at a public meeting.

The Royal Proclamation, therefore, set the stage for land surrender treaties signed by the Indians and the Crown. The reason for this is that under the Canadian legal system, English laws became a part of the law of Canada on the dates when various colonial governments were formed. Under this rule, the Royal Proclamation became a part of Canadian law. Without the passing of a specific law overruling such a law (which hasn't taken place), the Royal Proclamation is still valid.

However, this leaves us with several questions that have been and are being disputed in the courts. Despite its apparent clarity, there are several questions that arise. Did the proclamation provide the source of Native title to the land or did it merely recognize the pre-existing reality that the lands belonged to the Indians? Not surprisingly, Native activists and leaders, as well as anthropologists and other scholars, take the position that the land did in fact belong to aboriginal people and George III's proclamation simply affirmed this recognition.

Other questions need asking. Did the proclamation apply to all of what is now Canada (as Native people contend) or did it apply to simply lands that had been discovered by the British to that date? The province of British Columbia has long operated on the basis of the latter argument maintaining therefore that the proclamation does not apply to them.

THE INDIAN ACT

[handwritten: 1755 initially passed in 1876]

The Indian Act is a tool of a large bureaucracy created "to deal" with Indians. This bureaucracy predates confederation by over a hundred years, going back to 1755. Initially, the administration of Natives was in the hands of the military, reflecting the role and importance of Native people in inter-European wars. Additionally, after the American War of Independence (American Revolution) and the War of 1812, there was a belief that Natives posed a potential threat to European settlement. Hence their inclusion under military concerns.

In Upper Canada (Ontario), Native concerns remained in the hands of the military until 1830 when they were turned over to the lieutenant governor of the colony and the reserve system was implemented to encourage Indians to become farmers. Agrarianization and Christianization were seen as the best means of "civilizing" Indians.

In Lower Canada (Quebec), the military remained in charge of Indians until Lower and Upper Canada were united as the Province of Canada in 1840. At this time, all Native matters were transferred to the governor general. However, there was no budget for Native affairs and no establishment of an Indian Department.

It was not until 1860 that full control of Indian matters was given to the colonies. The transfer of full control marked a change in the nature of Native–White relations. Until that time, Natives had retained a fair amount of autonomy. As long as Indian matters had remained in the hands of the military and later the British Colonial Office (1840–1860), there had been little interference. The British Colonial Office was far away and could do little about colonial matters.

In 1867, the British North America Act made "Indians and lands reserved for Indians" a federal responsibility. From 1867 to 1873 they were under the jurisdiction of the secretary of state. In 1873, they were transferred to the Department of the Interior. In 1880, a separate Indian Affairs Department was set up under Minister of the Interior John A. Macdonald, who was also the prime minister.

The moving of the Indian Affairs Department to the Ministry of the Interior reflects a trend that persists to this day. The department or ministry that houses Indian Affairs invariably reflects the primary concerns of the government at the time. Thus, we find Indian Affairs a branch of the Department of Mines and Resources in 1936, Citizenship and Immigration in 1949 (which First Nations find ironic), Northern Affairs and National Resources in 1965, and, finally, the Department of Indian Affairs and Northern Development in 1966. Today it is called Indian and Northern Affairs Canada (INAC).

It is important to realize that the Indian Act of 1876, the tool with which the government controls Native people, was not a new piece of legislation. Rather, it was a consolidation of various pieces of existing federal and colonial statutes. The essential thrust of the legislation was to centralize and codify all legislation and to solidify the position of Natives as wards of the state. The powers allotted to band councils (or local governments) are minimal, restricted to the trivial and arcane, such as bee keeping and stray dog control. And, ultimately, even these are subject to higher authority.

It is a common complaint that the Natives are over-governed. Insofar as Natives and Native affairs are big business, there are 14 federal government departments, including Health and Welfare and the Secretary of State, which have Native programs. In addition, there are provincial agencies that run Native programs. Some provinces, like Ontario, have Native affairs secretariats that function as provincial Indian affairs departments. It is important to realize that these departments are run by non-Natives with Natives occupying only minor positions. However, a Mohawk from Kahnawâke has risen to the position of deputy minister in the Department of Indian Affairs. With this exception, most Natives never rise above middle management. Therefore, the paternalistic attitude that was created over a hundred years ago, and that was initiated with the arrival of the first Europeans, still prevails with Natives having little say in their own government.

Limitations of the Indian Act

The Indian Act has a history of restricting the personal freedoms of Native people, all in the name of assimilation or control. As we will see in Chapter 17, in 1884 the potlatch ceremony was banned, in large part because the giveaways involved were viewed as "communist," against the principle of private property that governments were trying to instill. During the course of the next few decades, the Sun Dance and other traditional dances and ceremonies were outlawed. The ban on these activities lasted until 1951 when a number of revisions were made to the Indian Act. Also ended that year were two other severe restrictions: the ban on raising money to fight land claims cases and the ban imposed on western Natives forbidding them to appear in their traditional dress off reserve without the permission of the Indian agent.

Indian agents were given a great deal of discretionary power to control various aspects of people's lives. Indian agent permission had to be asked if Native people wanted to sell the crops they had grown and harvested and the animals they had raised on reserve land. Fear of Natives brought on by the second Riel resistance in the Prairie provinces also gave power to the Indian agent in the form of the Pass System (see Chapter 22). Natives could not leave their reserves unless they had received a "pass" (like a visa) permitting them to do so.

The Indian agents also issued food vouchers. In the late nineteenth century Natives out west were low on food, even starving. This was the product of the near-extinction of the buffalo, the poor lands many bands were forced to live on, and the inadequate way the government delivered the assistance promised in the treaties—assistance that was supposed to enable Natives to become farmers. The Indian agent controlled who would receive these food vouchers and who would not. Offend the Indian agent and you could jeopardize your chances of receiving the food your family needed.

A number of recreational rights that other Canadians took for granted were also restricted by the Indian Act. Natives were forbidden to gamble, and people were encouraged to "snitch" on others. A person informing on a friend or family member could receive half of the fine the offender would have to pay (usually about 10 dollars). Indian agents could keep people from shooting pool in a pool hall. Not until 1951 could Status Indians drink in licensed bars.

Some restrictions lasted until 1960. Prior to that year, Status Indians could not vote federally without losing their status (they had obtained the right to vote provincially a number of years earlier, the dates varying for different provinces; Inuit had received the federal vote in 1950). Further, they would lose their status if they became doctors, lawyers, or ministers, or even if they obtained university degrees.

Indian Status: Who Defines Who Is an "Indian"?

Not surprisingly, there have been few issues that have generated as much controversy as who gets to define who is and isn't "Indian." Native people contend, rightly enough, that they are the best determiners of who is Native and who is not. Conversely, because the federal government funds Indians, it feels that it has a right to determine who should get status. Being "Indian" in Canada, in the eyes of the federal government, has nothing to do with biology or culture. "Indian" in Canada is a legal/political classification, subject to the Indian Act. It is the Indian Act that defines who is and is not Indian.

Government definition of "Indian" goes back to early legislation (1850) in Lower Canada (Quebec), which defined Indian in sweeping terms, including all persons of Indian ancestry, all persons married to Indians, anyone adopted by Indians and living in his or her adopted community, and, finally, anybody who was living with the band and was recognized as being Indian by the band.

Discriminating Against Women

Shortly thereafter (1851), the legal definition of who was "Indian" was amended. To be an Indian, a person was required to be of Indian blood or, alternately, show that at least his or her father was Indian. The law was also changed to provide that marriage only conferred status on non-Status Indian women, not vice versa. This set a precedent. Section 12 (1)(b) of the Indian Act was to read as follows:

12 (1) The following persons are not entitled to be registered, namely,

(b) a woman who married a person who is not an Indian. . .

Her children would likewise not have status, unlike the children of White women who married Status Indian men. Similarly, upon marriage, a woman lost her band status and became a member of her husband's band. These provisions violate notions of equality of the sexes and run counter to notions of matrilineality (you belong to the clan or lineage of your mother rather than of your father) held by a good number of Canadian First Nations.

Legal discrimination against women took a number of other different forms as well. Until 1951, the Indian Act forbade women from voting for band council.

In 1970, Jeannette Corbiere Lavell, a Status Indian from the Ojibwa reserve of Wikwemikong was going to marry a non-aboriginal man. She contested the discriminatory sections of the Indian Act on the grounds that it violated the Canadian Bill of Rights. In 1971, the Ontario County Court dismissed the case, essentially on the grounds that she had equal rights with other married Canadian women. She made an appeal to the Federal Court of Appeals and won, but the federal government decided that it would bring this case before the Supreme Court of Canada. Along with her case was that of Yvonne Bedard. She was a woman from the Six Nations Reserve who had lost her status when she married a non-aboriginal man. After their separation, she tried unsuccessfully to return to live in the house that was willed to her by her parents.

The federal government's appeal reflected its concerns that this could complicate and make more expensive its handling of Native matters, plus it was receiving pressure from the male-controlled and aptly named National Indian Brotherhood (NIB). The NIB had two main concerns. It was worried that this case might set a precedent for federal government tinkering with the Indian Act, not an unreasonable fear after the threats of the infamous White Paper of 1969, in which the federal government had proposed scrapping the Indian Act. Second, it was worried that this would result in further crowding on reserves, with non-Native men and their families moving into their communities.

In 1973, the Supreme Court voted five to four against the women, saying that they did not feel that the Bill of Rights could overrule the Indian Act in this way. Not surprisingly, the Native Women's Association of Canada was born around that time, writing its constitution that same year.

The United Nations condemned Canada in 1981 after Sandra Lovelace of the Tobique Reserve in New Brunswick complained that she was denied the right to live on her reserve after her failed marriage to a non-Native. Finally, the discriminatory clause was removed with the passage of Bill C-31 in 1985. However, the debate was not a peaceful one and, indeed, there are still bitter feelings within the Native community. When the debate was being conducted, Native leaders (especially male Native leaders) took the position that if Native women had made the decision to marry non-Natives they should be prepared to live with the consequences of that decision.

Perhaps the main cause of the anger had to do with the distribution of reserve and band resources as well as the limited benefits of being a Status Indian, such as post secondary education, a reserve home, etc. Some Alberta reserves have oil royalties, which some leaders feared having to share with recently returned Bill C-31s. The 1985 changes to the Indian Act allow some Indian control over status. The federal government decides whose names get on the Indian register. Bands may, however, by majority vote, decide to take control of band membership and establish their own rules for deciding who will be part of the band.

BOX 12-1　The Division of Bill C-31

The following is taken from something written by one of the authors:

> I was teaching in a summer program for Natives wanting to work as education counsellors. I remember two men of the same nation who were staying in the same house, almost always seen together, sitting together in my class. Both were proud of their nation and its heritage. Both taught me significant aspects of their heritage. In one class, it came out that one of these men lived on the nation's reserve, and had always had membership in the band, while the other was Bill C-31, and therefore had to live in a nearby town, although his heart was with the community that had no space for him. The first man made reference to his having a greater connection with his people and their heritage because he had always lived in the community of his nation. The other, who, because his mother had lost her status through marriage, had not been raised on the reserve, was hurt by what the first had said. He felt he was just as much a member of the nation as the "Status Indian." Some harsh words were said, but owing largely to their ability to draw upon the spiritual and conciliatory traditions of their people, peace between the two of them was finally achieved. (Steckley 1997:148)

ENFRANCHISEMENT

Reference was made earlier to enfranchisement, that is, the loss of Indian status and acquisition of the right to vote and full citizenship. This whole process goes back to 1857 when the United Canada passed a law entitled "An Act of the Gradual Civilization of the Indian Tribes in the Canadas" as a means of granting full citizenship to Native people. As a consequence of this act, local White authorities were obliged to report any Native ". . . of the male sex, not under 21 years of age, able to speak, read and write the English or French language readily and well, and is sufficiently advanced in the elementary branches of education and is of good moral character and is free of debt." Such people were to be reported to the governor who could then declare "that such Indian is enfranchised under this Act. . . and thereof." If the Native met the criteria, he was put on probation for a year, granted 20 hectares of land, and given full citizenship after one year. These were tough criteria, as Donald Purich points out, and only one applicant, Elias Hill, was accepted. Few Whites could meet the standard. The government, not surprisingly, blamed the Natives and it was partly right, for at least one band, Six Nations, was opposed to the whole scheme.

The government responded with another plan, the 1869 Act for the Gradual Enfranchisement of Indians. This imposed an elected municipal form of government on Indian bands. The chief and councillors were to be voted on by all males over 21 years of age, despite the fact that most nations didn't have chiefs. Of course, the government retained the right to remove any elected official. Nonetheless, this model has persisted to the present day.

In 1920, a law was passed to allow enfranchisement with or without consent. This was repeated again in 1922. The various reincarnations of the Indian Act continued to have provisions whereby Indians could voluntarily give up status. From the 1920s to the 1940s, some Natives gave up status in order to receive the right to go to school, vote, or to drink.

It wasn't until 1960 that Natives got the federal vote, while in some provinces the provincial vote was even later. Many servicemen who fought in World War I and the Korean War were persuaded to give up status.

Ç   Canada gave up enfranchisement in 1985 with the passage of Bill C-31. The Indian Act was amended so that people who had given up status could regain it. The enfranchisement provisions of the act were removed, making it impossible to give up status.

NATIVE VETERANS: LEGAL DEFINITIONS GETTING IN THE WAY

World War I (1914–1918)

The federal government originally had a policy that no aboriginal people become involved with the war. It is believed that the reason for this policy is that it was thought that Aboriginals would be considered "savage" by the enemy and would therefore be treated inhumanely if captured. This policy was not enforced and was eventually cancelled by 1915.

Unlike other Canadians, they were not conscripted in the war because of their legal status. Yet they volunteered in high numbers. Over 4,000 Status Indians did this, approximately 35% of all Status Indians of an age eligible to enlist. This number does not include the Métis, Inuit, or non-Status Indians, as well as the Aboriginals that lived in the Yukon, the Northwest Territories, and Newfoundland. In 1920, Canada's deputy superintendent general remarked on this patriotic spirit of volunteerism in the following way:

> The fine record of the Indians in the great war appears in a peculiarly favourable light when it is remembered that their services were absolutely voluntary, as they were exempted from the operation of the Military Service Act, and that they were prepared to give their lives for their country without compulsion or even the fear of compulsion. (Canada Sessional Papers 1920, as quoted in *Native Veterans*, http://aci.mta.ca/projects/Courage_Remembered/nativeveterans.html)

BOX 12-2   **Francis Pegahmagabow**

Corporal Francis Pegahmagabow (1891–1952), an Ojibwa from Parry Island, was the most decorated aboriginal soldier in World War I. A tribute to his courage, and his adaptation of traditional hunting skills to acting as a scout and sniper, he was awarded two bars, one at Passchendale. For his actions in France and Belgium, he was first awarded the prestigious Military Medal in 1916 and had added to that two bars for his bravery and fast thinking in two subsequent battles, in 1917 and 1918. His citation for the first bar stated that:

Before and after the attack he kept in touch with the flanks, advising the units what he had seen, this information proving the success of the attack and saving valuable time in consolidating. He also guided relief to its proper place after it had become mixed up. (Cited in "In Honour of Our Aboriginal Veterans")

After the war, he returned to his community, where he became chief and band councillor at different times.

They also contributed in another way. Reserve land was taken away from them by lease and by appropriation for purposes of farming for the war effort. The local bands involved were not asked for permission. The amount of land taken in this way totalled 25,142 hectares. This set a precedent for the world war to come, which, as we will see in the section on Dudley George, would have deadly implications.

World War II (1939–1945)

For the first three years of the war, Natives wanting to join up faced racism. The air force required that recruits be of "pure European descent" and the Royal Canadian Navy stipulated that their recruits be "a British born subject, of a White Race." Mi'kmaq Max Basque encountered this form of discrimination when he went to enlist with the navy. In his words, "The Navy recruiting officer looked at me. He said, 'Are you an Indian?' I said, 'Yes, sir.' 'Sorry, we don't take Indians in the Navy.'" When he noticed that the young man in front of him was not a "full-blooded" Indian, the navy recruiter said that it would be possible for Max to enlist as a Basque (a person from a group that lives in the north of Spain). Max replied:

> No. On the books, I was born on the Indian reservation and I've always gone as an Indian all my life. What in the world? Disown my own race, just to get in the Navy? I said, "I'm a Canadian, even if I am an Indian. Same as you are. . . I was born here in Canada." (*Cape Breton's magazine*, No. 52, p.58, as quoted in "Native Veterans")

Max never joined the navy, but he did serve his country in the army. His experience of being asked to enlist under a "false" race was not uncommon. Many Status Indians were called French, Italian, or Caucasian in the official records since Indians were considered unsuitable to go overseas to fight.

Again, enlistment figures are hard to calculate accurately. Native volunteers (and, after 1943, conscripts) came out in significant numbers. In 1945, the Department of Indian Affairs noted that there had been 3,090 Status Indians who had enlisted, but this would again not include all Aboriginals who joined up. Some estimates reach as high as 6,000.

During the war, the provisions of the Indian Act were used against Native people in ways that would disadvantage them after the war was over. The Veterans' Land Act rewarded non-Native veterans for their contribution to the war effort by providing them with a $6,000 loan (a large sum of money in those days) towards buying land and/or a house. This was later adapted to apply to fishing. Of this loan, $2,320 was an outright grant. The balance was payable over 25 years at the low interest rate of 3.5% per year. Once the money was paid off, the veteran's improved credit rating enabled him to more readily open commercial loans.

This was revised in 1942 so that the law would not act in the same way for Natives. Since reserve land, or Crown land, could not act as security for loans, the federal government decided that no loan could be awarded to Status Indians. It didn't have to be that way. The Department of Indian Affairs could have guaranteed the loan, or arranged it so the local band could have done so. What was left to the Status Indian veterans? They could be given a direct grant of $2,320 applicable to farming, fishing, forestry, or trapping. Still, there were strings attached. According to section 35A of the act, the money was not given to the Status Indian, as it would have been to the non-Native veteran. It was "to be paid to the Minister of Mines and Resources who shall have the control and management thereof on behalf of the Indian veteran" (as cited in the Royal Commission on Aboriginal Peoples, Final Report 1996). That was not the only string. The veteran could not apply directly to the minister but would have to go through the local Indian agent. The agent would submit, among other things, a certificate "that the applicant is qualified to engage in the occupation he proposes to follow." The process was a slow, complicated one, and one open to manipulation and even fraud by the Indian agent. And even if the aboriginal veteran were able to cut through all these strings, the Department of Indian Affairs still held ownership of all materials purchased under the grant for a period of 10 years.

Some Indian agents openly advised Status Indians that if they wanted the grants, it would be much easier if they enfranchised (gave up their status and their rights). There was a significant rise in the number of people who enfranchised (from 45 in 1942–3 to 447 in 1948–9), which might in part reflect the number of people who followed this advice. Things would not be easy for them. They would be separated from their reserve home, their extended family, and their community. Some were taken by force from their reserves.

Legal restrictions would harm Native veterans in other ways. They were not permitted to join the local Legion, as they were still prohibited from entering drinking establishments. These Legions were great places to find out about potential veterans' programs, as that was where such information was posted, and where veterans who had benefited from such programs would be around to pass on valuable tips as to how to take advantage of them. Their lack of access to Legions, among other factors, contributed to Status Indian veterans not fully benefiting from disability pensions, war service gratuities, dependents' allowances, re-establishment grants, and education and training provisions.

Native veterans then had to fight for their rights. The Parliamentary Hearings in 1946–7 and other official opportunities for the veterans to speak were instrumental in sparking some of the changes that were made in the Indian Act in 1951. The right to vote was not long in following.

But even with those changes, the Native veterans of the two world wars and the Korean War (1950–1953) were still treated as second-class veterans, still short-changed in terms of the benefits owed them and the official recognition of their role in the war, something that had long been downplayed, even ignored, in official ceremonies and in textbooks. This disparity was not really dealt with in any meaningful way until the 1990s.

The Royal Commission on Aboriginal Peoples spent a good deal of time listening to the veterans. The final report, published in 1996, contains a thoughtful look at the situation and made the following recommendations. First, there should be greater acknowledgement of the contribution of aboriginal peoples to the world wars and the Korean War. This was to be done by giving aboriginal veterans a higher profile at national Remembrance Day services (until 1992 they had not been permitted to place a wreath on the national cenotaph at the same ceremony with other veterans) and by funding aboriginal veterans' organizations and the construction of war memorials on reserves.

Second, the commission recommended that an ombudsman be hired to work with the appropriate federal departments to resolve the issues of veterans' benefits and "the legality and fairness of the sales, leases, and appropriations of Indian lands for purposes related to the war effort and for distribution to returning veterans of the two world wars." The commission also recommended that aboriginal people be hired in the Department of Veterans' Affairs, people who had both the language skills and cultural understanding necessary for dealing with Elders in their communities. Finally, there was a recommendation involving education. In part, this would entail education and research in aboriginal history as well as funding for aboriginal students.

Native Individuals 12-1

Yvonne Bedard: A Six Nations woman who fought her loss of status in the courts during the early 1970s.

Jeannette Corbiere-Lavell: A Wikwemikong woman who contested her loss of status; the case went to the Supreme Court.

Francis Pegahmagabow (1891–1952): A Parry Island Ojibwa who was the most-decorated aboriginal soldier in World War I.

On November 11, 1996, the federal government announced the establishment of the Aboriginal Veterans' Scholarship Trust, to be administered by the National Aboriginal Achievement Foundation. In 1998, that fund provided $254,831 in bursaries to aboriginal students. As of 1997, November 8 was declared National Aboriginal Veterans Day. Monies are being raised to construct the Aboriginal Veterans' Monument, with Native artist Lloyd Pinay hired for the project. Still, there is work to be done. In December 1998, the Federation of Saskatchewan Indian Nations and the Saskatchewan First Nations Veterans Association launched a lawsuit to obtain lost veterans' benefits for the 125 veterans who were still living (out of an original 800).

KEY TERMS

band
enfranchisement
status

CONTENT QUESTIONS

1. What is the significance of the Royal Proclamation of 1763?
2. What is the Indian Act?
3. How did the Indian Act discriminate against women prior to Bill C-31?
4. In what ways did the Indian Act limit Native people prior to 1960?
5. How were Native veterans of the world wars discriminated against?

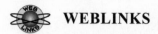 **WEBLINKS**

www.peak.sfu.ca/the-peak/96-3/issue12/native
"Saluting our Native Veterans" by Jolayne Madden-Marsh (from The Peak, vol. 94, issue 12, November 18, 1996).

www.ammsa.com/raven/NOV97
"Our soldiers slighted" by Matthew Stewart (from Raven's Eye, Nov. 1997).

www.escape.ca/~miko/articles/nativeamerican-soldiers
"In Honour of Our Aboriginal Veterans" (from Mesanagyun Indian and Métis Friendship Centre Newspaper, Winnipeg, November 1996).

aci.mta.ca/projects/Courage_Remembered/nativeveterans.html
"Native Veterans" (part of *Courage Remembered: The World Wars through Canadian Eyes*).

www.newswire.ca/government/federa...lish/releases/November1998/10/c3259.html
"Ministers Stewart and Mifflin pay tribute to Aboriginal Veterans."

www.indigenous.bc.ca/v1/Vol1Ch11s4.5tos6.asp
"4.5 The Veterans' Land Act" (from Royal Commission on Aboriginal Peoples, Final Report, vol. 1, Looking Forward, Looking Back).

www.bloorstreet.com/200block/sindact.htm
The Indian Act, with annotations by Bill Henderson, is reproduced in full; an excellent resource for detailed research.

C h a p t e r

THE
TREATIES

OVERVIEW

What is a treaty? Generally, in treaties, the Aboriginals involved would agree to give up their rights to a certain piece of land that was traditionally theirs. In return, they would have a much smaller area or areas reserved for their use. That is why the term **"reserve"** is used in Canada (as opposed to "reservation," which is used in the United States). Treaties 1 and 2 provided for 160 acres per family of five and treaties 3 through 11 provide for one square mile per family of five. The title, of course, remained with the government.

The location of reserves has been problematic. The Robinson Treaties specified where reserves would be located. Treaties 1, 2, 5, and 7 stipulated that reserves would be near specific lakes and rivers, while with treaties 3, 4, 6, and 8 reserve location was to be determined through consultation.

The location of reserves has caused great concern and problems. The Little Red River Band had its reserve determined by a government agent who, upon flying over a prairie, determined that it would be a good site. The Natives in question were Woodland Cree, not Plains peoples. The site had no water and was an alien environment.

The Attawapiskat Cree had their reserve located 200 kilometres inland from the coast. The Hudson's Bay Company Post was on the mouth of the Attawapiskat River on James Bay where the people traded and hunted for geese. After 40 years in which the inland reserve was never used, the government built another reserve one-sixteenth the size of the original reserve on the coast.

The Long Point Band in northwestern Quebec had its reserve built 70 kilometres from its traditional hunting grounds. The band packed up and went back to its traditional lands. The government built houses but the band still does not have reserve status.

The people signing the treaty would also receive a certain amount of money. In that sense, treaties were somewhat like land sales. They were different, however, in that the Natives involved were not permitted to get their hands on the money. It was held for them "in trust" by the government. From 1818 onward, Natives signing treaties would also receive **"annuities,"** or annual payments, typically involving a small sum per person. Monies usually are in the order of $12 for every man, woman, and child upon signing and $5 each year thereafter. The "chief" typically received slightly more.

Treaties also often involved hunting and fishing rights, which, as we will see with the Mi'kmaq treaties, can be problematic. An interesting example took place with the so-called Peterborough Bullfrog Incident (1977) in which two men were charged with taking bullfrogs out of season. This came under an 1818 treaty that makes no reference to hunting rights. However, the Natives contended that right to hunt was given verbally to their ancestors at the time of signing. Subsequent research proved them to be correct. They were acquitted and the right to hunt and fish was recognized by the court.

There are legal limits on these rights. For example, the Migratory Birds Convention Act (which applies to geese and ducks) overrides any treaty rights. So does the federal Fisheries Act. A case in 1962 involving the shooting of a mallard confirmed the supremacy of federal legislation over treaties.

THE MI'KMAQ TREATIES

The Mi'kmaq treaties are both the oldest in date and the newest in interpretation yet to be completely resolved. The first treaty they were involved with (although this was more of a Maliseet treaty) was the Treaty of Portsmouth, New Hampshire, in 1713. While it involved statements of "peace and friendship," as other treaties had before, it included allowing the Native peoples "free liberty for Hunting, Fishing, Fowling, and all other their Lawful Liberties and Privileges" (Dickason 1997:151). Statements to this effect were also included in the two treaties of 1725 that more directly affected the Mi'kmaq: the Mascarene Treaty of 1725, named after Major Paul Mascarene, the chief delegate from the colonial government of Nova Scotia to the treaty negotiations, and the Treaty of Boston. For years, all that was known about the conditions of those treaties was one side: the obligations of the Mi'kmaq and the Maliseet to keep the peace. In 1984, however, the "other side" of the Mascarene agreement was discovered in the public archives, which spelled out the obligations of the English to respect, among other things, the hunting and fishing rights of the people. This discovery would have a significant impact on how this treaty (and the 1752 Treaty that followed it as a reaffirmation) would be interpreted legally. Prior to that discovery, in the 1929 County Court decision in *Regina v Syliboy*, and in court decisions in 1958 and 1969, the treaties were not seen as guaranteeing aboriginal rights.

The 1752 Treaty was signed between Governor Peregrine Thomas Hopson and:

> Major Jean Baptiste Cope, chief Sachem of the Tribe of Mick Mack Indians inhabiting the Eastern Coast of the said Province, and Andrew Hadley Martin, Gabriel Martin & Francis Jeremiah, Members and Delegates of the said Tribe, for themselves and their said Tribe their Heirs, and the Heirs of their Heirs forever. . . . (Kulchyski 1994:195)

In *Regina v James Matthew Simon* (1985) the Chief Justice recognized the supremacy of the 1752 Treaty over provincial hunting laws:

> In my opinion, both the Governor and the Micmac entered into the Treaty with the intention of creating mutually binding obligations that would be solemnly respected. The Treaty was an exchange of solemn promises between the Micmacs and the King's representative entered into to achieve and guarantee peace. It is an enforceable obligation between the Indians and the white man and, as such, falls within the meaning of the word "treaty" in s.88 of the Indian Act. (Kulchyski 1994:192)

In 1988, a Nova Scotia Lands and Forests officer arrested 14 Mi'kmaq, charging them for illegal hunting. The charges were dismissed after the Nova Scotia Court of Appeal ruled in another case that the people did have the right to hunt and fish for food and were exempt from provincial regulations when doing so. This still did not settle matters in terms of how that supremacy would be worked out regarding actual hunting and fishing. In 1989, the Mi'kmaq were allowed a special limited hunting season but with no formal recognition of their rights to do so. They were allowed to hunt moose from September 24–29 and again from October 15–25, before and after the two-week season for non-Natives.

Several questions need to be asked here. Was this a reasonable resolution of the problem? How would non-Native hunters react to this? Does this make Natives active players in interpreting their rights, or just recipients of a "gift" that could be taken away? How would you resolve the issue?

The reaction to this treaty being upheld was small compared to the recognition of a treaty in 1760, which involved the Mi'kmaq, the Maliseet in Nova Scotia and New Brunswick, and the culturally related Passamaquoddy of Maine. In 1996, Donald Marshall Jr., the same man wrongfully imprisoned earlier for 11 years (see Chapter 20), was convicted for catching eels out of season. On September 17, 1999, this decision was overturned. The Supreme Court of Canada declared that the treaty right

> . . . is not a right to trade generally for economic gain, but rather a right to trade for necessaries. Catch limits that could reasonably be expected to produce a moderate livelihood for individual Micmac families at present day standards can be established by regulation. (Editorial, *The Toronto Star*, 29 September 1999)

The phrase "moderate livelihood" would appear in a good number of newspaper articles to follow.

As this was around the beginning of lobster season, the Mi'kmaq began to set up lobster traps. There was, understandably, a strong negative reaction on the part of non-Native lobster fishers, as they had a sense that their "livelihood" was being threatened. They reacted first with harsh words, then with destructive action. Over 3,500 Mi'kmaq traps were destroyed, processing plants thought to be handling Native-caught lobsters were vandalized, three Mi'kmaq were injured, and an arbour used for sacred ceremonies was burned. There was some retaliation, with the burning of a few trucks and of an Acadian flag (the latter a symbolic act).

Thirty-three of 35 affected Mi'kmaq communities eventually agreed to a 30-day moratorium. The two communities that did not agree were Burnt Church in New Brunswick, which was the scene of most of the confrontation (and the largest number of reporters) and Shubenacadie reserve near Indian Brook, Nova Scotia.

It is important to realize that the reaction was, to a certain extent, out of proportion to the numbers involved. Annually, about two million lobster traps are set in the Maritime provinces and, after the Supreme Court decision, about 12,000 Native traps were put in the water. Burnt Church, with a population between 1,200 and 1,300, was allowed to use 600 traps; Shubenacadie, a slightly larger community, was allowed 800. Generally, commercial lobster fishermen are permitted 300 traps each.

To date, this issue is still not resolved. Questions need to be addressed. How could the federal government have handled the situation differently? How can this be resolved in a way that is fair to non-Native fishers but that respects the legal rights of the Mi'kmaq?

THE NUMBERED TREATIES

While literally hundreds of small treaties exist, most of Canada was "publicly purchased" through a series of large land transfers. The first of these were the Robinson Treaties of 1850, involving the land immediately to the north of Lake Superior and Lake Huron. Mineral deposits had been discovered north of Lake Superior, leading the colonial government of Upper Canada to authorize mining activities on Ojibwa land. In 1846, Shinguaconse ("Little Pine," c.1773–1854), chief of the Ojibwa of Garden River (near Sault Ste. Marie) and other leaders made the long trip down to Toronto to ask for payment for the use of their land in this way. There was no official response. Three years later, they made the same trip and asked for a land settlement, and received none. Left with no apparent alternative, they closed a mine down by force. Troops were sent and the treaty process was hastened.

The expansion of non-Native Canadian interests westward after the foundation of Canada and the purchase of Rupert's Land was the impetus for what are called the "numbered treaties," 1 to 11, signed between 1871 and 1921. These covered the territory from the eastern part of British Columbia and parts of Yukon Territory and the Northwest Territories in the west, across the Prairie provinces to include most of northern Ontario. As was true of the Robinson treaties, there was a close connection between the federal government wanting something and the press for treaties. The settling of the prairies by European farmers made the signing of Treaties 1 to 7 imperative. The discovery of gold in the Klondike in 1897 resulted in Treaty 8 in 1899. The building of roads and railroads to gain access to northern Ontario brought about Treaty 9. The provincial status of Alberta and Saskatchewan was followed by the signing of Treaty 10 in 1906, while the discovery of oil in Norman Wells was followed by Treaty 11 in 1921.

WHEN TREATIES GO BAD: THE MISSISSAUGA TREATIES

To get a sense of the lack of trust that exists among Aboriginals that governments will keep their promises, it is useful to look in some detail at what happens "when treaties go bad." The people know enough stories like this, which tends to make them distrustful.

Piece by large piece, the Mississauga of southern Ontario had their land "publicly purchased." Two of the early transfers provided a much-welcomed home for the Mohawk and other Iroquois, who had been forced to abandon their ancestral territory after choosing to fight on the losing side of the American Revolution. On October 9, 1783, land stretching back from the northeastern shores of Lake Ontario, from the Gananoque River in the east to the Trent River in the west, was "purchased" from the Mississauga. John Deserontyon and his band of Mohawks settled in that winter. On May 22, 1784, the Mississauga announced at a council meeting at Niagara that they would permit a large tract around the Grand River to be transferred to the Crown for the purposes of giving it to the more than 2,000 Iroquois led by the Mohawk Joseph Brant.

The Mississauga signatories of this "public purchase" included the "Sachems and War Chiefs and Principal Women of the Messissauga Indian Nation"(Indian Treaties and Surrenders 1971, vol.1:5). It is noteworthy that Mississauga women had a say in the political decisions, while other Canadian women would have to wait for more than a hundred years before they would receive the right to vote.

Next, in a series of poorly recorded deals in 1784, 1787, and 1788, the northern shoreline from the Trent River west to what is now Scarborough changed hands. How far inland the transfer went is the subject of historical rumours. Some sources claim it reached "as far back as a man could walk, or go on foot in a day." Natives came to believe that it went the distance a gunshot could be heard. Another treaty had to be signed in 1923 to try to clear up the resultant legal mess.

On September 23, 1787, Toronto and surrounding townships, some 620,000 hectares, were negotiated for in a provisional land surrender. The deal, known as the Toronto Purchase, stayed in limbo until August 1, 1805, when eight Mississauga chiefs, headed by **Quinepenon** ("Golden Eagle") of the Otter clan, met with government officials on the flatlands beside the Credit River. The Mississauga were beginning to distrust the treaty process. They already felt confined on the land left to them. This is noted by Quinepenon, as is the suspicion held by the Mississauga women that the deal would further impoverish their nation:

> [I]t is hard to give away more land; the young men and women have found fault with so much having been sold before. It is true we are poor, and the women say we will be worse if we part with any more. . . . (Clarkson 1967:27)

Quinepenon had good reason to distrust both settlers and the government. He believed that the earlier treaties had promised that "the Farmers would help us" (Smith 1979:467), and that his people could "encamp and fish where we pleased" (ibid.) and felt that these promises had been violated. In 1797, the government passed a "Proclamation to Protect the Fishing Places and Burying Grounds of the Mississauga," but neither type of valued location was protected effectively by this legislation.

The meeting of August 1, 1805, was not just to confirm the Toronto Purchase. The rest of Lake Ontario shoreline was coveted by the incoming, mostly American immigrants and by the government, which was eager to welcome them. On August 2, land extending west from Etobicoke Creek to Burlington Bay was signed away. Fishing and corn-growing were vital to the survival of the Mississauga, so Quinepenon and other leaders fought hard to receive the concession of reserving to the "Missasague [*sic*] Nation":

> . . . the sole right of the fisheries in the Twelve Mile [Bronte] Creek, the Sixteen Mile Creek, the Etobicoke River, together with the flats or low grounds on said creeks and river, which we have heretofore cultivated and where we have our camps. And also the sole right of fishery in the River Credit with one mile on each side of said river. (Indian Treaties and Surrenders 1971, vol.1:36)

Quinepenon's fears were realized. By the time the August 2 treaty was confirmed the next year, a settler had destroyed the chief's cornfield as well as the field of a Mississauga widow who had to provide for four children. The same man, an illegal squatter by the rules of the treaty, had built a fish weir on Bronte Creek that prevented the salmon from swimming upstream to spawn. According to Quinepenon, another White man had so polluted the Credit River "by washing with [soap] and other dirt, that the fish refuse coming into the River as usual, by which our families are in great distress for want of food" (Smith 1983:467).

BOX 13-1   **A Nineteenth-Century Mississauga View of Government Promises**

The contrast between wartime promises and peacetime practices is summarized by Nahnebahwequay in her article published in the *Christian Guardian* of May 28, 1862:

> I cannot help thinking about those times, now past, when Governors and Generals used to meet our fathers in the Great Councils, and made great promises that were never, never to be broken while grass grew and waters ran. All our fathers who did not fall in the wars remained faithful to the British throne, and their children have followed their steps in loyalty. But the wars have passed away, . . . and advantage is taken of our weakness and ignorance, so that our fisheries, hunting-grounds, lands and homes are taken from us, whether we like it or not. They are first coveted, and then some plan is concocted to get them; and those pledges made to our grandsires by British noblemen have been and are still every day shamefully violated, so that the poor Indians have ceased to have any confidence in the Government. . . Little did those bold Indian warriors think when they were listening to the fine promises made by British noblemen that the successors of those Crown officials would, in a few years, rob their children of their birth-right. (Sutton 1862)

The next time the government came to ask for more Mississauga land was 1818. A lot had happened since 1806. Immigrants, mostly British, had swelled the ranks of White people in Upper Canada. By 1812, Natives made up barely more than 10% of that colony's population (Dickason 1992:224). The Credit River Mississauga continued to diminish in number. Their 330 had become 200. The toll on their chiefs was even heavier. Of the 10 leaders who had signed the last treaty, only two would be around to put their mark on paper in 1818. Among the dead was Quinepenon.

The land that the government wanted in 1818 was the "Mississauga Tract," a tract west of the Toronto Purchase and north of the land acquired during the other 1806 treaty. This introduced the notion of annuities. In return for obtaining possession of some 1.6 million hectares, the king, through his representative William Claus, promised to pay the Mississauga, ". . . yearly and every year *for ever* the said sum of five hundred and twenty two pounds ten shillings currency in goods at the Montreal price. . . ". (Indian Treaties and Surrenders 1971 vol.1:48; emphasis, authors)

"For ever" lasted a short time. This promise was broken. Two years later, William Claus, the deputy superintendent general of Indian affairs, came to speak with them again. The Mississauga were justifiably suspicious. What did he want now? So much had been taken. One leader summed up the feelings of many when he said:

> You came as a wind blowing across the great Lake. The wind wafted you to our shores. We . . . planted you—we nursed you. We protected you till you became a mighty tree that spread through our Hunting Land. With its branches you now lash us. (Schmalz 1991:105)

Claus wanted them to agree to give up their exclusive fishing rights and sell all of their remaining land:

Saving and reserving, nevertheless, always to the said Acheton, Newoiquiquah, Woiqueshequome, Pausetawnouguetohe and Wabakagige and the people of the Mississauga Nation of Indians and their posterity for ever a certain parcel or tract of land containing two hundred acres. . . .(Indian Treaties and Surrenders 1971, vol.1:52)

According to Claus, the proceeds from the sale of the land would

. . . be applied towards educating your Children & instructing yourselves in the principles of the Christian religion—and that a certain part of the said Tract never surrendered will be set apart for your accommodation & that of your families, on which Huts will be erected as soon as possible. (Smith 1987:39–40)

Two things are generally true about such Native land agreements. One is that the two parties, Native and government, have a different understanding about what took place. The second is that the government rarely delivers all that it has promised. Concerning the first, Claus felt that, with the 1820 treaty, the Mississauga had given up their rights to all the land but the "two hundred acres." The Credit River people thought differently. This can be seen in this quotation from a letter sent by two of their leaders to the lieutenant-governor in 1829. They believed that Claus had said:

The white people are getting thick around you and we are afraid they, or the yankees, will cheat you out of your land, you had better put it into the hands of your very Great father the king to keep for you till you want to settle, and he will appropriate it for your good and he will take good care of it; and will take you under his wing, and keep you under his arm, & give you schools, and build houses for you when you want to settle. (Smith 1987a:40)

The land that was supposedly reserved for the Mississauga forever did not remain theirs for more than a few years. The Mississauga still haven't received the promised 200 acres, or compensation for its loss.

Further, there seems to have been two different timetables for the two sides of this transaction. The government got its hands on the land surrendered fairly quickly, but six years passed (the "soon as possible") before the government began to fulfil even a part of its side of the bargain. Not until the fall of 1826 were 20 homes built for the Mississauga alongside the mouth of the Credit River.

Another part of the 1820 deal was that the Mississauga would receive annuities from the monies accrued from the sale of their lands. The monies were held for the Mississauga "in trust" by the government. But some of the government officials could not be trusted. Once they grasped the money in their hands, they treated much of it as if it were their own.

In 1826, Mississauga leader Peter Jones confronted Colonel James Givins, the Indian agent responsible for the Mississauga, concerning the fact that they were being paid £50 less in annuities than was agreed upon in the treaty. The reply given by the man the Mississauga called "the Wolf" smells of a cover-up. He claimed that he "was not at liberty to explain" (Smith 1987a:79) why they were not getting the sum of money owed to them. Doubtless, someone was skimming the money off the top like so much thick cream. Perhaps the Wolf himself was lapping some up.

The Mississauga of the Credit were growing concerned about what their rights actually were to the land. They were hearing nasty rumours. Chief James Ajetance (spelled "Acheton" in previous quote), Peter Jones' adoptive father, said to Givins, "Having heard some bad birds crying that we did not own any lands on the Credit, we wish to know from our great father how much land we really possess" (Smith 1987a:100).

Givins flatly stated that in his opinion the Mississauga had surrendered all their rights away. Despite its questionable legality, his opinion carried weight.

The Mississauga were feeling increasingly hemmed in. They had established a trade of salmon in exchange for flour, cattle, and other goods, but this mutually beneficial commerce was being interfered with in nasty ways. This can be seen from the words of a petition signed by Peter Jones and 53 others on January 31, 1829, and sent to Sir John Colbourne, the lieutenant-governor of Upper Canada. They were upset by what some White men were doing:

> They burn and destroy our fences and boards in the night; they watch the salmon and take them as fast as they come up; they swear and get drunk and give a very bad example to our young people, and try to persuade them to be wicked like themselves . . . Others go to the mouth of the river and catch all the salmon; they put the offals of salmon in the mouth of the river to keep the fish from passing up, that they may take them with a seine near the mouth of the river in the lake; and often in the dark they set gill nets in the river and stop all the fish. (Mackenzie 1833 in Fairley 1960:47–8)

Over the next two decades, the Mississauga came to realize that they were going to lose their land. They appeared doomed as a community. However, in 1847 they received an offer that seemed too good to be true. In April of that year the Six Nations Iroquois met in full council. They had heard of the desperate position of the Mississauga of the Credit. They remembered how the Mississauga had made land available to them when they had needed to move north away from the resentful Americans after fighting on the British side during the American Revolution. Their choice was clear. Feeling, in their words, "a great pleasure in returning the compliments to their descendants [i.e., those whose ancestors gave the land to the Iroquois]" (as quoted in Smith 1987a:212), they invited the Mississauga to take possession of some of the land on their reserve, near what is now Hagersville, Ontario. The Credit people accepted. That community today is known as the Mississauga of the New Credit.

BOX 13-2   A Brief History of Nisga'a Land Claims

The Tsimshian peoples are in the centre of aboriginal rights issues in British Columbia. The Gitxsan are, along with the We'tsuwet'en Carrier, the aboriginal parties involved with the Delgamuukw case. The Nisga'a are best known today by non-Natives in relation to the land claim settlement passed through Parliament in December 1999. It is important to understand that this is not a case that is "something new," nor part of a trend of "political correctness." First, consider that the following statement from **David McKay**, chief of the Greenville Nisga'a, was made in 1888:

What we don't like about the government is their saying this: "We will give you this much land." How can they give it when it is our own? We cannot understand it. They have never bought it from us or our forefathers. They have never fought or conquered our people and taken the land in that way, and yet they say now that they will give us so much land—our own land. It would have been foolish, but it has been ours for a thousand years. (Dickason 1997:325)

Now look at the following timeline:

Nisga'a Timeline 13-1

1763: Royal Proclamation of 1763 in which King George III recognizes that aboriginal peoples legally possess traditional territories until these lands are "ceded to or purchased by" the government.

1778: Captain James Cook lands on the coast of British Columbia and claims the land for Britain.

1793: British sea captain George Vancouver makes first European contact with the Nisga'a.

1871: British Columbia becomes a province.

1881: Chief Mountain leads a Nisga'a protest delegation to Victoria.

1886: Nisga'a resist surveyors and begin organized pursuit of land claims as no treaties have been signed with the Nisga'a (although they have been placed on reserves).

1887: Nisga'a (and Tsimshian) chiefs go to Victoria to discuss land claims and self-government with Premier William Smithe. Smithe responds with: "When the whites first came among you, you were little better than the wild beasts of the field", rejecting their claims to ownership.

1909: The Nisga'a Land Committee becomes part of the Native Tribes of B.C., who send a delegation to Britain to make a presentation on the land question.

1910: Prime Minister Wilfred Laurier promises to settle the Native land question in British Columbia.

1913: Nisga'a Land Committee submits petition to British Privy Council to resolve the land question. The petition is referred back to Canada.

1920: Bill 13, the British Columbia Indian Lands Settlement Act, is passed by the federal government. It allows reductions of reserves without consent of aboriginal people, contrary to the Indian Act.

1924: Nisga'a have 76 square kilometres cut off their reserve without their consent.

1927: Parliament amends Indian Act to make it illegal for aboriginal groups to raise money for the prosecution of land claims, so land claims activity has to go "underground" until 1951 when this amendment is repealed.

1955: Nisga'a Land Committee is re-established as the Nisga'a Tribal Council.

1967: Nisga'a leader Frank Calder takes the land question to court, seeking a declaration that they had held aboriginal title in the land prior to colonization, and that their title had never been extinguished. The Nisga'a lose the decision in the B.C. court, but appeal the decision, taking it to the Supreme Court of Canada.

1973: The appeal is lost on a split decision, but the Supreme Court judges agree that aboriginal title had existed but disagree as to whether that title continues to exist.

1976: The federal government and the Nisga'a begin negotiation regarding land claims under the new "comprehensive land claims policy." The province of British Columbia does not join in the negotiations.

1990: The province of British Columbia joins in the land claims negotiations

continued

continued

between the federal government and the Nisga'a.

1996: On March 22, the minister of Indian affairs, the B.C. aboriginal affairs minister, and Nisga'a Tribal Council President Joseph Gosnell Sr. sign an

The Nisga'a treaty involves "giving" the people title to 1,930 square kilometres in the Nass valley and $487.1 million in benefits and in money. It also gives them the right to make laws in several areas, including land use, employment, and cultural preservation. They will own the forest and mineral resources on their land (like a private owner would), but manage them, like other owners, within British Columbia's laws and standards.

agreement-in-principle for the first modern-day treaty in British Columbia.

1999: Parliament passes the bill for the Nisga'a treaty.

2000: The Senate passes the bill on April 13 and the treaty process is complete.

In exchange, they give up future claims on what amounts to more than 80% of their traditional territory (less than 10% of their original claim) and they give up their tax exemptions. Although the non-Native media have often presented this as a step towards separation or the breakup of Canada, it in actuality puts the Nisga'a in a position more like other Canadians in a number of ways, including their tax and ownership status.

Native Individuals 13-1

Jean Baptiste Cope: Leading Mi'kmaq saqmaw who signed the Treaty of 1752.

Kahkewaquonaby ("Sacred Feathers") or Peter Jones (1802–56): A nineteenth-century Mississauga writer, educator, and fundraiser.

Quinepenon ("Golden Eagle"): An important Mississauga leader of the eighteenth and nineteenth centuries.

KEY TERMS

aboriginal rights
annuities
public purchase
reserves

CONTENT QUESTIONS

1. Which acts override treaty rights?
2. In the case of *Regina v James Matthew Simon* (1985), which was ruled as having priority, the 1752 Treaty or provincial hunting laws?
3. In the Supreme Court decision of 1999, what rights did the Mi'kmaq have that came from the Treaty of 1760?
4. What happened with the Mississauga treaties?
5. When did the Nisga'a begin their organized fight for land claims?

 WEBLINKS

library.usask.ca/native/cnlch.html
A comprehensive listing of Native law cases, at the University of Saskatchewan's Web site.

ellesmere.ccm.emr.ca/wwwnais/select/indian/english/html/indian.html
A list of "Canadian-Indian Treaties."

www.inac.gc.ca/pr/trts/index_e.html
The numbered treaties are found online at the Web site of the Department of Indian and Northern Affairs.

www.inac.gc.ca/pr/trts/trmis_e.html
The federal government also provides an online copy of the treaty with the Mississauga.

THE GOLDEN LAKE ALGONQUIN AND ALGONQUIN PARK: MISSED BY TREATY

INTRODUCTION

As we have seen, groups with treaties face difficulty when trying to have their rights respected by governments. It is, of course, more difficult when a group has been missed by the treaty process. The Lubicon Cree of Alberta and the Temagami Anishinabe are examples of the long-running problems that such groups can have. In this section we will discuss the case of another such group: the Golden Lake Algonquin.

In the first half of the seventeenth century, several different bands referred to as "Algonquin" were living in the area of the Ottawa River and its tributaries. It is misleading that the river, the valley, and the city are called Ottawa, because the Ottawa Natives, who are related to the Algonquin, spent only a few years during the 1680s in the area. Their home country was Manitoulin Island and the Bruce Peninsula to the west. The river should be called the Algonquin River, because those people lived in the area for at least hundreds of years. Perhaps it would have been better for their land claims if the river were so named.

THE GOLDEN LAKE ALGONQUIN

The Golden Lake Algonquin live by the Bonnechere River, some 140 kilometres west of Ottawa. They have never surrendered their rights to the land, never having signed a treaty. But they did sign a good number of petitions, the first in 1772, trying to have their unsurrendered rights to their land recognized. Their message changed little, but governments changed in their response. In 1774 they were told by Lord Dorchester, then governor, that "if you anciently held the rights to these lands, and if you have not been paid, the rights belong to you still" (Sarazin 1989:173).

Their situation deteriorated after the War of 1812. The Algonquin had fought on the British side but were not rewarded for their efforts by any written guarantee of their rights. Instead, the government actively recruited veterans and others from Britain to come live on Algonquin land. Passage was paid for, land given, and assistance promised to the new-comers. In 1820 alone, 2,000 government-assisted Scots were brought to the Rideau district south of Ottawa. That same year, the Algonquin sent a petition to have their rights to their lands be recognized. They were turned down. In 1822, the government claimed that the land had been signed away by a few Bay of Quinte Mississauga, people who had never lived on or used the land.

Throughout the 1820s, the immigrant onslaught continued. Non-Natives in charge of Indian affairs became quite concerned about the effects of this rapid settlement on the Algonquin. In 1828, General Darling said that "[t]heir situation is becoming alarming by . . . rapid settlement" (Sarazin 1989:177).

For a while, the government made paper promises to keep squatters off of Algonquin land but by 1836 the government turned about-face and responded to Algonquin petitions with the inaccurate statement that "the claims of the present petitioners were fully settled and adjusted at the respective times when the lands were surrendered by those tribes to the Government" (Sarazin 1989:178).

In an 1857 petition, five heads of families asked for 80 hectares per family, the same amount of land many settler families had received. The local Crown Lands agent supported their petition, saying that "[t]hese men appear to be unusually intelligent and respectable; I have been informed that they are moral and industrious and well-deserving" (Sarazin 1989:186). But the commissioner of Crown Lands condemned them for being neither White men nor traditional Natives. He refused the land grant, saying he had heard that they were "half-bred, half-civilized Indians" (ibid.). The petitioners had to wait six years. Finally, in 1864, the Department of Indian Affairs used Indian funds to pay $156.10 (10 cents an acre) for 1,561 acres (631 hectares) that they could live on. They still had not signed their rights away.

Other families joined. By 1880 there were 83 people living there, 164 by 1924, and 475 by 1971. In 1986 there were 691 belonging to the band, with 285 living on the reserve and 406 off.

BOX 14-1   Chief Kaondinoketch's Petition of 1840

In 1840, Chief Kaondinoketch submitted a petition to the government. After outlining in grim detail what had happened to the resources where his people lived, he made the following observation:

> Brothers, we are partly the cause of these our present misfortunes. We were too good and generous. We permitted strangers to come and settle in our grounds and cultivate the land, and traders to destroy our valuable timber, who have done us much injury, as by clearing our rich forest, they have annihilated our beaver and our peltries, and driven away our deer. Had our hunting grounds belonged to the whites, they would not have allowed this, but we had good hearts and took pity on our white brethren. (Sarazin 1989:182)

ALGONQUIN PARK

Algonquin Park was created in 1893 out of Crown land that had been withdrawn from sale for settlement, to a large extent so that the timber it contained could be "harvested" and sold by logging companies. At that time there were at least three groups or bands of Algonquin living in what would later be Algonquin Park. Repeatedly, they sent petitions to have land granted to them in the same fashion as the Golden Lake people had to them, offering to give up their rights to a larger piece for a written guarantee for less land. They received three types of responses. Petitions were ignored, or the Algonquin were allowed to hunt for a while at "the pleasure of the Crown," as long as they didn't cut any wood or bother those who did, or they were told to go live with the people of Golden Lake. One Ontario official even admitted that the government didn't want to create official Native settlements with such a reserve grant, as that would "render the localities in which they are situated less attractive for settlement than other localities in which there is no Indian population" (Sarazin 1989:188). However, that hadn't stopped settlers from crowding out the Algonquin of the Ottawa Valley earlier that century.

The Golden Lake Algonquin needed to hunt deer in Algonquin Park in order to survive. They knew how to hunt so that the deer population would not be threatened. But these facts were not recognized by provincial game officials. In 1898, most of the Golden Lake men were summoned to court for hunting deer out of season. Most were convicted, given suspended sentences, and warned that they would be jailed if caught again. So the Algonquin learned how to hunt more carefully, like Canadian versions of Robin Hood, so they would not be caught. In the words of Chief **Greg Sarazin**:

> Our elders tell stories of hunting in Algonquin Park; of the man who used stilts to confuse the rangers who might try to track him, of the man who wore his snowshoes backwards, and of the family whose children were wrapped in "poached" furs under their snowsuits, which the rangers failed to search. At the portage store at Canoe Lake the Ontario Ministry of Natural Resources displays a birch-bark canoe blackened to avoid detection, seized from "an Indian poacher." (Sarazin 1989:190)

Petitions continued throughout the twentieth century. One, in the 1980s, yielded a surprising result. Provincial Court Judge Russell Meredew declared that the Algonquin still had aboriginal rights to the areas, including Algonquin Park, that had never been surrendered, that the Proclamation of 1763 held the status of a treaty with the Algonquin. Predictably, the Supreme Court of Ontario overturned this decision.

On September 2, 1988, the Golden Lake Algonquin, along with their Native and non-Native supporters, staged a protest on the road that led to Algonquin Park. They put forward a claim covering 34,000 square kilometres, including not only Algonquin Park but also the municipalities of Arnprior, Bancroft, Deep River, Mattawa, North Bay, Ottawa, Pembroke, and Renfrew. They did not want to take the land back, as some media pundits claimed. They consistently stressed that they were only negotiating to have unoccupied Crown land returned to the band. Private, corporate, and municipal lands would be untouched. The point of the exercise was to state dramatically that they had never signed that land away and that some recognition should be made of their rights. From their perspective, there were four issues involved: land, natural resources, self-government, and compensation for loss.

Nothing came of this until June 1991, when Ontario Minister of Natural Resources and Minister Responsible for Native Affairs Bud Wildman publicly acknowledged that the Golden Lake Algonquin had rights that needed to be dealt with. A Statement of Intent was signed, which outlined the intention to negotiate a land claim. It included an interim agreement allowing band members to hunt and fish in Algonquin Park. It was a first step towards resolution of the land claim and it was a form of recognition of Algonquin rights to hunt and fish for personal and community use. The hunt was to be regulated with specific sub-agreements specifying where hunting and fishing would be permitted, what limits would be placed on their "harvest," and what was needed to ensure public access and safety. Wildman assured concerned non-Native citizens and special interest groups such as tour operators that consultations with all parties would be a priority. It was a reversal of usual government policies across Canada, where an agreement would first be struck in favour of non-Natives, with Natives then assured that consultation would take place with them.

PUBLIC RELATIONS

Native groups involved with land claim negotiations must engage in public relations. They have to engage in complicated communication with a number of different parties: the federal government, the party whose legal responsibility for and to Native peoples is the greatest; provincial governments, the party primarily responsible for natural resources; non-Native special interest groups; and the Canadian public in general. Often the most difficult to deal with is the last-named group, for while studies tend to show that, on an abstract level, the Canadian public is sympathetic to "Native issues," those same studies also indicate that the public is fundamentally ignorant of the breadth, historical depth, and complexity of these issues. This ignorance has traditionally been used by governments and special interest groups to turn the public against the Natives, especially the case when the public comes to have perceptible self-interest in the outcome of the issue. Such was the case with the Algonquins and their negotiations concerning Algonquin Park.

INITIAL NEGATIVE RESPONSE

The initial response by local or special interest non-Native print media was predictably negative. A case in point is an editorial in the *Ontario Fisherman* (August–September 1991). The opening line set the tone: "With a bloodline that includes Ukrainian, Austrian, Irish Scotch [*sic*] and English, I don't believe that anyone has the right to call me racist." All the peoples referred to are northern Europeans who speak related languages—not much of an ethnic or "racial" mix. The writer made the following suggestion, which other non-Natives have made:

> If the natives are going to fish for subsistence, then let's go back to outfitting them with the same tools they used before the so-called white man arrived. If they don't want to fish by the white man's rules, then don't let them use the white man's inventions including mono-filament gill nets, iron hooks, or even the outboard motor in a rape of this resource. (op. cit.)

By that same logic, non-Native fishermen should not be permitted to use canoes, farmers should not be allowed to grow corn, potatoes, tomatoes, beans, squash, peppers, and tobacco, store owners should not be permitted to sell clothing made out of cotton, and White trappers should be banned from using snowshoes, since these were all Native inventions.

The same issue of that magazine carried an article dealing with alleged Native poaching in Ontario, but did not mention that most poaching is done by non-Natives.

More destructive to the Algonquin cause was how mainstream papers dealt with the issue. In *The Toronto Star*, on September 28, 1991, popular columnist Joey Slinger wrote an article with the leading headline of "Province Selling off our Algonquin Park Birthright" ("our" presumably meaning non-Natives). Slinger made the following comments:

> That old devil liberal guilt has let the Indians pull a fast one on the Ontario government . . . But the government bought it and lent credence to a claim on the park's territory that is about as reasonable as my family's claim on Stonehenge. The only way there could ever be a truly just settlement for Canadian Indians is for all the rest of us to pack up and go back where we came from. (ibid.)

Slinger might have had a case for his family's claim to Stonehenge if they had lived in that area for hundreds of years, maintained the grounds, buried their dead there, and then had it taken away illegally by Japanese tourists or Arab businessmen. The Golden Lake Algonquin were just asking for "the rest of us" to keep our legal promises.

THE INTERIM AGREEMENT

The Interim Agreement was unveiled early in October. It allowed members of the Golden Lake First Nation to hunt moose and deer between October 15, 1991, and January 15, 1992. Hunters were restricted to the eastern 40% of the park. The agreement restricted the use of all-terrain vehicles and snowmobiles for hunting within the park, placed limits on the use of cars, trucks, and motorboats, and limited the kill to 100 moose and 175 deer. This would not have an adverse effect on the population of those animals. In 1992, there were an estimated 3,800 moose in the park. A further agreement would be hammered out regarding fishing rights.

Reaction was swift. Special interest groups such as the Wildlands League, the Huntsville/Lake of Bays Chamber of Commerce, the Federation of Ontario Naturalists, and the more radical and anti-Native Ad Hoc Committee to Save Algonquin Park (hereafter called the Ad Hoc Committee), which labelled it "the blackest day in the history of Algonquin [Park]," voiced their concerns. The Ontario government and the Golden Lake Algonquin held public meetings to try to soothe feelings of anxiety among non-Natives. On February 4, 1992, one such meeting was held in Pembroke. According to *The Eganville Leader* published the next day, this seemed to have done little more than give non-Natives an opportunity to vent their ignorance and prejudice. Some of the speakers aired "gripes or prejudices against the Indian population in general." Accusations were made of anti-White discrimination, preferential treatment of Natives, and pleas for "equality for all people."

One of the main complaints was that the government was moving too quickly in bringing about the Interim Agreement. As **Clifford Meness**, then chief of the Golden Lake First Nation, was to say, 200 years seemed to be a reasonable amount of time.

The initial results of the Interim Agreement were favourable. *The Ottawa Citizen* of April 14, 1992, reported that the Golden Lake Algonquin took only 45 moose and 29 deer in the three-month season, considerably below the imposed limits. Of the roughly 300 people living on the reserve, Chief Meness estimated that only 20 to 30 were actually involved in the hunt. None of the fears of the opponents had come to pass, including the shooting of tourists mistaken for moose. However, this did not lessen the opposition. Scott Hayden, a resort owner and highly vocal representative of the roughly 1,000-member Ad Hoc Committee, suggested that the numbers indicated that the Golden Lake First Nation did not really need the hunt after all.

The Algonquin were ready to speak to any media that would listen, but their voice was most often the quietest one in articles claiming to give a balanced approach. The summer issue of *Outdoor Canada* had an article that began with the unreasonable assertion that "[i]f the land claims of an Ontario native band ever come to pass, Algonquin Park would become private fishing and hunting grounds." Considerable space was then given to the Ad Hoc Committee's attack on the Algonquin claim. It was probably too little too late for Greg Sarazin's reassuring statements near the end that "[i]f we get Algonquin Park, we're not going to sell it off in real estate development. We're not going to kick out the 300 cottagers. The broad principle is that it will remain a park-like access to the public."

The Ad Hoc Committee continued to incite fear about the park's fate if the Algonquin assumed control. In July 1992, the committee issued a report stating that, in order for the Golden Lake First Nation to maintain the park and guarantee financial stability, they would have to "introduce radically new revenue-generating activities—of which the most obvious would be massive real estate and rental development." In *Seasons*, the publication of the Federation of Ontario Naturalists, Scott Hayden claimed that "the Golden Lake band's so far successful attempt to turn Algonquin into their private hunting preserve is only a small part of their agenda for the park."

In order to counteract this flame of paranoia fanned by the Ad Hoc Committee, and to allay the genuine concerns of people in the area, Golden Lake Algonquin representatives addressed the public whenever possible. In the fall of 1992, they put together a newsletter and announced that they would have a full-time communications coordinator working on the reserve throughout the negotiation process.

Due to the success of the first Interim Agreement, a second was introduced in October 1992. This was done in spite of more protest, which included a 20-page "research" report from the Ad Hoc Committee disputing the claim.

The Ontario government again allowed the public one week to submit input on the agreement, which, with some modifications, closely resembled the first. The changes that were made reflected prior public input. The province would fund the Algonquin's cost for hiring and supporting an official to ensure that the rules of the agreement would be enforced. Additional enforcement would come from a tribunal set up by the Golden Lake band.

In December, the federal government entered the picture, with Minister of Indian Affairs Tom Siddon stating that "Canada is committed to establishing this agreement" and that "[t]he primary objective is to relieve historical injustice." He hoped that the claim would be resolved within two years.

Federal participation increased the credibility of the Golden Lake claim, but their task still remained to gain public support and eradicate fears of the loss of private lands, the dismantling of the park, and overhunting. That would not be easy with the Ad Hoc Committee's political manoeuvring. In an apparent attempt to incite fear and anger, Scott Hayden stated in *The Huntsville Herald* (March 31, 1993) that dignitaries attending the opening ceremonies at the new visitor centre and logging museum at Algonquin Park might "find themselves in the middle of a major political protest." He contended that the First Nation would seize the opportunity to protest "unless they're given a platform to condemn their land claim not being finished." He went on to say that he expected problems with crowd control and that he believed that a tent was being erected to keep politicians out of sight "in case of problems." But the problems existed only in his imagination. There was no Algonquin protest.

Howard Goldblatt, chief negotiator for the province, announced in April that there would be a series of open houses in the affected areas. They would enable people to speak their minds and meet with representatives of the Canadian, Ontario, and Golden Lake governments. In addition, a Native Affairs office was opened in Pembroke, in the middle of the claim territory, where people could go and ask questions about the claim and the process of negotiation.

The open houses seem to have worked well. They were well attended across the claim territory. In one report, based on approximately one third of 535 attendees at open houses who filled out evaluation forms, it was noted that 90% were satisfied with the quality and quantity of information given, as well as the format of the events. Federal representative Jacques Shore would note in a CBC Radio interview that at the open houses "[people] huff and puff and get upset. But nine times out of ten I find that people are walking away feeling a little bit lighter than when they walked in."

Significantly, to a large extent because of the open house process, local newspapers were more supportive of the Algonquin than they had been. *Barry's Bay This Week* (May 11, 1993) and *The Eganville Leader* (May 12, 1993), rather than playing upon the public's fears, as had often been done in the past, provided the historical context and legal background of the issue. On May 14, *The Pembroke Observer* carried an article with the headline, "Land Claim Open House Allays Fears." And, in an editorial celebrating the one hundredth anniversary of Algonquin Park, *The Ottawa Citizen*, which had not been supportive of the Algonquin in the past, published the following:

> Non-Native residents predicted the natives would clear the park of game and fish [after the Interim Agreement]. This hasn't happened. What will happen when they re-enter negotiations with the government . . . ? A cash settlement maybe; perhaps even the right to administer the park. Is this so bad? Harried urbanites looking for a little peace and quiet don't care who administers the park, they care that they have access to it. We hope that the government, and the Algonquins of Golden Lake, can cut a deal that guarantees that access: it's a big place, with plenty of room for all. (op. cit.)

Rather than portraying the Algonquin as a depersonalized "they," as had often occurred in the past, newspapers were printing positive articles about individuals. On May 29, *The Pembroke Daily News* published "A Leader for the Future," a laudatory piece on the new chief of Golden Lake band, **Robert Whiteduck**. In *The Bancroft Times* of June 8, Ernie Martelle, superintendent of Algonquin Park, was quoted as saying that "everyone speaks highly of **Dennis Sarazin**," the Golden Lake official in charge of enforcing the rules of the Interim Agreement.

The second hunting season of the Interim Hunting Agreement found the Algonquin again shooting less than the allowed limit, with 89 moose (11 under the maximum allowed) and only 39 deer. This led Grant Hopkins, outdoors writer for *The Ottawa Citizen*, to conclude an article on the hunt with the statement that "[a]ll in all, the Algonquin laws appear to be working" (August 8, 1993). In November, the agreement was renewed for the third year.

In December 1993, the situation looked positive for the Golden Lake Algonquin. The *Holmes Report*, a 2,500-page independent study commissioned by the Ontario government, supported the Golden Lake claim.

Rather than settling the matter, this seemed to spur on increased criticism of the Golden Lake Algonquin and of the N.D.P. Government. An editorial in *The Huntsville Forester* (January 5, 1994) claimed that the report "is showing what many in this region have thought all along. Those in power at Queen's Park have a biased political agenda." The Land O' Lakes Tourist

Association, writing in *The North Frontenac News* (January 25, 1994), argued that no special rights of access, possession, or stewardship should be given to the Algonquin as it felt that the First Nation's land claims were unrealistic.

Opposition was particularly vocal once it was reported that in Stringer Lake the Algonquin had caught their set quota of 50 fish. References were made in local newspapers to the "rape of Stringer Lake." Ed van Duuren, writing in *The Huntsville Forester* (May 25, 1994) stated that "[o]bviously, there are many natives who think themselves as outside the laws of Canada." He lumped together Algonquin fishing with the showdown at Oka as evidence.

On August 25, a "Framework for Negotiations" was signed by the Golden Lake Algonquin and the governments of Ontario and Canada. It set the scope, topics, and timetable for the actual negotiations. A companion document, "Shared Objectives," identified the areas that would guide the three parties in the negotiations. The second step, after the "Framework for Negotiations," would be an agreement in principle, to be followed by the third and last step, the final agreement. It was stated, optimistically, that the whole process would take about two years.

Then the soon-to-be-premier of the province, Mike Harris, appeared on the scene. Showing the attitude that he would later bring to his government's dealing with all Native groups, in speaking to a meeting of tourism officials in Peterborough in October, he said:

> There's a whole notion of guilt because Native people haven't fully adapted from the reservations [*sic*] to being full partners in this economy. We can't let that guilt preclude us from reaching a common sense solution. Too many Natives spend all their time on courts and lawyers and they just stay home and do nothing.

Howard Bernard, Golden Lake communications officer, responded by pointing out that his community had held nine open houses and had met with organizations such as the Wildlands League, the Ontario Federation of Anglers and Hunters, the Renfrew County Economic Development Committee, Natural Resources Canada, the Ontario Ministry of Natural Resources, and the Ontario Ministry of the Environment, among others, not really "staying at home and doing nothing."

The next summer, Harris asserted his wish to see Native land claim negotiations take place in public forums that required settlements to be approved through local referenda. Thus, any rightness of Native claims would be buried under the greater numbers of non-Natives. Justice would be sacrificed to popularity.

Harris also said that he wanted to put an end to interim policies such as the one in place at Golden Lake, despite the fact that it had worked efficiently each year.

The summer and fall of 1995 brought violent Native protests into the public eye (see Chapter 20 on Dudley George). Golden Lake Chief Robert Whiteduck assured non-Natives that "talking things out is the best way for Aboriginal people to resolve disputes" (*The Pembroke Observer*, September 12, 1995). He noted that through a quarter century of their talking with governments, the Golden Lake Algonquin had not instigated any confrontations, a policy they weren't about to change. Further, he stated that, "[i]f we can demonstrate in this process that there's a reasonable, constructive way to resolve the issues through negotiations, we can say we're doing it, and hopefully have an indirect impact on others. The only way I can see it being resolved is in a healthy fashion."

Resolution is still in the future. Since the Framework Agreement was put in place, the Golden Lake Algonquin have continued negotiations with the governments of Ontario and Canada. They have maintained their policy of educating non-Natives about Native culture

Timeline 14-1

1772: First Algonquin petition to have their rights to the area recognized.

1857: Five heads of families petition for land that would become the Golden Lake reserve.

1864: Land is purchased for them using funds from the sale of Native lands.

1893: Crown land is set aside for Algonquin Park.

1991: First Interim Agreement.

Native Individuals 14-1

Greg Sarazin: Chief of the Golden Lake Algonquin throughout much of their negotiation in the 1980s and 1990s for their rights to Algonquin Park.

and history, appearing frequently in schools and in public meetings. Their representatives travel throughout the land-claim territory and beyond, explaining the process of negotiation and the nature of their claim. In the meantime, however, they still face resistance from special interest groups, particularly hunters and anglers, who resent what they perceive to be special privileges for the Algonquin people. Recently, the issue has centred around deer hunting, which some non-Natives see as an area of unfair preferential treatment towards Natives and, despite the success of the Interim Agreement, as potentially harmful for the deer population. The issue is yet to be resolved. For the Algonquin, the waiting continues.

KEY TERMS

Interim Agreement

CONTENT QUESTIONS

1. Did the Golden Lake Algonquin sign a treaty?
2. Through what means did the Golden Lake Algonquin receive their land?
3. What were the results of the Interim Agreements?
4. What happened to the Interim Agreements?
5. What public relations moves did the Algonquin make?

 WEBLINK

www.ualberta.ca/~esimpson/claims/algonquins.htm
An overview of the Golden Lake Algonquin land claim, provided by a University of Alberta librarian.

FIGHTING FOR RECOGNITION: THE SHESHATSHIT INNU AND THE MEGAPROJECTS

OVERVIEW

The Mushuau-Innu, or "Barren Ground People," entered the twentieth century leading a traditional life, with their territory (which they called "Nitassinan") unceded to the government, still relatively untouched by outsiders. Several major projects would quickly alter that last fact but not the second one.

During the early years of this century, White trappers slowly encroached on the yet-to-be-signed-over territory around what is now **Sheshatshit** ("large inlet," pronounced sheh-shah-cheet), or Hamilton Inlet. Sheshatshit cuts deep into Labrador about half way up the peninsula. This outsider incursion into centuries-old Naskapi hunting and trapping country increased greatly in 1942 with the building of the U.S. Armed Forces Base at Goose Bay. Newfoundland, then independent of Canada, had signed over the land for that purpose. No Innu was notified of this passing on of their land from foreign hand to foreign hand.

Newfoundland joined Canada in 1949, but the official status of Native people in the new province was not dealt with, even though Native rights to the land had not been extinguished. There had been no treaties signed; no reserves had been created. So Newfoundland governments treated the Innu, Inuit, and Mi'kmaq of the province as if, unlike in every other province, they had no aboriginal rights.

This would be particularly destructive to the Innu when the megaprojects came to their country. To better understand the impact of these projects, we will be referring to statements from and about **Tshaukuesh Penashue**, a woman who is a key figure in the fight by the **Sheshashiwinnu** (Innu of Sheshatshit) for their well-being.

150

THE IRON MINES

In the early 1950s, the Quebec North Shore and Labrador Railway, which runs from Sept-Îles to Schefferville, was cut through about 500 kilometres of Innu territory. The intention was to remove 10 million tonnes of ore a year from the huge iron deposits around Schefferville. A few Innu found jobs, many of them seasonal or temporary, but many more saw and felt the despoliation of their traditional lands. And, as is so often the case in Canadian history, the original inhabitants were treated as second-class citizens by those who moved in to reap the wealth of their land.

For Euro-Canadians, the mines and spin-off industries would be profitable, at least for a while. During that time, Sept-Îles was considered to be one of the richest cities in Canada, based on per capita earnings. It is estimated that during the boom years (1975–1980) $257 million was made from mining (Wadden 1991:53). Predictably, the bottom fell out of the market during the 1980s; mines closed down and Sept-Îles saw a third of its population, mostly **Akaneshau** (Innu for White English-speakers), leave town for greener pastures, or more well-endowed mother lodes. The Innu, with a long-term investment in the area, had no such option.

It is ironic that an Innu hunter, **Mistanpeu (Mathieu Andre)**, had led geologists to the iron deposits in the late 1940s, receiving the Order of Canada for his efforts. He would later say that he had no idea of the negative effects that subsequent activities would have on his people and on his land (Wadden 1995:52–3).

During the 1950s and 1960s, the Sheshatshit Innu were increasingly forced into sanitation-poor shacks, thought by outsider "experts" to be much better than the tents that had served them in good health for a long time. Tuberculosis and alcoholism were the predictable results. In words that could be echoed by the parents of the children that drew national attention a few years ago at Davis Inlet, Tshaukuesh clearly contrasts the effects on children of the new life in the outsider-imposed community as opposed to the traditional life in **nutshimit** ("the bush," "inland," "the country"):

> Life is important in the country because you don't have to worry about the children, you know they're close somewhere in the camp. But in the community I start worrying. I worry my children will drink, then they get involved in vandalism and have to go to court . . . My children, they're totally confused. Whereas in the country they're busy all the time. (Wadden 1996:87)

BOX 15-1   **An Innu Reflects on the Iron Mines**

In 1998, Kathleen Nuna spoke (through a translator) about the railroad and iron mines experience of the Innu:

> When they talked about mining, the people were told, they were told you're not going to pay to train. So they didn't pay. No more than ten years and then they started paying training. 8 bucks. And first the Innu didn't understand because they were too excited at first. They bought it too early what has been said. Now here all the destruction is taking place in Schefferville. The only people that are there now is Innu and everywhere around them is like big holes and just like dump. They just—people just packed up and left. The only people there is Innu.

Media horror stories of reserve life and downtown outside-the-bar stereotypes of Innu, as of other Native groups, fail to give any indication that in nutshimit, or its equivalent among other peoples, Native life is more complete and the people more whole, both having purpose. In part because of this, insufficiently calculated in the number crunching of mega-projects balance sheets is the long-term value of nutshimit in providing both the material necessities of life as well as the less physical necessities of supportive family, community, a sense of purpose, and a spiritual balance.

CHURCHILL FALLS

The Churchill Falls Hydroelectric Project was built to fulfil the power demands of mining and other industries in Quebec and the northeastern U.S. Constructed over the period of 1966 to 1974, this project involved damming the Churchill River near spectacular falls and was a megaproject with all the usual superlatives: the world's largest underground power-house, creating the Smallwood Reservoir; the third-largest artificial body of water in the world, at 6,527 square kilometres; the tenth-largest freshwater body in Canada.

The Innu were not consulted nor notified, even though the land being flooded, some 1,300 square kilometres of black spruce forest, had not been signed over. Tshaukuesh's parents were, like many other Innu, unaware of the flooding. In 1973, as usual, they left their canoes, traps, tents, and other belongings behind. After their possessions and lands were covered with water, no compensation was paid to them or to the others who lost both supplies and hunting/trapping territory—their living—in this way. With typical outsider blindness, the writer hired by the company to write its "official" glorifying history wrote: "The Churchill Falls project did not deprive a single person of his home or livelihood" (as quoted in Wadden 1995:45).

Billions of dollars would be generated by this project and related industries, but that money flowed freely out of the Innu country like the waters of the Churchill River used to, not staying to benefit the Innu.

BOX 15-2   An Innu Reflects on Churchill Falls

In 1998, in the environmental assessment for the Voisey's Bay project, some Innu commented negatively about how they felt about the Churchill Falls dam. Here are the words of Peter Penashue:

> Many people today . . . look at Churchill Falls and they say there was a great river there. You could hear it for miles. What is it that benefits the Innu today from Churchill Falls? We pay the monthly bills that come from Newfoundland Hydro which is, in my view, a great wrong committed to the people because the governments flood the river and take the land then they turn around and send a bill to the people that own the land. But I look at it and I say, well what did we accomplish?

THE LOW-FLYING JETS

The Situation

In 1986, the Canadian government signed agreements with the governments of the United States, Britain, the Netherlands, and West Germany, permitting these NATO allies to train their air forces for 10 years over Innu land in Labrador. Again, there was no consultation or consideration of the Innu, who had still not signed away their land.

The pilot training consisted of low-level flying (30 metres above the ground) of 20-tonne jets streaking across the barrens at 900 kilometres an hour, achieving a noise level of between 110 to 140 decibels (Wadden 1996:36). To give some idea of the level of this noise, a jackhammer achieves 80 decibels and 120 decibels causes physical pain to human ears. The number of flights in 1986 was 6,000 and 7,000 in 1988.

The effect of these flights on the environment has been a hotly debated subject, but it is hard to convincingly argue against a few basic facts. Caribou tend to run without rest after being frightened by the jets. Thus, a typical caribou pace of 12 kilometres a day is extended to 55 or 60 kilometres a day without rest or food. Caribou that have starved to death have been found in increasing numbers and there is evidence of aborted births. Gas would be dumped near the end of the flights and the caribou would go out of their way to avoid the areas of this dumping. Migration paths and calving grounds have been altered in ways hazardous to both the caribou and to those who hunt them.

Judges, military leaders, and politicians have argued that not enough is "scientifically" known about the impact of the low-flying jets on caribou, that a people carrying the knowledge accumulated over thousands of years of hunting caribou cannot be considered "experts" because they don't bear pieces of paper saying that they are. Yet, farmers have received as much as $45,000 in compensation for the fact that domestic animals such as ranch fox and goats have aborted in jet-induced trauma, that turkeys have had heart attacks, and hens have stopped producing eggs (Wadden 1996:178). How much more might wild animals such as caribou be affected?

The Sheshatshiwinnu Fight Back

Innu resistance to the various outsider forces having a negative impact on their country has consistently followed a path of peaceful, non-violent civil disobedience. Not surprisingly, the first act of resistance involved hunting. The Innu were increasingly becoming more and more restricted in this critical area of their lives by rule-makers who did not consult them and by rules that often did not make any sense. One of the Sheshatshit band's foremost Elders, Tshaukuesh's father-in-law, had the proud name of **Kanatuakuet** ("Porcupine Hunter"), no doubt because he had often provided food for his family from that Innu-prized delicacy. But Newfoundland provincial game laws prohibited the killing of porcupine, even though that species was in no way threatened. Kanatuakuet could no longer legally live up to his name.

For 15 years, the Sheshatshiwinnu were not permitted to hunt the Mealy Mountain caribou herd. In March 1987, the Innu saw signs that the herd had recovered from earlier low numbers. Having a great need for the meat, they staged an act of peaceful political protest. They hunted openly, not trying to hide from the provincial wildlife officers. **Peter Penashue**, Tshaukuesh's son, states the following concerning the way they felt:

We were afraid, we'd never done anything like that before, actually provoking arrest. In the past, we would have hidden, but not any more, we're through hiding. It's time our rights are recognized on this land. So, when those Mounties finally caught up with us, you know, I felt they looked at us with some respect because they could see we were doing what we thought was right, and they could see we aren't afraid of them any more. (Wadden 1996:94)

They were arrested, convicted, and fined, but it was an important radicalizing first step. Their next step involved getting themselves heard concerning the low-level flying that was so destructive to their lives. In the autumn of 1987 and of 1988, Tshaukuesh and others of like mind made camp on the bombing range, obliging the military to temporarily cancel the bombing runs.

In 1988, NATO officials were given a grand tour of the military installation by government representatives, in the hope that Goose Bay would be chosen as the site for the NATO-sponsored Tactical Fighter Weapons Training Centre. The visiting dignitaries were kept safely away from the Sheshatshiwinnu, who sought to speak with them in order to voice their legitimate concerns.

On September 15, 1988, one of the most dramatic moments in the history of the Innu unfolded. More than 75 Innu, including Tshaukuesh, marched onto the runway at Goose Bay and refused to leave until they spoke with the NATO officials. After being made to wait, they were eventually given their chance to speak. They told the people from NATO that the land proposed for the centre was unceded Innu land and that NATO would be complicit in an act of "ethnocide" by the Canadian government if it went ahead with its plans for the Strategic Fighter Weapons Training Centre.

The Innu occupied the runway seven times that fall, determined to change the deteriorating social conditions at Sheshatshit. That year, 21 teenagers from the community would try to commit suicide. Tshaukuesh would be arrested on more than one occasion for her

---

BOX 15-3   **An Innu Reflects on Government Promises Concerning Low-Flying Jets**

Through a translator, Innu Mary Ann Michel spoke in 1998 at the environmental assessment of Voisey's Bay about the promises made by the government concerning the Innu ceasing their protests of low-flying jets. Her interpretation of that situation led to her distrust of the Voisey's Bay Nickel Company (note authors' emphasis):

> We fought low level flying . . . One year we were sitting—we got nothing and we were told. . ."Stop protesting. We will give you

housing." [We]re going to have nice housing, we were told. We're going to give you . . . lots of cars . . . we're going to have houses near the base. There's going to be land there . . . So we gave up the protest. On the 10th of December, we gave up protesting and when we gave up, one year, . . . and nothing happened. And today, still nothing. We didn't get anything and we were told we were going to get lots of money and lots of houses *and now, I hear you saying this. So we're told lies all the time like this. I hear them before . . .*

BOX 15-4 — Framework Agreement

On March 29, 1996, the federal government, the provincial government, and the Innu Nation, a political association representing the approximately 1,700 people of Sheshatshit and Davis Inlet, signed the Framework Agreement. This was the first step in the process of recognition of the aboriginal rights of the Innu. It appears to be a document of the three parties getting together, but if you look at the wording of the three leaders, you find that there appears to be two different attitudes towards the agreement. What do you think?

1) Peter Penashue, president of the Innu Nation:

Today we have taken a small but significant step for all future generations of Innu people. Our land and resources are our way of life . . . In the many months of negotiations that lie ahead we trust that Canada and Newfoundland will recognize our rights. We hope to enter an honourable treaty in which our rights are honoured, the wrongdoings of the past are corrected, and we agree to share our land and resources with the newcomers to our homeland Nitassinan, where we have lived in harmony with the land for thousands of years . . .

2) Brian Tobin, premier of Newfoundland and Labrador:

Signing this Framework Agreement today represents a very important and positive step in treaty negotiations with the Innu Nation, paving the way for agreement of substantive issues... My government has identified treaty negotiations with Aboriginal peoples in Labrador as a top priority. We are fully committed to achieving settlement which will provide the Innu with means necessary to attain self-sufficiency and create a stable and certain environment for economic development in Labrador.

3) Ronald Irwin, minister of Indian Affairs and Northern Development:

The Innu Nation Framework Agreement forms the fundamental structure for building a new relationship with the Innu, based on partnership and mutual respect . . . Reaching a treaty with the Innu will be a major catalyst for improving the social and economic well-being of the Innu and achieving the certainty non-Aboriginal land and resource users need.

acts of protest. One suicide attempt hit particularly close to her. Her son, Peter, had taken an overdose of pills, but fortunately not enough to kill him.

In court in the spring of 1989, the 44-year-old Tshaukuesh spoke in her people's defence concerning the reasons for their acts of civil disobedience:

We will lose our culture if the land is destroyed . . . We will lose our identity as Innu people and will not survive in the country any more if the wildlife is demolished by development. For you people, European people, white people, you take your meals from the store. You can survive that, but our people have to depend on the land. (Wadden 1996:145)

The judge of the trial of Tshaukuesh and three other Innu was an Inuk by the name of **James Igloliorte**. He granted an injunction to prevent the military from low-level flying over Innu land. In pronouncing his judgment, Judge Igloliorte observed:

Each of these four persons based their belief of ownership on an honest belief on reasonable grounds . . . Through their knowledge of ancestry and kinship they have showed that none of their people ever gave away rights to the land of Canada, and this is an honest belief each person holds. The provincial and federal statutes do not include as third parties or signatories any Innu people. (Wadden 1996:150)

Predictably, the decision was overturned in a higher court. Tshaukuesh was arrested again on the runway. In 1990, the number of low-level jet flights increased to 9,000. But the Innu continued to fight, beginning to reach a larger, even international, audience.

The news today is mixed. For the most part, the issue has been lost to the fickle consciousness of the Canadian public. On February 7, 1996, Canada signed a 10-year multilateral agreement following an environmental assessment. The low-level flying will continue, April to November, with a maximum of 18,000 sorties a season. You don't have to be an Innu hunter to know that the caribou herds will be affected.

VOISEY'S BAY

There are two new megaprojects on the horizon for the Innu to deal with. One is another dam on the Churchill River, this one on a slightly smaller scale, flooding only 1,146 square kilometres. The other project, one that is moving ahead more quickly, is mining at Voisey's Bay, 335 kilometres northwest of Sheshatshit. In 1993, rich deposits of nickel, cobalt, and copper were discovered there. Voisey's Bay Nickel Company (owned by Inco Limited) is planning to develop an area it refers to as the Claims Block, an area measuring 18 kilometres by 29 kilometres.

Voisey's Bay Nickel Company has acted more responsibly and sympathetically to Innu concerns than its predecessors in the other megaprojects. During the environmental assessment hearing held in October 1998, the company made fair-sounding proposals concerning jobs and job training. But the Innu, justifiably, were suspicious. They had been led down that path before. The Innu presentations at the hearing spoke of how badly they had been treated before (see boxes 1, 2, and 3). In the following presentation (given in translation), **Francis Penashue** compared the Voisey's Bay Nickel Company representatives to the first priest that came to live with her people:

Native Individuals 15-1

James Igloliorte: An Inuit judge who awarded a decision in favour of the protesting Sheshatshit Innu.

Mistanpeu: Mathieu Andre, an Innu who led geologists to the huge Schefferville iron deposits.

Peter Penashue: President of the Innu Nation during the signing of the Framework Agreement.

Tshaukuesh Penashue: A Sheshatshit Innu woman who has been at the forefront of the protest movement against low-flying jets.

Timeline 15-1

1949: American Armed Forces Base is built at Goose Bay.

1950: Newfoundland joins Canada.

Early 1950s: The Quebec North Shore and Labrador Railway is cut through about 500 kilometres of Innu territory.

1973: The Churchill Falls dam floods Innu country.

1975–80: Boom period for the mines in Innu territory.

1986: The Canadian government signs an agreement with NATO countries permitting low-flying jets over Innu territory.

1987-89: Innu peacefully protest low-flying jets.

1993: Rich deposits are discovered at Voisey's Bay.

1996: The Framework Agreement is signed by the Innu Nation, the province of Newfoundland and Labrador, and the federal government.

I want to talk about 1950s towards today. I remember what this gentleman said, that he said it would be one year or two years that the work will be working and that people would be able to get jobs, and I was just thinking about what he had just said. 1950s, the first one was, I guess the priest came to our communities, permanently, and those people like my grandmother and my grandfather were very committed to the church and very respect[ful] to the church much as if it was God, . . . and they thought that if they didn't listen to the church and today I heard the gentleman here, and I was thinking about, he reminded me about the priest, 1950s . . . and so I was thinking, it was almost 50 years now, I guess and today just look at us now and see all the misery you see in the community of other people's culture coming into our communities and for us trying to adopt jobs and the way of life of others.

KEY TERMS

Innu

Mushuau-Innu (Innu)

nutshimit (Innu)

CONTENT QUESTIONS

1. What unique situation has caused the Sheshatshit Innu to be treated, until recently, as if they had no aboriginal rights?

2. In what sense would the Innu feel that they had already paid for their electricity from Churchill Falls?

3. What three megaprojects have had an impact on the Innu in the twentieth century?

4. Why are the Innu suspicious of the promises from the Voisey's Bay Nickel Company?

5. What do you think the Voisey's Bay Nickel Company representatives needed to learn from the Innu?

 **WEBLINKS**

www.innu.ca/mining.html
The Innu Nation maintains a Web page specifically about Voisey's Bay development concerns.

www.innu.ca/llfindex.html
The Innu also have an excellent collection of information and Weblinks about the low-flying jets issue.

www.capitalnet.com/~pmogb/website/environment/earp/earp_panel/ panel_ch1-3_e.html
The federal environmental assessment on the impact of low-flying jets on Northern communities.

THE JAMES BAY
AND NORTHERN QUEBEC
AGREEMENT

OVERVIEW

The Cree have lived in the James Bay region for approximately five to six thousand years. While we can never be sure of their population at the time of contact, it is estimated that they numbered at least 20,000 people. However, it was not until 1971 that the Cree who occupy present-day Quebec ever came together for a common cause. Until that time, the Cree of Quebec had been living in less than a dozen villages in an essentially traditional way, hunting and trapping for food and income. They would spread out over the land for the winter months, exploiting territories that had been in families for generations. The care of the land was vested in an older man, whose job it was to maintain and perpetuate it.

When northern Quebec was handed over to the province by the federal government in 1898 and 1912, it was under the strict stipulation that the Cree, along with the Inuit and the Innu, have their rights dealt with through some sort of treaty. Prior to 1971, not one Quebec provincial government had done anything to fulfil these requirements.

THE PROJECT OF THE CENTURY

In April 1971, Quebec Premier Robert Bourassa announced that the province was going to initiate a huge hydroelectric development project that would involve harnessing the rivers of the James Bay watershed. The government was totally oblivious to the fact that these rivers ran through the Cree hunting territories and, in fact, were essential to the Cree way of life. The government's position was that the project would be constructed on provincial lands and would be beneficial to everybody, including First Nations people.

The Cree leaders met in Mistassini on June 29, 1971, two months after Bourassa's announcement. During the three-day meeting, the Cree leaders decided that they would fight with all of their ability to protest and derail the government's plans. They would not tolerate the flooding of the area. Through a petition, they requested that the minister of Indian affairs intervene on their behalf.

The Native battle over the James Bay project would take nearly five years and would involve the province of Quebec, the federal government, the Cree, and the Inuit. The culmination would be the first major settlement of a Native land claim in recent years. The James Bay and Northern Quebec Agreement (1975) has generated dispute and debate since it was signed. Initially, it was believed that it would pave the way for all subsequent land claims settlements, but since its signing it has come to be reassessed and reconsidered. The agreement was signed by the government of Quebec, three Quebec Crown corporations, the Grand Council of the Crees of Quebec, the Northern Quebec Inuit Association, and the Government of Canada. It involved 6,650 Cree from eight communities and 4,386 Inuit from fifteen communities.

A couple of facts must be acknowledged before a discussion of the events. First, there had never been any treaty or surrendering of land by the First Nations people who occupied the Quebec portion of James Bay. Under Canadian law, as per the Royal Proclamation of 1763, the land was *ipso facto* Native land. Second, the Quebec government had had no prior consultations with the Cree or Inuit people. This was very much consistent with previous actions on the part of the Quebec government in its dealings with Native people.

Perhaps the most remarkable aspect of the history of the project is the rapidity with which the Cree and Inuit responded to the threat by Quebec. The provincial government was totally unprepared for the response on the part of the First Nations. Implicit in the government's total disregard for the concerns of the Natives is a belief that these were unsophisticated and politically naive peoples. They were quite wrong.

The Inuit reacted by forming themselves into a number of associations, which were then coordinated by the Inuit Tapirisat of Canada, a blanket organization for a number of groups, representing the Inuit across Canada. The Cree, as noted above, also reacted quickly. They were led initially by a number of young people who had had experience with the "outside world." The Cree decided at their initial meeting that the project would not benefit them in any way and would destroy land, animals, and their culture. Their strategy was to organize at a grassroots level, within their communities, and to solicit support not only from other Native groups but the public at large.

Also, it was decided that talks with the government must be undertaken. The attitude of the provincial government was negative to say the least. In January 1972, one of its first moves was to refuse to discuss a claim for compensation that was put forward by the Indians of Quebec Association (IQA). However, a month later, a joint federal and provincial committee on environmental effects of the project stated that it would have a substantial impact on Native peoples of the region. The Cree did not want to convey the impression of being in total opposition to the project, and so adopted a position of moderation and accommodation. Above all, they wanted to discuss with the government alternative plans or modifications to the project so that the impact might be lessened. The government, for its part, refused to do anything but inform the First Nations of the plans developed. As a consequence, the Cree were obliged to assume a position of opposition.

Under the auspices of the IQA, the Cree met at Fort George in 1972. **Chief Billy Diamond** raised the possibility of a court case to stop the project and a general mandate for this purpose was extended to the IQA. At the same time, the Cree set up community liaison workers. The following month, the IQA formed a task force and called upon McGill University researchers to conduct environmental and social impact studies. The McGill University Department of Anthropology was a major player in these. During this month, May 1972, the Cree and Inuit initiated action in the injunction.

In late October 1972, the government announced its policy of no modifications to its plans. That same week, the Cree, Inuit, and executives of the IQA met in Montreal to review the work of the task force. They subsequently met with Premier Bourassa, a meeting that was essentially fruitless because of the government's no-modification policy. At this point, the Cree decided that they had no other alternative than to pursue court action wholeheartedly. To this end, a week later they filed papers for an injunction stopping the development. Justice Albert Malouf of the Quebec Superior Court granted a hearing on the petition by the Cree and Inuit. This would end up being the longest temporary injunction hearing in Canadian history. It lasted 71 days, from December 11, 1972, until May 24, 1973, and heard testimony from 167 witnesses, of whom nearly 100 were Cree and Inuit hunters. The First Nations had to prove that they had a *prima facie* (evidence adequate to establish a fact) claim to rights to the territory, and that the project would damage the exercising of these rights. Furthermore, they had to prove that these damages would be irreversible and unremediable.

What would be the cause of this damage? The work to be undertaken by the government was enormous. Among other creations was a 700-kilometre-long road through traditional hunting territories, a new town to house the project's headquarters, a number of scattered construction camps, and airports and communications infrastructures that were also needed. Additional long-term plans included mines and forestry operations.

The hydroelectric project itself involved diverting three major rivers into the La Grande River in order to increase its flow by 80%. What did this involve? It meant the construction of four main dams, 130 kilometres of dykes, and eight main reservoirs that would flood 8,722 square kilometres, or 5%, of the land surface. These reservoirs would be filled during the summer and released during the winter to produce electricity needed for heating in more southerly cities and towns. This necessitated the construction of 960 kilometres of power lines through the bush, intersecting Cree hunting territories. All of these activities constituted only the first phase of the project.

The Cree argued their case based on the concept of aboriginal rights, the essence of which is rights to the land based on traditional use and occupancy. They contended that, among other things, flooding would destroy much of the wildlife, including beaver and other fur bearers and game. The variability in water levels would be particularly dangerous, as animals would not be able to predict their levels. Fish levels would decline, vegetation would be lost, and the Cree's subsistence would be destroyed. In sum, their culture would be lost.

The government's response was predictable. It argued that the Cree lived in settlements, made use of modern technology, and did not take much from the land. It stated that employment or government assistance provided much of their income. Furthermore, any damage would be temporary and reparable.

Justice Malouf agreed with the Cree and Inuit. In November 1973, he ruled that the government was trespassing since the Cree and Inuit did have title to the land. They had been occupying and using it to a full extent, hunting was of fundamental cultural and economic importance, and they had demonstrated their interest in pursuing their way of life. Any interference would compromise and interfere with their culture and way of life. He accorded the interlocutory injunction based on the evidence.

The Malouf Judgment was far more than anybody expected. The government appealed and a week later the Quebec Court of Appeal suspended the Malouf Judgment on the basis of the "balance of convenience" without specifically treating the issue of Native title to lands.

Between the date of the Malouf Judgment (November 15, 1973) and the Quebec suspension (November 22, 1973), the Bourassa Government had submitted an 11-page proposal for a settlement to the IQA executive and to the Cree and Inuit representatives. On December 10, the Cree chiefs met in Val d'Or and agreed to enter negotiations and to extend a mandate to the IQA to seek funds and to undertake negotiations. The Cree also set the requirement that the IQA *must* consult with the villages prior to negotiations.

In the meantime, the Cree tried to appeal the suspension of the Malouf Judgment, but to no avail. The Cree chiefs met in Fort George (Chisasibi) and developed a counterproposal, which they titled *Our Land, Our Demand*. At this point, Billy Diamond held a press conference and stated that the Cree rejected the province's 11-point proposal, stating that "the land is not for sale." At the same time, the minister of Indian affairs made threatening noises about cutting off funds to the Cree if they did not seriously consider the Bourassa proposal. However, he later backed down.

For six months, from February to July 1974, negotiations were undertaken with the Cree, who were represented by the IQA. Committees and subcommittees were struck and utilized. Equally important, the IQA undertook consultations with all communities regarding offers and negotiations positions. However, early on during the negotiations, a rift developed between the Cree and the IQA. Some people have interpreted this as being a rift that was the product of Iroquois versus Cree interests, north versus south, urban versus rural. Regardless, as a result of dissatisfaction with the IQA in the negotiations, the mandate was withdrawn at a meeting in Fort George of the Cree chiefs, and a three-man Cree negotiating team was created. *Our Land, Our Demand #2 for Crees* was drawn up. On August 16, 1974, the Grand Council of the Cree of Quebec (GCCQ) was created. It included a chief and another leader from each community on its board of directors and an executive group of four regional leaders. From then on, the council took over the negotiations. However, at all times, the Cree recognized that decisions had to be made at the grassroots level and the Cree people remained the final decision makers.

On October 14–15, promises between the Cree and the province were exchanged. For the rest of the month, the Cree entered into consultations with their various communities. On November 15, an Agreement in Principle was signed, with the Cree leaders declaring it a victory for the Cree. The IQA, however, denounced the agreement in a press conference.

A week after the signing of the Agreement in Principle, the Quebec Court of Appeals overturned the Malouf Judgment, based upon what it called (again) "the balance of convenience." The justices declared that Native rights to the land were extinguished at the time of the Hudson's Bay Company Charter, or were, at best, "rights to live on the territory."

The entire year of 1975 was spent hammering out the final details of the James Bay and Northern Quebec Agreement. Negotiations for the final agreement were undertaken with subcommittees, working groups, and task forces. In August, the General Assembly of Crees decided to proceed with negotiations to reach an agreement and the Grand Council of the Crees of Quebec was authorized to sign on behalf of the Cree Nation. In the final stages, beginning in September, the main committee moved into a Montreal hotel to review, edit, and negotiate final matters prepared by the subcommittees and working groups. For a month, from October 15 to November 11, 1975, all Cree band councils converged in Montreal for a close review of the agreement and signing of the agreement. Finally, on November 11, 1975, the James Bay and Northern Quebec Agreement was signed in Quebec. Between December 15–18, 1975, a 70-page text of this agreement was circulated and a ratification vote was held. Voter turnout was 24%, with 922 in favour and one opposed.

It is important to remember that while all of this was going on, the Cree had also turned to the public for support. There were massive demonstrations in Montreal, Quebec City, and Ottawa. Native peoples put on theatrical performances depicting both traditional and contemporary Cree life. In a move that fully demonstrated the Quebec Government's ignorance of the people it was dealing with, it sent a communiqué to the Cree written in the wrong dialect. The Cree capitalized on this gaffe in a brilliant way, by burning it in front of the print press and television cameras. While the goof was insulting in a huge way, it provided the Cree with a wonderful opportunity to demonstrate the government's ignorance of them and their culture. At the same time, public support was being found at colleges, universities, environmental groups, and elsewhere. Books were being written and films were being made. The "Project of the Century" was rapidly becoming the issue of the century.

TERMS OF THE AGREEMENT

The agreement provides that, not only all persons enrolled under the Indian Act are included, but also "any person of Cree or Indian ancestry who is recognized by one of the Cree communities as having been on such date (November 15, 1974) a member thereof." Further, the natural and adopted descendants of persons so eligible would continue to enjoy benefits of the agreement. Thus, the benefits of the agreement were not only extended to non-Status Indians and Métis, but the provision giving the community the right to recognize particular people as beneficiaries in effect leaves the definition of "beneficiaries" largely up to the local community.

So, what did the Cree win in the case? The James Bay and Northern Quebec Agreement of 1975 has been described as the last of the old-time treaties, although it has at the same time been hailed for breaking new ground. It is both the last of the old and the first of the modern aboriginal claims settlements in Canada, for it granted to the Cree and the Inuit communities of Quebec substantial control over economic, political, and social affairs (although final say rests with the government). In addition to a cash settlement greater than $230 million to be paid over 21 years, and special economic assistance, Natives maintained ownership of certain sections of land. These have been designated as Categories 1 (a and b), 2, and 3. Category 1a lands are those transferred to federal jurisdiction for the use of the Cree bands. They are reserves in the conventional sense. Category 1b are lands transferred to Cree Village Corporations, essentially "reserve" lands but under provincial jurisdiction. The principal distinction between sub-categories 1a and 1b relates to the role of the federal or provincial government. On 1b lands, the Cree are subject to provincial law, although they are regarded as full owners of the land. Category 1 lands may not be bought or sold. The general public is restricted in its access and, if expropriated or subjected to public servitude, the lands taken in this way must be replaced by equivalent tracts. The province retains ownership of all subsurface rights but a prospective developer must obtain the consent of the Cree before undertaking exploitation of these resources.

Category 2 lands are those on which the Cree enjoy hunting, fishing, and trapping rights, as well as priority in certain development activities. They have the right to set conditions under which non-Cree sports users may have access. These lands are under provincial jurisdiction and may be readily appropriated for development activities. However, land taken for development must be replaced by equivalent lands or, if the Cree choose, monetary compensation.

The remainder of the territory is classified as Category 3 lands, which are those governed by provincial legislation and regulations concerning public lands. The Cree have important protection for their harvesting activities without restriction but within social and environmental protection guidelines.

In addition, provision was made for a minimum family income plan for those in wildlife harvesting, for Native languages to be included as official languages of administration, and for a James Bay Native Development Corporation to handle investments.

Financial compensation takes a number of forms. The sums are payable to the Native population as a whole and then divided between the Cree and the Inuit on the basis of their respective populations. The split was roughly 60:40, with the Cree receiving the larger amount. The actual amount was $225 million, of which $150 million was basic compensation and $75 million was considered compensation for future development.

The initial $150 million would best be perceived as compensation for the surrender of aboriginal title. The payment was essentially broken down in two chunks of $75 million, the first for loss of title in the strict sense (Canada paid half), and the second being, essentially, a royalty payment in reference to installed hydroelectric generating capacity. The third $75 million was made to cover the cost of negotiations and $4 million was paid in compensation to take into account the non-Status Native population in the region. The total compensation to the James Bay Cree then was $137.4 million. However, by 1983, unforeseen costs, particularly in the forms of new or unplanned medical, housing, educational, and others brought the total cost to over $500 million, or nearly $50,000 per Native person living in the region.

Native critics have not been kind to the agreement. They point to the cost involved, including the flooding of thousands of kilometres of prime habitat. Furthermore, the entire project involved a number of projects eventually affecting an area the size of France. Critics suggested that the Cree sold out. Some media accused them of simply being money hungry.

Critics also point out that Native rights fell far short of being entrenched in the agreement. Furthermore, time has shown that the government has not met its end of the bargain, and Natives contend that the government has not allowed them to have any say in the developments.

FIGHTING THE SECOND PHASE

The Great Whale Phase was strongly protested by the Cree, beginning in 1989. The Cree had decided that there was no fairness in the dealings by either Hydro Quebec or the government. In 1981, eight children in Cree villages died of diarrhea. The cause was determined to be open sewers that had been left by construction camps when money was cut off for completion of the construction. From a Cree perspective, as soon as the work on delivering power was completed, everybody ran to the south.

Mercury poisoning was also a problem. Tests on Chisasibi residents found high levels of mercury in 64% of the population. That was in 1984. The land was not cleared before flooding and bacteria from the drowned decomposing vegetation transformed the insoluble mercury in the rocks into methylmercury. The methylmercury then evaporated and returned to the waterways as rain, poisoning the food system. Elders in Chisasibi exhibited the symptoms of poisoning, including numbness, shakiness, and loss of peripheral vision. No one could eat river fish. Hydro Quebec initially said it would take six years for the methyl-mercury to dissipate, but now says it will take 30. More recent studies suggest that it will be 100 years.

Mercury poisoning is known as **nimass aksiwin**, "fish disease" in Cree. According to Cree fisherman George Lameboy:

> Nimass aksiwin strikes at the very heart of our society. It's like being told that Armageddon has started, and people are scared as hell. The scientists come in here and tell us we're getting better [by eating less fish], but hey, you can't measure the effects of nimass aksiwin by taking hair samples. How can you measure a man's fear? How can you measure your way of life coming to an end? (Richardson 1991:xi)

The protests to stop Great Whale have been far-reaching and dramatic. The most dramatic was a specially made canoe, named *Odeyak*, which sailed down the Ottawa and Hudson rivers to New York City, capturing the attention of the international media. The Cree have questioned the environmental, ethical, economic, and social benefits of Great Whale. People seem to be listening; the Second Phase was blocked.

The Cree's fight continues. Not long prior to the Referendum in Quebec in the fall of 1995, the Cree issued a declaration that if Quebec separated from Canada, they would separate from Quebec. The main legal argument they put forth in their massive document was that Quebec had failed to live up to its part of the bargain concerning the James Bay and Northern Quebec Agreement of 1975. More recently, the Cree have been trying to stop the sale of environ-mentally sensitive forests in Northern Quebec to forest-product companies.

Native Individuals 16-1

Billy Diamond: Chief of the Waska-ganish band of the James Bay Cree during the negotiations for the James Bay Agreement.

KEY TERMS

Category 1
Category 2
Category 3
nimass aksiwin (Cree)

CONTENT QUESTIONS

1. Under what conditions was the province of Quebec given its northern territories?
2. What had been done to resolve Cree aboriginal rights prior to the announcement of the James Bay project in 1971?

3. What was the Malouf Judgment?

4. How did the Quebec provincial government counteract the Malouf Judgment?

5. What has been the main environmental problem affecting the health of the Cree?

 **WEBLINKS**

arcticcircle.uconn.edu/CulturalViability/Cree
An excellent starting point for issues relating to the Cree in Quebec, including articles on the James Bay Agreement.

http://www.waseskun.net/cree.htm
Information about the Cree legal struggle in opposition to the Great Whale project.

www.gcc.ca/Political-Issues/jbnqa/jbnqa_menu.htm
The Web site of the Grand Council of Cree concerning the James Bay and Northern Quebec Agreement, which includes the text of the agreement.

COLONIALISM

OVERVIEW

In this section, you will read about the negative influence of European, or Euro-Canadian colonialist forces (sometimes the word "settlers" is used) on Natives in Canada. It is good to keep in mind when reading this that there are numerous examples of Natives successfully resisting outsider influence. As this introductory piece shows, "resistance is (and was) not futile" (see Box 17.1).

RELIGIOUS COLONIALISM: THE SUPPRESSION OF THE POTLATCH

There are no mainstream Western cultural events that can directly compare with the potlatch ceremony of the peoples of the Northwest Coast. The potlatch is both sacred and a good time. It is like a combination of a Christmas mass, a christening, a confirmation, and the Bible, a country's constitution and a legal contract, a movie based on a true story and live theatre, a drug- and drink-free rave, the ballet and an art exhibition, an old-style storyteller and a mandatory course in local history. It is unique.

Potlatches are traditionally centred on hereditary names. They are religious ceremonies, often brought about by births, coming-of-age events, marriages, and deaths. They demonstrated that the individuals and groups hosting the potlatch were socially, economically, and spiritually worthy of such an important inheritance. Names are connected with specific

BOX 17-1   Resistance Is Not Futile: The Case of Mikak, a Labradormiut (Labrador Inuit)

Mikak was born around 1740. She met her first Kablunat (European) in September 1765 when Moravian missionaries were forced by a storm to stay in a tent in her camp. She got along well with the German-speaking Moravians, but her next meeting with Kablunat would not be so friendly. The next year, 200 to 300 American whaling vessels worked the Labrador coast, killing Inuit as well as whales. The Inuit struck back against all Kablunat. In November 1767 they attacked a fishing station in the southern part of Labrador, killing three, driving off the rest, making off with the boats, and burning the establishment to the ground. The British commander of the timber blockhouse fort built in Chateau Bay the year before sent out troops under Lieutenant Francis Lucas in retaliation. They killed at least 20 Labradormiut and captured nine women and children. Included in their number were Mikak and her son, Tootac. They spent the winter in the fort.

Mikak impressed her captors so much that she was selected by Newfoundland Governor Hugh Palliser, along with her son and an older boy, Karpik, to travel to London. Palliser's purpose was to impress upon Mikak that the English were so numerous and powerful that her people should respect them, be at peace with them, and trade with them.

In London, Mikak received two kinds of treatment. On the one hand she was treated royally in London, receiving an expensive, gold-trimmed dress from the Dowager Princess of Wales, Augusta,

was given a king's medal, and had her portrait painted in her new dress by society artist John Russell. On the other hand, people reacted to her very much as if she were some species of zoo animal. According to Moravian missionary James Hutton, the Labradormiut woman was "stared and gaped" at rudely by the English, in a way that was "offensive to modesty and Humanity." In London, Mikak encountered Moravian missionary Jens Haven, whom she had met in Labrador, and learned of his desire to obtain a land grant for a mission post on the Labrador coast. Mikak seems to have been sympathetic to Haven's cause. She had reason to be. The times were dangerous on the Labrador coast. Inuit travelling in reported numbers of 200 and 300 suggests as much a defensive as an offensive strategy. A young woman with a family would have good reason to argue for peace. While meeting with English high society, she promoted the cause of the Moravian land grant. Her efforts helped them receive 100,000 acres on May 3, 1769.

Mikak and her son were returned to Labrador by Lieutenant Lucas in the spring of 1769. She did not perform the propaganda role Governor Palliser had planned for her. Like other Natives who had been taken to Europe, she was not overawed by alleged European "cultural superiority." This was apparent in July of 1770 when she was visited by Haven and Christian Drachart at Byron Bay. She graciously greeted them wearing her fancy gown and medal. However, the

continued

continued

two Moravians made a speech concerning their mission plans, sternly warning Mikak's people that they would severely punish theft or murder by the Labradormiut. Mikak was not appreciative of this insulting accusation of her people and replied to the missionaries that she was "sorry to hear that we had such a bad opinion of their country people," pointing out that the Kablunat also stole from her people. Still, she expressed support for their mission, as they offered a way of peace.

Once the missions were set up at Nain (1771), Okak (1776), and Hopedale (1782), raiding between the Inuit and Europeans essentially stopped. Sometime after her arrival back in Labrador, she married her second husband, Tuglavina. The two of them guided the missionaries north and helped them pick a suitable site, which would become the first mission post of Nain. Both Mikak and Tuglavina enrolled in baptism class but chose to live apart from the mission and neither proceeded far along the Christian path at that time.

Mikak would never be baptized. Perhaps this was because of the restrictions the Moravians placed on their Inuit mission charges. While the Moravians were a source of European goods, they put what (to the Inuit) were severely restrictive conditions on the trade. They didn't provide gifts of food or other valued objects, as Inuit traders did their partners and as European traders in the south did as well. They likewise did not provide credit, both standard practice and a necessary aspect of trade. The Moravians did not trade in guns or ammunition, a sign of mistrust. They also tried to limit Inuit movement away from the supervised area of the mission post, even though the Inuit needed to travel to hunt caribou, a staple of their diet. They wanted to separate Christians from the influence of non-Christians. Traditional food-sharing feasts were forbidden because they brought Christian and traditional Inuit together.

Mikak and Tuglavina frequently quarrelled. Eventually she separated from him, marrying a man named Serkoak in 1783. Despite her early support of the Moravian cause, she chose not to live at a mission station and regularly travelled to the European trading posts on the south coast. She only moved to Nain in the year of her death, in 1795. Upon her return, she was reported as saying that she had not forgotten her early Christian lessons. It seems that while accepting the peaceful alternative of the Moravians to the more violent European ways that preceded them, she would not let them dominate her life, anymore than she would her ex-husband Tuglavina.

stories, songs, dances, carved and painted images, and the rights to fish, hunt, or harvest plants in a particular territory. Along with these rights come the responsibilities of passing down and performing well those art forms, conserving the life forms in their territory, and maintaining the strength and social unity of the group. The potlatch reinforced the values of those sacred duties. James Sewid, a Kwakiutl of high rank, received the following names during the ceremony that followed his birth in 1913. The Kwiksutainuk and Mamalilikulla are Kwakwaka'wakw peoples.

I received my father's father's name from the Kwiksutainuk people, Owadzidi, which means "people will do anything for him because he is so respected." My mother's father Jim Bell, was from the Mamalilikulla people and I received the name Poogleedee from him, which means "guests never leave his feasts hungry." I received the name Waltkeena, which was from Chief Goatlas of the Mamalilikulla and means "something very precious has been given to us." I received the name Sewid after my father and his father, which means "paddling towards the chief that is giving a potlatch." (Spradley 1969:16)

What happens at a potlatch? Stories are told, stories that go deep in time, often relating back to the first ones who held the names being validated. These stories are not just told, they are also acted, sung, and danced. Sacred masks are often used to depict the characters involved. Sometimes strings are pulled that change the face of the mask to indicate some change that happened to the person portrayed by the mask.

A key component in the potlatch is giveaway. The word "**potlatch**" means "to give" in the Chinook trade language. While giveaway is a major component of Native ceremonies across North America, the amount of giveaway involved in a potlatch was on a scale un-equalled elsewhere. The Kwakiutl word for potlatch is derived from **pasa**, meaning "to flat-ten," implying that the ones receiving the gifts would be flattened by the large number of gifts given to them. One of the most lavish potlatches ever recorded by non-Native writers was, not surprisingly, given by Maquina of the Nuu'chah'nulth. In his potlatch of 1803, he was reported to have given away 200 muskets, 200 yards of European-manufactured cloth, 100 shirts, 100 looking glasses, and seven barrels of gunpowder. How much he gave away in Native goods such as wooden carvings, Chilkat blankets, and salmon was not written down, possibly reflecting the bias of the non-Native writer as to what was important.

Some misleading assumptions should be cleared up. No one individual owned the large amount of gifts that were given away. The person hosting the potlatch traditionally drew upon his connections of family, secret society, clan, or moiety to get those gifts together. This collection could take a long time as more and more people were included in the giving circle. Traditionally, two kinds of people attended a potlatch: hosts, who were involved with the bringing together of the gifts, and guests, who received the gifts. Second, no one did without anything important for survival in order to give something away. The gifts tended to be more luxury items than necessities. Blankets, either Native-made or obtained through trade with the Hudson's Bay Company, were major potlatch gifts. And the gifts circulated around. At one potlatch you might be of the hosting party, then a guest at the next.

The Competitive Element

The fact that the Northwest Coast peoples were hierarchical contributed to an element of com-petition in the potlatch. One proof that a high-ranking man was worthy of his position was how much he could give away at a potlatch, particularly to other people of high rank, who would be given the largest number of gifts.

The greatest gifts were coppers. These treasured items are sheets of copper shaped like shields and covered with designs painted on with black lead. They traditionally came from copper that was mined in Alaska. Coppers have names, just as people do, putting them in the class of non-human persons, an important element in Northwest Coast as in all Native spirituality. One copper is particularly famous to anthropologists and to students of anthropology, as a part of its story was recorded by the famous anthropologist Franz Boas in his stay with the Kwakiutl in the winter of 1894–5. The name of the copper was **Maxtsolem**, meaning "One of whom all [other coppers] are ashamed [to look at; i.e., because they are not Maxtsolem's equal]." At a potlatch held that winter, a high-ranking man named

Owaxalagilis was attempting to buy Maxtsolem. He began by placing 1,200 blankets in front of the chief who was hosting the potlatch. Walas Nemogwis of the Wewamasquem clan of the Mamalilikulla nation then owned Maxtsolem. The speaker in the following quote is Yaqalenlis, a high-ranking man who had once purchased Maxtsolem and who wanted to encourage Owaxalagilis to really prove his worthiness by purchasing the copper with more gifts than anyone else had ever done before. He began his speech by announcing his name and telling of its history:

> The name began at the time when the world was made. I am a descendant of the chiefs about whom we hear in the earliest legends. The Hoxhoq came down to Xoxopa, and took off his bird mask and became a man. Then he took the name Yaqalenlis. That was my ancestor, the first of . . . [the Kwiksutainuk]. He married Laqoagilayuqoa, the daughter of Walas Nemogwis, the first chief of the great clan Wewamasquem of the . . . [Mamalilikulla] . . . . (Kehoe 1992:439)

He then challenged Owaxalagilis by bragging about what he paid for the copper:

> I know how to buy great coppers. I bought this copper Maxtsolem for 4,000 blankets . . . What is it, Owaxalagilis? Come, did you not give any thought to my copper here? You always say that you are rich, Chief. Now give more, that it may be as great as I am. Give only ten times 100 blankets more, Chief Owaxalagilis. It will not be much, give 1,000 more for my sake . . . . (ibid.)

Owaxalagilis ended up paying 4,200 blankets for the copper.

The level of competition involved in the giveaway part of this religious ceremony rose with European contact. This is partially because more goods became available with Native success in the fur trade, as the people obtained more and more European luxury goods. But there was another, more negative cause. European diseases hit the people hard. The Kwakwaka'wakw, for example, dropped in population from 8,000 in 1835 to around 2,000 in 1885. This disturbed the usually straightforward process of the inheritance of names, typically a choice between brothers, with the eldest having the best chance. However, when diseases wiped out whole lineages, more distant relatives could sometimes vie for prestigious names. The possibility existed for competition for names that would be socially divisive and destructive. Another factor that could possibly result in heightened competition would be when formerly separate peoples within nations would move into the same area, as happened at Fort Rupert with the Kwakwaka'wakw. While the ranking of names within any one of these peoples was clearly established, there were no traditional rules to follow when several peoples all participated in the same potlatch.

One point should be made here. There were incidents in the nineteenth century in which property was destroyed to show wealth and in which competition took a violent turn. But such incidents were rare. Unfortunately, they were over-reported in local mainstream papers and by anthropologists, who were often interested in the study of conflict. Both kinds of reporting could make outsiders overlook the overall good that came from the potlatch. Condemning the potlatch for these incidents would be like using the conflict between Irish Catholics and Protestants as a reason for banning Christianity.

The Banning of the Potlatch

Missionaries who came to the Northwest Coast tended to see the potlatch as "the enemy," or at least the competition. William Duncan, who worked with the Tsimshian, wrote in 1875 that the potlatch was "by far the most formidable of all obstacles in the way of Indians becoming Christians, or even civilized." Some missionaries made giving up sacred potlatch items, such as masks, as a condition of becoming a Christian. During the 1870s, government officials involved with Natives would have been nervous reading newspapers about what was going on in the American West. It was the decade in which the Apache leaders Cochise and Geronimo and the Nez Perce Chief Joseph successfully eluded the American army for years on end. In June of 1876, Lakota Sioux leaders Sitting Bull and Crazy Horse triumphed at the Battle of the Little Bighorn. In Canada, the First Riel Rebellion of 1869–70 was fresh in people's memory and government officials would be hearing rumours and reading reports of discontent among the Métis that would lead to a second conflict in 1885. So the missionaries and officials pushed for and successfully achieved the banning of the potlatch in 1884. The law read as follows:

> Every Indian or other person who engages in or assists in celebrating the Indian festival known as the "Potlatch" or in the Indian dance known as "Tamanawas" [the Spirit Dance of the Salish] is guilty of a misdemeanour, and shall be liable to imprisonment for a term of not more than six nor less than two months in any gaol or other place of confinement, and any Indian or other person who encourages, either directly of indirectly, an Indian or Indians to get up such a festival or dance, or to celebrate the same, or who shall assist in the celebration of same, is guilty of a like offense, and shall be liable to the same punishment.

The U.S. government was slower to act against the potlatch, waiting until the early twentieth century to do so. In Canada, the ban was extended to the Sun Dance of the Prairies in 1895. By 1914, Natives could not wear traditional clothing or perform dances even at fairs or stampedes without the written permission of the Indian agent.

The people resisted. When Franz Boas came to study the Kwakiutl in 1886, he was told that if he was there to oppose the potlatch, he should leave. Their often-quoted declaration to him includes the following words:

> We will dance when our laws command us to dance, we will feast when our hearts desire to feast. Do we ask the white man, "Do as the Indian does"? No, we do not. Why then do you ask us, "Do as the white man does"?

> It is a strict law that bids us dance. It is a strict law that bids us distribute our property among our friends and neighbors. It is a good law. Let the white man observe his law, we shall observe ours. (Nabokov 1991:227)

In 1896, three Nisga'a Elders sent the following petition, which was published in the *Victoria Daily Colonist*:

> If we wish to perform an act moral in its nature, with no injury or damage, and pay for it, no law in equity can divest us of such a right. We see the Salvation Army parade through the streets of your town with music and drum, enchanting the town . . . We are puzzled to know whether in the estimation of civilization we are human or fish in the tributaries of the Na'as River, that the felicities of our ancestors should be denied us. (Dickason 1997:261)

Most resistance was covert and the potlatch went underground. For that and other reasons, the anti-potlatch law was difficult to enforce. In 1889, Kwakiutl Chief Hamasak was convicted and sentenced to the maximum sentence of six months. But Chief Justice Matthew Baillie discharged him on a technicality, noting that the law was imprecise.

James Sewid records the following almost comic situation concerning the potlatch that inducted him at 16 into the very important Hamatsa Society. The potlatch had been reported and an R.C.M.P. officer was sent from Ottawa to investigate. He asked the people to show him what they did. According to Sewid:

> He demanded to see it that night, so we put on a good show for him. The dances we did were all mixed together and not in the right way we had been doing them. I was dancing with a fool's mask on along with a group of [people wearing] masks. The mounted police was standing on one side of the house while the big dance was going on and one of our people was interpreting to him what it was all about . . . . (Spradley 1969:92–3)

At the conclusion of the ceremony, the R.C.M.P. officer declared:

> I'd like to see the young man that went through this thing. I'd like to see him dance for me tonight because I was sent here to investigate this young man. I want him to dance with everything he had on, all his masks and everything. I want him to do it just like the way he did it last week. (93)

James Sewid then heard from the village leaders that he would have to dance for the officer:

> So I got all my stuff on and the others who were dancing my dances and came out [and] started dancing. After I came out my masks came out and danced. At the end he got up and thanked the people and said, "It was a wonderful dance. I really enjoyed it. I can't see anything wrong with it." (ibid.)

After that, the officer left for Ottawa.

But not all cases ended so positively. In 1921, 45 of the highest-ranking Kwakiutl were arrested. Twenty-two were sentenced to prison terms of two to three months. The tragedy was twofold. First, the leaders of a community were taken from their people. Compare it with going to a small town and locking up the CEOs of the most successful businesses, the mayor and councillors, priests and ministers, police chief, fire chief, and teachers. Second, their sacred items were also taken. The condition upon which the others were let go was that the coppers, masks, and other objects integral to the ceremony had to be surrendered. Compare that with taking the company ledgers, the local law books, the Bibles and altars, and the textbooks and lesson plans. The comparison isn't completely fair, as the potlatch items were one of a kind. The items were dispersed as personal possessions of the minister of Indian affairs, art collectors, and museums.

In 1951, the potlatch ban was repealed (some 17 years after the Americans did it). In 1969, the people started negotiating for the return of their sacred things. In 1975, the National Museum of Man declared that it would return the items on the condition that they would be kept in museums. One, the Kwakiutl Museum of Cape Mudge, opened in 1979, and the other, the U'mista Cultural Centre ("u'mista" means "a special return") opened in the 1980s. In 1988, the Royal Ontario Museum returned the items it had and the National Museum of the American Indian in New York repatriated some objects in 1993. Some items have still not been recovered.

Selling the Sacred Objects of the Tsimshian

The fight for respect for the potlatch still goes on. Consider the following case. In the 1860s, Reverend Robert Dundas, a young Anglican missionary from Britain, received some goods. The person who is believed to have given him those goods was Tsimshian Chief Paul Legaic of Fort Simpson by the Nass River in northern B.C., the richest and most powerful of the

Tsimshian leaders in the nineteenth century. The goods included beautifully crafted wooden masks, rattles, dolls, and wooden instruments. Dundas was able to obtain these goods in this way because Legaic had become a Christian. The missionaries forced Tsimshian, who became Christian, to give away sacred objects related to the potlatch ceremony, the most treasured cultural objects of the people. Giving away the objects was a condition of becoming a Christian. Being a Christian could give a Tsimshian some advantages in trade with non-Natives and Legaic wanted to maintain his strong position in the trade. To do so, he sacrificed his people's traditions. Still, it would not be fair to judge him harshly. We don't know how much freedom of choice he really had.

Dundas took these items back to Britain, where he sold some, gave others away to museums, but kept the better part of his collection, displaying them in his home. After his death, they were kept in a box. When his daughter died in 1948, they were saved from being discarded by Dundas' great-grandson Simon Carey. He kept them at his home and his children played with them.

Carey is now a retired professor of psychology and has been trying to sell the collection in one piece. He has entertained Canadian offers from the Museum of Civilization, the Royal Ontario Museum, and Canada Heritage, but they could not pay the price he was asking.

He has put the collection, now worth an estimated $5,000,000, in the hands of the prestigious auction house of Sotheby's, which will publish a catalogue and mount an exhibit, giving Native scholars and anthropologists an opportunity to study the pieces. Carey says that he is willing to provide Native carvers and scholars access to the collection so they can make copies. However, Sotheby's has made a point of having the collection travel only to London, Paris, and New York, with no Canadian destinations, fearing the Canadian government would seize the collection. The director of Sotheby's American Indian art department says "We wouldn't want to put the collection at risk."

Who owns the collection? What should be done with the pieces? These questions can only be answered once other questions are asked. Did Legaic have the right to give away the pieces? According to Art Sterrit, former president of the Tsimshian Tribal Council, they did not really belong to Legaic, but to the clan to which he belonged. He only had the rights to use them in ceremony. Is that similar to a priest and the sacred objects that belong to his church, or with the British Queen and her crown? Were the objects coerced from him through "undue duress"? Can we say that they were "stolen" by the missionaries? Morally, we can readily say that they were. How should the Canadian courts interpret this?

An example to follow might be that of the Zuni in the United States. The Zuni, a nation of more than 7,000 people living in the southwestern United States, have had legal success in retrieving their Ahayuda. These are 18-inch wooden war gods, carved once each year during their winter ceremony. In 1968, they sought all Ahayuda that had left their reservations to go to art galleries and museums. In their words, "Putting a war god under glass is not preserving culture. The way you preserve Zuni culture is by using the war gods in the living ritual for which they were created" (Rajotte 1998:94). They stated that Ahayuda belonged to the whole nation, so by definition, all Ahayuda not on tribal land would be considered stolen. In 1978, agents of the United States government halted the auctioning of an Ahayuda in a gallery in New York. Dozens more have been returned from museums all over the U.S.

Native Individuals 17-1

Paul Legaic: A rich and powerful Tsimshian chief of the nineteenth century.

Mikak: An eighteenth-century Labrador Inuk woman.

Timeline 17-1

1860s: Tsimshian leader Paul Legaic is pressured into giving up sacred potlatch goods as a condition of becoming a Christian.

1884: The potlatch is banned in Canada.

1889: Kwakiutl Chief Hamasak is convicted and sentenced to the maximum sentence of six months, but is discharged on a technicality.

1895: The Sun Dance is banned in Canada.

1914: Natives are prohibited from wearing traditional clothing or performing dances publicly without the written permission of the Indian agent.

1921: Forty-five of the highest-ranking Kwakiutl are arrested. Twenty-two are sentenced to prison terms of two to three months.

1951: The ban of the potlatch is repealed.

1975: The National Museum of Man declares it will return sacred items on the condition that they are kept in museums.

1979: The Kwakiutl Museum of Cape Mudge is built and receives sacred potlatch items.

1980: The U'mista Cultural Centre is built and receives sacred potlatch items.

1988: The Royal Ontario Museum returns sacred potlatch items.

1993: The National Museum of the American Indian in New York returns sacred potlatch items.

1999: A descendant of the missionary who received sacred potlatch items from Legaic puts together, with Sotheby's, a travelling show of the collection with the aim of selling the items at auction.

KEY TERMS

Ahayuda (Zuni)
copper
pasa (Kwakiutl)
potlatch (Chinook)
u'mista (Kwakiutl)

CONTENT QUESTIONS

1. What is the potlatch?
2. Who worked to have the potlatch banned?
3. For how long was the potlatch banned in Canada?
4. What else was banned?
5. What happened to the sacred potlatch items that Legaic was forced to give away?

 WEBLINKS

www.anu.edu.au/~e950866/potlatch
An excellent resource for learning about the potlatch ban, this site is the product of combined law-school courses in B.C. and Australia.

www.civilization.ca/membrs/fph/tsimsian/intro00e.html
The Museum of Civilization's virtual exhibition, "From Time Immemorial: Tsimshian Prehistory."

www.inac.gc.ca
The Web site of the federal Department of Indian and Northern Affairs.

www.si.edu/nmai/nav.htm
A revealing example of a leading museum, the Smithsonian's National Museum of the American Indian.

NATIVE
HEALTH ISSUES

COLONIALISM AND HEALTH

The Smallpox Story

No European disease had a larger impact on peoples in the Americas than smallpox. From the first case in Mexico in 1520 until 1618 (after the Cortés conquest), it reduced the population there from about 20 million to about 1.6 million. At various times and places, as we will see, it had a similar impact in Native Canada.

Why was the impact so high? The disease was a European one, an offshoot of cowpox. As Europeans and Asians had cows and Natives did not, the disease first struck people of those lands. The descendants of people that had survived the great smallpox infestations in European and Asian countries had to a significant extent inherited the immunities with which the survivors were lucky enough to have been born. No such immunities existed for Natives; they were completely vulnerable.

One of the nastiest stories concerning smallpox that can be found in the historical literature relates to Jeffrey Amherst, the commander-in-chief of the British forces in America during the so-called "Pontiac Uprising" (named after an Odawa leader). This uprising consisted of a series of battles in which a number of First Nations of the Great Lakes were using the struggle between the French and British as an opportunity to assert their own independence. Amherst, who had a very poor understanding of aboriginal peoples and the lack of sympathy that so often goes along with such a state of ignorance, distrusting and alienating his own Native allies, suggested in June of 1763 that blankets infested with smallpox be distributed to Natives as presents. While smallpox did hit a number of groups at that time, to the best of our knowledge a deliberate policy of germ warfare was not practised by the British at that time. Still, the very idea that such a practice was being considered says a lot.

Accurate figures concerning the death toll of smallpox are hard to come by. Non-Native writers recording the numbers at the time often lacked contact with all the bands or groups of a particular First Nation and thus were unable to arrive at a reliable figure. The oft-repeated one-third death toll in the interior of British Columbia in 1862 has been challenged by some historians (Fisher 1977:21–2). Still, it can be stated that the effect was uniformly devastating where it hit. The following are figures from across the country at different times. Even if they only represent part of a people or are somewhat high, they still document a series of tragedies.

TABLE 18-1	Smallpox Chart	
Date	**People**	**Estimated Decline**
1640s	Mohawk	75%
1781	Chipewyan	90%
1782	Stó:lo	62%
1837	Blackfoot	50%
1835–40	Tlingit	50%

The Inuit and Tuberculosis

While tuberculosis has hit all Native groups hard, it has been particularly devastating for the Inuit. During the 1940s, the mortality rate from this disease was roughly 1,000 per 100,000 population, about 25% higher than that of other Natives and about 20 times that of the general Canadian populace. About 20% were said to have been infected in 1950. During the 1950s, they had the highest rate of tuberculosis in the world.

The negative effects of tuberculosis were not just physical. The loss of family, language, and culture were also results. Beginning in 1947, when x-ray surveys to detect the disease were conducted across Inuit territory, most people identified as having tuberculosis were flown away from family, friends, and community to sanatoriums in the south. They stayed there, with little or no contact with the north, for long periods of time. In the Charles Camsell Hospital in Edmonton, for example, the average length of stay was 28 months.

Some never returned home. One in five Inuit were said to have been afflicted in 1950. One in seven were flown south for treatment. Most returned, but some disappeared. Children were adopted into White families even though their Inuit parents were not dead. Some families never discovered what happened to those who died. In 1989, a program was initiated that attempted to uncover the records of those Inuit who had died of tuberculosis at the Mountain Sanatorium in Hamilton, Ontario, and had vanished from the view of their relations. Seventy bodies have been tracked down through that program. In 1995, **Joanasie Salomonie** travelled to Hamilton to attend the dedication of a monument erected as a memorial to 39 Inuit buried anonymously in the poor person's section of a cemetery there. One of the graves belonged to his father. In Salomonie's words:

I buried something there . . . I buried all my negative feelings and thoughts. I felt a lot of anger for a lot of years. But I'm OK now; it cured me of the negative things. I'm satisfied. (Bergman 1996:67)

Alcohol

Wilfred Pelletier, Ojibwa writer, educator, and activist of the 1960s and 1970s, wrote the following in 1973 of White hunters and their attitudes towards giving alcohol to him, their Native guide:

Most of them wouldn't offer me any drink at all because I'm Indian—like I go wild when I drink! So they wouldn't offer me the drink. But then sometimes a guy would. He'd ask me, though; he'd say, "This stuff won't get to you, will it chief?" And I'd say, "Well, I don't know. Don't you ever get drunk?" and he'd say, "Oh yeah." "Well, I get drunk sometimes," I'd say. (Pelletier and Poole 1973:91)

One of the most damaging stereotypes of all concerning Natives is the stereotype of the drunken Indian. A trip to downtown Toronto, Winnipeg, Regina, or Vancouver confirms it with a few examples, for non-Natives who have walked by many Natives they didn't "see" because those Natives didn't fit into the stereotype.

The myth that Aboriginals generally are "biologically helpless" to resist alcohol is believed by many people, including, unfortunately, many Natives. However, it has never been clearly established that Natives as a group metabolize alcohol significantly differently from other groups.

As the quote above illustrates, one of the more destructive aspects of this stereotype is the myth of biological helplessness in the face of alcohol, which is a belief that Natives have no control when they drink. This myth is well developed in literature. Look at the following words from Diamond Jenness, whose *Indians of Canada* was probably the single-most influential book about Natives in Canada in the twentieth century. Although first published in 1932, reprints continue to be made and can be found in bookstores even now. According to Jenness:

The Indians . . . had no alcoholic beverages in prehistoric times, and from the earliest days of settlement they abandoned every restraint in their frenzy for the white man's firewater. (Jenness 1932:253)

BOX 18-1   Trapped by the Law

Sometimes drinking patterns affected by the old laws helped to contribute to the stereotype of the drunken Indian. Consider the following scenario described by Wilfred Pelletier in 1973:

There are still some reserves where drinking is against the law, so Indians go into town and buy a bottle or maybe two. They can't take it home and drink it, and it's against the law to drink in a public place. So what do they do? They go in a back alley or maybe in a men's can and they knock the whole bottle off real quick. So then there are some drunken Indians staggering around the town, because drinking that fast will knock anybody on his ass. (Pelletier and Poole 1973:90)

Federal policy was influenced by this misconception. Parts of the Indian Act strictly restricted Native contact with alcohol. Section 94 of the Indian Act reads as follows:

94. An Indian who

a) has intoxicants in his possession,

b) is intoxicated, or

c) makes or manufactures intoxicants off a reserve, is guilty of an offence and is liable on summary conviction to a fine of not less than ten dollars and not more than fifty dollars or to imprisonment for term not exceeding three months to both fine and imprisonment. (as quoted in Kulchyski 1994:51)

The Flow of Profits: Alcohol in the Fur Trade

The myth of biological helplessness developed within a specific historical context: the fur trade. There was a brutally profitable economy to including alcohol in the trade. One keg of brandy could fetch as many furs as an entire canoe-load of useful goods. From at least the 1660s on, when English traders literally poured alcohol into their trade with the Mohawk, an overwhelming amount of alcohol was part of the fur trade. This was especially true when there was competition between companies, primarily the Hudson's Bay Company and the Northwest Company. The amounts of alcohol traded were staggering. At the Hudson's Bay Company trading post of York Factory, on the west side of Hudson Bay, the amount of rum traded per year rose to a peak of 864 gallons by 1753. Between 1720 and 1774, 21,634 gallons of rum were traded from that post alone. It was only in 1822, after the merger of the Hudson's Bay Company and the Northwest Company, that the H.B.C. seriously attempted to restrict the amount of alcohol that was involved in its business.

The destructive influence of alcohol was very real, of course, as can be seen in this sad story told by **Pahtahsegua** (Reverend Peter Jacobs), a Mississauga teacher, preacher, and writer, in a letter published in the *New York Christian Advocate* of June 17, 1836. After speaking generally of the devastating effect alcohol had on the Mississauga, he spoke in more personal terms:

[M]y father and mother died when I was very young, in drinking the fire water to excess . . . My sister and brother-in-law then took me to bring me up. But in a short time they died also in drinking the fire water to excess. My sister was frozen to death on a drinking spree, on new year's day . . . And in about one year from this time one of my sisters, in a drunken spree, was struck with a club on her head by her husband, which caused her death. And in the same year my brother was tomahawked in a drinking spree . . . . (Schmalz 1991:133)

BOX 18-2	**Terms for Alcohol**	
Language	**Term**	**Translation**
Ojibwe	shkodewaaboo	fire water (Rhodes 1985:617)
Blackfoot	naapiaohkii	white man's water (for whisky)

Although Pahtahsegua went on to publish a small volume describing his travels and to preach to the Saulteaux out west, he eventually "became 'constantly bedevilled by heavy drinking and sank into poverty and oblivion'" (ibid.).

Still, claims of Native biological helplessness were exaggerations, connected in part with the notion that Natives were a vanishing inferior race, doomed to extinction. The hypocrisy of loading up the trade with alcohol and then blaming the results on Natives' nature was seen quite clearly by nineteenth-century Ojibwa writer George Copway, in a best-seller for its time, *The Traditional History and Characteristic Sketches of the Ojibway Nation* (originally published in 1850):

> The ministry of this country, and the sluggards in the cause of humanity, say now: **There is a fate or certain doom on the Indians, therefore we need do nothing for them**. How blasphemous! First you give us rum by the thousand barrels, and, before the presence of God and this enlightened world, point to God, and charge him as the murderer of the unfortunate Indians. (Copway 1972:264–5)

Historical examples of individuals or groups resisting alcohol seem to have been down-played or ignored, even in some relatively recent works. Consider the following quote from Isabel Thompson Kelsay's biography of the Mohawk leader Joseph Brant, winner of several prestigious awards and published in 1984. The quote here is about Handsome Lake, the Seneca prophet who recovered from an alcohol problem through a series of visions of the Creator from 1799 to 1801. Among other benefits to his people, the teachings he developed based on his visions resulted in his lifetime in an effective temperance and sobriety move-ment. This had a dramatic, positive impact on the Seneca and related peoples (see Wallace 1969:303–10) for quite some time. Still, Kelsay felt compelled to toss off this one-liner about Handsome Lake in his pre-vision years:

> No one thought any the less of a head man of the Senecas who bore the name of The Drunkard and, indeed, *it appears that almost any Indian anywhere could have borne that name.* (Kelsay 1984:29; authors' emphasis)

Perhaps one factor in the perpetuation of the myth of Native biological helplessness with respect to alcohol lies with its connections to some of the romantic heroism of part of Canadian history. As Daniel Francis, in *The Imaginary Indian: The Image of the Indian in Canadian Culture* (Francis 1992) points out, some early historians of the R.C.M.P. (such as Sir Cecil Denny, himself former R.C.M.P.) colourfully exaggerated Native helplessness in the face of American whisky traders in Alberta in order to enhance the heroic image of the beginnings of the force. The Northwest Mounted Police, precursor of the R.C.M.P., did shut down the infamous Fort Whoop Up in a display of praiseworthy courage. However, distorting that fact with allusions to Native inferiority does not do justice to that brave tale.

The Brutal Statistics

The statistics concerning Natives and the negative impact of alcohol are brutal. Alcohol's relationship to high rates of kidney problems, injury, crime, accidental death, murder, and suicide cannot be ignored. Rather than dragging out the numbers at length, one statistic will be used here: alcohol involvement in homicides. The numbers used here are from Ontario between 1980 and 1990:

	Natives on Reserves	Natives off Reserves	Non-Natives
Drinking involved	67%	65%	20%
Suspect drinking	64%	57%	15%
Victim drinking	57%	59%	15%
Both drinking	54%	52%	11%

Two points need to be made here. One is that there are striking differences between communities. Some have fewer problems with drinking than do most non-Native communities. Further, there are a number of ways in which numbers such as arrest records related to alcohol, particularly off-reserve, reflect discriminatory practices that should be stopped. The problem lies as much with the non-Natives as with the Natives. Consider the following picture depicted by David Stymeist in his classic portrayal of "Crow Lake," a railway town in northwestern Ontario in the 1970s:

> Ontario Provincial Police cars park outside the entrance to the Crow Lake Hotel, the town's largest central pub, for an hour or so before and after the pub closes. The waiters will ask a drunk white man, who is perhaps a relative, friend or steady customer, if he wants to call a cab. The cab will arrive at the back door of the hotel and the man in question will leave unseen. Many Indians, however, are arrested as they leave the pub, and some have been arrested for public drunkenness as they were climbing the stairs to their rooms in the hotel. (Stymeist 1977:79)

Natives brought into the police station for drinking are also more likely to be charged and brought to court. A study by University of Regina Professor James Harding, published in 1980 (*Unemployment, Racial Discrimination and Public Drunkenness in Regina*), revealed that 30% of the Aboriginals arrested for drunkenness were charged and sent to court, while the figure was only 11% for non-Natives (as reported in York 1990:148).

BOX 18-3   Ted Nolan:
The Power of a Stereotype

Ted Nolan is an Ojibwa who has both played and coached in the National Hockey League (N.H.L.). He won the Jack Adams Trophy for the N.H.L. coach of the year in 1997 and was fired that same year. From that time until the writing of this piece (March 2000), he has not been able to get another N.H.L. coaching job, even though 30 have opened up. He feels this has racist connotations. Perhaps the following story has had an impact on his ability to return to the N.H.L. He has spent about 15 years visiting reserves and advising Native children, particularly teenagers, against the abuse of drugs and alcohol. When he was still coaching in Buffalo, he missed a couple of practices. The rumour began that he had been drunk for three days. His response in an article written in February 2000 was as follows: "That really hurt. It never happened but the damage was done; because I'm a Native guy, people assume that I drink too much. And that's not true."

THE STORY OF MINNIE SUTHERLAND:
DEATH BY STEREOTYPE?

On New Year's Day in 1989, Minnie Sutherland, a 40-year-old Cree woman from Moose Factory, was struck by a car in downtown Hull, Quebec. She was struck on one side of her head and then hit her head again on the road. It was about 3:30 a.m. and Minnie, her cousin, whom we will call "Jean," and a few hundred others were milling around the street, unwilling or unable to get home.

The car that struck her was driven by two off-duty nurses, who quickly stopped and got out of their car when they heard the bump and saw the Cree woman fall. They checked her over a bit but could discern nothing other than her eyes showing that she had severe eye trouble (she had been declared legally blind but could still see using her thick glasses) and that her breath indicated that she had been drinking. Three male university students saw the accident and moved towards the scene to see if Minnie was okay. Two stayed with her while another went to call 911. Two young male police officers noticed the sudden stoppage of traffic and got out of the van they were driving to see what had happened. One of the students told him, in English and in French, that a car had hit the woman. One of the officers asked Jean what had happened. Minnie's cousin wasn't sure (she hadn't actually seen the accident) and just made reference to the fact that they had been drinking.

The officers then attempted to lift Minnie up to a sitting position. One of the students was upset by this, knowing that accident victims should not be moved until medical help arrives, and shouted words to that effect at the officers. One officer told the student to leave and said that he would be arrested if he didn't keep quiet. Their confrontation would go on and off over the next little while.

The officers asked the nurse who had been driving whether the car stopped was hers and then requested that she move it. The nurse didn't want to leave until she knew for sure that Minnie was okay and wondered at the casual attitude of the officer concerning an accident victim. According to John Nihmey, author of *Fireworks and Folly: How We Killed Minnie Sutherland*, who had access to the transcripts of the hearing that would follow, the attitude of the officers was that:

> They were perplexed by what seemed to be an overreaction to a drunk woman who had either slipped on an ice patch and fallen, or walked into a car that couldn't have been going very fast given all the traffic. (Nihmey 1998:82–3)

The officers first picked Minnie up and deposited her in a snowbank at the side of the road, then asked Jean whether she and her cousin wanted them to call a taxi. Jean said that she did. At about the same time, the third student returned, saying that Hull didn't have 911 yet so his attempt to get help had failed. Another one of the students suggested an ambulance. That sounded like a better offer than a taxi so Jean changed her mind and told the police. The officer called into Hull Police Headquarters concerning the call for a taxi, saying "Cancel the taxi now. The squaw decided otherwise" (Nihmey 1998:84). The police then left, satisfied that the matter was finished.

The students and the two Cree women went into a restaurant, with the students and Jean supporting Minnie in a standing position. The students, feeling that Minnie was looking a little better (although she was barely conscious), and wondering whether the police might have been right in treating the matter lightly, left. Two men then picked up the two women and drove them to Ottawa. But seeing the state that Minnie was in and not getting a positive response from Jean, the men called 911 and dropped the women off beside a restaurant on Nelson Street.

Native Individuals 18-1

Ted Nolan: An Ojibwa who played hockey and coached in the N.H.L.	**Minnie Sutherland**: A Cree woman living in the Hull-Ottawa area whose death from a car accident and subsequent neglect was the subject of a book.

A female police officer responded to the call. What she encountered was a Native woman with alcohol on her breath and another one who had passed out. The conscious woman said that they had been drinking. The officer tried to rouse Minnie to consciousness but failed. An ambulance pulled up and a paramedic checked Minnie over. He stated that she was drunk and suggested that the officer take her to a detoxification centre. The ambulance then left.

The officer took Minnie to the detox centre but staff wouldn't admit her because of a policy of not taking non-ambulatory people. It was now about 5:00 a.m. The officer then drove Minnie to her station and conferred with her sergeant. He checked Minnie over and seems to have concluded pretty much that he saw what he expected to see: a Native woman, smelling of alcohol, who had passed out, and another drunken Indian. Still, he recommended that the officer drive Minnie to a nearby hospital.

Minnie arrived at the hospital at approximately 5:45 a.m. She stayed there until she died on January 11 of a cardiac arrest, ultimately the result of a blood clot in the back of her brain caused by her accident. The doctors at the hospital had been unaware of the blood clot and hadn't felt her case was serious enough to warrant an MRI (Magnetic Resonance Imaging). This was new technology at that hospital with a long waiting list. On January 17, a doctor from the hospital sent the following letter to the Hull police:

> There is no doubt that the lack of information about the traumatic event was of great significance in making the initial diagnosis of the abnormality and in following this up to a logical conclusion which may have been able to prevent her demise. It is also unfortunate that Mrs. Sutherland received powerful antibiotics for her condition which would not have been necessary had this history been available. The antibiotics do have their own particular risks.
>
> In particular, if the allegations of the conduct of the Hull Police are correct, then a serious error of judgment has been made by the officers concerned and this should be investigated. (Nihmey 1998:163)

An investigation was held. A coroner's jury ruled in March that Hull police should offer compulsory courses to sensitize officers to the needs of visible minorities, but four out of the five jurors felt that racism was not a factor in the case. The Quebec Police Commission also cleared its officers of racism charges in 1990.

KEY TERMS

myth of Native biological helplessness

CONTENT QUESTIONS

1. Why did smallpox have such a devastating effect on Native peoples?
2. How did the treatment of tuberculosis hurt Inuit families?
3. Is there any physical reason why so many Native people have problems with alcohol?
4. In Stymeist's account, why is it that more Natives than non-Natives were arrested for drinking in the Crow Lake hotel?
5. How did the stereotype of the "drunken Indian" contribute to Minnie Sutherland's death?

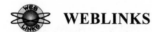 **WEBLINKS**

www.health-sciences.ubc.ca/iah/indexnf.html
The Institute for Aboriginal Health is part of the University of British Columbia. It works on Aboriginal health issues at both the policy and the practical levels, and the site contains a very good list of other health-related sites under the heading "Links."

http://afn.ca/Programs/Health%20Secretariat/Default.htm
The Assembly of First Nations Health Secretariat's home page, including links to various reports.

http://www.hc-sc.gc.ca/msb/fnihp/index_e.htm
Health Canada's "First Nations and Inuit Health" Web page, including discussion of its tuberculosis elimination strategy.

19

COLONIALISM, NATIVE EDUCATION, AND "CHILD WELFARE"

INTRODUCTION

A good introduction to this section comes from the words of Ojibwa writer George Copway, or Kahgegagahbowh ("He who stands forever," 1818–69), from his 1850 best-seller *The Traditional History and Characteristic Sketches of the Ojibway Nation*:

> Much has been lost to the world, through a neglect of educating the red men who lived and died in the midst of educational privileges, but have not been allowed to enjoy them. They hold a key which will unlock a library of information, the like of which is not. It is for the present generation to say, whether the last remnants of a powerful people shall perish through neglect, and as they depart bear with them that key.
>
> Give the Indian the means of education and he will avail himself of them. Keep them from him, and let me tell you he is not the only loser. (Copway 1972:viii)

Look at how similar the sentiments of that last sentence are to those articulated by Reverend Edward Ahenakew, a Cree graduate of the University of Saskatchewan, in an article published in the *Saskatchewan Daily Star* on June 1, 1918. In arguing for the government to put more money into Native education, he said:

> Surely the government is not thinking of being hampered by a race of ignorant and non-self supporting people for all time to come . . . Conditions as they are are neither fair to the Indians nor to the white people who have to live in the same country with them. (as quoted in Barman, Hébert, and McCaskill 1986:12)

TWO SEVENTEENTH-CENTURY STORIES

From the early 1600s in New France, Europeans coming to Canada felt that they needed to take Native children away from their homes, their parents, their families, friends, and community in order to better educate them. From that early beginning it was an overwhelming failure but the Europeans never seemed to learn that important lesson. This would have devastating results in the twentieth century. Two stories from the seventeenth century will serve as early illustrations of repeating patterns.

The first is the story of **Pastedechouan**. His story shows the dangers of education making a person neither Native nor non-Native. He was an Innu (Montagnais) sent to France as a child in 1620, where he was baptized as Pierre Antoine and where he studied French and Latin for five years. When he returned, he spoke French well but had nearly lost his language, which he had to relearn. He had also missed an important part of his traditional education as a hunter and would repeatedly fail at that activity. One of his brothers would once tell a missionary that he "gets lost in the woods like a European" (JR7:173). He spent some time with the English when they controlled the Quebec area for a short time. They encouraged him to question what the French priests had taught him. They also introduced him to alcohol, which he would have difficulties with on a number of occasions.

In the 1630s he was torn between two groups of people. Jesuit Father Paul Le Jeune wanted to learn the Montagnais language from him and aid in the religious conversion of Pastedechouan's people. Pastedechouan translated for Le Jeune and instructed the missionary in the language and in some of the customs of his people. His older brothers took care of him and felt that he would rot if he adopted the sedentary life of the French (JR7:91). In honest words that would reveal the turmoil that would be echoed in the minds of twentieth-century students of residential schools, Pastedechouan said:

> I see clearly . . . that I am not doing right; but my misfortune is that I have not a mind strong enough to remain firm in my determination . . . When I was with the English, I allowed myself to be influenced by their talk; when I am with the Savages, I do as they do; when I am with you, it seems to me your belief is the true one. Would to God I had died when I was sick in France, and I would now be saved. (JR7:89–91)

Le Jeune lived and travelled with Pastedechouan and his brothers and was quick to condemn him, typically referring to him as the Apostate and the Renegade. Pastedechouan's life was difficult. He would be the speaker who would translate the words of antagonism between his eldest brother (a shaman) and Le Jeune. His ineptness in the skills of his people made him the butt of jokes made by the women living with them. A council of those women condemned him for not bringing back food from a feast for his wife to eat. He got married several times but could not keep a wife.

Eventually, as his brothers died young of European diseases and other causes, he was left on his own. In 1636, he died alone in the woods.

The second story comes from Mother Marie de L'Incarnation of the Ursuline order, who had, in 1668, around 30 years of experience trying to educate Native children by boarding them apart from their people. While couched in prejudicial terms of "civilized" and "savage," it contains the vital message that separating Native children from their families for education purposes is wrong, a message that should have been listened to 300 years later:

> [W]e have remarked that out of a hundred that have passed through our hands scarcely have we civilized one. We find docility and intelligence in them, but when we are least expecting

it they climb over our enclosure and go to run the woods with their relatives, where they find more pleasure than in all the amenities of our French houses . . . [T]hey cannot be constrained, and if they are they become melancholy . . . [T]he Savages love their children extraordinarily and when they know that they are sad they will do everything to get them back....(as quoted in Jaenen 1986:58)

Unlike their colleagues in the twentieth century, the Ursulines would give the children back in such situations.

ONTARIO SCHOOLS FOR OJIBWA IN THE FIRST HALF OF THE NINETEENTH CENTURY

During the first half of the nineteenth century in what is now Ontario, a number of schools for the Mississauga developed, largely through the efforts of the Methodist church. These schools were arguably as good as any in the country at the time, but they still tended to promote Christianity and Western culture generally at the expense of Native culture. In 1830, there were 11 such schools, none better than the school that was found in the middle of the community of the Mississauga of the Credit. The following description of this school comes from William Lyon Mackenzie in a *Colonial Advocate* article of December 30, 1830. It well illustrates the culture of the school. He describes the one-room school building as being large:

with tiers of raised benches in the rear; on one division of which sit the girls, and the boys on the other. There are also desks and slates for ciphering and copy books and copper-plate lines for those who write. The Bibles and Testaments are chiefly those of the London Society for Promoting Christian Knowledge . . . Among the school-furniture, are a handsome map of the world . . . attractive alphabets on pasteboard; regular figures illustrative of geometry . . . a clock . . . . The walls of the school are adorned with good moral maxims . . . [including] *"No blankets to be worn in school."* (Mackenzie in Fairley 1960:46; authors' emphasis)

A number of well-educated people would graduate from those schools (including the best-selling writer George Copway, who was quoted at the beginning of this chapter), but they would often have a hard time fitting in as people "between two worlds." A good example of this is Kahkewaquonaby ("Sacred Feathers") or Peter Jones (1802–56). He went to the United States and Britain and successfully raised funds for Native education. An accomplished writer, he translated hymns and parts of the Bible, and wrote the popular, posthumously published *History of the Ojebway Indians*. Yet there was a low cloud ceiling to his flights of accomplishment. He was denied a mission of his own, even though he was more than qualified for the position. Likewise, the Indian Affairs department didn't give him the job he very much wanted, despite the support of the influential Egerton Ryerson, his good friend. An ex-military man, scarcely experienced with Natives, and not knowledgeable in Native matters, was given the job. Such a clipping of his eagle wings was a source of frustration for Sacred Feathers in his later years.

Furthermore, he seemed to have something of an ambivalent attitude towards the culture of his people. The following idea about how Native schools should be run sounds very similar to one of the main goals set by later residential schools: "Let all the children be placed entirely under the charge and management of the teachers & missionaries, so that their parents shall have no control over them" (memorandum: "Thoughts on Indian Schools" (1835) as quoted in Miller 1996:80).

BOX 19-1 — Oronhyateka ("Burning Cloud"): How Peter Martin Became a Doctor

Oronhyateka (Burning Cloud) or Doctor Peter Martin (1841–1907) was a Mohawk whose success story is one of determination and courage. He became the head of the Independent Order of Foresters (I.O.F.) in 1881 at a time when it had a debt of $4,000 and a Canadian membership of 369. At his death, the I.O.F. had accumulated funds of $11 million and a membership of more than 250,000. His early ambition was to be a doctor, but a lot of obstacles were in his way. This is the story of how he got his education:

> Attending a local school until he graduated at 14, on his own youthful initiative he took himself far afield to the Wesleyan Academy in Wilbraham, Massachusetts. With little money, he earned much of his board and tuition by cutting wood and performing similar chores [he would jokingly say that it kept him in bread, no butter]. After two years he graduated first in his class.
>
> A year's teaching at a newly-opened school on his home reserve [of Six Nations] was just a momentary break for money and family. Soon he was off to Kenyon College in Gambier, Ohio, from which he graduated in three years. Always possessing a showman's flair, he earned money running a "Wild West" show in which he dressed up white men as Natives.

Oronhyateka's greatest ambition was to become a doctor. But no Native had ever received a university degree from a Canadian university. Lack of money and opportunity, and no lack of prejudice, had proven formidable obstacles. In 1860 Oronhyateka had just managed a year at the University of Toronto, straining his always meagre financial resources. Opportunity and his own ability were soon to bring him the chance of a lifetime.

He had been chosen by the Six Nations leaders to address the visiting Prince of Wales, later Edward VII. As the most educated person in the community, he was probably picked because of his facility with formal, educated English. But that was not what the Prince was to hear. Proud of his heritage, Oronhyateka addressed the Prince in Mohawk, translated by an interpreter.

The Prince of Wales was so impressed by this, and by the story of the young man's determined fight for education, that he invited Oronhyateka to study at Oxford, under the supervision of Sir Henry Acland, Regius Professor of medicine and the Prince's personal physician.

After three years at Oxford and a final year at the University of Toronto, Oronhyateka became a doctor. (Steckley 1987)

Industrial and Boarding Schools

Gradually, a system of "industrial schools" was developed during the nineteenth century. In many ways, these schools combined academic studies with more practical matters, like what you might find in a technical high school or at a community college. From 1879 on, they were modelled after the Carlisle Indian School in Pennsylvania, established in 1878 by Lt. Richard Henry Pratt. What could be called the mission statement of this influential school was Pratt's motto of what the school should do for the Native student: "Kill the Indian in him and save the man." The most effective weapon for "killing the Indian" in the students was taking the children away from their homes and often their home communities, thus separating them from their supports.

But, literally, the most deadly aspect of these schools was the death rate. The federal government funded these schools and religious denominations ran them. Students weren't forced to go to school. In 1900, of the roughly 20,000 Status Indians between the ages of 6 and 15 at that time, only 3,285 were in the 22 industrial schools and 39 boarding schools. Students numbering 6,349 went to 226 day schools. The schools, which were paid according to the number of students attending, recruited even sick children. The tough economics of these schools meant that dormitories were poorly heated and overcrowded, ideal conditions for tuberculosis, which was the leading killer. The same economy meant that the food was less than adequate when it came to nutrition.

In 1904, Doctor P.H. Bryce was appointed medical inspector for Indian Affairs and the Department of the Interior. He was conscientious about his job, so, in response to his superior's request in 1907 that he inspect health conditions in the industrial and boarding schools, he performed a thorough job. His alarming report found its way to the national media, the *Montreal Star* and *Saturday Night* in particular. In the latter magazine, one editorial read that "Even war seldom shows as large a percentage of fatalities as does the educational system we have imposed upon our Indian wards" (as quoted in Fournier and Crey 1997:49).

The figures in question included a 24% death rate of aboriginal children in 15 prairie schools. At File Hills industrial school in Saskatchewan, 69% died of tuberculosis during one decade (Fournier and Crey 1997:58).

Indian Affairs, hearing horror story after horror story, seems to have developed a callous attitude in its approach to the problem, as is indicated in the following often quoted remark from a deputy superintendent general of Indian Affairs:

> It is quite within the mark to say that fifty per cent of the children who passed through these schools did not live to benefit from the education which they had received therein. (as quoted in Miller 1996:133)

Nothing significant was done to improve the situation. Although the death rate would decline, death would become part of the residential school tradition.

Sifton's Two Faces

Sir Clifford Sifton was brought to a federal ministerial position with the election of Wilfred Laurier's government in 1896. He opposed the relatively "good" (relative to the residential schools) education that Natives were receiving in the industrial schools. Two reasons he gave for this opposition were contradictory, leaving the reader to suspect deep anti-Native prejudice on his part. On the one hand, speaking to the House of Commons in 1897, he clearly displayed a "there is only so much room in the lifeboat" mentality when he stated that "we are educating these Indians to compete industrially with our own peoples, which seems to me a very undesirable use of public money" (as quoted in Barman, Hébert, and McCaskill 1986:7–8). On the other hand, in a speech to the House of Commons in 1904, he spoke of the inherent "racial" inability of Native people to get educated and prosper (perhaps he did not know about Burning Sky and others like him). He felt that:

> . . . the attempt to give a highly civilized education to the Indian child . . . was practically a failure. I have no hesitation in saying—we may as well be frank—that the Indian cannot go out from school, making his own way and compete with the white man . . . [The Indian] has not the physical, mental or moral get-up to enable him to compete. He cannot do it. (House of Commons, *Debates 1904*, 6948, 6956; as quoted in Miller 1996:134–5)

The failure of Native students of industrial schools to get jobs had a lot more to do with the "we-they" attitude of people like Sifton, who were much more willing to hire "our people" than they were to hire Natives.

Dumbing Down the Native Schools

In 1910, the federal government decided that a series of changes was needed in its schools. It decided to put most of its Native education eggs into the basket of residential schools. It would provide the money while religious groups such as the Catholic, Anglican, United Church, and Presbyterian churches would deliver the education. The government generally provided funding that was insufficient so schools had to run themselves like self-sufficient businesses. "Student workers" were removed from classes so they could do the laundry, heat the buildings, and perform the farm work in order to cut down expenses.

These schools would have an even greater impact on Natives in Canada once attendance was made compulsory in 1920.

The curriculum would suffer in this new regime. Following the notions of Sifton and others like him, the academic goals of residential schools were "dumbed down" from those of their predecessors. The statement was that they would be educating the Native student "to fit the Indian for civilized life in his own environment." What did this mean? It meant that they felt that although the students should learn mainstream Canadian culture, they should be prepared for life on reserves only, apart from the bad influences in Canadian towns and cities. The protective aspect was particularly aimed at Native women. Minister of Indian Affairs Duncan Campbell Scott felt that they should be kept on the reserves away from White men of the "lowest type" (Barman 1986:120).

What did this mean for the curriculum? In Scott's words:

> To this end the curriculum in residential schools has been simplified and the practical instruction given is such as may be immediately of use to the pupil when he returns to the reserve after leaving school. (ibid.)

They didn't want students who would be, as Scott stated about the girls, that were "made too smart for the Indian villages" (ibid.).

This ran counter to what was going on elsewhere in Canada, where, throughout the twentieth century, it was increasingly felt that students required more education, not less, to succeed.

ABUSE

The worst aspect of the residential schools, why they might readily qualify as the single-worst thing that Europeans did to Natives in Canada, was the abuse: emotional, physical, and sexual. J.R. Miller, in his classic study of residential schools, identifies emotional abuse of enforced loneliness as the form of abuse "that probably did the most harm because it was the most pervasive and enduring done to students" (Miller 1996:337). The residential schools

BOX 19-2   Punishment for Speaking Mi'kmaq

Isabelle Knockwood attended the Shubenacadie residential school in Nova Scotia. Her book, *Out of the Depths*, is an eloquent and tragic portrayal of life in a residential school. During her first year at Shubenacadie, she witnessed the following violent punishment of a little girl who had spoken Mi'kmaq:

> The nun came up from behind her and swung her around and began beating her up . . . then the Sister pinched her cheeks and her lips were drawn taut across her teeth and her eyes were wide with terror . . . Then the nun picked the little girl clean off the floor by the ears or hair and the girl stood on her tiptoes with her feet dangling in the air . . . The nun was yelling, "You bad, bad girl." Then she let go with one hand and continued slapping her in the mouth until her nose bled. (Knockwood 1992:97)

were basically designed to keep children from the "bad" influence of their parents. Children were taken from their parents and extended families for periods of time that often lasted the whole school year, even when the residential schools were located in the students' own communities. Parental visits, when they were permitted, were typically closely monitored in a special "visiting room." Brothers and sisters were often kept apart in strict sexual separation, sometimes meaning that the children could only communicate with each other by waving from one building to another or through secretly arranged meetings.

Miller tells the story of a Cree woman who went to File Hills residential school. Her community was only 19 kilometres away but it might as well have been on the other side of the world. A fence surrounded the school property and the students. For hours on end, she and her friends would stand at the corner of the fence that was closest to their reserve. According to Miller:

> She would put her hand through the fence, because that meant she was closer to her home and family by the length of her arm and hand. Other times, she would observe the place where the road emerged from the trees and watch for her parents. She would say to herself, "the next black horse that comes along" will be drawing her parents' wagon on a visit. Disappointment only led to repetitions of the childlike incantation, a wish and a prayer that never seemed to come true. (Miller 1996:338–9)

All studies show that a very high percentage of physical and sexual abusers were abused once themselves. Sexual abuse has been identified as the number one social problem in a good number of Native communities. Studies conducted at Hollow Water in Manitoba and Canim Lake have reported that at least 75% of their members experienced unwanted sexual contact as a child. The chain of abuse began with the residential schools. Girls and boys alike were sexually assaulted by priests, nuns, doctors, teachers, and principals who worked for residential schools.

Short of funds and often desperate for staff, particularly after 1945, the residential schools were often careless when hiring. As J.R. Miller cleverly words it, the schools would often end up employing the "devoted and the deviant" (Miller 1996:321). These could range from the merely incompetent to sexual predators and outright sadists. Punishment was not merely strict, it could be brutal and cruel, life-threatening and life-ending. Children had pins stuck in their tongues for speaking their Native language, they were punched in the face, and scarred for life by studded belts. Punishment could be humiliating, as when bed-wetters had to walk around the school with their damp sheets on their heads, and sadistic, as when a boy was forced to eat porridge onto which he had poured salt. He threw it up and was forced to eat that twice until he fainted. Punishment could also be sexualized, as when girls were caught stealing food and were forced to stand in a line in front of the whole school with their skirts up and their genitals in full view.

It is small wonder why a good number of former residential school students have, like war veterans or police officers, been diagnosed as suffering from Post-Traumatic Stress Disorder. They exhibit symptoms such as panic attacks, insomnia, uncontrollable/un-explainable anger, alcohol and drug abuse, sexual inadequacy or addiction, the inability to form intimate relationships, and eating disorders.

When the students left the schools, they often had little experience of the caring parenting traditional to the people. Instead, they had been "parented" by outsiders, a few of them "nice," some of them "nasty," much more of them strict and impersonal. Three generations of parents would be influenced by these models when they became parents.

Legal charges began in the late 1980s, a few years after the last residential school closed. One of the more spectacular cases involved a Catholic bishop, the former principal of St. Joseph's residential school in British Columbia. After four years of prosecution, he was finally convicted of raping one girl (now a chief) and sexually assaulting another, resulting in a sentence of two-and-a-half years. In 1995, a male supervisor at Port Alberni school was imprisoned for 11 years after pleading guilty to sexually assaulting 18 boys between the ages of 6 and 13 between 1948 and 1968. Around the same time, the churches that ran the schools all issued formal apologies, beginning with the United Church in 1986 and followed over the next eight years by the Anglican Church, the Canadian Conference of Catholic Bishops, and the Presbyterian Church.

STEALING THE CHILDREN: THE SIXTIES SCOOP

> The harm we do children always becomes known in the end, even though we believe it to be well-hidden.
>
> –Huron-Wendat writer Georges Sioui, summing up one of the main moral messages of the traditional stories of his people (Sioui 1999:37)

In 1951, the Indian Act was changed so that provincial authorities would be responsible for the welfare of Indian children. This had little effect initially. This can be seen in the British Columbia statistic for 1955 in which 29 of the 3,433 children placed in protective care in the province were Native, less than 1%. Starting in the 1960s, however, aggressive policies of taking Native children from their families, communities, and from the Native world generally came into play. In British Columbia in 1964, the figure became 1,446 Native children out of a total of 4,228 children, or 34.2%. In his book *Native Children and the Child Welfare System,* writer Patrick Johnston coined the term "Sixties Scoop" to refer to the forced migration of aboriginal children.

The situation was the worst in Manitoba. Between 1971 and 1981, over 3,400 Native children were taken from their homes and removed from their province. More than a thousand of these children were sent to the United States, where there was a demand for children to adopt. American agencies could get $4,000 for every child placed. Native children in the United States had been adopted in a similar way until 1978, when the Indian Child Welfare Act was passed, protecting the children from being taken from their people (see Box 19.3).

About 300 of the Canadian Native children went to Pennsylvania alone. A study of 100 of those children showed that they suffered more problems than any other children "of colour," including African-Americans, Vietnamese, and Koreans. By 1995, five had died, about one half had experienced "difficulties involving identity issues," only about one third had completed high school, and about the same percentage had lost all touch with their adoptive parents.

In 1982, the Manitoba government finally agreed to impose a moratorium on the export of children outside of the province, the last province to do so. There was an investigation into the practice. Justice Edwin C. Kimelman wrote a report in 1985 entitled *No Quiet Place*, based primarily on looking at the 93 children that were "exported" in 1981. He did not mince his words in his conclusions, saying:

> cultural genocide has been taking place in a systematic routine manner. One gets an image of children stacked in foster homes as used cars are stacked on corner lots, just waiting for the right "buyer" to stroll by. (as reported in Fournier and Crey 1997:88)

Two Manitoba Stories

Cameron Kerley

Two well-reported biographies of Manitoba Native children born in 1964 tell the stories for the others. **Cameron Kerley** was removed from his family when he was eight years old. His father had been killed in a fight and his mother was drinking heavily, creating a

---

BOX 19-3   Indian Child Welfare Act

The Indian Child Welfare Act (I.C.W.A.) was passed in 1978 by the government of the United States. It applies to any un-married person under 18 who belongs or is eligible to belong to an "Indian tribe" in the United States. The declared pur-pose of the I.C.W.A. is "to protect the best interests of Indian children and to promote the stability and security of Indian tribes and families." In an infor-mation sheet put out by the Wabanaki of Maine, under the question "What does the law do?," this answer is given:

> The I.C.W.A. requires that placement cases involving Indian children be heard in tribal courts if possible

[some of the First Nations in the United States have their own courts], and permits a child's tribe to be involved in state court proceedings. It requires testimony from expert witnesses who are familiar with Indian culture before a child can be removed from his/her home. If a child is removed, either for foster care or adoption, the law requires that Indian children be placed with extended family members, other tribal members, or other Indian families. (see web site www.ptla.org/wabanaki/icwa.htm)

There is no such law in Canada.

physical condition that would kill her two years later. Cameron and his three sisters were placed in non-Native foster homes. At the age of 11 in 1975 he was sent for adoption to a single man in Wichita, Kansas. While living there he was beaten and sexually abused by the man whose surname he still bears. The authorities should have been aware of the signs of trouble. He was skipping school and running away from home for days on end. This happened before the adoption was made legal in 1977; they could have taken him away. School counsellors and social workers attempted to help him but he couldn't speak of what was happening. In Cameron's words:

> I didn't trust them, . . . I wasn't able to tell them. I felt helpless. At that point there was nobody I could turn to for help. I was a kid, taken away from home . . . and put into a situation I didn't ask to be in. (Yorke 1990:211)

He was afraid to tell them what was happening for fear it would get worse. He had run-ins with the police. In 1978, at 13, he ran away only to be picked up by the police. At 17 he dropped out of school and was soon arrested for burglary. At 19 he moved away from his abusive adoptive father. His initial plans were to find his way back to the Manitoba reserve in which he was born. But he got drunk one night, returned to his "home," and killed his adoptive father with a baseball bat. He was sentenced to 18 years but after two years was transferred to Stony Mountain Penitentiary, north of Winnipeg. At least there he would be with others who would know from their own experiences what he had been through.

Carla Williams

Carla Williams was a Saulteaux from southern Manitoba. Her parents were alcoholics who had their four children taken from them in 1968. Her father hanged himself a few years later and her mother also committed suicide at a later date. In 1972, Carla was placed in "permanent" adoption with a Dutch couple who were in Canada but were returning to the Netherlands. It looked good on paper for the child welfare agency as the man was a prominent physician. But the adoption broke down after six months and Carla was fostered out. Unfortunately, her adoptive father received visitation rights. He got her pregnant twice, the first time when she was 14, the second time when she was 15. Both children were taken away from her. She was placed in a series of Dutch orphanages and mental institutions, worked as a prostitute for a while, and tried unsuccessfully to commit suicide.

Her luck changed somewhat when she met a group of Natives from Manitoba at a conference. They put her in touch with a Native-run agency that enabled her to obtain a passport and the funds necessary to return to Canada. In 1989, at Winnipeg International Airport, she saw her brothers and sisters for the first time in over 20 years.

Stó:lo Stories

Ernie Crey is a Stó:lo who co-authored the powerful book *Stolen from Our Embrace: The Abduction of First Nations Children and the Restoration of Aboriginal Communities* (Fournier and Crey 1997). It is a book of incredible tragedy as well as a book offering hope, an amazing combination. In Chapter 1, "The Perpetual Stranger: Four Generations in My Stó:lo Family," Crey courageously tells his own story. His father died in 1961 when Crey was 12. His mother, without the strong support of her husband, and without any job skills, fell into depression and alcoholism. All but one of her children were taken away from her within a few months of the death of her husband. They would never be reunited as a family. Crey was driven away in an R.C.M.P. cruiser to spend his first week away from home in a prison cell. He had been skipping school and had shoplifted (so did John Steckley, one of the authors of this book, at the same age, during the same year). The judge sentenced him to Brannan Lake Industrial School, which was rife with physical and sexual abuse.

Crey would not see his mother or any other member of his family for four years. They grew up within a few miles of each other but didn't know where the others were. Crey would go through several foster homes and a group home run by an eventually convicted pedophile. His brothers and sisters lived in foster homes where one was sexually abused and where their punishment for "misbehaving" included being locked in a closet, having their heads stuck in a toilet bowl while the toilet was being flushed, and being forced to shovel chicken excrement throughout the night.

One of the most moving elements of this story involves his mother's letters. She wrote letters to each of her children and gave them to the social workers, hoping they would be passed on. They weren't. Crey was shown those letters as an adult by a sympathetic social worker. According to Crey, in those letters:

> . . . my mother poured out her fears and concerns for me and tried to reassure me that she still loved me, that I should never think she did not. She told me how much she missed me and thought of me. And in one letter, she had an ingenious plan. The social workers would not tell her exactly where I was, but she proposed that I meet her one Saturday at a tiny park in Abbotsford . . . I couldn't help but wonder how many times she had driven by that park, looking for me. (Fournier and Crey 1997:35)

WHY TAKE THE CHILDREN AWAY?

Why did they take these children from their homes and from their people? There are a number of reasons. Part of it is cultural. Non-Native social workers and agencies have in their minds a set of ideas as to what a "family" and a "good home" are like. For family, they think of two parents and their children, the nuclear family. However, there are strong traditions in Native cultures in Canada that think of family as something larger than this (see Box 19.4). This is well expressed in the words of **Wilfred Pelletier**, an Odawa from Wikwemikong on Manitoulin Island who wrote in 1973 (when he was 45) of what family was like when he was growing up. The same story could be told in many places across Native Canada.

> If a man was having a hard time financially, it was quite common for someone in better circumstances to offer to take one of that man's kids and raise it as one of his own. So the child would have two sets of parents, and usually he'd end up with the name of his adopted parents just through usage. Of course, the child was free to stay where he chose, and often he would live with one set of parents for a while and then go home to the others. Either way, he went home. (Pelletier and Poole 1973:124–5)

Then there is the "good home" in terms of physical resources. For non-Native Canadians, this would include a separate bedroom for each child, sewage or a septic tank, and running water. Most Native houses, often structures designed by Indian Affairs, could not meet those "standards." In 1981, 33% of all on-reserve dwellings had more than one person per room, as compared with 3% in all of Canada (Frideres 1998:171). In 1963, less than 10% of all on-reserve houses had access to sewers or septic tanks, a figure that rose to around 55% by 1980 (174). Similarly, around 12% of those houses had running water in 1963, rising to about 70% by 1981 (ibid.).

BOX 19-4   My Mothers

Traditional aboriginal notions of family were different from what modern North Americans would expect. It is hard to use a few words to try to teach this idea. One way of doing this is with the term "my mother." The Huron in the seventeenth century used the term **"annen-en"** to address or refer to the woman who gave birth to them. But she wasn't the only one a child would refer to that way. It was also used for your mother's sisters as well. They would reciprocate with a term meaning "my child." Often, that person would live with you in the traditional longhouse, which could house 40 or more people. If you needed a mother, there was bound to be one around.

The notion of having a mother term used for mother's sisters is not unique to the Huron, nor restricted to the past. In contemporary Blackfoot, the noun **"iksísst"** refers both to one's mother and her sisters and the term **"miksísstsiksi"** means "my mothers" and refers collectively to one's mother and her sisters (Frantz and Russell 1995:51).

A similar linking together of terms occurred in some languages and cultures with fathers and their brothers. Likewise, the children of the mother's sisters and father's brothers (what were "cousins" in English terminology) would be considered "brothers" and "sisters." Take for example the word **"ndawemaa."** In Ojibwe, traditionally it was used in the following ways:

> Female's use: brother, mother's sister's son, father's brother's son

> Male's use: sister, mother's sister's daughter, father's brother's daughter

It had the meaning of "sibling of the opposite sex." There was a like term for "sibling of the same sex." The key thing to remember is that it meant including people that English speakers would call "cousins" into the circle of brothers and sisters.

Sometimes the children were taken away "for health reasons." This could mean that newborn infants needing to be in or near an urban hospital for treatment would be fostered to a non-Native family who lived nearby and would never be given back to their Native parents. This despite the fact that those parents had done nothing to abuse or even harm the children. In Manitoba, 79 Sixties Scoop children were removed in this way.

There were, of course, many cases where children were physically, emotionally, and sexually abused and should have been removed from their parents and other potentially dangerous members of their family. But that did not mean that the children would be better off away from their extended families, their reserves, and their people.

DIFFICULTIES FOR RECOVERY IN MANITOBA

Manitoba Natives, who had borne the major brunt of the Sixties Scoop, would also have the hardest time in overcoming its effects. On July 1, 1981, Dakota Ojibway Child and Family Services (D.O.C.F.S.) received its legal mandate and took over the care of 49 Native children who had been apprehended by Children's Aid societies. The road ahead of them would be difficult. Within three years, the number of children in their care rose to 115.

Between 1983 and 1987, the five Native child welfare agencies that had come into being had to face an increase in the number of registered Indian children in care, from 863 to 1,563.

The agencies were swamped with incidents of child abuse that were beyond their meagre resources to cope with adequately. The lack of formal training of many of their workers diminished their effectiveness. When the agencies were first formed, it was believed that "Native-run" would be a panacea that would soon solve everything, so they were not prepared for the increasing numbers of children needing care.

Much of the negative side of what was happening in Manitoba was revealed through the inquest following the death of **Lester Desjarlais**. Lester Desjarlais was Saulteaux, born in Sandy Bay, Manitoba, on June 7, 1974. He had an older brother and three younger sisters so he was the "baby" of the family. He had a hard life, particularly when he was 12 and 13. Before you read the following list of what happened to him during that period of his life, picture the kind of life you had and what happened to you at 12 and 13.

When he was 12 and 13, Lester

- weighed about 45 kilos and was a little over five feet tall
- often got drunk and high by sniffing solvents such as gas, cleaning fluid, plastic cement, etc.
- was raped by a large man from his community and was sexually molested by a male teacher
- got into a good number of fights and was beaten up several times at drinking parties at his mother's place
- was placed in several foster homes in his own community as well as one in Brandon
- was placed three times in the Seven Oaks Centre for Youth in Winnipeg
- was put in a group home in Sioux Valley, which he escaped from, stole a bicycle, and rode 200 kilometres towards home
- was twice admitted to the Brandon Mental Health Centre
- had his much-loved mother call the police on him
- committed suicide by hanging

The inquest into his death, beginning in April 1992, told a story of how the system had failed him, as it was continuing to fail other Native children. Painful truths were revealed by the actions of a few courageous women who faced the opposition of influential people in their communities for what they would reveal. The inquest showed the dark side of band and provincial politics. The band council was engaged in a power struggle with the D.O.C.F.S. Abusers were protected and child abuse continued because of the political power of certain male band councillors in the community. The D.O.C.F.S. did not want to go to non-Native agencies or professionals because this was felt to be a step backwards. For good historical reasons, it did not want to rely on outsiders; distrust was high. As the D.O.C.F.S. was the first of its kind, it had attracted a lot of attention from the media, academics, politicians, and Native leaders. As the "great Native success story," it had a lot of face to lose if it looked bad. Undoubtedly, the people, who had long rightfully criticized non-Native institutions, could imagine smug looks with "I told you so" written all over them. Outside agencies and the provincial ministry did not want to be seen as meddling, as racists, for stepping in and trying to resolve problems that were being reported. The provincial government did not want to have the opposition of Native leaders during an election year. All of this meant that the children were being sacrificed.

Native Individuals 19-1

Ernie Crey: A Stó:lo man and co-author of *Stolen from Our Embrace* (Fournier and Crey 1997).

Lester Desjarlais: A Saulteaux boy whose tragic story was told in *Flowers on My Grave* (Teichroeb 1998).

Kahgegagahbowh ("He who stands forever," 1818–69): George Copway, a best-selling Ojibwa writer.

Cameron Kerley: One of the Manitoba Native children involved with the Sixties Scoop, he was convicted of killing his abusive adoptive father.

Isabelle Knockwood: A Mi'kmaq writer/educator who wrote *Out of the*

Depths (Knockwood 1993), a moving book about the residential school experience.

Oronhyateka ("Burning Sky/Cloud," 1841–1907): Doctor Peter Martin, a Mohawk whose hard work made him a doctor and the successful head of the Independent Order of Foresters.

Pastedechouan: A seventeenth-century Montagnais whose education in France forced him to live between two cultures.

Carla Williams: A Saulteaux woman whose failed adoption through the Sixties Scoop led her to the Netherlands and a great deal of hardship.

KEY TERMS

annen-en (Huron)
miksisstsiksi (Blackfoot)
residential schools
Sixties Scoop

CONTENT QUESTIONS

1. What two contradictory reasons did Clifford Sifton give for changing industrial schools?
2. What happened to the curriculum in residential schools in 1910?
3. To what does the term "Sixties Scoop" refer?
4. How many Native children were taken out of Manitoba between 1971 and 1981?
5. What is the Indian Child Welfare Act?

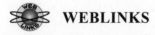 **WEBLINKS**

www.ptla.org/wabanaki/icwa.htm
See this Web site for information on the Indian Child Welfare Act.

afn.ca/Programs/Residential%20School%20Issues/Default.htm
The Assembly of First Nations on the residential-schools issue.

SOCIAL ISSUES:
THE DUDLEY
GEORGE STORY

THE NINETEENTH CENTURY

This story begins in the 1820s. Anishinabe originally from northern Ontario had moved south around a century and a half before and had become known in the south as Chippewa or Mississauga. Mixing with them a short time later were the Potawatomi, a closely related people being forced out of the United States.

The relationship between the Anishinabe people and the British government was changing. From the American Revolution to the War of 1812, they had been valued allies against the Americans. Now the land they lived on was considered more valuable than the services they could render to the Crown.

The "Chiefs and Principle Men of the Chippewa" signed a Provisional Agreement in 1825, which became the Treaty of Amherstburg in 1827. The Elders who signed this treaty had been born in a time when their people far outnumbered the newcomers. Now their people made up less than 10% of the population of Upper Canada (the heart of what is now Ontario). There were four bands and four reserves created by this treaty: Sarnia, Walpole Island, Kettle Point, and Stoney Point. The latter reserve was "two miles square at the River aux Sable which empties into Lake Huron."[1]

THE APPROPRIATION OF LAND

Slightly more than 100 years after the Treaty of Amherstburg, the people of Stoney Point band #43, whose name in Ojibwe is Aazhoodenaang Enjibaajig, were pressed by the federal and

BOX 20-1	A Soldier Returns Home

In 1993, a reporter covering a speech given at Trent University by Native Elder Clifford George, wrote:

> He told the crowd about when he returned home after fighting overseas in World War II. Upon his return, he found his people and his home uprooted and (mis)placed elsewhere. He said he'd been promised a forty acre plot of land when he returned from the war, and his father had also written to him overseas telling him not to worry as their land would be returned to them after the war.[2]

provincial governments to sell 377 acres in 1928 to "private interests." They really didn't have much say in the matter, as the federal government, through the Department of Indian Affairs, held primary responsibility for the reserve. Natives couldn't even vote in federal elections. In 1936, without the permission of the Stoney Point band, 108 of those acres were purchased to make Ipperwash Park. The people were not too happy about this situation, particularly because a cemetery had been dug into and violated during the making of the park in 1937.

Then came World War II. Natives volunteered to fight in numbers proportionately higher than any other group. In 1942, the federal government asked the Natives of the Stoney Point to make another sacrifice for their country, one not asked of others. The Department of National Defence, invoking the War Measures Act, appropriated the remaining land of the Stoney Point band, even though 85% of the members of the band were opposed to the appropriation. They would receive $50,000 in compensation for about 2,211 acres of land (about $23 an acre), plus they were promised that "if, at the termination of the war, no further use of the area is required by the Department of National Defence, negotiations will be entered into with the Department of Indian Affairs to transfer the lands back to the Indians at a reasonable price determined by mutual agreement" (Leaflet #4, PC2652).

On May 31, 1946, the "Advanced Infantry Training Centre" was closed but negotiations were not to follow. The armed forces continued to make peacetime use of the land that had been appropriated for war. From 1960 on it was used as a six-week cadet training camp and recreation facility.

It is hard for outsiders to understand the feeling concerning what happened. Imagine that your home is expropriated and you are forced to live in your parents' or some other relative's home. The Stoney Point people were forced to live in the less-than-prime territory of their Kettle Point neighbours and were not given the same number or quality of houses as those they had been compelled to give up.

TRYING TO REGAIN LOST LAND

While the Stoney Point people never stopped trying to regain their land and their community, it wasn't until 1981 that they achieved a measure of success. The federal government agreed to pay $2.4 million in compensation for the nearly 40 years of use they had had of the land. But the return of the land was delayed pending an environmental assessment and cleanup, which was necessary since the land had been used for shooting practice of a number of different weapons. This would put plans on long-term hold.

In 1985, a small step was made in that the members of the Kettle and Stoney Point band were permitted to hunt and fish on the land during provincially approved seasons. The Department of National Defence agreed to review the need for the camp for military purposes every four years. This wasn't much of a concession, as it would not voluntarily want to give up the land.

No changes were made in the situation until 1992. In March of that year, the Standing Committee on Aboriginal People tabled its report recommending that the federal government return the land to its former Aboriginal inhabitants and their descendants, saying that the government's reasons for continuing to occupy the land were "spurious and without substance." The Department of National Defence initially held its ground, literally. It replied to the Standing Committee in August, claiming that there was a continuing need for it to retain the Camp Ipperwash lands for military purposes. Eventually, the cadet camp was closed, but the department continued to assert possession of the land, agreeing merely to "consult" with the Kettle and Stoney Point First Nation, a word that Native people have learned to distrust.

In 1993, the Stoney Pointers took more radical steps to regain their land. On May 6, they moved on to the old firing range, living in makeshift dwellings such as small trailers and tents. They would be opposed on two fronts: Native and Armed Forces. In the former front, Tom Bressette, Chief of the Kettle and Stoney Point First Nation, showed his opposition to the move by asking the premier of the province to demand that it stop issuing general welfare to the Stoney Point people occupying Camp Ipperwash.

Why would he take such a position? Consider the following. Media attention could cast his band in a bad light, as it had done with the earlier confrontations at Oka and Gustafsen Lake. He knew that it was often not a good thing for a Native community to draw federal government attention to itself and for local non-Natives to see a First Nation as having a militant element. Finally, any action to split the band in two would diminish his budget, his power, and his general capacity to get things done in his community.

Chief Bressette and most of his council appear to have resented what they construed as "outsider" influence from the broader Native community. Gord Peters, Regional Chief of the Chiefs of Ontario, publicly advocated for resolution to the conflict. The council wrote to him, asking him to "refrain from your involvement with matters directly related to our First Nation."

On September 12, the Stoney Pointers occupying the base walked from Stoney Point, by the shores of Lake Huron, across the breadth of Southern Ontario to Ottawa, to press the federal government to recognize their rights. The trip took two and a half weeks. Along the way, they stopped at Peterborough, as the Trent University Native Studies department had organized a rally for them. Media coverage was light.

The relationship between the Armed Forces personnel and the Stoney Pointers deteriorated. Time, slowly escalating incidents of aggressiveness, and uncertainties concerning turnover upped the tension at Camp Ipperwash. On June 27, 1995, Glenn Morris George, then 34, angered by the fact that the army had placed iron "tire slashers" on the roadway leading to a burial ground, started to remove them. Captain Allan Howse saw this and got into a verbal fight with him. Following a series of events that took place between Glenn, Howse, and at least one other Armed Forces personnel, Glenn was charged with two counts of assault, one of mischief, and one of uttering a death threat. Howse alleged that Glenn drove a tractor that bumped an army truck, causing $900 damage.

BOX 20-2	Why Is Everyone Called "George"?

Why does everyone in this community seem to have the last name "George"? Do they all belong to just one family? No. Often there is a limited number of surnames in a Native community. In the same area the surname "Simon" and "Jacobs" also developed. Surnames were imposed on the people by missionaries and officials only over the last two centuries, a combination of administrative demands, plus an ethnocentric sense that Natives should be like "everybody else." Surnames for Europeans themselves are only a few centuries old. Think of the Bible, where no one has a last name.

Traditional Anishinabe naming traditions involve a person having one name, which could reflect a vision that the individual had or it could be something passed down.

On July 29, faced with a mutually confrontational atmosphere, the military (from 15 to 20 people) moved out and roughly 100 Stoney Pointers moved into the barracks. Cleve Jackson would later be charged with reckless driving when it was alleged that he drove a bus through the drill hall that day. Stoney Pointers would claim that he was not the driver of the bus, that the only reason that he was charged was because the Military Police saw his picture on the cover of the *London Free Press* and then decided that he was the culprit. Judge Louise Eddy dismissed the charges the next year.

The summer came to an end, unfortunately, with a passing written shot that would have repercussions later on. Kettle and Stoney Point Band Councillor Gerald George printed a letter in the local *Forest Standard*, which contained the following inflammatory remarks: "I am glad that these Army Camp Indians call themselves separate from my First Nation because I would not want any of my fellow band members to act like animals" (Forest Standard, August 30, 1995).

THE OCCUPATION OF IPPERWASH PARK

On September 4, 1995, at least 24 Stoney Pointers would occupy Ipperwash Park, which was closed because the summer tourist season was over. The Natives posed no physical threat to anyone. They expressed their concern about a sacred burial ground that was located in the park. This burial ground had been well documented in archaeological site reports on file at Queen's Park in Toronto and in Ottawa, but both the provincial and federal governments would deny knowledge of these reports until after the issue came to a head and the damage was done.

On September 5, the newly elected Progressive Conservative government of Mike Harris held a closed, secret session to set out how it would handle the occupation of Ipperwash Park. Members of the new government had talked tough during the election campaign and the next few months would show that they were anxious to demonstrate that their actions followed their words. Members of the cabinet, representatives of the Ministry of Natural Resources (who ran the park), the Ontario Native affairs secretariat, the attorney general, and the Ontario Provincial Police attended. While what was said exactly is yet to be revealed, pending a long-delayed and much-demanded inquiry, subsequent evidence suggests the provincial police received a clear message of "Get those Indians out of the park." No mandate was given to negotiate or to respect the claims of the Stoney Pointers.

BOX 20-3

The Tensions of the Times: Gustafsen Lake

The summer of 1995 saw another Native hot spot in British Columbia. For six years, Natives of a number of different First Nations had held a Sun Dance at a ranch at Gustafsen Lake owned by an American, Lyle James. To that time there had been no problems. But in 1995 there was tension. Ranch hands were harassing Natives and, on June 13, a forestry worker was shot at. Following the eight-day ceremony, some people refused to leave the site, claiming that it was sacred ground. James had them served with trespass notices.

It was a complicated issue, with a number of divisive elements separating Native people. The Sun Dance was not traditional to the local First Nation, the Shuswap. Some of the dancers were not from the area. Not all dancers supported the occupiers. Some Shuswap Elders stated that the site was not a sacred one, but the occupiers claimed that three people had had visions there.

A division between Native officials and militants seemed to be forming. The occupiers issued a press release under the name of Shuswap Traditionalists, stating that the land had never been officially ceded or surrendered. The elected officials of the local band and tribal council failed to negotiate peace with the occupiers. Ovide Mercredi, Chief of the Assembly of First Nations, tried too, and likewise failed.

On September 11, four days after Dudley George died, 400 R.C.M.P. officers, with helicopters and armed personnel carriers, closed in. Shots were exchanged. It was the costliest police operation in British Columbia and in R.C.M.P. history. Six days later, the occupiers surrendered. Of the 18 arrested, 14 were Native and 4 were non-Natives (13 men and 5 women). Sixty charges were laid. They went to court on July 18, 1996, and the trial lasted 10 months. There were 39 acquittals and 21 convictions.

On September 6, Chief Tom Bressette was notified that an order had been given to get the protesters out of the park. He did not inform the Stoney Pointers of this order, not that they would have obeyed it had he done so.

"Escalating Violence Against Police"

Prior to the confrontation in Ipperwash Park, the O.P.P. had gone through a very thorough preparation for battle, requesting from the army 50 gas masks, 50 pairs of night vision goggles, equipment for intercepting cellular telephone calls, 100 bulletproof vests, two Huey helicopters, and two Bison personnel carriers. Two hundred and fifty officers were mobilized from across Ontario to face about 30 people with no firearms.

Ipperwash Park was like a dry forest after a hot, dry summer—only a dropped match was needed for conflict to rage like a forest fire. At 7:55 p.m., that match was lit. Stoney Pointer Stewart George got into an argument with Gerald George, the man who had referred in the paper to Stewart's group as "animals". Stewart would take his anger on Gerald out on

Gerald's car. The next day, the O.P.P. issued a news release stating that "A private citizen's vehicle was damaged by a number of First Nations people armed with baseball bats. As a result of this, the O.P.P. Crowd Management Team was deployed. . .". Stewart George later pled guilty to one count of mischief (another charge was dismissed) and was fined $300.

At 8:19 p.m., Gerald George lodged a complaint with the O.P.P. At about 10:45 p.m., a team of 32 officers of the Crowd Management Unit, in riot gear that included shields, batons, and sidearms, advanced on about 30 unarmed Native men, women, and children. The officers were protected by a more heavily armed eight-man Tactics and Rescue Unit (a SWAT team).

Cecil Bernard George, a Kettle and Stoney Point band councillor, walked into the middle of the oncoming confrontation, in an attempt to defuse the potential human explosion, but he was too late. The O.P.P. beat him with clubs and kicked him. He later filed a civil action suit, in which a doctor's report revealed that he had injuries to 28 different places on his body.

The assault on Cecil George would cause Warren George, 22, to drive slowly onto the scene, trying to put his car between his people and the police. An officer pointed a gun directly at Warren, who then swerved and braked, making contact with five officers, one of whom suffered a sprained ankle. In February 1998, Warren was found guilty of criminal negligence causing bodily harm and assault with a weapon (his car). A charge of dangerous driving was stayed. He was sentenced to six months and was banned from driving for two years. Strangely, although he was unarmed during the incident, he was prohibited from possessing firearms for 10 years. Judge Greg Pockele, in pronouncing sentence, said that Warren lacked "remorse" for what he had done and had become part of the "escalating violence against police" in the situation.

At about the same time, a youth made a similar attempt to block the advance of the police. This time the vehicle was a bus. Seven officers drew their weapons and fired and a bullet struck the young man in his lower right back. The youth was acquitted of charges, with Judge Graham stating that "It is reasonable for [the youth] to assume that a breach of the peace was occurring and that Bernard George was being assaulted."

The Killing of Dudley George

On March 17, 1957, Anthony O'Brien (Dudley) George was born in Sarnia. He had been involved with every aspect of Stoney Point resistance, the occupation of Camp Ipperwash, the march, and was a face familiar to all, including the police. He looked the part of the "militant Indian": long hair, short beard, and sunglasses. His familiarity and his "militant look" would make him an easy target for police anxiety. It is alleged that before the police advanced, the O.P.P. said to him, "Dudley, you are going to be first."

Acting Sergeant Kenneth Deane was second in command of the Tactics and Rescue Unit. He later testified that he saw muzzle flashes coming from the bushes and moments later Dudley stepped onto the road and scanned the police, pointing a rifle. Deane alleged that Dudley threw the rifle away after being hit in the collarbone by Deane's shot. This was proven untrue in court. The Natives fired no shots, although the police are rumoured to have fired 1,000 (perhaps Deane mistook one of those for unfriendly fire) and Dudley was not carrying a gun.

Deane shot Dudley but the Stoney Pointer did not die right away. No ambulances appear to have been called by the police. Marcia Simon, a Stoney Pointer, tried to call an ambulance but was grabbed and arrested while trying to do so. Dudley's brother, Pierre, his sister, Carolyn, and a youth proceeded to drive him to the nearest hospital, some 50 kilometres away. A tire went flat but still they lumbered on.

When they got to the hospital, the O.P.P., who had been monitoring the progress of the car, took Pierre and Carolyn into custody, claiming that they would be charged with attempted murder (although they had possessed no weapons and hadn't tried to harm anyone). They were held overnight and then let go. Dudley died at 12:45 a.m.

The Investigation

The Special Investigations Unit arrived within hours of the shooting but was prevented by the O.P.P. from entering the park until two weeks later. Although police are required to file a report within 90 days of a shooting incident, their report wasn't released until July 23, 1996, more than 10 months later.

Deane was charged the next day with criminal negligence causing death, for which the maximum penalty is life imprisonment. The trial began on April 1, 1997. On April 29, 1997, he was found guilty. Judge Hugh Fraser stated that Deane had "concocted a story...in an ill-fated attempt to disguise the fact that an unarmed man was shot."[3] The judge told Deane, "You were not honest in your statements to police investigators, to the S.I.U., and to this court." Brian Adkin, president of the O.P.P. Association, said outside the court that he felt that government inaction on the land claim had created a "tragedy on both sides, a tragedy for the George family and a tragedy for Sgt. Deane."

On July 4, sentence was passed down. Deane was given a conditional sentence of two years less a day to be served in the community and told to perform 180 hours of community work. Deane appealed the decision and lost the appeal on February 18, 2000. By then, he had served his sentence, with no penitentiary time.

For their activities of the summer and of September, the Stoney Pointers faced 62 charges. Most of those charges were dropped. For example, 20 charges of forcible entry were dropped because the police were unable to establish how the people got into the park. More significantly, 23 charges of forcible detainer were dropped because "The accused have raised the defence of colour of right on the basis that there is a Chippewa burial ground within Ipperwash Provincial Park and that therefore *they were justified in being in the Park during the time set out in the charges*" (authors' emphasis).[4]

On June 18, 1998, after roughly two years of negotiations, Minister of Indian Affairs and Northern Development Jane Stewart and Chief Norm Shawnoo of the Kettle and Stoney Point First Nation signed an Agreement-in-Principle on the return of the former Camp Ipperwash lands. It was anticipated that a Final Agreement would follow, as would an environmental assessment and cleanup, as was said in the government news release "because of the likelihood of contaminants and unexploded ordnances which accumulated during the time the site was used as a military training base."[5] There is no news yet of a Final Agreement. The official land transfer is still a work in progress.

Native Individuals 20-1

Dudley George (1957–1995): a Stoney Point Ojibwa whose occupation of Ipperwash Park in Ontario led to his shooting death by the police.

Timeline 20-1

1680: Mississauga and related peoples move south from Northern Ontario.

1827: Mississauga sign Treaty of Amherstburg.

1928: Stoney Point people forced to sell 377 acres of their reserve.

1936: 108 of those acres purchased to form Ipperwash Park.

1937: Mississauga cemetery violated during the making of Ipperwash Park.

1942: Federal government uses War Measures Act to expropriate the Stoney Point band's land for military training purposes, forcing them to live with the Kettle Point band.

1946: Advanced Infantry Training Centre closed, but military possession is maintained.

1993: Stoney Point people begin to occupy Camp Ipperwash.

1995:

In July, the army moves out of Camp Ipperwash.

On September 4, 24 Stoney Point people occupy Ipperwash Park.

On September 5, the provincial government holds closed meeting to deal with the occupation.

September 7, Dudley George dies.

1997: O.P.P. officer found guilty of criminal negligence causing death and is given a suspended sentence with 180 hours of community work.

1998: Agreement-in-Principle signed for return of the Camp Ipperwash lands to the Stoney Point people.

ENDNOTES

1. See Web site www.web.net/nacaa/info-leaflets/04.html.
2. See Web site www.web.net/nacaa/info-leaflets/04.html.
3. See Web site http://kafka.uvic.ca/~vipirig/SISISI/Ipperwash/tapr2997.html.
4. See Web site www.web.apc.org/~ara/spoint/sppr1.htm.
5. See Web site www.inac.gc.ca/news/may98/1-9854.html.

KEY TERMS

War Measures Act

CONTENT QUESTIONS

1. How did the Ipperwash Park land get transferred away from the Stoney Point band?
2. How did the Stoney Point people get the Camp Ipperwash land taken away from them?
3. How long did it take for the Stoney Point people to get their land back from the Department of National Defence?

4. Why did the Stoney Point people occupy Ipperwash Park?

5. What was the court's decision on the people's right to be in Ipperwash Park?

WEBLINKS

www.web.apc.org/~ara/spoint/background.htm
"Aazhoodena Background," Stoney Point Web site giving a background to the story.

www.inac.gc.ca/news/May98/1-9854.html
"Agreement-in-Principle Reached on Return of Former Camp Ipperwash Lands."
DIAND news release, June 18, 1998.

www.inac.gc.ca/NEWS/may98/RFCIL.html
"Chronology: Return of Former Camp Ipperwash Lands." DIAND news release, June
1998.

http://kafka.uvic.ca/~vipirg/SISIS/Ipperwash/dghist.html
"Dudley George—A history." Harold Koehler, September 3, 1996. A biography of
Dudley George.

www.web.apc.org/~ara/spoint/Ifpapr498.htm
"Ipperwash Protester Sent to Jail, Natives Angered Over 'Injustice.'" John Hamilton,
London Free Press, April 4, 1998. A report on Warren George case.

www.web.net/~acaa/info-leaflet/0.html
"Justice for the Stoney People." Anti-Colonial Action Alliance information leaflet no. 4.
May 1996, with files from Stoney Point First Nation, the *London Free Press, Toronto
Star, Globe and Mail,* and Arthur.

http://kafka.uvic.ca/~vipirg/SISIS/Ipperwash/tapr2997.html
"OPP Officer Kenneth Deane Found Guilty in 1995 Murder of Dudley George." From
Anti-Racist Action Toronto—April 29, 1997. "Lying Officer Convicted." Julie Carl.
London Free Press, 1997, report on Deane Case.

http://kafka.uvic.ca/~vipirg/SISIS/Ipperwash/arch01.html
"The Police Attack on Indigenous Resisters at Stoney Point (Aazhoodena)." Anti-Racist
Action Toronto 1996–1998 chronology.

www.mcc.org/pr/1998/08-13/2.html
"Return of Confiscated Land Salves Wounds But Doesn't Heal Them." Mennonite
Central Committee—News Service, August 12, 1998.

www.web.apc.org/~ara/spoint/sppr2.htm
"Stoney Point Trial Update." Stoney Point press release, Oct 24, 1996.

www.web.apc.org/~ara/spoint/sppr7.htm
"Stoney Point Trial Update #7." Stoney Point press release, March 13, 1997.

www.web.apc.org/~ara/spoint/sppr1.htm
"Stoney Point Trials Begin, 43 charges withdrawn by the Crown." Stoney Point press
release, Oct 22, 1996.

FIGHTING FOR THE SACRED WATERS: THE PEIGAN AND THE OLDMAN RIVER DAM

OLDMAN RIVER, SACRED RIVER

According to the traditions of the Peigan, the nation first came to life in the waters and surrounding plains of the Oldman River. To them, the river, which winds through Peigan land in southwestern Alberta, is as sacred as the Jordan is to Christians or as the Ganges is to Hindus. They even named it **N'api,** meaning "Old Man,"[1] their name for the hero who was said to have created the first Peigan. The Peigan came to the N'api River to pray, to drink its water, and to take the plants and animals it nourished for medicine and food. In the N'api River, religion, history, and the necessities of life came together.

There was a special relationship that the traditional Peigan had with bodies of water. They did not use canoes, nor did they eat fish. Yet, in the words of American Blackfoot writer Darrell Robes Kipp:

> . . . [R]ivers and lakes hold a special power because they are inhabited by the Suyitapis, the Underwater People. Painted lodge covers, medicine bundles, and other sacred items were transferred to the tribe from the Suyitapis. In turn their power and domain are respected by the tribe. Today, the reservation waterways and lakes are touted as premier fishing spots. Yet most tribal members maintain the traditional ban on fishing. (Kipp 1996:76)

THE LONEFIGHTERS SOCIETY

Peigan Elders can recount stories of **Ni'taiitsskaaiks** (literally "lone-fight," plural) or Lonefighters Society (see Chapter 9, "The Plains") that trace it back at least to the 1700s, when

---

BOX 21-1   **Blackfoot Names**

There are a number of long-standing jokes about Native names. This is largely because the meanings of these names are so apparent, the result of their recently being translated from the language of their origin. Sometimes Native people feel pressured into changing their names because they believe they are targets because of this aspect of their names. A student of one of the authors had the last name Bigwin. It wasn't until the end of the semester when he discovered her Native ancestry, and she learned that a member of her family had changed the name so they would not be harassed for having the name "Big Wind," traditionally a name that gave the bearer pride.

Non-Natives should realize that at one point virtually all names held meaning of some kind. It is just that many English speakers (and, to a lesser extent, French speakers) have lost the cultural meaning and significance of their names.

---

horses first came to Peigan culture. According to **James Bad Eagle**, a descendant of the Lonefighters, the name came from a time when one lone warrior fought against impossibly heavy odds and did not give up. Today, the Elders can point to a one-kilometre stretch of the Oldman River as being the original home of the society. By the banks of the river, this society buried its dead, performed the sacred Sun Dance, held meetings, and prepared for war against threatening peoples. The Lonefighters were expected to protect their land and their people to the last warrior's last breath. This earned them the respect of other Plains nations.

The Peigan were hit hard by the nineteenth century. The buffalo were killed off. Strangers took their land and made them sign a treaty and put them on reserves. Their most sacred ceremony, the Sun Dance, was made illegal. The Lonefighters struggled to maintain Peigan ways. However, in the words of James Bad Eagle, they eventually disappeared "like ghosts."

FIGHTING FOR THE RIVER

The fight for the river began essentially in 1976, almost a century after the Peigan had signed the treaty surrendering most of their land but keeping rights that they believe include the Oldman River. In that year, the Alberta government declared its intention to dam the Oldman River, claiming that the project would create about 500 temporary construction jobs, increase the province's hydroelectric power potential, guarantee that Alberta could meets its water commitments to neighbouring Saskatchewan, and that the resulting irrigation would benefit farms.[2] The Peigan were not considered, even though the dam would be a mere four kilometres upstream from their reserve and the flooding created by the project would mean the loss of sacred tribal burial grounds, 5,000-year-old tipi rings, vision quest sites, and more than 200 archaeological sites.

The first battle between the provincial government and the Peigan over the river took place in 1978. That involved a 23-day blockade initiated by Chief **Nelson Small Legs** over a diversion weir and canal, on what the Peigan believed to be their land. Following a series of confrontations, Alberta agreed in 1981 to pay the band a cash settlement of $4 million over an extended period of time and an annual user fee of $300,000 for the water rights. The band, in return, would allow the province to use about 300,000 acres of land. Think of that as a payment of $13.33 per acre, plus a $1-a-year user fee, and it looks like a good deal for the government—especially as government monies promised sometimes get paid in services and in goods, the value of which can be inflated and sometimes don't get delivered.

There were environmental concerns that needed to be addressed, such as the impact of the dam on the local mule deer population (estimated at 500), the trout fishery, and on six rare and threatened species of animals, not to mention the pollution possibilities that have come from other such projects (see Chapter 16, "The James Bay and Northern Quebec Agreement"). These concerns were articulated by the Friends of the Oldman River (FOR), a protest group that included environmentalists, ranchers, and First Nations people.

The Environmental Council of Alberta, a semi-autonomous government body, heard over 250 briefs and technical submissions pertaining to the project. In 1979, it ruled that "a dam on the Oldman River is not required now or in the foreseeable future . . . A dam at the Three Rivers site would be the worst possible location from environmental and social perspectives." The provincial government ignored the report, refused to conduct an environmental assessment, and, in 1984, announced its decision to go ahead with construction. In 1988 work was underway, the cost of which was estimated to be over $350 million.

Opponents of the project continued to mount protests. The largest of these occurred in June 1989, when FOR held a very successful "This Oldman" benefit concert on the banks of the river, attracting a crowd of between 15,000 and 18,000. Journalist David Suzuki and Peigan Elders addressed the crowd. An editorial in the *Edmonton Journal* stated that "The Oldman River Dam has potential to be an economic and environmental disaster. The dam's only benefit may be political, ensuring by its largess that southern Alberta remains solidly Tory."

Treaty rights were also involved. The Peigan band insisted that Treaty #7, validated in the Constitution Act of 1982, granted them aboriginal rights to the water. In 1989, the band sued the provincial government for illegally taking away those rights.

There was legal precedent for them to do so, although only in court cases tried and won by American First Nations. No Canadian First Nation had ever filed such a case.

In 1990, the Lonefighters entered the picture. **Milton Born With a Tooth** was the person who decided to resurrect the society, inspired, no doubt, by the Mohawk Warriors who had launched their own battle for land at Oka. There would be about 30 to 40 Lonefighters involved in the protest, ranging in age from 20 to about 45. Prominent among these would be **Devalon Small Legs**, the spiritual leader, and **Glenn North Peigan**, who frequently acted as spokesperson.

On August 2, with the dam mostly completed, the Lonefighters Society took action. Armed with a bulldozer and allegedly financed with $5,000 by FOR, the Lonefighters started diverting the river in an attempt to sabotage the project. The plan was to cut a diversion ditch on Peigan reserve land, reconnecting the river to its natural creek bed, which had been blocked in the early 1920s. This would divert water away from the waterworks system managed by the provincial government, rendering the highly sophisticated and expensive dam useless.

The provincial government responded by obtaining a court injunction the next day, declaring the diversion illegal. Born With a Tooth countered that it was not illegal, because the work did not affect the weir and canal of the 1981 deal. In an interview at the Lonefighters' encampment, he told reporters that what his people were doing was "re-healing" the river and that the R.C.M.P. were not bothering them because they were aware that no laws were being broken. Rather, he said, the government was breaking the law because it allowed construction of the dam without a proper environmental assessment study being conducted.

The 2,300 Peigan of the local reserve were split concerning the tactics of opposition. **Chief Leonard Bastien** told reporters that the Lonefighters Society did not have the backing of the chief and council, that what they were doing was violating the 1981 agreement with respect to the supplying of water to 900 farm families in the Lethbridge Northern Irrigation District. The chief said that he and the council intended to meet with federal and provincial negotiators to try to bring about a peaceful resolution to the situation. Nonetheless, Bastien made it very clear that he understood the reasons for the protest. "Personally, I am against the Oldman River Dam because of the cultural genocide on our people," he told reporter Jackie Red Crow from *Windspeaker* (August 17, 1990).

The crisis at the Oldman River climaxed in violence on September 7 and 8, 1990. There are two versions of what happened, each represented in Native and in non-Native press, each with their own "we" and "they." An article in *Windspeaker* reported that a Lonefighter runner spotted what he claimed to be 16 R.C.M.P. cruisers and vans, along with Lethbridge Northern Irrigation District officials. They had with them heavy equipment and were going towards the weir. The runner sounded the alarm to the rest of the Lonefighters' camp. The Lonefighters then assumed predetermined defensive positions and built bunkers. The R.C.M.P. added to the tension by flying their helicopters over the camp.

As the R.C.M.P. began to close the distance between the two groups, the Lonefighters began to yell at them, warning them off Peigan land. After some time, a number of the Lonefighters began to throw rocks at the advancing police. Then, Milton Born With a Tooth fired at least two warning shots "that sent the R.C.M.P. scurrying for cover" (Woodward 1990).

Kenneth Whyte, writing for the conservative *Alberta Report* (September 17, 1990) gave a differing account, predictable in how it painted the picture:

> By last Friday, the R.C.M.P. were comfortable enough with the situation to accompany a small army of provincial environmental workers and several pieces of heavy equipment to the reserve to repair damage done by Indian bulldozers. They were greeted with gunfire . . . As R.C.M.P. and environment workers moved in . . . two or three shots were fired at them from across the river, one just missing a policeman . . . Milton Born With a Tooth, who was until very recently serving time for criminal negligent homicide, admitted in front of television cameras to sending the bullets. Soon after, some 40 riot-equipped police officers arrived on the Lonefighters' encampment in more than a dozen vehicles . . . A standoff was underway.

Following the initial outburst of gunfire, the Lonefighters claimed a number of small victories. The R.C.M.P. removed the heavy equipment. They also complied with two Lonefighter demands. Some of the Lonefighters felt that Ray Gauthier, an officer from the Pinscher Creek detachment, was unduly biased against them. When they asked that he be taken away from the front lines, this was done. They also asked that the helicopter not fly in "Peigan air space." The R.C.M.P. again complied.

At the same time, the Peigan closed ranks. While initially, according to Chief Bastien, about 76% of his community was opposed to the diversion, the majority swung around to the Lonefighters' position. The band council passed a resolution that day, stating that the R.C.M.P. was trespassing. The resolution was read to the officers by Chief Bastien. Three days later, chief and council voted 9–1 to pass another resolution supporting the diversion. The Lonefighters said they were proud of the band and council, adding that "They literally threw away a promise of hundreds of thousands of dollars (from the government) to support the diversion."

All day during September 7, the R.C.M.P. sealed off the area and dug in for a siege, setting up a roadblock and constructing an observation tower. The Lonefighters heard that the Mounties were moving a tactical squad, riot police, and an ambulance into position. Police squad leaders were seen poring over a map and a helicopter was again flying overhead. It didn't look like they were interested in a peaceful resolution of the matter.

There was a lighter side to the conflict as well. Traditional Prairie Native practice was to "count coup" (pronounced "coo") on enemies by sneaking into their camp unarmed and touching them with a "coup stick." During the night, one Lonefighter touched the sleeve of an officer. Some of the Lonefighters praised some of the R.C.M.P., whom they saw as unwitting federal tools of a provincial government. Raymond Crow Shoe, who had been involved in a shoving match with some officers, had good words to say for R.C.M.P. Superintendent Owen Maguire who had ordered his men to back away, adding that Maguire had "reasoned with me in a friendly manner." Lonefighter spokesman Glenn North Peigan would say in front of a group of officers that there were many good police.

However, the situation worsened on September 8. Overnight, the R.C.M.P. tightened their position around the Lonefighters' camp. A warrant was issued for Born With a Tooth, but the Lonefighters refused to surrender their leader. Harsh words were exchanged when Glenn North Peigan encountered officer Ray Gauthier, who had supposedly been withdrawn from the action the day before.

THE TRIALS OF MILTON BORN WITH A TOOTH

After a tense, 33-hour standoff, Milton Born With a Tooth was arrested. He was denied bail on the basis of the "public interest" and spent over three months in jail, some of it in solitary confinement. The Alberta government attempted to charge him with civil contempt for violating their August 29 court injunction preventing attempts at diverting the Oldman River. Judge Roy Dewell threw out the application, saying that it lacked detail and was deficient. Born With a Tooth was released on bail on December 18, only to have weapons charges laid against him. He was ordered to return to his home on the Peigan reserve.

He was found guilty on seven charges ranging from pointing a firearm to obstructing police officers, and was sentenced to 18 months in jail. But there was evidence that racism was at play in this decision. When the verdict was appealed, the Alberta Court of Appeal quashed the seven convictions and ordered a new trial. In the opinion of that court, the presiding judge in the original case, Justice Laurie MacLean, had cut too short cross-examination designed to raise doubt about police intentions and had unjustly deemed much of Peigan culture and traditions "irrelevant" to the case.

Justice MacLean was eventually reproached by the Canadian Judicial Council in 1993. The council's judicial conduct committee concluded that the record of the case was "filled with examples of how a judge should not conduct himself during the course of a high profile trial involving sensitive and cultural issues." The matter had been brought to the attention of the council by the Canadian Alliance in Solidarity with Native People, which accused the judge of having "displayed an insensitivity to cultural and religious differences" during the trial (Western Report, vol. 10 #3, 1995). The alliance claimed that Justice MacLean had said that "Native spirituality is as irrelevant as Satanism" and that he used the word "fantasy" in reference to Native spiritual beliefs.

The new trial had difficulties from the beginning that also appeared to have a racial taint to them. The defence tried unsuccessfully to have the trial moved out of Fort McLeod, alleging that there was significant prejudice against First Nations' people there and that the community had vested interests in the dam. Chief Justice Kenneth Moore of Alberta's Court of Queen's Bench had instructed that half the jurors at the retrial be Native. However, the trial judge, Willis O'Leary, dismissed that order, claiming that it was incompatible with Canadian judicial practice and that no provision exists for "tailor made" juries based on race. He did, however, let Born With a Tooth take a traditional Blackfoot oath, involving the burning of sweetgrass and the touching of a sacred pipe, allowing that it was just like taking a biblical oath.

On March 14, 1994, after deliberating for four hours, the jury found him guilty of seven weapons charges. When the judge polled the jurors to see whether they had concurred, a Native woman broke down, sobbing "I don't know. You don't understand" (Hutchinson 1994). The judge ordered jury members back to chambers. They returned an hour-and-a-half later with the woman accepting the verdict. The defence attorney, Karen Gainer, suggested that the woman might have been pressured into compliance.

Before the sentence was imposed, Born With a Tooth addressed the government with the following statement:

> Why do I have to go to jail when Ralph Klein is the real criminal? Who administers the policies like the ones that govern the Oldman River dam? The government of Alberta still has a one-sided agenda and that's not just me saying that, that's society. I wasn't in it to win or lose. I've taken the responsibility and I have to take what comes with it . . . I've been used as a scapegoat. Who are they going to use after I've gone? (*Windspeaker*, October 9, 1994)

He also suggested that the police were responsible for much of what happened, saying "They should have sent a couple [of] R.C.M.P. officers down to the camp that day; instead they sent an army" (ibid.). He received a 16-month sentence.

REPERCUSSIONS

Today, the dam is operational. However, some small victories have been won. In December 1991, the Supreme Court of Canada made a ruling that could affect similar projects in the future. In response to a series of lawsuits submitted by the Friends of the Oldman River,

---

Native Individuals 21-1

James Bad Eagle: A Peigan Elder, descendant of the Lonefighters.

Milton Born With a Tooth: Peigan leader of the Lonefighters in their confrontation with the R.C.M.P. in opposition to the dam being built on the Oldman River.

Nelson Small Legs: Peigan chief who led a 23-day blockade in 1978.

Timeline 21-1

1700s: Origin of the Lonefighters Society with the coming of the horse.

1976: Alberta government declares that it will build a dam on the Oldman River.

1978: Peigan initiate a 23-day blockade over a diversion weir and dam.

1981: Agreement is signed between the Peigan and the Alberta government.

1988: Work begins on the dam on the Oldman River.

1989:

In June, Friends of the Oldman River hold a rally to oppose the dam.

The Peigan sue the Alberta government for taking away rights to the water guaranteed in Treaty #7.

1990:

August 2: Lonefighters Society diverts the river with a bulldozer.

September 7–8: Confrontation between the Lonefighters and the R.C.M.P.

1994: Milton Born With a Tooth found guilty of weapons charges.

the court concluded that the federal government had the constitutional power to review the environmental repercussions of any provincial project affecting territory such as reserves over which the federal government has regulatory powers. The Oldman River Dam affected federal jurisdiction over inland fisheries, Native lands, and navigable waters, and thus was an issue for Ottawa. It also stated that all reviews of such matters should consider the physical, economic, and social environment.

The decision was received with mixed emotions by the Native community. It was hailed for its broad definition of the environment, but, in the eyes of Born With a Tooth, it "didn't consider culture." Nor did it support Ottawa's fiduciary responsibility to First Nations people for environmental damage, according to Doris Ronnenberg, head of the Alberta branch of the Native Council of Canada. Nonetheless, she called the decision a "tool for the future." In the five years leading up to the ruling, Alberta spent $1 million fending off legal challenges from First Nations, environmentalists, and economists who questioned the wisdom of constructing the dam. It would not be so easy in the future with similar issues.

While the dam is in place, a number of steps are being taken to lessen its negative effects. Environmental mitigation work is underway and socioeconomic studies are being conducted. There is an environmental Assessment Committee, which is meant to include all interested parties. The Peigan have been invited to participate, but so far they have declined to send official representation.

ENDNOTES

1. This is cognate with the **-nabe-** of Ojibwe and the **-ape** of Delaware. It is found in words depicting the male of a species, such as in the term (in Blackfoot) **naapim** ("male animal") and **naapissko** ("male gopher") (Frantz and Russell 1995:132).

2. Estimates vary from 150 to an optimistic 300 as to how many farmers would allegedly benefit from the irrigation produced by the dam.

KEY TERMS

Na'pi (Peigan)
Ni'taiisskaaiks (Blackfoot)
Suyitapis (Peigan)

CONTENT QUESTIONS

1. What is the significance of the name "Oldman" applied to the river?
2. What is the Lonefighters Society?
3. What was the result of the first conflict in 1978?
4. What action did the Lonefighters Society take in 1990?
5. What were the end results of the confrontation?

WEBLINKS

www.finearts.uvic.ca/~vipirg/SISIS/sov/allmilt.html
The text of a radio interview with Milton Born With a Tooth.

www.lis.ab.ca/afp/justice.htm
A comparison of the treatment of Milton Born With a Tooth and Dudley George, from the *Alberta Free Press*.

home.uleth.ca/~andrjd/Web/OldmanDam/OldmanDam.html
A basic description of the Oldman River dam itself.

NATIVE
POLICING

THE R.C.M.P.

The Image of the Mountie and the Indian in Canadian Culture

One of the few relatively distinct images of Western Canada's past is that of the "Mountie and the Indian." It is an image flattering to the Mountie but not complimentary to the Indian. As Daniel Francis describes the image in the chapter entitled "Red Coats and Redskins" in his excellent work *The Imaginary Indian: The Images of the Indian in Canadian Culture* (Francis 1992), there is the image of the Mountie being the saviour of the drunken Indian victimized by the unscrupulous American whisky trader at places such as Fort Whoop-Up, near present-day Calgary. While there is some truth to the fact that the North West Mounted Police (N.W.M.P.), formed in 1873, did act bravely in taking on the often well-armed traders, the image of the drunken and helpless Indian is an exaggeration and contributes to a negative stereotype.

Also negative is the image of the confrontation, with the Mountie facing down the "wild savage." It is part of the Mountie "always gets his man" mystique of the N.W.M.P., later their descendant group, the Royal Canadian Mounted Police (R.C.M.P.). Again, it contributes only to negative stereotyping of Aboriginals. Further, it can be an exaggeration, even out-right fiction. Such is the case with one story about Piapot.

Piapot (c.1816–1908) was a Plains Cree leader who rose to prominence in the last half of the nineteenth century. In 1874, he signed Treaty #4. In that treaty, the leaders were promised they could choose their reserve lands. In 1879, he was one of a group of leaders who requested reserves side by side, which would allow them to continue to hunt the remaining buffalo in southern Saskatchewan. The federal Indian commissioner didn't want them there because then the people would be harder to control, they might cross the paper border into the United States, and because the railroad was going through that area. Rather than negotiate with Piapot and the others, he reneged on the treaty promise of choice of reserve and declared that Piapot and his people had to move north, near Regina. He enforced his policy through not providing the rations of food that the people needed in the transition time between buffalo hunting and learning another way to provide food. Piapot resisted, in part because some of his people died from the diet of fatty and salty bacon that could not replace the more nutritious buffalo and partially because he knew that what he was being forced to do was not in the agreement.

Eventually he was forced to give in, but not by military might or Mountie bravery. Because he believed in keeping his word, he did not join the Riel Rebellion of 1885.

His leadership, his honesty, and his loyalty were not well recorded in the history books produced in most of the next century. Instead, a fictitious story was composed by journalist William Fraser, first printed in 1899, and was reproduced in often well-read histories of the R.C.M.P. It became part of the "Mountie mystique" in later history books. It was about a confrontation between a brave Mountie and a Native leader, the fictional stuff of the Wild West.

Piapot and his people were camped by the Canadian Pacific Railroad (C.P.R.) lines, refusing to leave. Two Mounties were sent to defuse the situation, one by the name of William Wilde. In Francis's rendition of the story:

> When Piapot refuses to move,...Wilde pulls out his watch and tells the Indians they have fifteen minutes to clear out. As the minutes slowly pass, Indian braves try to intimidate the Mounties by bumping their horses and firing guns into the air. Finally, when the time is up, Wilde calmly gets down from his horse, walks over to Piapot's tent and kicks down the lodge pole, collapsing the tent in a heap. He proceeds to knock over another tipi, and then another, until Piapot gets the message and shamefacedly orders his braves away. (Francis 1992:66-7)

It is important to make mention of the image of the "Mountie and the Indian" because both the R.C.M.P. and Natives are aware of this image. It has contributed to an atmosphere of confrontation that has existed between them. Trust is hard won between the two.

The Pass System

It is not just image that creates that atmosphere, it is also memory. Some of the most bitter of the memories that Natives in the West have concerning the R.C.M.P. include the removal of children from homes to go to residential schools and, in the Sixties Scoop, the removal of a later generation of children from homes considered unsuitable. Another bitter memory, not yet discussed, is that of R.C.M.P. enforcement of the Pass System that existed in the West.

General Middleton introduced the Pass System in 1885 during the second Riel resistance. Under the system, Natives could not leave their reserves without first obtaining a pass permitting them to do so. The main idea behind it was to control Natives, particularly the Plains Cree and the Blackfoot, so they would not join the Métis in their fight. In 1886, books of passes were issued. In order for Natives to obtain a pass, they would have to get permission from their farming instructor. The police enforced this rule, even though in 1892 government lawyers made it known that the system was illegal. Neither the Indian Act nor

BOX 22-1 — The Police: To Serve and Protect?

The meanings of terms for groups of people have implications for how we see those people. We have fairly recently replaced the word "policeman" in English with "police officer" because the former term conveys the idea that only men can work as police officers. Terms for a police officer in Native languages communicate some interesting perceptions. The word in Blackfoot is **iyínnakiikoan**. It is derived from the verb stem **yinnaki**, which means "to grab, seize, hold, capture something living" (Franz and Russell 1995:266). An almost identical term is found in Ojibwe, where the word **dkonwewnini** is used (Rhodes 1985:115). It, too, stems from a verb (**dkonaad**) meaning "to grab, seize, capture something living" and means "a man who captures, grabs, seizes something living."

any other legislation allowed the Department of Indian Affairs to institute such a system. The N.W.M.P. temporarily stopped trying to enforce it, but there were howls of non-Native public protest and statements of outrage. During the period of non-enforcement, the restriction of food rations was the sole means of forcing people to stay on the reserves.

The N.W.M.P. then returned to applying the rule, even though they, as well as some Natives, were aware of its illegality. As Natives were not permitted at that time to become lawyers, they could not fight it in the courts. The system continued until the 1930s, when many of today's Elders were children.

Other memories are more recent. In 1974, about 200 Aboriginals travelled to Ottawa from British Columbia on what was called the "Native Peoples' Caravan," a peaceful protest against poor living conditions. An R.C.M.P. riot squad was summoned and a clash ensued. There was also a clash between the R.C.M.P. and the Peigan over the Oldman Dam in 1990 (see Chapter 21) and between that police force and the Shuswap at Gustafsen Lake in 1995.

Joining the Force

One significant part of Native demands for self-government has been the right to police themselves, a right enjoyed by many non-Native cities and towns but not Native bands. It was a long time coming and it came in small steps.

It should first be stated that the concept of policing is not new to Canada's First Nations. Whether it was through the warrior societies that policed the buffalo hunt in the Plains (among other things) or the more subtle influence of the Elders in council, the functions of policing were well handled prior to contact with Europeans.

In 1971, the Department of Indian Affairs and Northern Development issued Circular 55, which gave band councils the authority to create "special constables" who could enforce band by-laws, a far cry from the authority of a police officer. They were not permitted to carry firearms. Very little money was available for them, so they had very low salaries, were expected to provide their own vehicles, and sometimes did not even have uniforms (York 1990:147). From the mid 1970s to 1990, through the R.C.M.P. (see below), the Ontario Provincial Police (O.P.P.), and the Sûreté du Quebec (S.Q.), Special Constable programs were

BOX 22-2   The J.J. Harper Story

In 1988, there were between 40,000 and 50,000 Aboriginals in the city of Winnipeg (Frideres 1998:241). The 1,140-member police force had nine Native constables at that time.

It was roughly 2:30 in the morning on March 9, 1988. John Joseph Harper was walking home in downtown Winnipeg after having a few coffee-and-whiskys at a local tavern. He was 36, the father of three, a leader in the Indian Lake Tribal Council, and a well-respected man in Native circles.

Meanwhile, elsewhere, a 22-year-old Native man had stolen a car and had been apprehended. The police were still in the area.

A police officer walked towards J.J. Harper. He ignored the officer, as he had committed no crime. The constable asked him to show identification and Harper refused. The constable asked him again and Harper just walked away. The officer grabbed him by the arm and turned him around. Harper was dead within a few minutes, shot to death by the officer's gun.

The investigation was minimal. The scene of the death was hosed down before morning light, possibly washing clean clues that could have revealed what happened. The officer claimed in court that Harper, who the officer felt matched the auto thief's description more closely than the suspect did, had pushed him down and tried to grab his gun. In the ensuing struggle, according to this story, the officer's finger found its way to the trigger and the gun accidentally went off. Yet the gun was not dusted for fingerprints to corroborate the story.

Within 36 hours of Harper's death, the police chief said his officer was innocent of any wrongdoing and the mayor of Winnipeg agreed with him.

Reframe this picture with a Native constable and with a Native unit in the Winnipeg police force. How might it have proceeded differently?

---

developed, but they still had limited authority, less than that of a regular officer. According to Geoffrey York, the regular officers would often use the Special Constables "merely as translators and intermediaries in their dealings with the Indian communities" (York 1990:148).

In the late 1980s, Native people were distinctly under-represented as police officers in Canada. In 1988, the city of Calgary had two treaty Indians on its force of about a thousand (Comeau and Santin 1990:51), its Native population being between 30,000 and 40,000 (Frideres 1998:241). In Ontario, that same year, just 26 of the 4,450 members of the O.P.P. were Aboriginal. In Thunder Bay, a city in northwest Ontario in the middle of Native country, with about 10% of its population Aboriginal, only one of its 200 police officers was Native, less than 0.5% (York 1990:148).

Changing the Relationship With the R.C.M.P.

Following a 1973 federal task force report recommending changes be made to on-reserve policing, the R.C.M.P. came up with the "3(b) Option," which was implemented in all provinces except for Ontario (where authority over on-reserve policing was being transferred to the O.P.P.), Quebec (where the Sûreté du Quebec had authority), and New

Brunswick. It developed the position of Special Constable, a position with limited authority but still more than had existed earlier. This program was terminated in 1990, as it was found to have a number of flaws. In an inquiry into the deaths of five Blood, or Kainai, a former Special Constable testified that he had had to put up with a constant barrage of racist remarks and anti-Native jokes from his fellow R.C.M.P. officers (York 1990:170).

Shortly after the Solicitor General initiated its comprehensive policy to change policing services to Native communities (see First Nations Policing Policy in next section), the R.C.M.P. developed its own policy: the Royal Canadian Mounted Police First Nations Community Policing Service (R.C.M.P.–F.N.C.P.S.). It "incorporates the principles and objectives of the First Nations Policing Policy including service levels equivalent to those of non-First Nations communities; compatibility and sensitivity to First Nations culture and beliefs; flexibility to accommodate local variations in policing needs; and a framework which allows for transition to an independent First Nations-administered police service where this is desired by the community" (R.C.M.P. First Nations Community Policing Service). The elements of the R.C.M.P.–F.N.C.P.S. correspond very closely with those of the F.N.P.P. Prior to this, the R.C.M.P. policed Native communities pursuant to provincial policing agreements. Later, this was enhanced by the Indian Special Constable Program, which was phased out during the 1980s.

The R.C.M.P. also has a number of initiatives offered through its Aboriginal Policing Branch. The Aboriginal Cadet Development Program is operated through funding provided by Human Resources Development Canada. Under this program, Natives interested in a career with the R.C.M.P. who don't meet basic entrance requirements, but who are otherwise suitable candidates, can upgrade their qualifications. Following a three-week assessment, candidates are sent to their home areas with a program designed to bring them up to the appropriate qualification level. They are granted two years to meet the standards, whereupon they proceed to Regina to undergo basic cadet training.

The Aboriginal Youth Training Program provides Native young people with 17 weeks of summer employment, including three weeks of training in Regina. Once stationed at a detachment near their home, they are under the supervision of a regular member of the R.C.M.P. for the remaining 14 weeks. Major funding for the program comes from the Department of Indian Affairs and Northern Development.

Changing Policy

In 1991, the First Nations Policing Policy (F.N.P.P.) was initiated through the federal solicitor general. It represented a culmination of proposals by First Nations leaders and groups and the recommendations of a number of commissions on justice and policing in Native communities. It was initiated "to provide First Nations across Canada with access to police services that are professional, effective, culturally appropriate, and accountable to the communities they serve" (Canada, Minister of Supplies and Services, 1996:1). It has been administered by the Department of the Solicitor General since April 1992 and operates on a principle of partnership involving First Nations, the federal government, and the provincial governments. These three enter into tripartite agreements for police services that meet the needs of the particular Aboriginal communities involved. The policy applies to all Native reserves, to certain other First Nations communities on Crown land, and to Inuit communities. By the end of 1999 there were 52 such agreements across the country.

Funding for the agreements is roughly evenly split: 52% comes from the federal government with the remaining 48% coming from the provincial or territorial government. The First Nations will, where possible, be encouraged to pay the cost of maintaining their police services, particularly for enhanced services. A number of criteria exist in order for an agreement to qualify for funding. First, all police officers in non-Native administered policing services must be Native, except where the First Nation agrees to and participates in the staffing of a non-Native person. An example of this exists in the Nishnawbe-Aski Police Service (N.A.P.S.) in Northern Ontario. In 1998, they appointed as the Commander of their "B" Division a man who had come to the N.A.P.S. after serving 25 years with the R.C.M.P. in areas such as Winnipeg, Brandon, Kenora, and Yukon, areas where there was a distinct Aboriginal presence.

Second, the First Nations police service must meet the standards of its home province or territory. In Ontario, for example, all Native constables must attend the Ontario Police College in Aylmer and take the same courses as the non-Native students. The Anishinabek Police Service in that province requires that all its potential applicants, like applicants for non-Native police services, successfully complete the Constable Selection System (involving a pre-interview and interview stages and a background reference check) and possess the newly instituted Ontario Association of Chiefs of Police Certificate of Results.

Third, Native police officers must be properly appointed as peace officers and be empowered to enforce all applicable laws. And, finally, the police service must consult with and be accountable to the community it serves through a police board commission or advisory board.

There are a number of models for agreements that are eligible for federal funding. These include a First Nations Administered Police Service organized on a band, "tribal," regional, or provincial basis, including arrangements providing for one First Nation to contract for the policing services of another. In Nova Scotia, the Unama'ki Tribal Police Service consists of 15 officers who provide service to five Mi'kmaq communities in Cape Breton. In Ontario, those police services following this model include the Nishnawbe-Aski Police Services in

BOX 22-3	Two Ways of Dealing with a Contentious Issue

What does a Native police service do when its band council is seen as "breaking the law"? Two Native police services followed two different strategies in the case of bingo licensing.

The provincial government issues gambling licences for bingo. In 1998, the process of negotiating for such a licence was proceeding very slowly for a number of First Nations in Ontario. In the Nipissing First Nation, which was unwilling to wait for the provincial government to establish a clear policy, the people ran a charity bingo. It was raided and equipment was seized by the O.P.P., with the assistance of the Anishinabek Police Service (*Tribal Council News*, vol.2, issue 4, December 1998). The United Chiefs and Councils of Manitoulin (U.C.C.M.) gave explicit instructions that same year that the U.C.C.M. Anishinabek Police (which was the product of a tripartite agreement) not participate in any such bingo bust.

the northwest, which covers 46 communities, and the Anishinabek Police Service, which administers 20 communities in north, central, and southwestern Ontario. In 1996, in a very important breakthrough, the troubled community of Kanehsatake or Oka, which had major conflict with the Sûreté du Quebec (and with the Canadian army) in 1990, was able to achieve a tripartite agreement with the governments of Quebec and Canada.

Another model provides for a special contingent of First Nations Officers within an existing police service. This may include Native officers employed within a provincial or municipal police service with dedicated responsibilities to serve a Native community or a group of Native police officers employed through a contractual arrangement to provide a policing service to a First Nations community. Third, there is the Developmental Policing Arrangement, which is designed to smooth the transition from one type of policing arrangement to another.

THE ANISHINABEK POLICE SERVICE: A CASE STUDY

On March 30, 1992, the Anishinabek Nation, along with several other Ontario Native regional groups, signed a five-year tripartite agreement. By 1994, the Ojibwa communities of Garden River, Curve Lake, Sagamok, and Saugeen First Nations had withdrawn from using the Ontario Provincial Police and formed the Anishinabek Police Service. In 1996, they signed a new three-year agreement, which allowed them to include 13 more First Nations. In 1997, two more First Nations joined. As of February 2000, there are 20 communities involved. The force's headquarters is located in the Garden River (near Sault Ste. Marie), which is situated in the middle of the widespread participating communities that stretch from the northwest through central to southwestern Ontario. Currently working out of the headquarters is the police chief, an administrator, one staff sergeant for the north and one for the south, a court case manager, financial assistant, pay and benefits clerk, computer systems manager, and an office assistant.

Table 22.1 charts the communities involved, their on-reserve population as of 1991, and the staff that works out of each detachment. The communities of Henvey Inlet, Magnetawan, and Wahnapitae are also served by the Anishinabek Police Service.

THE FIRST NATIONS CHIEFS OF POLICE ASSOCIATION

In 1992, the First Nations Chiefs of Police Association (F.N.C.P.A.) was incorporated. It set the following objectives:

1. To encourage and develop establishment of First Nations Police Services to provide adequate police services to First Nations communities and territories throughout Canada.

2. To encourage, promote, and foster adequate and meaningful training programs to meet the needs of First Nations Police Services.

3. To encourage and establish liaison among all Canadian First Nations Police Services and other First Nation governments and organizations.

4. To encourage high efficiency in First Nations law enforcement.

5. To promote and maintain a high standard of ethics, integrity, honour, and conduct in the profession of First Nations policing, taking into account traditional values and First Nations traditional law.

TABLE 22-1	The Anishinabek Police Service	
First Nation	**On-Reserve Population**	**Detachment Staff**
North		
Fort William	506	1 commander, 2 constables, 1 court officer/secretary
Garden River	901	1 commander, 4 constables, 1 court officer/secretary
Heron Bay	378	1 commander, 2 constables, 1 court officer/secretary
Long Lake #58	321	1 commander, 4 constables, 1 court officer/secretary
Long Lake #77	179	combined with Long Lake #58
Pic Mobert	292	1 constable
Rocky Bay	240	2 constables, 1 court officer/secretary
South		
Christian Island	554	1 commander 2 constables, 1 court officer/secretary
Curve Lake	751	1 commander, 3 constables, 1 court officer/secretary
Dokis	183	1 constable
Kettle Point	798	1 commander, 5 constables, 1 court officer, and 1 secretary
Nipissing	539	1 commander, 3 constables, 1 court officer/secretary
Sagamok	993	1 commander, 3 constables, 1 secretary/court officer
Saugeen	651	1 commander, 1 detective sergeant, 5 constables, 1 secretary, and 1 court officer
Shawanaga	89	1 commander, 1 constable, 1 secretary/court officer
Wasauksing	259	1 constable

6. To foster and encourage policing and other programs to ensure the safety and security of residents of First Nations communities and territories. (www.soonet.ca/fncpa/objective.htm)

In 1997, the F.N.C.P.A. entered into partnership with Human Resources Development Canada (H.R.D.C.) to study the human resource needs and challenges facing First Nations policing services. They want to come up with a concrete action plan for addressing those challenges. The report is to have seven separate phases. The first phase, already completed, examined the historical background of First Nations policing in Canada. The title of this first phase publication is *Setting the Context: The Policing of First Nations Communities*. In 1998, along with the Department of the Solicitor General, the F.N.C.P.A. sponsored a national conference on crime prevention in aboriginal communities.

OTHER FORMS OF NATIVE POLICING

Not all forms of Native policing come from tripartite agreements and uniformed cops following a European model. Other forms of policing, based in part on traditions, but also innovative, have appeared in the last 20 years. Two of these are the Mi'kmaq Warrior Society and the Native Youth Movement.

The Mi'kmaq Warrior Society

In the recent disturbance in New Brunswick and Nova Scotia concerning the treaty rights of the Mi'kmaq to fish and trap lobster, the Mi'kmaq Warrior Society was seen in the television coverage of one of the hot spots, the Burnt Church reserve in New Brunswick. They looked like the familiar images from Oka, wearing army fatigues and headbands, so the television cameras focused on them. But those cameras and the pictures they created did not create understanding. If anything, they facilitate a process of misunderstanding.

The Mi'kmaq Warrior Society probably owes its origin, as much as anything else, to a confrontation in 1981 at the Mi'kmaq reserve of Restigouche in Quebec. The rules for fishing on the Quebec side of the river that separated the two provinces were different than those on the New Brunswick side. The Mi'kmaq chose to follow the New Brunswick rules and were raided at dawn, in what was described as being like a scene from *Apocalypse Now*. Four hundred heavily armed Sûreté du Quebec officers deployed helicopters and bulldozers and used tear gas, confiscating some 250 kilograms of salmon. Eventually the rules changed and were made the same for both sides of the border. Perhaps more significantly, a strong sense was developed at that time that the Mi'kmaq would need to have peacekeeping forces to defend themselves from outside aggression.

But the Mi'kmaq Warrior Society is more a diplomatic police force than anything else. The members are chosen because they can handle themselves coolly under trying situations. During the tense times at Burnt Church in 1999, they were unarmed. They were asked to keep the peace, to make sure that equipment and boats were not vandalized by outsiders, and to keep tension from getting out of hand.

The Native Youth Movement

The Native Youth Movement (N.Y.M.) was founded in 1990 in Winnipeg but it seems that it's the British Columbia branch, formed in Vancouver in 1996, that has been getting the most press. The N.Y.M. represents a sometimes confusing (to the outsider) mixture of elements. Members have the "Oka look" with camouflage outfits and scarves covering their faces. They sometimes perform policing functions such as guarding Native fishermen from Department of Fisheries and Oceans (D.F.O.) officers, carry handcuffs and police-issue batons, army knives, and two-way radios, and are trained in military techniques. Still, they do not carry or use firearms. They are educated, too; some are still in college or university.

In British Columbia, the N.Y.M. has identified a number of "enemies." The first is the British Columbia Treaty Commission (the N.Y.M. refers to itself as "the official opposition" to the B.C.T.C.). It also opposes chiefs and councils it feels are selling out the rights of future generations in order to receive money now and even opposes the Assembly of First Nations (A.F.N.), which the N.Y.M. feels is involved with the sellout. One N.Y.M protester's sign read that "A.F.N." stands for "Another Financial Network."

The N.Y.M. has been engaged in civil disobedience without violence in a series of actions. In April 1997, it occupied the B.C.T.C. office for 40 hours. On January 30, 1998, it interrupted a meeting of top Native leaders. In April of that same year, members occupied the B.C.T.C. office again, this time for five days, with 14 members arrested. The charges were eventually dropped. On May 25, 43 N.Y.M. members occupied the Westbank Indian Band band office, chanting "Sellouts, get the hell out." Thirty-three hours later, 20 left voluntarily and 23 were arrested, and again the charges were eventually dropped. In the summer of

BOX 22-4	**Initials and Their Meanings**
A.F.N.	= Assembly of First Nations
B.C.T.C.	= British Columbia Treaty Commission
F.N.C.P.A.	= First Nations Chiefs of Police Association
F.N.N.P.	= First Nations Policing Policy
H.R.D.C.	= Human Resources Development Canada
N.A.P.S.	= Nishnawbe-Aski Police Service
N.W.M.P.	= North West Mounted Police
N.Y.M.	= Native Youth Movement
O.P.P.	= Ontario Provincial Police
R.C.M.P.	= Royal Canadian Mounted Police
R.C.M.P.–F.N.C.P.S.	= Royal Canadian Mounted Police–First Nations Community Policing Service
S.Q.	= Sûreté du Quebec
U.C.C.M.	= United Chiefs and Councils of Manitoulin

1999, when the Cheam First Nation decided to disregard the ban on salmon fishing in their area, 20 N.Y.M. members were there. In the words of one member, named "Shrubs," "We have been invited here to show a political and physical presence." R.C.M.P.-trained D.F.O. officers, wearing bullet-proof flak jackets and carrying tear-gas canisters and semi-automatic weapons, tried to stop the salmon fishing by cutting and seizing Cheam nets and by trying to arrest those whose nets were in the water or who had fish. Still, there were no arrests and no violence erupted throughout that tense summer.

In the fall of 1999, the N.Y.M. received some bad press because of some small, photocopied posters that appeared in Penticton. On the posters were written the words, "Get off our land or we will burn you out one house at a time." It was signed "Native Youth Movement." This seems inconsistent with the N.Y.M. approach and was probably either the work of a single hothead or an attempt to discredit the N.Y.M. by its opponents, Native or non-Native. Monty Joseph, an N.Y.M. leader in Penticton, said that the N.Y.M. had nothing to do with the posters and that "This definitely is not the message I want to convey to the people of Penticton."

Native Individuals 22-1

Piapot (c.1816–1908): A prominent Plains Cree leader.

J.J. Harper: A Native man living in Winnipeg who was killed by a policeman in March 1988 after refusing to stop for the officer.

KEY TERMS

the confrontation
dkonwewnini (Ojibwe)
iyínnakiikoan (Blackfoot)
pass system

CONTENT QUESTIONS

1. What distorted image of Mountie/Native interaction is illustrated in the fictional Piapot story?
2. What is the First Nations Policing Policy and when was it initiated?
3. What three criteria must be met for a tripartite agreement to receive funding?
4. What is the Native Youth Movement?
5. What is the Mi'kmaq Warrior Society?

 **WEBLINKS**

www.soonet.ca/fncpa
The Web site of the First Nations Chiefs of Police Association.

www.sgc.gc.ca/whoweare/aboriginal/eaboriginal.htm
The federal Solicitor General's "Aboriginal Policing Directive."

www.apscops.org
The Anishinabek Police Services official Web site.

23

THE JUSTICE SYSTEM AND NATIVES

HEADLINES

Native peoples and justice issues are closely linked. Consider the following headlines that appeared in the *Globe and Mail* on February 19, 2000:

"Retired Mountie called in to probe Winnipeg police: Inkster to review handling of case in which two Métis women died" (p. A2, Canadian Press)

"RCMP to face snags in probe of native deaths: Officers looking at alleged police link may have a hard time unearthing evidence" (p. A3, David Roberts)

"Ontario to appeal hunting rights ruling: Acquittal of aboriginals threatens wildlife conservation effort, Attorney-General says" (p. A7, Canadian Press)

"Ipperwash officer loses conviction appeal" (p. A7, Martin Mittelstaedt)

"Homeless alcoholic pleads guilty to bashing lover to death" (p. A30, an article by Jane Gadd in which a picture of the killer—an alcoholic who had been abused by his parents before and after his six years of residential schooling—clearly shows his Native identity)

In the following section, we will discuss the main justice issues with which Native people are confronted. It will be seen that very real progress has taken place over the last 10 years or so but, as the headlines above attest, there is still a long way to go.

TRADITIONAL JUSTICE

Non-Natives often believe that prior to contact with Europeans, First Nations peoples lacked any system of justice or social control. This misrepresentation would seem to be based primarily on one of two stereotypes. One is that Native peoples lived in some sort of idyllic Garden of Eden, where crime or aberrant behaviour was completely unknown. The second stereotype is based on the notion that they lived in a fierce and primitive world in which there were only the laws of the jungle, no social rules. Neither stereotype is true.

There were laws, recorded in oral tradition and interpreted by the Elders. While these laws differed from nation to nation, it is a fair generalization to say that across cultures these laws tended to emphasize social harmony and the restoration of peace over punishment or retribution, although the latter did exist. We will use the description of one culture to illustrate how this could function.

Traditional Native Justice for the Huron-Wendat

Restoring the community to the way it was before the crime was committed is a key element in restorative justice. That this has long been an important aspect of Native traditional justice can be seen in the following illustration of how the seventeenth-century Huron-Wendat dealt with murder in their society. The restoration was done with gifts presented by the family or village of the murderer to that of the murder victim. These gifts were expensive, at least the value of a new beaver robe (JR10:215–7; cf. JR28:49). The number of gifts varied. If the victim was a man, the usual number was 30. For a woman, it was 40. It was said that the murder of a woman required more gifts as they peopled the country (JR33:243).

Each gift had a name, which informed those in attendance of its purpose. Each was presented with a long speech, probably of further explanation of the purpose. The judicial ceremony could last an entire day. What follows are the names of the first nine, the most important gifts, the only ones whose names survive. They illustrate Huron-Wendat notions of justice.

The first gift was named **condayee onsahachoutawas** (JR10:217), meaning "this is that which he uses to withdraw the axe" (authors' translation). The axe stood symbolically for all murder weapons. This is a statement of apology and regret on the part of the murderer and the murderer's family/village. Accepting the gift was probably a statement of accepting what it said. The second gift was similar in purpose. It was named **condayee oscotaweanon** (JR10:217), meaning "this is that which he uses to wipe off the head" (i.e., of blood).

The third gift shifts the focus from the victim's family to the country generally. Its name was **condayee onsahondechari** (ibid.), meaning "this is that which he uses to reunite the country" (see Chapter 1 for a discussion of the meaning and significance of -**ondech**-, "country"). This speaks to the mutual goal of all participants in restoring order to the society. The fourth gift reiterates this important goal. It was named **condayee onsahondwaronti, etotonhwentsiai**, meaning "this is that which he uses to put a stone in the split in the earth or country."

In Huron-Wendat culture, vengeance was a respected aim when it came to warfare with outside nations, but had to be held back within the circle of their own society so that social harmony would be maintained. The next three gifts all speak to the need to reduce the possibility of vengeance. The fifth gift was named **condayee onsahannonkiai** (JR10:219), meaning "this is that which he uses to clear away, cut down the brush" (i.e., from around the paths that people walk). It was a metaphorical statement of the shared goal of keeping people from hiding in the bushes beside the paths, ready to ambush those upon which they wanted to exact revenge.

The Huron-Wendat believed in the existence of two soul/spirits within each individual: **yandiyonra**, "the mind," and **eiachia**, "the heart." The former was the spirit of peace and wisdom; the latter was the spirit of strong emotions such as sadness, anger, bravery, and vengeance. When the mind was at peace, feelings of vengeance would be in check. The sixth gift was an offer of tobacco to smoke. Its name was **condayee onsahoheronti** (ibid.), meaning "this is that which he uses to fill his stone" (i.e., his pipe bowl). The seventh gift was called **condayee onsahondionroenkha** (JR10:221), meaning "this is that which he uses to restore his mind" (i.e., after it has been driven away by the strong, negative emotions of the heart).

The last two gifts are directed to the mother of the person killed and thereby to the lineage and the clan, as Huron-Wendat society was matrilineal. The eighth gift was named **condayee onsaweannoncwa d'ocweton** (ibid.), meaning "this is that which gives a medicinal drink to the one who gave birth to him/her." The ninth gift was **condayee onsahohiendaen**, meaning "this is that upon which she can lie on as a mat."

A FOREIGN SYSTEM

It should be stressed the extent to which the British system of justice was, and is, foreign to Native peoples. Prior to contact with Europeans, Natives had no jails, judges, juries, or lawyers. According to Mohawk lawyer and law professor Patricia Monture-Angus, some of the basic premises of the legal system are foreign. In an article about legal education for Natives, she takes issue with the writer of a then (1990) standard textbook who stated that conflict between individuals and between individuals and the community were natural and universal, the fundamental core around which the legal system is based:

> To Aboriginal people, this ideology is nothing short of ridiculous. Harmony is the centre of our relations with the universe and all other beings, be they human, animal, or plant. Not only is this the basis of Aboriginal legal relations, but it is a total and integrated philosophy around which all social relations are constructed. (Angus-Monture 1995:101)

Further, as the highly technical, formal legal language of English and French is deeply embedded in a European social context, the terms used do not translate easily into aboriginal languages. To illustrate, let's take the word "guilty." It is loaded with meaning that comes from European cultures.

According to Bernie Francis, a Mi'kmaq who was a Native courtworker in Nova Scotia, his people often used to misunderstand the word "guilty" because there was no such word in their language. The word closest to it meant "blame." So when some people were asked whether they were guilty, they answered "yes," as they felt that the question they were being asked was whether they were being blamed for the offence.

Other Algonquian languages seem to tell a similar story. In Rhodes' excellent dictionary of the Ojibwe language (often used in the instruction of the language), if you look up "guilty," the closest word you can find is **naammendaagzid**, "be considered guilty" (Rhodes 1985:269), derived from a verb root meaning "to accuse or to blame." In Frantz and Russell's dictionary of Blackfoot, there is no entry under the English word "guilty," but there is a verb **otói'm**, meaning "accuse/blame" (Franz and Russell 1995:176). In John O'Meara's extensive dictionary of Delaware, under "guilty" you will only find **maashiingwéexiin**, meaning to "have a guilty look on one's face, look guilty of something" (O'Meara 1996:482). The literal meaning is "to have a strange face." Again, there is a verb **akwíimeew**, meaning "blame" (O'Meara 1996:403). One might surmise from this that the issue to be resolved for these people traditionally might have been less that a person was "guilty" of a "crime" and more that the harmony in society was disturbed because something had happened that upset someone and someone else got blamed for it.

DEVELOPMENTS SINCE 1975

Prior to 1975, "[l]ittle attention was paid in any official or programmatic way to the distinctive problems, needs, and participation of Aboriginal people in the criminal justice system" (Clairmont and Linden 1998:4). In 1975, there was a three-day federal-provincial conference held in Edmonton, entitled "The National Conference on Native Peoples and the Criminal Justice System." More than 200 delegates attended this important conference and they came up with 58 specific guidelines. These included the need to hire more Native people throughout the criminal justice system and the need to teach non-Natives already working in that system about aboriginal customs and values. Those and similar guidelines would be repeated over and again over the next 25 years. They still need to be addressed today. But, as is so often said, it was a beginning.

1988

In 1988, there was suddenly a coalescing focus on Native justice issues. In Manitoba, the outcry following the J.J. Harper (see Chapter 22) and Helen Betty Osborne (see Box 23.1) cases brought about the Manitoba Aboriginal Justice Inquiry. From September of that year to April 1989, two provincial judges, one a 37-year-old Saulteaux, Murray Sinclair, listened carefully to over 800 witnesses tell some unusually horrific stories about the sad state of justice for Natives in Manitoba. They heard of judges who were drunk when they sentenced Natives for drinking, of other judges who refused to go to a reserve to hear cases because there were no indoor washrooms. The band had to pick up the expensive tab for people to fly south where the conditions were more suitable for the judges. They listened to tales of gun-happy police officers and of one instance in which two Native teenagers sitting in a convertible were ordered by the police to stand up against a wall to be searched. It was assumed that they had stolen the car. A witness told the inquiry that, "They said there's no way two Indian kids could own a car like that, it was too expensive" (York 1990:168–9).

They identified that, for some young Native people in Manitoba at the time, crime was a way of getting out of isolated communities where there was nothing to do and no future in sight. In his book, *The Dispossessed*, Geoffrey York reported the story of Stan Sinclair, a 26-year-old Métis who had been in prison for 16 years of his life. He lived in a community in northwestern Manitoba where there was no running water, few jobs, and few recreational opportunities. In Sinclair's words:

> We have nothing to look forward to when we wake up in the morning. We get frustrated and scared. We don't give a damn what happens to anybody any more because nobody gives a damn about us. The only thing we know is to cause trouble and go to jail, where you have three meals a day and a place to sleep and a T.V. to look at. (York 1990:143)

BOX 23-1   Helen Betty Osborne: Conspiracy of Silence

On November 12, 1971, four young White men who were drinking heavily in The Pas, Manitoba, went cruising for Native girls, a common practice in the area. They saw a 19-year-old Cree woman, Helen Betty Osborne, out walking. They tried to coax her into the car, but she refused. They grabbed her, forced her into the car, and drove out of town. They tore her clothes off and at least one of the men sexually assaulted her. She was eventually killed, stabbed 56 times with a screwdriver.

The identity of the guilty parties soon became public knowledge. One of the four men, Lee Colgan, described the slaying to just about everyone: friends, acquaintances, people he met in bars, even a local sheriff and a civilian employee of the R.C.M.P. At a party in 1972, Dwayne Johnston, then around 17, described how he killed the Cree woman, boasting about the act. Yet nothing was done about it, even though there were physical clues linking the men to the scene of the crime.

The non-Native community protected the men. A friend threatened someone who wanted to tell. A local lawyer counselled the men to remain quiet.

It took 14 years before anything concrete was done about the crime. In 1985, the police put an ad in the local newspaper and received a response from a woman who had heard the story in 1972. Colgan made a deal with the prosecution. He agreed to testify if all charges against him relating to the killing were dropped. Johnston and Jim Houghton (who, along with Johnston, had been outside with the victim) were arrested in 1986. The fourth man was not charged with anything as he claimed to have been too drunk at the time to remember any details.

One hundred and four prospective jurors were considered. Twenty of them were Aboriginal, but they were rejected by the lawyers. The jury let Jim Houghton go free and convicted Dwayne Johnston. He served a 10-year sentence and was released on full parole in October 1997 to considerable protest from Native peoples across Canada.

That same year, the very conservative Canadian Bar Association issued a fairly radical 119-page report, *Locking Up Natives in Canada*, based on a two-year study and written by Professor Michael Jackson. This report became well known because of its suggestion that a separate, totally Native-run justice system might be one model for the future, a statement that ran into a lot of resistance from many non-Natives in the Canadian justice system. Jackson made an important observation concerning the inability of those non-Natives to consider such an option:

> Those in criminal justice typically see Native people at the worst part of their lives...Police, sheriffs, judges and prison staff don't see Native communities and their leadership solving their own problems. They see the people who have failed. They rarely come into contact with the Native leaders responding to problems in positive, effective ways. From that viewpoint, the response is predictable: "How can Native people do this when they can't stand up straight?" (Comeau and Santin 1990:132)

BOX 23-2 The Donald Marshall Case: Justice Denied[1]

On May 28, 1971, 17-year-old Mi'kmaq Donald Marshall Jr., along with a friend of his, Sandy Seale, were walking through a park in Sydney, Nova Scotia. They spotted two White men in the park and decided to ask them for some money. This led to a scuffle in which Seale was stabbed to death by one of the men, Roy Ebsary, who was carrying a large knife. There were no witnesses to the murder other than the three who had been directly involved.

Marshall quickly became the prime suspect. Three teenagers who had been in the area, but had not witnessed the stabbing, gave their testimony to police concerning what they knew, which was little. Gradually, they were coerced by the police into implicating Marshall with stories that became the same tall tale. One of them, 14 years old, would eventually testify that he had been threatened with a jail sentence if he did not tell the story the Sydney police wanted to hear. In the trial that followed that November, the prosecutor, violating the ethics but not the letter of the law of his profession, refused to let the defence see the original versions of the teenagers' testimony. Marshall was convicted of murder by a jury of 12 White men. The judge sentenced him to life.

Ten days later, Jimmy MacNeill, who had been Ebsary's companion on the night of the stabbing, went to the Sydney police to tell them that Ebsary had committed the act. His description of the killing matched the one that Marshall had given during the trial. The police questioned Ebsary but accepted his denials as truth.

Eleven years later, a man came forward to say that when he had lived in Ebsary's house, he had heard the man brag of killing someone in 1971. He knew Marshall, so he visited him in prison. They contacted Marshall's lawyer and the R.C.M.P. reopened the case. They spoke with the three key witnesses, who admitted that they had lied.

The case went to the Nova Scotia Court of Appeal in the spring of 1982. While the Crown prosecutor acknowledged that the Mi'kmaq man should be acquitted, he also asked the five judges involved to exonerate the criminal justice system of any blame on the grounds that its reputation must be upheld, that "[i]t seems reasonable to assume that the public will suspect that there is something wrong with the system if a man can be convicted of a murder he did not commit" (York 1990:161–2). The judges accepted this position and blamed Marshall more than the system for the lack of justice he received. They felt that he had initiated the series of actions that had led to his conviction and that he had been "evasive" in his answers during the trial.

Fortunately, the matter did not end there. A two-year study followed, revealing the anti-Mi'kmaq prejudice that was deeply embedded in every aspect of the justice system. In the words of the three Nova Scotia judges who released their seven-volume report on January 26, 1990, "The criminal justice system failed Donald Marshall Jr. at virtually every turn" (Comeau and Santin 1990:126).

---

[1] See Harris 1986.

As York points out, a sports and recreational program organized by a University of Manitoba professor, Neil Winther, was a factor in the 1987 drop of 17.4% in the crime rate in four Native communities where the program was in place. In contrast, in 26 other Native communities in the area, the rate increased by 10.6% (York 1990:143–4).

Another one of the many problems they identified as existing in the justice system as it applied to Natives was the fact that monetary reasons were a key factor in the disproportionately high number of Aboriginals in prisons. Making bail, even if the figure set was only for a few hundred dollars, was also found to keep more Natives in prison longer. Non-payment of fines is also a cause of incarceration. In one provincial jail in Manitoba, up to 60% of the Native inmates in 1987 were serving jail terms because they were unable to pay fines (York 1990:145). This was true even though Manitoba at that time had a kind of "fine option" program, in which people could perform community work if they could not afford to pay a fine, something 3,700 Aboriginals did in that same year in Manitoba (York 1990:144). This seems to be a continuing problem, as Frideres reports in 1998 (with no date attached to the figures) that nearly one third of aboriginal males and two thirds of aboriginal females sentenced to jail were because of fine defaults (Frideres 1998:188).

The judges also looked at options for change. They studied the various forms of courts run by the Pueblo peoples (the Zuni, Hopi, Keresan, and Tanoan peoples) of the American southwest: the traditional or customary courts, the Courts of Indian Offences (set up in 1883), and, more extensively, the tribal courts, which communities with a population as small as 500 could have access to (sometimes by renting the tribal court officials of a larger Native community).

In April 1988, the Kainai, or Blood, were finally able to pressure the Alberta government into calling for an inquiry into police relations with the province's Native people. It would examine a claim that police had improperly conducted murder investigations concerning five band members. The inquiry lasted 11 months, involved more than 15,000 pages of transcripts, and cost about $2 million.

BOX 23-3	**The Statistical Picture**

For 1991, Department of Solicitor General research estimated that the national Native crime rate was 165.6 per 1,000 population (Department of Solicitor General, 1991). At the same time, the national non-Native crime rate was 92.7 per 1,000 population (*Crime Publication*, C.C.J.S./Statistics Canada).

The rate of violent crime in Native communities is five to six times higher than the non-Native rate of eight offences per 1,000 population (ibid.). Out of 588 homicides reported in Canada in 1995, 88 involved Native victims (about 15%).

Natives made up 17% of incarcerated people and 20% of those on probation in 1993 (*Examining Aboriginal Corrections in Canada*, User Report APC14 CA, Department of the Solicitor General, 1996).

Source: *Crime Prevention in First Nations Communities: An Inventory of Policing Initiatives*, Canada: Solicitor General, n.d.

STEPS FORWARD IN THE 1990s

In response to demands from Native communities and to recommendations of the various reports and commissions of the late 1980s and early 1990s, the federal government, through the Department of the Solicitor General and through the Department of Justice, has put forward a number of effective initiatives. Under the sponsorship of the solicitor general, new Native-based penitentiaries have been constructed for both men and women in western Canada, supplementing existing policies and programs of penitentiary liaison, and Native counselling and spirituality (e.g., involving sweatlodges and sweetgrass ceremonies). The penitentiaries were developed in partnership with Native people and place an emphasis on healing.

In 1992, the federal government established the Aboriginal Justice Initiative in both the Justice and Solicitor General departments, renewed in 1996 as the Aboriginal Justice Strategy. Both departments have undertaken a number of initiatives (e.g., the Aboriginal Justice Learning Network and the Aboriginal Corrections Policy Unit) directed at such goals as supporting and evaluating Native community-based justice projects, getting Natives and non-Natives working together to improve justice institutions for Aboriginals, and generally moving towards greater self-sufficiency of Native communities in the area of justice.

Sentencing Circles

It is not so much what government initiates but what the people develop that will determine how well the justice system will serve Native people. One of the most promising developments in this area comes in the form of what are variously called youth justice committees, community peacemaking circles, or, more usually, sentencing circles. They provide alternatives to incarceration through adaptations of traditional notions of restorative rather than punitive justice. They typically involve community members such as Elders and Native social workers, lawyers, health care workers, and those affected by the crime, including both offender and victim(s) and their families. Guilt or innocence is not at stake; they follow guilty pleas. The circles are more informal than traditional courts. People sit in a circle, with no one above or "at the head of the table." Usually, those involved sit while speaking, and, instead of titles, personal names are used.

The participation in sentencing circles has been uneven in different parts of Canada. The Yukon had, by the end of 1994, around 300 circle sentencing experiences, more than the rest of all of Canada at that time, with about 100 in Saskatchewan and a handful in Manitoba, British Columbia, and Quebec. The first case (1992) in the Yukon that set that up was *R. v Moses*, in which an offender with a long history of substance abuse, violent acts, and incarceration had committed an assault with a bat on an officer, had stolen something, and had breached his probation. It came as a more or less spontaneous act of desperation.

Initial reports of the effectiveness of sentencing circles have been overwhelmingly positive, but during the last few years a few challenges to this good news have been made. Gordon Green, in the 1998 paper, "Community Sentencing and Mediation in Aboriginal Communities," expresses concern for the victims who are involved in the circles, especially in cases of domestic violence. He worries how the emphasis on the healing of the offender might take away from supporting the victim and about whether or not there might be power imbalances between the victim's and the offender's "sides." The Native ideal is for there to be no such imbalance, but this remains a challenge that needs to be faced openly and honestly.

A more serious critique comes from Roberts and LaPrairie (1997) who point to the fact that, in the Yukon and Saskatchewan from 1990 to 1995, the number of incarcerations increased among Native people as an indicator that the sentencing circles might not be living up to what they term "extravagant claims." There are several good responses to this critique. One is that the rate of incarceration might have gone up even more if not for the sentencing circles; it is hard to tell. Second, such a radically new form of justice requires time to mature before its effectiveness can truly be measured. Third, there are other benefits that have to be brought into the picture in any measure of the effectiveness of these circles. Greater community participation in justice has clearly been demonstrated. What the long-term positive effects of this participation will be can only be imagined at this point. That positive effects will take place would be difficult to doubt.

In what follows in this section, two specific sentencing circle programs will be discussed: the Hollow Water Community Holistic Circle Healing Program and the United Chiefs and Councils of Manitoulin Justice Project.

The Hollow Water Community Holistic Circle Healing Program

Hollow Water First Nation is a Saulteaux community of about 600, situated on the east side of Lake Winnipeg, some 190 kilometres north of Winnipeg. What they developed in their community, the Community Holistic Circle Healing (C.H.C.H.), has become a useful model for other Native communities interested in developing sentencing circles.

The birth of the C.H.C.H. goes back to 1984, when a group of people in the community who were involved with providing health and social services got together to discuss how they could bring about a more positive future for the youth of the community. They soon started to put their main focus on ending the sexual abuse that had a negative impact on most of the people in their community, young and old. They developed a circle composed of a team of people, mostly women, involved with child protection, community health, nursing, policing, and spirituality, so that their approach would be holistic, not divided into separate aspects of the self.

They came up with a 13-step program promoting a kind of healing justice for sexual abuse "victimizers." The first step is Disclosure, where the victimizer admits the offence. For the team to work to support the victimizer, the individual must enter a plea of guilty rather than deciding to take the case to the courts and must express a willingness to accept full responsibility for what he or she has done. In Rupert Ross's brief look at C.H.C.H. in 1993, he noted that virtually all those accused of sexual abuse had requested the team's support in this matter, so that trials were rare.

The second step is the Healing Contract, designed by people who were affected by the offence, people who have to make commitments themselves to the healing process of the victimizer and others affected, including themselves. This contract is meant to last for more than two years. Special attention is placed on the feelings and thoughts of the victim(s), non-offending spouse, and the families of both victim(s) and victimizer. The team puts together a Pre-Sentence Report, which appraises what the victimizer's chances of rehabilitation are and what it will require to effect that rehabilitation. An action plan is put together based on this report and on the Healing Contract. Upon completion of the Healing Contract, a Cleansing Ceremony is held to "mark a new beginning for all involved" and to "honour the victimizer for completing the healing contract/process" (Ross 1993).

A 1993 position paper gives some interesting insight into how the attitudes of those working for the C.H.C.H. have changed concerning the need for incarceration of individuals whose cases might be considered "too serious" for the C.H.C.H. process:

> In our initial efforts to break the vicious cycle of abuse that was occurring in our community, we took the position that we needed to promote the use of incarceration in cases which were defined as "too serious." After some time, however, we came to the conclusion that this position was adding significantly to the difficulty of what was already complex casework. (as recorded in Ross 1993)

They have come to believe that:

> Removal of the victimizer from those who must, and are best able to, hold him/her account-able, and to offer him/her support, adds complexity to already existing dynamics of denial, guilt, and shame. The healing process of all parties is therefore at best delayed, and most often actually deterred. (ibid.)

The United Chiefs and Councils of Manitoulin Justice Project

The United Chiefs and Councils of Manitoulin (U.C.C.M.) Justice Project was first funded in 1994 by the federal Department of Justice and the Ontario Ministry of the Attorney General. However, it wasn't until January 1998 that the U.C.C.M. Justice Project began diverting cases from the courts to justice circles. The objective of the Justice Project is:

> to contribute to building healthier communities by promoting Anishinabe values of healing, making amends and respect for self and others, and encouraging the active participation of community members in justice and expanding aboriginal control of criminal justice. (*Tribal Council News*, vol.2, issue 6)

From January 1, 1998, to the end of June 1999, the project diverted the cases of 87 people belonging to seven different communities. Seventy-seven justice circles were created, involving 110 members of the community. The kinds of cases involved were typically property offences (i.e., break and enter, theft, and vandalism) and relatively minor instances of assault, but did not include more serious crimes such as murder, manslaughter, sexual or spousal abuse, or impaired driving, which, in the words of one *Tribal Council News* article, "the government is intent on prosecuting" (*Tribal Council News*, vol.2, issue 8).

The wording of articles written by the U.C.C.M. Justice Project for the *Tribal Council News* indicates the positive approach that the people give to their work. The people whose cases they are diverting are referred to as "clients" rather than "offenders" and their "sentences" are referred to as "plans of action."

These plans of action are traditional based, but also creative and new. For instance, there are public apologies made by the clients, not only to the victims involved but to the police and others affected by the harmful actions. Some of the apologies have even been aired on a local cable T.V. station.

In the words of one writer, "since healing the community is as important as healing the victim and client, the plans of action often require some form of community service" (*Tribal Council News*, vol.2, issue 8). This community service has involved doing such things as cleaning up the results of vandalism, painting a new detox centre, and participating in a walk held annually to raise awareness of violence against women.

Native Individuals 23-1

Donald Marshall Jr.: A Mi'kmaq who was falsely imprisoned for 11 years for the murder of his friend.

Helen Betty Osborne: A young Cree woman who was killed by young White men in northern Manitoba in 1971. Her murderers were not apprehended until 1986.

Murray Sinclair: A Saulteaux who was one of two provincial court judges who led the Manitoba Aboriginal Justice Inquiry of 1988–89.

Making amends is a key feature of the plans of action. This has even involved assisting victims with their traplines. In one case, a woman had assaulted another woman, a close neighbour she had known for a long time. Had she decided to fight the charge, which was her initial intention, she probably would have been put on probation and would have been told to stay away from the victim. Instead, with the apology, the two women have managed to remain on good terms. The benefits of making amends were articulated by the client when she stated that "[t]hey don't resolve anything in court. It wouldn't have been right if we had hated each other. In court, I would never have got the chance to apologize" (*Tribal Council News*, vol.2, issue 10).

The healing element has included referrals to drug and alcohol addiction treatment centres or mental health facilities, but has also entailed traditional activities. The intent of these activities is to heal the clients "by enabling them to learn more about themselves and their culture, thereby raising their self-esteem and sense of identity" (*Tribal Council News*, vol.2, issue 8). Examples of the traditional activities recommended are helping to gather traditional medicines in the bush, participating in an arduous canoe trip around Manitoulin Island (the largest island in the world in a freshwater lake), and researching a family tree. Some clients have done more than was required of them as they felt rewarded by the activity.

An easy criticism of this system of alternative Native justice would be to say that the people get off lightly. A client of the Justice Project in one *Tribal Council News* article spoke of how it was more difficult to face people he knew, rather than a judge and jury, "a bunch of strangers. Who cares what they think?" (*Tribal Council News*, vol.2, issue 10).

There are difficulties. The staff of the Justice Project want to do more, but with only two lawyers on staff, along with three courtworkers, they are hampered by an extensive workload that has required them to cut back on the number of new cases that they handle. A lot of time is taken in putting together reports and proposals for the funding necessary to continue and to grow. Still, the outlook is positive. No one has had to return to the court for non-compliance with their plans of action and 41 files have been formally closed.

KEY TERMS

naammendaagzid (Ojibwe)

restorative justice

sentencing circle

sweat lodge

sweetgrass ceremony

CONTENT QUESTIONS

1. How did the Huron-Wendat deal with murder in the seventeenth century?

2. How do the expressions relating to guilt in the four Algonquian languages differ from the English justice notion of "guilty"?

3. What reasons have proven to be a factor in the disproportionately high number of Aboriginals in prison?

4. What important observation did Professor Jackson make concerning the inability of non-Natives to consider a Native-run justice system as an option?

5. What are sentencing circles?

 WEBLINKS

www.sgc.gc.ca/epub/Abocor/e199805/e199805.htm
Clairmont, Don and Linden, Rick. 1998 "Developing & Evaluating Justice Projects in Aboriginal Communities: A Review of the Literature" APC 16 CA (1998), Solicitor General Canada. Review of the literature on sentencing circles.

Tribal Council News. This is published by the United Chiefs and Councils of Manitoulin, and contains valuable articles on the Justice Project:
  <http://uccm.on.ca/features1.htm> (February 2000, vol. 3, issue 6)
  <http://uccm.on.ca/Archive/December 1998/features5.htm>
    (December 2000, vol. 2, issue 4)
  <http://uccm.on.ca/Archive/February1999/feature3.htm> (February 1999, vol. 2, issue 6)
  <http://uccm.on.ca/Archive/March%201999/inside2.htm> (March 1999, vol. 2, issue 7)
  <http://uccm.on.ca/Archive/April1999/web2.8.5.htm> (April 1999, vol. 2, issue 8)
  <http://uccm.on.ca/Archive/June%201999/feature2.htm> (June 1999, vol. 2, issue 10)
  <http://uccm.on.ca/Archive/July1999/inside5.htm> (July 1999, vol. 2, issue 11)

www.usask.ca/nativelaw/jah_ross.html
Ross, Rupert. 1993. "Aboriginal Community Healing in Action: The Hollow Water Approach." A review of the Hollow Water justice and healing project.

www.ajic.mb.ca/volume.html
A detailed examination of the justice system's treatment is provided in the Report of the Aboriginal Justice Inquiry of Manitoba. It contains Aboriginal concepts of justice, over-representation of Natives in jails, and the justice system's treatment of Aboriginal women.

www.usask.ca/nativelaw/jah_scircle.html
The University of Saskatchewan maintains an excellent Web site on sentencing circles.

NATIVE GOVERNANCE

EARLY POLITICAL LEADERS

It is easy for people to think that Native political activism is a recent phenomenon. Throughout the nineteenth and twentieth centuries, Native political leaders have risen to the huge challenges involved. The following are four examples.

Nahne's Trip to Meet the Queen

Nahne was born in 1824 beside the Credit River, which flows south into Lake Ontario. Her Mississauga name was **Nahnebahwequay** ("Upright Standing Woman"), but many people just called her Nahne. She married at 15 and eventually had six children. In 1845, Nahne and her family were forced to move from their Credit River home because their rights to the reserve there were not guaranteed. They accepted an invitation from another Ojibwa community that lived near the shores of Lake Huron. In 1857, Nahne and her new community were forced to auction off their land. Nahne was determined to buy some of this land. Initially, all went well. Nahne's bids were the highest. But government bureaucrats opposed her, telling her she could not buy the land because she was an Indian. Appeals failed. What could she do?

When Canadian First Nations signed treaties, the government officials signed them in the name of the "Great White Mother," or Queen Victoria. So when her people selected Nahne to speak about the problems they were having, it seemed right for her to go to meet the

Queen. This would not be easy. She had neither the money for the trip nor the contacts to get her an appointment with the Queen. That did not stop her. She went to New York to raise funds for her trip. While there she met some influential Quakers who saw the rightness of her cause and who had friends in high places. Money and contacts became available. The date arranged was June 19, 1860. Many questions and worries must have rushed through her mind: What do you say to the Queen? How do you curtsy when you are eight months pregnant?

Nahne's thoughts are recorded in a letter she wrote:

> So you see I have seen the Queen. The Duke went before us, and he made two bows, and then I was left in the presence of the Queen; she came forward to meet me, and held out her hand for me to kiss, but I forgot to kiss it, and only shook hands with her. The Queen asked me many questions, and was very kind in her manners and very friendly to me . . . ("An Indian Woman's Audience with Queen Victoria" in the *Brantford Courier*, August 1860)

The Queen was favourably impressed. When Nahne returned home, despite government resistance, she was able to buy the land for her family.

Deskahe ("More Than Eleven"), a Cayuga Sachem

This name was held by **Levi General** (1873–1925), who became the official speaker of the Six Nations Iroquois in 1922. At that time, the community was still governed by hereditary sachem government that had been set down through the Great Law of Peace. The community was fighting with the federal government and decided to seek sovereignty. In 1923, Deskahe went to the League of Nations headquarters in Geneva to plead their cause. He received the support of nations that knew what outsider control was like—Estonia, Ireland, Panama, and Persia—but Britain intervened and the proposal was dropped. Deskahe went the next year to speak with the king, but with no effect.

The federal government struck while he was away. It ruled that the Six Nations must be governed by elected council, not by the system that had been serving them well for hundreds of years. The people of the community were not consulted. The R.C.M.P. changed the locks of the council house so the sachems could not get in. An election was staged on October 21, 1924. The population of Six Nations had been recorded as 4,615 in 1920. In the imposed election, only 52 people voted. The community has been divided on that issue ever since.

Levi General died the next year, but named his brother Alexander (1889–1965) to replace him. He bore the name Deskahe well. In 1928, as a guiding influence of the Indian Defense League of America, he helped gain legal recognition in the United States for the part of the Jay's Treaty that permitted Natives to cross the border between Canada and the United States without paying customs. In 1930, on a Six Nations-issued passport, he went to see the King. His passport was recognized, as they have been ever since, but his appeal wasn't. After that time he became an important anthropological informant, teaching the famous anthropologist Frank Speck and others about the traditional customs of his people.

Andy Paull: The Last of the "One Man Shows"

Squamish leader **Andy Paull** (1892–1959) was an early political activist that George Manuel referred to as the last of the "one man shows." He was one of the founding members of the Allied Tribes of British Columbia in 1916, working extensively on the "Indian Land

Question" unique to that province. It was difficult work, as, from 1927 to 1951, it was illegal to "receive, obtain, solicit, or request from any Indian any payment or contribution for the purpose of raising a fund or providing money for the prosecution of any [land] claim" without the consent of the superintendent general of Indian Affairs. His train trips across the country to Ottawa were dramatic affairs. He would get off the train to meet with other activists and would dress up in flashy suits to meet with federal officials in the country's capital. Having worked for four years as a legal assistant, he had good legal training for dealing with those officials. While he had the knowledge and experience to become a lawyer, he was ineligible to become one because he was a Status Indian and, therefore, legally only a minor and not able to vote or practise law.

He was considered a radical, even by other Native leaders, but most of what he fought for seems reasonable today. He advocated such measures as the right to vote in federal elections (this wouldn't happen until 1960), the abolition of the culturally destructive residential schools (this took place in the 1960s and 1970s), the end of the federal power to determine band membership (this took place in the 1980s), giving Indian bands the power of local, municipal governments (the Sechelt achieved that in 1986), and hiring more Natives in administrative positions in the Department of Indian Affairs (this has been slowly, gradually taking place during the 1990s). He was ahead of his time.

Frank Calder: Nisga'a Leader

Frank Calder, the man who initiated the procedure that eventually led to the Nisga'a treaty, was born in 1915. He was adopted by his mother's older sister, Louisa, for traditional Nisga'a reasons. Louisa, as the eldest daughter of a prominent lineage, would have her son become the chief of the clan. But her son died in childhood, so she adopted Frank from her sister.

He often tells the story of how he was formally introduced to the land question when he was 12. It was 1927, the year the fundraising for claims issues was declared illegal. His father placed a box of claims-related documents down in front of him, telling Frank that he had to learn their content.

He was fortunate enough to attend the University of British Columbia, something very few of his Native contemporaries were in a position to do. Initially, he studied theology but became involved with the politics of getting his people the right to vote. In 1949, when the British Columbia government finally gave aboriginal people the vote in the provincial election (they wouldn't get the federal vote until 1960), he was elected as the Co-operative Commonwealth Federation (C.C.F.) (forerunner of the N.D.P.) candidate in the predominantly aboriginal riding of Atlin, where he served for 26 years. That made him a groundbreaker, as he was the first Native to be elected to the provincial legislature and was, in fact, the first Native to be elected to any Canadian legislature. Interestingly, he had not been given the endorsement of the Native Brotherhood of British Columbia, who supported the Liberal-Conservative coalition candidate out of appreciation for giving them the vote.

In 1955, Frank Calder founded the Nisga'a Tribal Council, making use of the four traditional clans in doing so. He was its president from that year to 1974, holding the position very much like the hereditary chief he would have been at an earlier time in Nisga'a history.

In 1967, he brought the Nisga'a land question to the British Columbia court system. This did not receive the complete agreement of his people, as some held the very realistic fear that if they lost in the courts, they would lose their rights forever.

In 1972, Calder became a cabinet minister in the British Columbia N.D.P. government, but that didn't work out for him, in part because he was a minister without a portfolio and so had no readily defined tasks to perform. Curiously, another cabinet minister handled Native matters. In 1973, the year when the Supreme Court handed down its decision, he was held by the police for being found drunk in a public place. One wonders whether a non-Native cabinet minister would have been apprehended in the same way. He was not formally charged with a crime, but ended up being kicked out of the cabinet in disgrace. He quit the N.D.P. and ran as a Social Credit candidate in 1975 and won.

In an interview held shortly after the passing of the treaty through parliament, he said:

> We've been liberated, that's what's going on here . . . Now we're free to exercise what we wanted to do, instead of remaining under the confinement of the reservation. The reservation and to get out of it, that's the main theme of what we're doing. (Matas 1999)

NATIVE GOVERNANCE: NUNAVUT

On April 1, 1999, Canada saw the creation of its third territory: **Nunavut**. This was a major political event in the lives of Canadians as it redrew our map for the first time since Newfoundland joined in 1949. For the Inuit of the Eastern Arctic, it had a greater significance, changing their relationship with the Canadian government and with other Canadians.

The landmass involved is huge. It is larger than any other Canadian province or territory, roughly twice the size of British Columbia, about one fifth of Canada. It covers, roughly, everything north of the treeline in the old Northwest Territories, stretching from a line north of the Manitoba border east and north. It includes half of Victoria Island and all of the big islands of Ellesmere, Southampton, Baffin, and Devon. Its population is small, about 25,000; the caribou (about 750,000 of them) outnumber the humans by about 30 to 1. There are 28 communities.

The word Nunavut (pronounced noo-nah-voot) means "our land" in Inuktitut. There are several important reasons why the Inuit can name it so. They have been on the land for thousands of years. They are usually estimated as making up between 82% to about 85% of the population, numbering 17,500. And, prior to the signing of the Nunavut agreement, the Inuit still had aboriginal rights to the land, having never been conquered and having never put pen to any treaties.

The agreement involves in part the settlement of the largest and richest land claim in Canadian history. In this settlement, the Inuit retain a number of rights. First is the right to hunt, fish, and trap throughout Nunavut. While the number of hunters is not as great as it used to be, nearly 60% of all Inuit households still rely upon the land for their meat. Nearly 85% of households are still involved in hunting and fishing to some extent and over 15% still trap. Inuit will not require any licence to hunt for basic needs. In addition, the Inuit will retain outright ownership of 353,610 square kilometres of land, about 18% of Nunavut. In a move unusual in the signing of treaties and like agreements by Native people, the Inuit got to choose which lands they desired. The remaining 82% remains Crown land, but the people will have joint control with the federal government over land use planning, wildlife, environmental protection, and offshore resources. On 36,257 square kilometres, or 10.5% of Inuit-owned land (about 2% of Nunavut), the Inuit will own subsurface rights to oil, gas, and minerals. It is believed that the land over which the Inuit hold rights contains as much as 80% of Nunavut's mineral resources. Of equal importance, the Inuit will receive a royalty from the government on any oil, gas, or mineral development on Crown land within Nunavut. This amounts to 50% of the first $2 million and 5% thereafter. In terms of cash, the Inuit will theoretically receive (these things have ways of diminishing) $1.15 billion over 14 years. The Nunavut Trust will be set up by the Inuit to receive the money and to manage and invest it. The money will be put into such concerns as Inuit-owned businesses, a scholarship program for Inuit students seeking college or university education, and an income support program for hunters, similar to what was developed for the Cree of James Bay.

A number of boards have been, or will be, established to help govern the new territory. The land claim agreement included a proviso that requires the relevant governments to negotiate a political accord (the Nunavut Accord), which would establish Nunavut as a new territory. In practice, this means that the territory, under the Nunavut Legislative Assembly, would have the same powers as those held by the Northwest Territories. The Nunavut Implementation Commission designed the new government, prepared for the first election, determined the capital, and began training the territory's new leaders. The Inuktitut language would be recognized as official, the first Native language to receive such recognition in Canada (although it is not unusual in South America). Being the official language entails such things as having legal documents published in the language, having the right to be tried in court in the language, and having the language taught in schools.

The choice of capital was an issue of many debates. There are only 20 kilometres of highway in Nunavut, so for the most part travel is by plane. Nunavut residents use aircraft five or six times as often as do other Canadians. Because there are almost 30 communities throughout the territory, accessible only by air, the choice of capital was a touchy subject. The contenders were Rankin Inlet (on the west coast of Hudson Bay), Iqaluit (on Baffin Island), and Cambridge Bay (on Victoria Island, at the extreme west of Nunavut). In 1995, Iqaluit (known as Frobisher Bay until 1987) was chosen at a plebiscite, with 60% of the 79% who voted choosing it. The choice is not surprising. It is the largest community in Nunavut, with a population of about 4,500 and is far removed from Yellowknife, which has been as vilified in Inuit country as Ottawa has sometimes been for the rest of Canada.

A number of boards and commissions have been established to oversee crucial social and environmental concerns. The Nunavut Wildlife Management Board has responsibility for management of the wildlife throughout Nunavut. The Inuit are a majority on the board. Five of the nine members are to be appointed from either the regional Inuit organization or the Nunavut government. Current quotas and restrictions remain in effect until this new board changes them.

The Nunavut Impact Review Board (N.I.R.B.), Nunavut Planning Commission (N.P.C.), and Nunavut Water Board (N.W.B.) are all essentially Inuit-controlled. The N.I.R.B. has the mandate to review and assess all projects throughout the territory to determine their impact on the environment or on socioeconomic conditions. The N.P.C. will review land use plans to ensure they conform to their criteria and their plans and to identify cleanup requirements. The N.W.B. works in association with the other two boards, but its mandate is to license the use of water for purposes other than navigation and to approve the disposal of waste into waterways and water systems.

The Inuit have a say in all future developments before projects begin. This applies to such concerns as parks (three of which are planned) and, of course, hydroelectric projects. Any developer must negotiate impact and benefit agreements with the Inuit before any such projects begin. The Inuit are especially concerned with the hiring and training of local Inuit and with the potential social and economic gains to be had.

A lot, then, has been planned. And this has been done without a great deal of awareness in the south. We need to address the question, then, of what led to Nunavut.

THE ROAD TO NUNAVUT

The road to Nunavut can be said to have begun in 1969 when then Minister of Indian Affairs
Jean Chretien introduced his infamous "White Paper" on Indian policy. Among other things,
it proposed doing away with special status for Native people, doing away with treaties,
denying the existence of aboriginal rights, and making the provinces responsible for Natives.

The reaction was loud, sometimes confrontational, but not in the north. The Inuit quietly
chose a peaceful political route. In 1971, they formed the Inuit Tapirisat of Canada, an
organization with representation from the four corners of the N.W.T., along with Labrador
and Quebec. It became the prime political vehicle for the Inuit. In 1976, the Inuit Tapirisat
published a 60-page document entitled *Nunavut: A Proposal for the Settlement of Inuit
Lands in the Northwest Territories.*

The document was received very coolly by the Trudeau government, ostensibly on the
basis of its "racial bias." The government contended that it assigned legislative and gov-
ernmental jurisdiction based on racial differentiation, something out of place in democracy
as the government saw it. However, Liberal M.P. Bud Drury was appointed to conduct a study
on the subject. He was to talk with recognized Native leaders and attempt to get a consensus
from Native people. While not supportive of division of the N.W.T., he did not reject the idea
outright. He concluded that Native aspirations could be met merely by settling land claims
and setting aside land for Native peoples. The Inuit Tapirisat rejected his plan.

Three major developments took place in Inuit country in 1979. First, the Inuit of Baker
Lake appealed to a federal court judge, claiming that 78,000 square kilometres in the area was
theirs. They were protesting prospecting that was being conducted by uranium companies.
They sought a court order prohibiting further exploration because the helicopters and
prospecting camps were frightening the caribou.

For the first time, Inuit went to court suing for aboriginal title. Testimony went on for
weeks, with Elders demonstrating their knowledge of the land. The federal court judge
demanded that four criteria be satisfied to determine aboriginal title. The Inuit had to prove
that their ancestors formed an organized society, that they occupied the claimed land, that
all other organized societies were excluded, and that the occupation was a fact at the time that
Britain asserted sovereignty over the land. The Inuit were able to satisfy these four criteria,
so the judge declared that Inuit title did exist in the lands surrounding Baker Lake. However,
he refused to stop the prospecting. While acknowledging that the caribou herds had declined,
he failed to recognize that mining was a significant factor in that decline. He also stated
that federal and territorial mining legislation could abrogate aboriginal title. It was a partial
victory. While recognizing Inuit aboriginal rights, it still allowed that governments were
within their legal rights to issue exploratory permits to mining companies on Inuit land.
Second, the Inuit Tapirisat adopted a position paper entitled *Political Development in
Nunavut,* proposing a three-stage, 15-year period in which the Eastern Arctic would grow into
provincehood. The first stage would be the recognition of Nunavut. The second would be the
transfer of territorial powers to the new territory and finally the achievement of provincial
status. Third, rather than following the usual practice of boycotting territorial elections as
irrelevant to their needs, the Inuit and Dene voted in large numbers, with the result that a
majority of Members of Legislative Assembly (M.L.A.s) were Native. For the first time, First

Nations issues became a priority. Territorial division was then put on the table. A vote was called for and a plebiscite was held in 1982. The question asked was, "Do you think that the Northwest Territories should be divided?" Over half the eligible voters turned out, with 56.5% voting "yes." The demographics tell an interesting story. Voter turnout in the Inuit east was 76%, with 82% supporting division, compared to a turnout of 45% in the west, where only 44% supported it. In western Inuit and Dene communities, support was 60%; in non-Native communities it was 25%. After the plebiscite, the Assembly voted 19–0 in favour of division and asked the federal government to recommend the new boundaries after consultation with the people of the N.W.T.

A group called the Constitutional Alliance, which had lobbied for division, set up two forums, one for the east (the Nunavut Constitutional Forum, or N.C.F.) and one for the west (the Western Constitutional Forum, or W.C.F.). The N.C.F. became very active in consulting communities and elders, publishing widely in newspapers, broadcasting through television and radio, and producing position papers. In 1987, the Iqaluit Agreement was signed by the N.C.F. and the W.C.F. It set the tentative boundaries and the principles under which the territories would operate.

Support for the division continued. In 1989, the Legislative Assembly again affirmed its support for Nunavut by a vote of 20–0, with one abstention. This was reaffirmed two years later by Territorial Commissioner Dan Norris. In November 1992, a plebiscite was held with 69% of voters in favour of division.

Nunavut has not been without its detractors within the Inuit community, particularly concerning the signing away forever of any future claim to aboriginal title. Some have felt that the loss of so much land involves the severing of the spiritual connection between the Inuit, their ancestors, and the land. Opposition to the surrender took on a very public face, when the lone Inuit Member of Parliament, **Jack Anawak**, questioned whether the Inuit were being asked to pay too high a price for Nunavut.

On the other side was **John Amagoalik**, referred to as the "father of Nunavut." His passion is inflamed by the fact that his family was one of those that faced hunger and deprivation after being forcibly removed from Inukjuak in northern Quebec to Ellesmere Island in 1953 (see Chapter 5). He is co-chair of the Inuit Committee on National Issues and has been involved with the issue for 20 years. While battling for Nunavut, and for a capital far removed from Yellowknife, he has also demonstrated that he has a more-than-local perspective, supporting the notion of a Dene and Métis homeland in the west. On a global scale, he sees his struggle as not only one for the Inuit, but perhaps as a model for other indigenous peoples worldwide. At the same time, he sees Nunavut as providing an education for non-Natives, reducing the fears that the term "self-government" brings to the un-informed.

The First Election

On February 15, 1999, Nunavut held its first election. The voter turnout was incredibly high, with 88% of eligible voters showing up at the polls. One unusual feature of the Nunavut Legislative Assembly is that no political parties are represented, making it more like a municipal than a provincial political body. Several names were proposed for the first premier, **Paul Okalik** and Jack Anawak being the finalists. Okalik, a 34-year-old lawyer, was voted in.

Native Individuals 24-1

John Amagoalik: Called the "father of Nunavut," a long-time Inuk activist promoting Nunavut.

Jack Anawak: An Inuk M.P. who questioned whether the gains of Nunavut were worth giving up aboriginal title forever.

Frank Calder: Nisga'a activist and provincial cabinet minister, he started the land claims case in 1967 that ended up with the Nisga'a treaty.

Deskahe ("More than eleven"): A Cayuga sachem title. It was held by Levi General (1873–1925) who went to the League of Nations to try to gain sovereignty for his people. The title was then held by Alexander General (1889–1965), who helped gain recognition for the Native rights that came from the Jay's Treaty.

Nahnebahwequay: A nineteenth-century Mississauga woman who had to speak with Queen Victoria in order to buy land.

Paul Okalik: Inuk, the first premier of Nunavut.

Andrew Paull (1892–1952): Squamish leader, one of the founding members of the Allied Tribes of British Columbia in 1916.

Timeline 24-1

1969: Minister of Indian Affairs Jean Chretien tables the "White Paper."

1971: The Inuit Tapirisat is formed.

1976: The Inuit Tapirisat puts forward its first proposal for Nunavut.

1979: The Inuit of Baker Lake put forward their first land claim proposal.

1982: A plebiscite is held in which the division of the Northwest Territories is approved.

1987: The Iqaluit Agreement is signed by Inuit from the west and east.

1999:
On February 15, Nunavut holds its first election.

On April 1, Nunavut is officially born.

The elected candidates, called M.L.A.s, included 18 men and one woman. In 1997, showing how willing the Inuit are to at least entertain issues of equity unheard of in the rest of Canada, the people of Nunavut held a plebiscite concerning whether each riding would have both a male and a female M.L.A. It had some support, losing only by 2,662–1,978.

Interestingly, four of the M.L.A.s were non-Inuit, slightly more than their percentage of the population. Jack Anawak has expressed his concern about the future of non-Inuit in Nunavut:

Because of the articles in the Nunavut Land Claim there's a feeling of unfairness for people who are not Inuit and who have made this place their home . . . I think there has to be some recognition of people who have made this their home and grown up here. Right now there is no mechanism to give that cognition. Something has to be put in place to acknowledge that . . .

Of the many challenges that the leaders of Nunavut face, this is one that many people from outside Nunavut will be looking at closely.

KEY TERMS

Inuit Tapirisat
Jay's Treaty

CONTENT QUESTIONS

1. Why was Nahnebahwequay not allowed to buy land in 1857?
2. How did the federal government take authority away from the traditional sachems of the Iroquois?
3. What are the terms of the Nunavut agreement?
4. What percentage of the population of Nunavut is Inuit?
5. What is unusual about how the Legislative Assembly of Nunavut is composed?

 WEBLINKS

www.carc.org/pubs/v21no1/nunavut2
Discusses the Nunavut Political Accord.

www.nunatsiaq.com/archives/nunavut 990228/nvt9021901.html
February 18, 1999 edition of Nunatsiaq News "Lookout Canada—Nunavut's coming," regarding the first vote in Nunavut.

npc.nunavut.ca/eng/nunavut
The official Web site for Nunavut.

afn.ca
The Assembly of First Nations is the leading political body for status Indians in Canada.

UNDOING THE PAST

A REASON TO HOPE: ALKALI LAKE, POUNDMAKER'S LODGE, AND THE NECHI INSTITUTE

The Native battle against alcohol began to turn around during the 1970s. The major hot spot for the turnaround was in the area of Alberta and the interior of British Columbia. We can start this story with Alkali Lake.

Alkali Lake

Alkali Lake is a community of the Shuswap, or Secwepemc people. Their tough battle with alcohol is said to have begun when their hereditary chief, Sxoxomic, died in 1940, after decades of his tough anti-alcohol leadership. He had developed a policy of imposing harsh penalties on anyone who was found drinking on the reserve. The federal and provincial legal systems, somewhat ironically, lent alcoholism a hand by giving Natives equal rights in access to alcohol. In 1951, the Indian Act was amended so that it was legal for Status Indians to drink alcohol in licensed bars. A British Columbia provincial law passed in 1962 allowed Status Indians to purchase alcohol outside of bars. By the end of that decade, Section 94 of the Indian Act had been successfully challenged in the *Regina v Drybones* case. Joseph Drybones, a Dene, had been charged under 94(b) for being intoxicated in a hotel bar in Yellowknife, Northwest Territories, on April 8, 1967. As 94(b) differed significantly from the territorial Liquor Ordinance, Drybones's lawyers argued that this contravened the 1960

Canadian Bill of Rights. They won the case in 1969, liberalizing alcohol-related laws concerning Status Indians across the country.

Another factor that helped earn Alkali Lake the local nickname of "Alcohol Lake" is the influence of the nearby Williams Lake residential school. Throughout the 1950s and 1960s, Native children at that school were sexually and physically abused. (A priest was convicted in 1989.) Alcohol was a way of trying to escape that pain.

By the late 1960s, Alkali Lake existed in an alcoholic haze. Although alcohol could not be purchased legally on the reserve, taxis and buses brought in a great supply, and there were always the local makers of homebrew. Drinking parties lasted several days, women and children were beaten and raped, people died due to alcohol and alcohol-related incidents. Francis Johnson described the following recurring incident of his childhood:

> Many times our parents left us children alone when they went to town. When they went in the bar, we would spend hours waiting in the truck, not knowing when they would be back. Many times we went to bed hungry and without knowing when our parents would get back. (York 1990:178)

The turnaround began in 1972 and it began with one family, the Chelseas. Phyllis Chelsea stopped at her mother's to pick up her seven-year-old daughter but the girl refused to go, saying "You and Daddy drink too much" (York 1990:179). Phyllis Chelsea poured her bottle of liquor down the sink, becoming sober from that day on, the first in her community to walk down that path. A strong sense of family would also help others, later, to walk that path (Johnson and Johnson 1993:228–9).

A few months later, Phyllis's husband, Andrew, joined her on the road to recovery. He saw a group of children with bruised faces walking to school after their parents had been drinking all night. When he asked them whether they had had anything to eat that morning, and they replied "no," he decided to stop drinking. The place on the road where he saw the children became a sacred place to him. He would revisit it to remind himself why he had quit drinking.

He was elected chief in 1973 and quickly took action against the local bootleggers, arranging a sting operation with the local R.C.M.P., and banning from the reserve a bus driver who made runs carrying thousands of dollars of alcohol. His wife, Phyllis, became the welfare supervisor and arranged to have welfare cheques replaced with food and clothing vouchers.

The next big step came from the community, which developed a supportive series of Alcoholics Anonymous-style "Alcoholism Awareness" meetings. And when people went away to treatment centres, they received a constant flow of cards and letters and the community painted and repaired their houses.

In 1985, more than a thousand Native people and addiction counsellors from Canada and the United States came to Alkali Lake to attend an international conference on alcohol abuse. That same year they made a video entitled *The Honour of All: The Alkali Lake Story*, which has since been used effectively to teach other Native communities that such a change is possible. By 1988, three quarters of the band members (in a community of over 400) had completed an alcohol treatment program. By 1989, more than 90% of band members were sober.

Spiritual revival played a very important role. When members of the community of Alkali Lake began on their path to conquer the negative effects of alcohol, there was almost no practice of traditional spiritual ceremonies. With the help of Shuswap Elders from other communities, reviving spiritual practices such as the sweat lodge, sweetgrass, and pipe ceremonies played a key role in the rehabilitation of the community. A 1992 study of the success of Alkali Lake's fight with alcohol, conducted by Jean and Fred Johnson, counsellors in their drug and alcohol programs, demonstrated this. When the people were asked "What significant event or thing caused you to want to be sober?," 31% responded "spiritual support." When asked "What have been the most effective factors in your after-care programs?," 34% also answered "spiritual support" (Johnson and Johnson 1993:229).

The effectiveness of traditional spiritual ceremonies and a consequent strengthening of cultural identity in helping Native people fight alcohol, of course, is not confined to Alkali Lake. A 1995 study sponsored by the Department of the Solicitor General of Canada and researched by the Nechi Institute and KAS Corporation Limited found similar stories of personal rehabilitation. Twenty Native people studied who had come into serious conflict with the law and served time in Canadian penal institutions had subsequently turned their lives around using traditional cultural means. In the words of one of these former prisoners:

> What helped me into sobriety was the spiritual part this program offered—the Sweat Lodge and the sweetgrass and the stories the Elder used to share with me. Some stories I already heard from my late grandfather. I was amazed those stories were even over here [in prison]. . .[T]hat brought back a lot of strength with me again. I grew up as a little spiritual person and bringing that back to me was welcoming. It hit home. In a spirituality sense, I knew now that I found myself. This is me and I knew then, too, that I will never drink again. (Solicitor General of Canada, 1995)

This change was also made possible through the development in the area of Native-run alcohol treatment centres such as Poundmaker's Lodge (named after Pitikwahanpiwiyin or Poundmaker, a Plains Cree leader of the nineteenth century), and the Hobbema Centre in the early 1970s, both in Alberta. They were the first such institutions that were run by Natives. Their success rate soon surpassed comparable institutions that were run and staffed by non-Natives.

What the people running these centres quickly found was that they needed Native people with special training as alcohol and drug counsellors if they were going to continue to succeed in their programs. This need would begin to be met when, on October 15, 1974, the Nechi Institute was incorporated as a non-profit society. It would provide the first Addictions Diploma in Alberta. The founding principles of the Nechi Institute are that:

1. Native alcohol and drug abusers can be most effectively counselled and rehabilitated by our Native people.

2. Native people can best manage and direct their own community programs and businesses.

3. Native people will research the most effective methods of dealing with community problems (i.e., employee assistance).

Since its inception, the Nechi Institute has trained over 1,500 people. It currently shares its facilities (which include training rooms, a gymnasium, a large ceremonial room, three sweat lodges, and residences for 44 training program participants and 54 treatment clients) with Poundmaker's Lodge and has over 30 staff members.

TAKING OVER THE SCHOOLS

In September 1970, after a month-long sit-in by around 300 people, Blue Quills (situated on the Saddle Lake Reserve, in northeast Alberta) changed from being a residential school

BOX 25-1   **A Montagnais Elder Talks About Young People and Education**

Julienne Malec, a Montagnais Elder in the community of Natashquan, actively promotes the inclusion of Montagnais culture in the local school. She believes:

> [c]ulture has to be taught like other school subjects. Otherwise, how will the children remain Innuat? Both cultures must be passed on for the

well-being of young people, so that we can communicate with them . . . Ten years ago, suicide was unknown here. Now, not a year goes by without a young person killing himself. I don't know why they do it, but perhaps if they felt more strongly that they were Innuat, proud of their culture, they would feel better.

(which it had been since 1931) to the first Native-run school in Canada. It marked an important beginning in Native education in Canada, the beginning of Native control over their own education. In 1973, the National Indian Brotherhood produced a document, entitled *Indian Control of Indian Education*, which set forth a plan for the gradual takeover of Native education by the parents and local Native communities. It was later accepted by the federal government and adopted as official educational policy.

The change can be documented by the numbers. By 1980 there were well over 100 band-operated schools. Ten years later there were about 300. In 1975–76, only 2,842 of the 71,817 on-reserve Indian children enrolled in schools went to band-operated schools, roughly 5% (Frideres 1998:153). By 1989–90, their numbers were 34,674 of 88,158, slightly less than 40% (ibid.). During that same period, the number of children in federally run, on-reserve schools declined sharply (around 18,000) while provincially run schools where Natives could attend decreased slightly.

A number of positive statistics go along with that development. The enrollment rate of school-age (i.e., 4 to 18), on-reserve Natives rose about 8%, from 81% to 90.2% from 1975–76 (Frideres 1998:155). Likewise, over the same years, the number remaining until grade 12 or 13 of consecutive schooling leaped ahead, from 15.8% to 41.6% (Frideres 1998:158). Similarly, the number of Native students in high school, as a percentage of total school enrollment, rose from 17.1% to 22.4%, from 1975–76 to 1990–91 (Frideres 1998:159).

The Challenge of Native Post-Secondary Education

There has been a similar rise in the number of Native students involved with post-secondary education. For example, from 1975–76 to 1990–91, the number of Native students enrolled in university climbed from 2,071 to about 23,000 (Frideres 1998:159). However, there are some real problems occurring at the post-secondary level, as Frideres points out in the following:

> Today [1995] 40,000 Aboriginals are enrolled in post-secondary educational institutions. Of these about 9 percent graduate, compared to a graduation rate of well over 18 percent for non-Aboriginals. Clearly, an Aboriginal student's chances of finishing university are still quite small. For individuals having attended university, non-Indians are about 2.4 times as likely as Indians to earn a degree. (Frideres 1998:165)

BOX 25-2   Yellowquill College Philosophy

The Dakota-Ojibway Tribal Council believes that education of Native people is both the right and responsibility of Native people as they are capable of determining their own educational needs. Education and training are seen as an integral part of the process of Indian self-government and economic and social development. Native people have the leadership and knowledge needed to implement and maintain an effective post-secondary institution.

Mission Statement

Yellowquill College, a First Nation place of LEARNING, provides culturally sensitive EDUCATION and TRAINING for ADULTS and ABORIGINAL COMMUNITIES.

Goals and Objectives

The overall goal of Yellowquill College is to provide educational and training opportunities which are uniquely suited to the aspirations of Aboriginal people in Manitoba. In order to meet this goal, the College must provide each student with the opportunity to assess his/her abilities, to determine his/her career or occupational goal, and to plan a course of study which will provide him/her with the necessary skills and knowledge to attain that goal.

General Goals

1. To provide an environment which allows for all types of learning to occur.

2. To provide education and training that accepts and promotes the adult learner's cultural differences.

3. To provide curriculum and uniquely designed programs based upon identified adult and aboriginal community needs.

Source: http://www2.portage.net/~quill/philos.html.

Native students, then, are having difficulties adapting to post-secondary institutions. One solution that has been suggested to address this problem is Native-run colleges and universities. There are institutions called "tribal colleges" that exist in the United States. Although they operate under less secure funding formulas than do most other post-secondary institutions in the United States, enrollment figures suggest that they are where Native students increasingly want to go. From 1990 to 1996, enrollment at the 31 tribal colleges (two of which are in Canada: Red Crow community college in Alberta and Saskatchewan Indian Federated College in Saskatchewan) went up 62% (to about 25,000), a figure that is more than 10 times the figure of 1982 (2,100), while in mainstream colleges the rate for the same six-year period was only 36% (Matthews 1999:3).

In Canada, many leading Native educators are critical of the possibilities that non-Native post-secondary institutions can provide a suitable education. Doctor Vivian Ayoungman, a prominent Blackfoot educator in Canada, states the following in her words to the "Proceedings of the Standing Senate Committee on Social Affairs, Science, Technology: Subcommittee on Post-Secondary Education" (1997):

It is our opinion that after more than 100 years of ignoring its obligations, Canada and its post-secondary institutions are no longer in a moral position to affirm that they will eventually do the right thing. (Ayoungman 1997)

Credentials and accreditation concerning who can teach Native courses and what those courses should contain are currently sore spots for educators with views similar to those of Ayoungman and Don Fiddler. He is the executive director of the En'owkin Centre in the interior of British Columbia. It is a reasonably successful, Native-run educational institute that offers courses in the Okanagan language, as well as providing Adult Basic Education, pre-college, and university transfer programs. For funding and accreditation purposes it is affiliated with Okanagan University College. It is not on par with colleges or university colleges in British Columbia. His sense of frustration with that situation, with the system as it is, even with the successes, can be seen in the following:

> What we are saying, when we talk about accreditation of those issues, is that we have the expertise. In our communities throughout North America, we have many scholars who have already been educated in mainstream universities and have recognized that if we wish to pursue aboriginal education we need to take radical alternatives . . . . We are talking about the freedom to develop education that is particular to our own people and whose direction may differ very widely from what is commonly called education. (Fiddler 1997)

Elders in Post-Secondary Education

Most Native post-secondary educators work in non-Native institutions and have been trying to find ways in which they can reach out to Native students. One of the most innovative ways is the use of Elders. What is an Elder? The following definitions are useful in establishing this important concept:

> A label given to men or women who, recognized by others, possess knowledge of Aboriginal stories, values, and the history of communities and nations. (Draft proposal, *The Ontario Curriculum*, Grades 11 and 12, Native Studies, January 1999, p.69)

> Elders are repositories of cultural and philosophical knowledge and are the transmitters of such information. (Medicine 1987:142)

BOX 25-3   **Ray Peter: Elder-in-Residence**

Ray Peter (Qwul Shi Mut) is Elder-in-Residence at the Nanaimo Campus of Malaspina University-College in British Columbia. He aptly demonstrates what being an Elder means:

> In the past Ray has worked at the Victoria Friendship Centre, the Native Heritage Centre in Duncan, as well as driving [a] truck, logging, and various other seasonal labours. Ray also heads a Tzinqwa Dance Group out of Duncan, and we can all attest to his beautiful singing voice.

Ray actively participates in his culture and traditions, and never lets us forget that while he is an Elder, he is continually learning as well.

As well as working at Malaspina, Ray teaches the Hul Qami? Num language at John Barsby Secondary School in Nanaimo and has been working within the district for the last five years.

Source: www.mala.bc.ca/www/discover/firstnat/elders.htm.

[Elders are] those people who have earned the respect of their own community and who are looked upon as Elders in their own society. (Mark, cited in Medicine 1987:146)

Taken together, then, we can say that, for purposes of education, Elders are people who:

1. have significant wisdom in areas of traditional aboriginal knowledge
2. are recognized as having that wisdom by their community, their Nation
3. have the capacity to transmit this knowledge to others

WHAT ROLES SHOULD ELDERS PLAY?

It is vitally important that Elders as leaders in post-secondary education are not decorative, not symbolic, but are deeply entrenched in the workings of the post-secondary institution. Two ways in which this is done are programs of Elders-in-Residence and Visiting Elders. Some institutions, particularly those with a significant percentage of Native students and with a number of Native stream programs, have both. Others, with a lower percentage of Native students and fewer programs, opt for just the latter status. A good example of the former is Lakehead University in Thunder Bay in northwestern Ontario, deep in the traditional country of the Ojibwa or Anishinabe people. Lakehead has an Elders-in-Residence Program, a Visiting Humanities Fellowship in Native Philosophy, an Annual Elders Conference, and Elder/Healing Circles.

How much that type of program can involve the Elder-in-Residence can be seen in the following description of some of the work done by Louise Underwood (Thulih-wul-wut), Elder-in-Residence, Cowichan Campus, Malaspina University-College. In addition to her close connection with the Child and Youth Care–First Nations Diploma program, she

> also is a resource on subjects of First Nations cultural practices, traditions, and protocol to faculty and staff. Louise has taken a lead in directing cultural events, hosting guests and other visiting Elders. Louise has provided a link between Malaspina University-College and First Nations organizations and assists in building the vision of cultural and Elder participation [into a] university-college setting. (www.mala.bc.ca/www/discover/firstnat/elders.htm)

The University of Ottawa, while only having an estimated 100 Native students, runs a Visiting Elders program through its Aboriginal Resource Centre. During the 1998–1999 academic year, the university had eight Elders come in from various First Nations for periods of a few days. The stated goal of the program is ". . . to provide aboriginal students with support and also to educate non-aboriginal people in an effort to promote respect and awareness of aboriginal culture" (Heartfield 1998).

Visiting Elders programs are available at a number of community colleges, particularly those, such as Georgian College in Ontario, that have Native students at a number of different campuses.

TAKING BACK THE CHILDREN

The Spallumcheen Story

Spallumcheen, a Secwepemc or Shuswap community, is one that was particularly hard hit by the Sixties Scoop. It would be little exaggeration to say that they almost lost an entire generation to overzealous, non-Native social workers in the 1960s. Imagine the impact of losing 50 children in one year from a community of about 300, of having a social worker rent a bus one weekend to take away 38 of their children, to be deposited among non-Native Mormon families in southeastern British Columbia and the United States.

This story turned around in 1979 when the band council passed a by-law that seems to have been modelled after the Indian Child Welfare Act in the United States. It proposed the takeover of their own child welfare from the British Columbia Ministry of Children and Families. The by-law reflected the community's recognition of and support for the traditional role of the extended family. They proposed that if a child had to be taken away from its home that the child be placed with the following priorities of placement applied:

1) a parent

2) a member of the extended family living on the reserve

3) a member of the extended family living on another reserve, although not a reserve to the Indian Band

4) a member of the extended family living off the reserve

5) an Indian living on a reserve

6) an Indian living off a reserve

7) a non-Indian living off the reserve

Remarkably, the minister of the Department of Indian Affairs approved this by-law. The success of this policy was soon evident. They reduced the number of children taken into care and the children that were taking from their homes were increasingly kept within the social circle of the community. The path was not an easy one. They still had to fight for recognition of their rights. And they pretty much stood alone in what they were able to achieve. It wasn't until the 1990s that other Aboriginal communities in British Columbia were able to introduce similar plans.

In 1998, there was a high-profile court case in which members of the Spallumcheen Band Council had to fight to protect their authority over children who belonged to the band. At that time they were responsible for 25 children in care. The case involved a complicated story. A girl was born to a young Spallumcheen woman on October 27, 1996. The mother, who felt unable to take care of her child at that time, asked a non-Native couple to act as foster parents. The agreement was formalized through the provincial ministry, as the child had not been registered as a member of the band. When she was registered in 1998, the responsibility for her welfare passed to the band. Initially, the band was content to leave the child with the foster parents but entered into an agreement with them that would eventually see the child reunited with her mother. It would involve an increasing number of parental visits, initially supervised.

In the spring of 1998, the relationship between the foster parents and the band began to deteriorate. In June, the band council decided that the girl should be placed with her mother's sister living off the reserve. The foster parents did not have access to the child, so they applied to the court for access and also applied for custody. They wanted a ruling that said that the by-law was discriminatory in not allowing them to adopt the child. The court case was picked up by the British Columbia media, which, rather than clarifying, muddied the waters. According to Judge L.P. Williamson, who presided over the case, the press coverage ". . .disclose[d] an apparent lack of verisimilitude and could be interpreted as reinforcing negative stereotypes of Native peoples. Certainly there are blatant errors."

BOX 25-4	It's How a Foster Family Works

In an article in an aboriginal newspaper, Ted Dellaire, a Native living in the Edmonton area, spoke about how his family treats Native children they take into foster care in their home:

We are all related as Native people. We never identify the kids as foster kids because it has such a negative connotation to it. Within the circle, we are all the same . . . (Burle 1999)

The band admitted it had been too abrupt in taking the child from the non-Native foster home, but felt that the foster parents' antagonism to the band would become apparent to the child, which would not be in the child's best interests. The judge ruled in favour of the band council, reaffirming the authority of their child welfare by-law.

XOLHMI:LH FAMILY AND CHILD CARE SERVICES

A real success story as a Native-run child care agency is Xolhmi:lh (pronounced roughly hoth-meeth) Family and Child Care Services of the Stó:lo Nation. Xolhmi:lh means "the special relationship of caring, respect, and love that exists between a caregiver and a child" (Fournier and Crey 1997:233). The agency was first formed in 1994 and then achieved a breakthrough deal in 1997 in which aboriginal families of a nation living inside Stó:lo traditional territory could choose to be served by them rather than the B.C. Ministry for Children and Families. It is currently responsible for child protection services for 23 of the 24 Stó:lo First Nations. It runs Ma and Pa Xolhmi:lh foster homes, 60 of which are Native and 40 non-Native; three group homes for high-risk teens and youths; a repatriation program; a wide variety of preventative and remedial programs, ranging from camps for children, parenting education, and sweat lodges; and it has a connection with street kids with Xolhmi:lh Reconnect, which acts as a liaison between the youth and non-Native institutions and agents (e.g., social workers, school staff, and probation officers). A lot of the agency's positive, non-judgmental approach can be seen in the following, which comes from its Web site:

> Have you ever felt your family was falling apart and you have been close to harming your child? Have you ever wanted to reach out for help because you have harmed your child but are afraid of the consequences? Do you know someone who is needing help because children in the home are not safe but they don't know how to get this help?

Native Individuals 25-1

Andrew and Phyllis Chelsea: Shuswap couple who spearheaded the Alkali Lake community's successful fight against alcohol.

Joseph Drybones: Dene man whose court case liberalized the liquor laws concerning Status Indians.

Timeline 25-1

1951: The Indian Act was changed to allow provincial child welfare agencies to deal with Status Indians.

1978: Indian Child Welfare Act is passed in the United States.

1979: The Secwepemc, or Shuswap, community of Spallumcheen passes a by-law taking responsibility for child welfare away from the province.

1981: Dakota Ojibway Child and Family Services becomes the first Native-run child welfare agency.

1994: Xolhmi:lh Family and Child Care Services is formed.

Initiatives such as this are appearing in Native communities across the country. They bring hope that children will not be lost to their people. These initiatives also bring innovations that might inspire non-Native communities and urban centres to find new ways to "rescue" their own children.

KEY TERMS

Elder
hereditary chief
xolhmi:lh (Stó:lo)

CONTENT QUESTIONS

1. What is the Nechi Institute?
2. What has played a significant role in the rehabilitation of Native alcoholics at Alkali Lake and elsewhere?
3. What roles do Elders play in post-secondary education?
4. What did the Spallumcheen band do to change child welfare in its community?
5. What services are provided by Xolhmi:lh Family and Child Care Services among the Stó:lo?

  WEBLINKS

Alcohol Programs

www.nechi.com/hisover.html
A history of the Nechi Institute.

www.sqc.qc.ca/EPub/AboCor/eAPC11CA/eAPC11CA
"Healing, Spirit and Recovery: Factors Associated with Successful Integration," 1995 Solicitor General Canada, put together by the Nechi Institute and KAS Corporation Limitied, a study of Natives formerly in jail who successfully made it back into society.

Education

http://fleming0.fleminc.on.ca/ssr/nec/necinfoa.htm
Native Education Council, Sir Sandford Fleming College, Terms of Reference on the
Role of Elders at Sir Sandford Fleming.

www.ankn.uaf.edu/elders.html
Alaska Native Knowledge Network Web site.

www.georgian.org/online/native.htm
Native Education Department. Student and Community Services. Georgian College. On
Elders and their role at Georgian College.

www.lakeheadu.ca/~firstnation/main.html
On Elders and their role at Lakehead University.

www.mala.bc.ca/www/discover/firstnat/elders.htm
Malaspina University-College Web site "First Nations Studies: Malaspina University-
College, Our Elders." On Elders and their role at Malaspina University-College.

www.sasked.gov.sk.ca/docs/native10/invit.htl
Meadow Lake Tribal Council Web site: "The Invitation of the Elders. On Elders and
education.

www.parlgc.ca/english/senate/con-e/educ-e/06evb-e.htm
Ayoungman, Vivan and Fiddler, Don (as quoted in) 1997 Proceedings of the Standing
Committee on Social Affairs. Science, Technology: Subcommittee on Post-Secondary
Education in Canada, February 11, 1997 (Internet).

www2.portage.net/~quill/philos.html
Web site for Yellowquill College, a Native-run post-secondary institution.

Child Welfare

www.courts.gov.bc.ca/jdb%2Dtx/sc/98/17/s98%2D1771.txt
The 1998 Spallumcheen trial.

hicks.valleynet.bc.ca/~connect/Ch...lhmilh%20Family%20and%20Child%care.htm

www.fvconnect.bc.ca/Chillliwack/fi...nations/
Stolo%20Xolhmilh%20RECONNECT.htm
Web site for the Xolhmi:lh Family and Child Care Services of the Stó:lo Nation.

Glossary

Note on Languages

Both authors of this book have the strongly held belief that in order for non-Natives to be able to understand Native culture and Native people, they should learn at least a few words from the languages, in part because they have no equivalent terms in English or French. The words presented here have equal value to the more technical English terms in the comprehension of the material of this textbook.

Aboriginal rights A good sense of what aboriginal rights are and how they are interpreted comes from Dickason:

> As originally used, "aboriginal rights" referred only to land; in 1972 it was defined as "those property rights which inure to Native peoples by virtue of their occupation upon certain lands from time immemorial." Today, most Native speakers use the term to include rights to self-determination and self-government. (Dickason 1997:366)

Ahayuda A Zuni word for sacred wooden carvings that represent spirits associated with war. They are carved in ceremony every year. The Zuni people have had a good deal of success in retrieving the Ahayuda from museums and private collections.

Algon(qu/k)ian The largest Native language family in Canada. It includes Mi'kmaq, Maliseet, Innu, Attikamek, Cree, Delaware, Ojibwe, Blackfoot, Piegan, and Kainai. The word is based on "Algonquin" (possibly derived from a Maliseet term meaning "they are relatives or allies"), which only refers to one group.

Angajuqqaq An Inuktitut term for a relatively hierarchical leader, one who has the capacity to give orders to another.

Anishinabe An Ojibwe term for themselves, often translated as "real people" or "original people."

Annen-en A Huron/Wendat word meaning "my mother." It could be used to address or refer to both one's biological mother and her sister(s).

Annuities Small, yearly payments that came with treaties.

Âtalohkâna A Cree term referring to stories about events supposed to have taken place at a time when the world was being transformed into what it is today.

Atha(b/p)aska A Woods Cree word usually translated as "[where] there are plants one after the other" or as "there are reeds here and there," referring to the lake of that name. From that word is derived **Athapaskan,** which refers to languages spoken by the Dene peoples.

Atlatl A Nahuatl or Aztec word referring to the spearthrower, a device that creates an extension of the arm, thus enabling the person using the device to throw the spear harder and farther than would otherwise be possible.

Awokanak A Cree word referring typically to domesticated animals, which came to be translated as "slaves" when referring to Dene peoples the Cree were fighting in the eighteenth century.

Band In Dickason's words, interpreting the legal definition of "band" as set down in the Indian Act: "According to the Act, a band is a body of Amerindians for whom the government has set aside lands for their common use and benefit; or which has been declared a band by the governor-in-council for the purposes of the Act" (Dickason 1997:259).

This legal entity differs from the anthropological definition of a band, referring to a socio-political unit in traditional cultures. (See use of the terms *microband* and *macroband* in the text).

Kottak supplied the following typical anthropological definition of the term "band": "Basic unit of social organization among foragers [i.e., those that live by hunting and gathering]. A band includes fewer than 100 people; it often splits up seasonally" (Kottak 2000:501).

Bilateral An anthropological term referring to: "[a] system in which kinship ties are calculated equally through both sexes: mother and father, sister and brother, daughter and son, and so on" (Kottak 2000:501).

Bitterroot This plant (*Lewisia rediviva*) has a pink or white flower, short stems, and a starchy root that looks like a forked radish, is sweet (and edible) in the spring, but becomes bitter by the summer.

Camas The word for this plant (*Camassia quamash*) comes from a Nootka word "chamas", meaning "sweet." The Camas is a member of the lily family and has a large, edible underground bulb, narrow leaves, purplish flowers, and long stems (up to 90 cm).

Category 1 According to the James Bay and Northern Quebec Agreement, this category of land (amounting to 5,543 square kilometres) was kept in Cree possession.

Category 2 According to the James Bay and Northern Quebec Agreement, on this category of land (amounting to 62,160 square kilometres) the Cree had exclusive rights to hunt, fish, and trap.

Category 3 According to the James Bay and Northern Quebec Agreement, this category of land, by far the greatest amount, was surrendered by the Cree but would have special consideration in terms of their traditional activities.

Clovis points Fluted or grooved spear points that were used for hunting big game from roughly 11,600 to 10,200 years ago. These spear points have been found from the extreme north to the extreme south of the Americas.

Cognates Words or parts of words that sound alike, have similar meaning, and ultimately come from the same word (e.g., *chant*, en*chant*ment and in*cant*ation in English and *chant*er in French, ultimately derived from

the Latin *cantare,* a form of the verb "to sing").

(The) Confrontation A mythologized encounter between a non-Native official (typically an R.C.M.P. officer) and a Native who is "in trouble with the law." The non-Native triumphs through shear heroism, typically without the use of arms.

Copper A copper shield (from copper traditionally mined in Alaska) that bears a personal name and is given away in a potlatch ceremony as a highly valued item.

Dene A term in Athapaskan languages meaning "people." Often the names that Athapaskan-speaking First Nations give themselves have some form of this word in them. This includes the following from the text:

Dunne-za	"Real People," the Beaver
Kawcho*dinneh*	"Hare Big People," the Hare (term given to them by other Athapaskan speakers)
K'ashogo*tine*	"Willow Big People," the term used by the Hare to refer to themselves
Sahtú *Dene*	"Bear Lake People"
Thlingcha-*dinneh*	"Dog Side People," Dogrib term for themselves

Dialect A version of a language, differing somewhat in pronunciation (i.e., accent), in grammar, or in words used in other versions of the language.

Dkonwewnini An Ojibwe term for police officer, meaning "a man who captures, grabs, or seizes something living."

Elder This term is used to refer to Native people recognized as having grown to wisdom over a relatively long life. Typically this growth to wisdom has been nurtured by areas of traditional aboriginal knowledge.

Enfranchisement This term refers to losing the status of being legally "Indian." In some ways it is like having a contract one has signed declared no longer legally binding. It was called "enfranchisement" because (prior to 1960 in federal elections) the individual, upon losing Indian status, was then legally enfranchised to vote in elections.

Epicanthic eyefold Driben and Herstein define this feature in the following way: ". . . a fold of skin on the upper eyelids that droops down over one or both corners of the eyes and makes them appear to be almond shaped" (Driben and Herstein 1994:422).

While this feature is not unique to Asia (e.g., it is found among the San (bushmen) of the Kalahari Desert in Africa and among some Native peoples), and not all Asians have this feature, it is associated with "looking Oriental" for many English-speakers.

Gaiwi:yoh A Seneca term meaning "it is a good, great, or beautiful matter." It refers to the teachings that sprang from the visions of the Seneca prophet, Handsome Lake, about the beginning of the nineteenth century. (The ":" after the "i" means that the vowel is long.)

Gayanerengo:wa A Mohawk word meaning "it is a great good," but is typically referred to in English as "the Great Law of Peace." It refers to the story of how the five nations of the Iroquois came together, the rules they set in place, and the teachings that come from both these components.

Guilty See **Naammendaagzid.**

Hereditary chief This is someone whose lineage provides the leader of a particular group. Usually this term is used when speaking about the more hierarchical First Nations, such as the Iroquoians and the peoples of the Northwest Coast.

Hierarchical This refers to a people who have relatively clear distinctions among different ranks or classes of peoples within their society. These distinctions relate to a greater number of privileges of authority and the use or ownership of material and non-material (e.g., songs, dances, or stories) possessions. The opposite of this term is "egalitarian."

Hierarchy of person An Ojibwe pronominal feature in which the morpheme or word part for "you" is always placed before the morpheme for "I" or "we."

Hominids This term refers to the family of primates to which, today, only humans

(e.g., *homo sapiens*) belong. The australopithecines, who lived until about one million years ago, and Neandertal, who lived until about 30,000 years ago, were also hominids.

Hunter's response A physical adaptation of Inuit and other Northern peoples in which the hands warm up quickly after being exposed to the cold.

Ice creepers Pieces of ivory attached to footwear. The ivory is notched to form treads that grip the ice.

Iniskim A Blackfoot term meaning "buffalo stone." It refers to a sacred rock, usually one containing fossils bearing a spiral shell.

Innu An Innu (i.e., Montagnais or Naskapi) word meaning "person." It is used to refer to the people generally. It appears in the words **Mushuau-Innu** ("barren ground person") **Sheshatsiwinnu** ("great inlet person").

Interim agreement An agreement between a government body and a Native group that lasts for a fixed period of time. Sometimes it leads to a more permanent agreement, but that certainly is not always the case.

Inuit Tapirisat An Inuit political group, formed in 1971, that provided the primary push for the development of Nunavut. In Hugh Brody's words, Tapirisat is an Inuktitut word meaning, "literally 'the people's team' or 'collaboration'" (Brody 1987:233).

I(s/h)umataq An Inuktitut term roughly translated as "one who thinks." It refers to a type of egalitarian leader who leads by suggestion rather than by giving orders. In order to understand what the root -**ihuma**- means in Inuktitut, see Jean Briggs' important discussion on the subject (Briggs 1970:358–64).

Íyinnakiikoan A Blackfoot term for police officer. It is derived from the verb stem **yinnaki,** which means "to grab, seize, hold, capture something living" (Franz and Russell 1995:266).

Jay's Treaty This was an agreement, concluded on November 19, 1794, between U.S. Chief Justice John Jay and British Foreign Minister Lord Grenville, in which issues were settled that had not been resolved after the end of the American Revolution in 1783. Some of the issues related to border crossing between what would become Canada and the United States.

Language family A group of languages that have been demonstrated to be related. English, for example, is in the Indo-European language family, related to such diverse languages as French, Russian, Greek, and Hindi.

Language isolate A language that has no known relatives.

Manly hearted woman See **Ninauposkitzipxpe.**

Matrilineal A way of determining kinship following the line of the mother. If, for example, a father belongs to the Bear clan and a mother belongs to the Turtle clan, then their children are of the Turtle clan.

Microblades Small pieces of rock that have been flaked off a rock core and then fashioned to work as tools (e.g., scrapers) or as attachments in other tools (e.g., lances).

Miksísstsiksi This word means "my mothers" in Blackfoot, and refers, collectively, to a person's mother and her sisters.

Moiety Derived from a French term meaning "half," it refers to two social groups that a society is divided into, typically for burial, ritual, and political purposes. These groups can be subdivided into clans.

Morpheme A part of a word that has meaning or grammatical function. For example, in the word "words" there are two morphemes, the noun "word" and the plural marker "-s."

Mothers See **Annen-en** and **Miksísstsiksi.**

Mushuau-Innu An Innu term meaning "barren ground person," referring to Innu peoples who live in the barrens area of Labrador.

Muyine' A Dunne-za or Beaver term meaning "his/her song" and referring to a person's spiritual power or medicine bundle (i.e., collection of sacred items that connect a person with the spiritual).

Myth of native biological helplessness The belief that Native people generally have no physical resistance to alcohol and cannot control how much they drink.

Naammendaagzid An Ojibwe verb meaning "to be considered guilty." This is the closest term in the traditional language to the European legal sense of someone "being guilty."

Na'pi A Blackfoot term meaning "Old Man," referring to the cultural hero of the Blackfoot.

Nimass aksiwin Literally meaning "fish disease," this Cree term refers to mercury poisoning. The Cree use this term because the fish in the East James Bay area have dangerously high amounts of mercury in their system.

Ninauposkitzipxpe This Blackfoot term means "manly hearted woman." It refers to women who take on roles usually associated with men.

Nitapiksisako A Blackfoot term meaning "real meat." It refers to buffalo meat, showing the significance of buffalo to the traditional diet of the Blackfoot.

Notka The standard derivation of the term *Nootka* states that it came from an instruction by the Nuu'chah'nulth to Captain James Cook to "circle around" the area of what is now Nootka Sound.

Nutshimit This Innu word is sometimes translated as "the bush" or "the country" in English. Its significance is hard to translate. A good English translation would also have to incorporate such diverse notions as: "(at) home," "my country," "my homeland," "the cottage," "where I can be myself." Some further sense of this term can be seen in the following East Cree cognates that, with a slightly different spelling, incorporate the same morpheme:

*nuuhchimiiu*iinuu	"inland hunter, trapper" (with -iinuu- "person")
*nuuhchimiiu*nitunkuin	"bush medicine" (with -nitunkuin- "medicine")
*nuuhchimiiu*maakusuu	"s/he smells like the bush"
*nuuhchimiiu*naakusuu	"s/he looks like someone from inland, from the bush.

(Cree School Board 1987:406)

Okan A Piegan word referring to the centre pole of the Sun Dance lodge (the most sacred object of the ritual) and to the Sun Dance itself. In Blackfoot, the cognates are the following:

ookaa: [to] sponsor the primary religious ceremony associated with the Sun Dance

áakookaawa: she [/he] will sponsor a Sun Dance

ookáán: the primary religious ceremony associated with the Sun Dance. (Franz and Russell 1995:168)

-ondech(r)- A Huron noun stem referring to "country" in the physical, social, and spiritual senses of the word.

On,8e n'on,8e (Huron) or **Ongwehon:we** (Mohawk) Loosely translated, this term means "humans who are humans." The Huron term referred to Native peoples and the Mohawk term can be used to refer to Six Nations peoples or Natives in general.

Oolichan (also eulachon, oolakan, or oulakan) This Chinook word has entered the English language and refers to the candlefish (*Thaleichthys pacificus*), a fish related to the smelt. When it goes on its spawning run, this fish is so oily that it can be used to make an oil that was an important food item for Northwest Coast peoples. It got its name "candlefish" because when it is dried, a wick can be stuck in it and the fish can be used as a candle.

Pasa This is a Kwakwaka'kw word for the potlatch. It means "to flatten" and is an exaggerated statement of the effect of all the gifts that will be given to those who are receiving the gifts.

Pass system Introduced in 1885 and lasting until the 1930s, it was a legally questionable practice of not allowing Natives in prairie reserves to leave the reserve without a pass issued by their non-Native farming instructor or Indian Agent.

Pâstâmowin A Cree word referring to stories in which something bad happens after someone breaks the rules.

Patrilineal Reckoning kinship along the husband's or father's line.

Pemmican A Cree word referring to buffalo jerky, made from dried buffalo meat, rendered fat, and saskatoon berries. It was a staple of the fur trade in the eighteenth and nineteenth centuries.

Pine Tree Chiefs A term used to refer to members of the Iroquois Confederacy who take on leadership roles, not because they hold one of the 50 chiefly titles, but solely because they have made a name and role for themselves.

Police officer See **Dkonwewnini** and **Íyinnakiikoan.**

Potlatch Based on a Chinook trade jargon term meaning "to give." Because of the importance of generosity and giveaway in the ceremony, potlatch refers to the most important ceremony of most of the Northwest Coast peoples. It was banned from 1884 to 1951.

Phratries These are like moieties in that they are a way of dividing up society for social, political, and ritual purposes. Typically phratries have clans that belong to them. The eighteenth-century Wyandot of the Windsor/Detroit area had three phratries: Deer, Turtle, and Wolf. Each phratry had a chief and various member clans:

Deer phratry	Deer, Bear, and Snake clans
Turtle phratry	Porcupine, Large Turtle, Striped Turtle, and Prairie Turtle clans
Wolf phratry	Wolf, Hawk, and Sturgeon clans

Public purchase This refers to the government acquiring ownership of land by entering into a treaty or other formal agreement with a Native group.

Reserves Called "reservations" in the United States, these are plots of land reserved to particular Native bands.

Residential schools These were boarding schools of Native students financed by the federal government and run by various churches. Not only did these schools have a lower standard of education than schools intended for non-Native children, but they were also places where a significant number of Native children were abused—physically, emotionally, and sexually.

Restorative justice This is the principle of justice that stresses that the offender, the victim and the general community need to be "healed" or restored to a healthy state. It is in contrast to retributive justice, in which the main idea is that someone gets punished.

Root The central part of a word, the main building block upon which other parts (e.g., prefixes or suffixes) are added. For example, in the word *building, -build-* is the root.

Sachem Derived from an Eastern Algonquian word for "leader" (see **Saqmaw**). This term is often used to refer to the 50 chiefs titles of the League of the Iroquois.

Saqmaw A Mi'kmaw word for "leader." Cognates have entered English as *sachem* and *sagamore.*

Saskatoon Derived from the Cree word "misaskwatomi" (lit. much-wood-berry) referring to the service or saskatoon berry, which is used in the making of pemmican and is used on its own as a sacrament in the Sun Dance.

Sheshatshit This is an Innu word meaning "Great Inlet," and is the name of the community in Labrador known in English as Northwest River.

Sheshatsiwinnu This is an Innu word meaning "Great Inlet Person."

Sixties scoop This term, coined by writer Patrick Johnston, refers to the taking of thousands of Native children from their families, communities, and peoples during the 1960s to early 1980s.

Slave See **Awokanak.**

Suyitapis This Piegan word meaning "Underwater People" refers to the spirit figures who live in the water and who gave the Piegan people sacred images and items.

Sweatlodge This word is used to refer to a traditional ceremony in which water is poured on hot rocks producing steam that makes people sweat. An Elder or some other spiritual leader usually directs people in terms of what they are experiencing. The sweatlodge itself was traditionally a small curved structure covered with hides, but now may be covered by anything that keeps the steam in.

Sweetgrass ceremony The sweetgrass ceremony, also called "smudging," involves the burning of sweetgrass with a ceremonial bathing in the smoke. The practice, often done at sunrise or at the beginning of important meetings or events, ritually cleanses the people so that they can be pure in what they think and do. It can also be used to invoke the spirits.

Tipâcimôwina A Cree word typically translated as stories, news, historical narratives or personal experiences

Totem An Ojibwe word for "clan." It has come to be associated in English with the Northwest Coast poles, which have carved symbols of clans or moieties.

Tun(n/r)it A gentle, seal-hunting people in traditional Inuit stories, thought to be the Dorset people.

Umiak An Inuit word referring to a large sealskin boat that could hold 12 people and could be over nine metres in length.

U'mista A Kwakwaka'wakw word meaning "special return." It is used in the name of the U'mista Cultural Centre, constructed in 1980 to receive the special return of the sacred potlatch items.

War Measures Act This is an act that the federal government can invoke to suspend the usual rights of the people in order to serve the needs of war or a special emergency.

Weir A trap, typically constructed out of poles or rocks, that gathers fish together in one spot where they can be easily speared.

Xolhmi:lh A Stó:lo or Halkomelem word referring to the special relationship of caring, respect, and love that exists between a caregiver and a child.

Yandarachrio A seventeenth-century Huron word meaning "it is great in existence"; referring to a people as the original or First Nation in a particular place.

References

Abel, Kerry. 1993. *Drum Songs: Glimpses of Dene History.* Montreal: McGill-Queen's University Press.

Barbeau, Marius. 1915. *Huron and Wyandot Mythology.* Ottawa, Dept. of Mines, Geological Survey, Memoir 80.

Barman, Jean. 1986. "Separate and Unequal: Indian and White Girls at All Hallows School, 1884–1920." In J. Barman, Y. Hébert, and D. McCaskill. *Indian Education in Canada.* Vol. 1 *The Legacy*, pp.110–127.

Barman, Jean, Yvonne Hébert, and Don McCaskill. 1986. "The Legacy of the Past: An Overview." In *Indian Education in Canada,* Vol. 1, *The Legacy.* Vancouver: Univ. of British Columbia Press, pp.1–22.

Benton-Banai, Edward. 1988. *The Mishomis Book: The Voice of the Ojibway.* Saint Paul, Minn.: Red School House.

Bergman, Brian. 1996. "Dark Days for the Inuit." *Maclean's*, March 4, p.67.

Blondin, George. 1996. "When the World Was New: Stories of the Sahtú Dene." In K. Coates and R. Fisher, eds. *Out of the Background: Readings on Canadian Native History*, 2nd ed. Toronto: Copp Clark, pp.245–278.

Briggs, Jean. 1970. *Never in Anger: Portrait of an Eskimo Family.* Cambridge, Mass: Harvard University Press.

Brody, Hugh. 1987. *Living Arctic: Hunters of the Canadian North.* Vancouver: Douglas & McIntyre.

Burch, Ernest S., Jr. 1995. "The Caribou Inuit." In R.B. Morrison and C.R. Wilson, eds., *Native Peoples: The Canadian Experience*, pp.115–142.

Burke, Marie. 1999. "It's how a foster family works." *Alberta Sweetgrass*, Oct. 11.

Carl, Julie. 1999. "Ipperwash conviction, sentence appealed." *London Free Press*, Sept. 15.

Chaumel, Gilles, and Germaine Mesténapéo. 1996. "The Four Seasons of Julienne." *Rencontre*, vol.17, no.2, pp.4–5.

Clarkson, Betty. 1967. *Credit Valley Gateway: The Story of Port Credit.* Toronto: Univ. of Toronto Press.

de Coccola, Raymond, and Paul King. 1986. *The Incredible Eskimo: Life among the Barren Land Eskimo.* Surrey, B.C.: Hancock House.

Comeau, Pauline. 1993. *Elijah: No Ordinary Hero.* Vancouver: Douglas & McIntyre.

Comeau, Pauline, and Santin Aldo. *The First Canadians: A Profile of Canada's Native People Today.* Toronto: James Lorimer.

Copway, George (Kah-ge-ga-gah-bowh). 1972. *The Traditional History and Characteristic Sketches of the Ojibway* (orig. 1850). Toronto: Coles Publishing Ltd.

Cree School Board. 1987. *Cree Lexicon: Eastern James Bay Dialects.* Baie-de-la-Poste, Mistassini Lake.

Crowe, Keith. 1974. *A History of the Original Peoples of Northern Canada.* Montreal, Arctic Institute of North America. McGill-Queen's Univ. Press.

Cruikshank, Julie. 1990. *Life Lived Like a Story: Life Stories of Three Yukon Native Elders.* Vancouver: Univ. of British Columbia Press.

Curnoe, Greg. 1996. *Deeds/Nations.* London: London Chapter, Ontario Archaeology Society.

Day, Gordon M. 1978. "Western Abenaki." In *Handbook of North American Indians.* Vol. 15, *Northeast*, B.G. Trigger, ed. Washington: Smithsonian Institute, pp.148–159.

——. 1994. *Western Abenaki Dictionary: volume 1: Abenaki-English.* Hull, Canadian Museum of Civilization.

Dempsey, Hugh. 1972. *Crowfoot, Chief of the Blackfeet.* Norman: Univ. of Oklahoma Press.

——. 1995. "The Blackfoot Indians." In R.B. Morrison and C.R. Wilson, eds., *Native Peoples: The Canadian Experience,* 2nd ed. Toronto: McClelland & Stewart, pp.381–413.

Dickason, Olive. 1992. *Canada's First Nations: A History of Founding Peoples from Earliest Times.* Toronto: Oxford University Press.

Douglas, Mark, n.d. *Mnjikaning: The Fish Fence at the Narrows* pamphlet.

Driben, Paul, and Harvey Herstein. 1994. *Portrait of Humankind: An Introduction to Human Biology and Prehistoric Cultures.* Scarborough: Prentice-Hall Canada.

Ellis, Douglas C. 1995. *Âtalohkâna nêsta Tipâcimôwina: Cree Legends and Narratives from the West Coast of James Bay.* Winnipeg: Univ. of Manitoba Press.

Fairley, Margaret, ed. 1960. *The Selected Writings of William Lyon Mackenzie, 1824–1837.* Toronto: Oxford University Press.

FH1693 ca1693. *French-Huron dictionary.* ms., Archive Séminaire de Québec.

FH1697 ca1697. *French-Huron dictionary.* ms., John Carter Brown Library, Brown University, Providence, Rhode Island.

Fisher, Robin. 1977. *Contact and Conflict: Indian-European Relations in British Columbia, 1774–1890.* Vancouver: Univ. of British Columbia Press.

Fournier, Suzanne, and Ernie Crey. 1997. *Stolen from Our Embrace: The Abduction of First Nations Children and the Restoration of Aboriginal Communities.* Vancouver: Douglas & McIntyre.

Francis, Daniel. 1992. *The Imaginary Indian: The Image of the Indian in Canadian Culture.* Vancouver: Arsenal Pulp Press.

Franz, Donald G., and Norma Jean Russell. 1995. *Blackfoot Dictionary of Stems, Roots and Affixes.* 2nd ed., Toronto: Univ. of Toronto Press.

Frideres, James S. 1998. *Aboriginal Peoples in Canada: Contemporary Conflicts,* 5th ed. Scarborough: Prentice Hall Allyn and Bacon.

Friesen, John W. *Rediscovering the First Nations of Canada.* Calgary: Detselig Enterprises Ltd.

Green, Gordon. 1998. "Community Sentencing and Mediation in Aboriginal Communities." *Manitoba Law Journal.*

Harris, Michael. 1986. *Justice Denied: The Law versus Donald Marshall.* Toronto: Macmillan.

Heartfield, Kate. 1998. "Aboriginal elder visits U of O campus." *Fulcrum Online* Issue 59-09, October (*www.thefulcrum.com/98-99/59_09_05.html*).

Helm, June, and Vital Thomas. 1991. "The Bewitched Pale Man from 'Tales of the Dogribs.'" Orig. published in 1966, in Peter Nabokov, ed., *Native American Testimony: A Chronicle of Indian-White Relations from Prophecy to the Present, 1492–1992.* Toronto: Penguin Books, pp.47–48.

Hodge, F. W., ed. 1971. *Handbook of Indians of Canada* (orig. 1913). Toronto, Coles Pub. Ltd.

——. 1971. *Indian Treaties and Surrenders* 3 vols., (orig. 1891 and 1912). Toronto: Coles Pub. Ltd.

Jaenen, Cornelius J. 1986. "Education for Francization: The Case of New France in the Seventeenth Century." In Barman, Hébert & McCaskill, *Indian Education,* Vol. 1, *The Legacy,* pp.45–63

Jenness, Diamond. 1932. *The Indians of Canada.* Ottawa: King's Printer.

Johnston, Basil. 1991. "One Generation from Extinction." W.H. New, ed. In *Native Writers and Canadian Writing,* Vancouver: Univ. of B.C. Press, pp.10–15.

Johnson, Joyce, and Fred Johnson. 1993. "Community Development, Sobriety and After-Care at Alkali Lake Band." *The Path to Healing: Report on the National Round Table on Aboriginal Health and Social Issues.* Royal Commission on Aboriginal Peoples, Ottawa.

Kehoe, Alice. 1992. *North American Indians: A Comprehensive Account.* Englewood Cliffs: Prentice Hall.

Kelsay, Isabel Thompson. 1984. *Joseph Brant 1743–1807: Man of Two Worlds.* Syracuse: Syracuse University Press.

Kipp, Darrell Robes. 1996. "Blackfoot." In *Encyclopedia of North American Indians.* Frederick E. Hoxie, ed. Boston/New York: Houghton Mifflin Co., pp.75–76.

Knockwood, Isabelle. 1992. *Out of the Depths: The Experiences of Mi'kmaw Children at the Indian Residential School at Shubenacadie, Nova Scotia.* Lockeport, NS: Roseway Publishing.

Kottak, Conrad Phillip. 2000. *Cultural Anthropology,* 8th ed., Boston: McGraw-Hill.

Kulchyski, Peter, ed. 1994. *Unjust Relations: Aboriginal Rights in Canadian Courts.* Toronto: Oxford Univ. Press.

MacGregor, Roy. 1989. *Chief: The Fearless Vision of Billy Diamond.* Toronto: Penguin Books.

Maclean, John. 1970. *The Indians of Canada: Their Manners and Customs* (orig. 1889). Toronto: Coles Publishing.

Manuel, George, and Michael Posluns. 1974. *The Fourth World: An Indian Reality.* Don Mills: Collier-Macmillan Canada.

Matas, Robert. 1999. "He carried the torch for the Nisga'a." *The Globe and Mail,* Dec. 14, 1999, A18.

Matthiason, John S. 1992. *Living on the Land: Change among the Inuit of Baffin Island.* Peterborough: Broadview Press.

——. 1995. "The Maritime Inuit: Life on the Edge," in Morrison and Wilson, pp.78–114.

May, Philip A. 1998. "The Epidemiology of Alcohol Abuse among American Indians: Mythical and Real Properties" (orig. 1994). *Native American Voices: A Reader.* Susan Lobo and Steve Talbot, eds., Don Mills: Longman, pp.388–399.

Mercredi, Ovide, and Mary Ellen Turpel. 1993. *In the Rapids: Navigating the Future of First Nations.* Toronto: Penguin Books.

Miller, J.R. 1996. *Shingwauk's Vision: A History of Native Residential Schools.* Toronto: Univ. of Toronto Press.

Miller, Virginia P. 1995. "The Micmac: A Maritime Woodland Group." In Morrison and Wilson, pp.347–374.

Milloy, John. 1988. *The Plains Cree: Trade, Diplomacy and War, 1790–1870.* Winnipeg: Univ. of Manitoba Press.

Monture-Angus Patricia. 1995. *Thunder in My Soul: A Mohawk Woman Speaks.* Halifax: Fernwood Publishing.

Moran, Bridget. 1996. "Justa: A First Nations Leader" ("Dakelhne butsowhudilhulh'un"). In Coates and Fisher, eds., *Out of the Background: Readings on Canadian Native History.* Toronto: Copp Clark Ltd., pp.297–309.

Morrison, R. Bruce, and C. Roderick Wilson, eds. 1995. *Native Peoples: The Canadian Experience.* 2nd ed. Toronto: McClelland & Stewart.

Nabokov, Peter, ed. 1991. *Native American Testimony: A Chronicle of Indian-White Relations from Prophecy to the Present, 1492–1992.* Toronto: Penguin Books Canada.

Nihmey, John. 1998. *Fireworks and Folly: How We Killed Minnie Sutherland.* Ottawa: Phillip Diamond Books.

Niquay, Marie-Louise. 1996. "Kokomino Judith Kawiasiketct, Preserving the Atikamekw Soul." *Rencontre.* vol. 17, no. 2, pp.8–9.

O'Hara, Jane. 1999. "Trade Secrets." *Maclean's,* October 18, pp.20–29.

O'Meara, John. 1996. *Delaware-English/English-Delaware Dictionary.* Toronto: Univ. of Toronto Press.

Ontario Ministry of Education. 1999. *Draft Proposal, The Ontario Curriculum, Grades 11 and 12, Native Studies.* January 1999.

Ormsby, Mary. 2000. "Nolan waits, others wonder: Could racism be blamed for lack of NHL offers?" *Toronto Star.*

Pelletier, Wilfred, and Ted Poole. 1973. *No Foreign Land: The Biography of a North American Indian.* New York: Pantheon Books.

Plainspeak. 2000. *The Métis Hunt for Justice: A Plainspeak of the Powley Decision.* Pamphlet.

Potier, Pierre. 1920. *The Fifteenth Report of the Bureau of Archives for the Province of Ontario.* Toronto: C.W. James.

Priest, Lisa. 1989. *Conspiracy of Silence.* Toronto: McClelland & Stewart.

Rajotte, Freda. 1998. *First Nations Faith and Ecology.* Toronto: Anglican Book Centre.

Rhodes, Richard. 1985. *Eastern Ojibwa-Chippewa-Ottawa Dictionary.* Amsterdam: Mouton Pub.

Richardson, Boyce. 1991. *Strangers Devour the Land.* Vancouver: Douglas & McIntyre.

Roberts, Julian, and Carol LaPrairie. 1997. "Raising Some Questions about Sentencing Circles." *Criminal Law Quarterly.*

Rudes, Blair. 1987. *Tuscarora Roots, Stems and Particles: Towards a Dictionary of Tuscarora.* Memoir 3. Winnipeg, Algonquian and Iroquoian Linguistics.

Sarazin, Greg. 1989. "220 Years of Broken Promises." In Boyce Richardson, ed., *Drumbeat: Anger and Renewal in Indian Country.* Toronto: Summerhill Press. pp.139–166.

Schmalz, Peter S. 1991. *The Ojibwa of Southern Ontario*. Toronto: Univ. of Toronto Press.

Sioui, Georges E. 1999. *Huron-Wendat: The Heritage of the Circle*. Trans. by Jane Brierley, Vancouver: Univ. of British Columbia Press.

Smith, Donald. 1979. "Wabakinine," *Dictionary of Canadian Biography,* vol. 4, Toronto: Univ. of Toronto Press, pp.755–756.

——. 1987. *Sacred Feathers: The Reverend Peter Jones (Kahkewaquonaby) and the Mississauga Indians,* Toronto: Univ. of Toronto Press.

Smith, James G. E. 1981. "Chipewyan." In *The Handbook of North American Indians*. Vol. 6. *Subarctic.* Washington: Smithsonian Institute, pp.271–284.

Spielmann, Roger. 1998. *You're So Fat: Exploring Ojibwe Discourse*. Toronto: Univ. of Toronto Press.

Spradley, James P. 1969. *Guests Never Leave Hungry: The Autobiography of James Sewid: A Kwakiutl Indian.* New Haven and London: Yale Univ. Press.

Steckley, John L. 1987. "Burning Cloud." In *Indian Record.*

——. 1993. "Leaders, Origins, Customs and Unity: Traditional Huron Notions of Country," *Arch. Notes* 4:18–21. 1997.

——. "Aboriginal Peoples." in Paul Angelini, ed., *Our Society: Human Diversity in Canada.* Toronto: ITP Nelson, pp.131–158.

Stevenson, Marc. 1997. *Inuit Whalers and Cultural Persistence: Structure in Cumberland Sound and Central Inuit Social Organization.* Toronto: Oxford Univ. Press.

Stewart, Hilary, ed. 1987. *The Adventures and Sufferings of John R. Jewitt, Captive of Maquinna.* Vancouver: Douglas & McIntyre.

Stymeist, David. 1977. *Ethnics and Indians: Social Relations in a Northwestern Ontario Town.* Toronto: Peter Martin Associates.

Sutton, Catharine. 1860. An Indian Woman's Audience with Queen Victoria. *Brantford Courier,* August 1860.

——. 1862. "Is There Hope for the Indians?" *Christian Guardian,* May 28.

Talbot, Francis X. S.J. 1956. *Saint Among the Hurons: The Life of Jean de Brébeuf.* New York: Image Books.

Teichroeb, Ruth. 1998. *Flowers on My Grave: How an Ojibwa Boy's Death Helped Break the Silence on Child Abuse.* Toronto: Harper Collins.

Thwaites, Reuben G., Jr. 1959. *The Jesuit Relations and Allied Documents.* New York: Pageant Book Company.

Tooker, Elisabeth. 1978. "The League of the Iroquois: Its History, Politics, and Rituals." *Handbook of North American Indians*. Vol. 15, *Northeast.* Washington, Smithsonian Institute, pp.418–441.

Upton, L.F.S. 1979. *Micmacs and Colonists: Indian-White Relations in the Maritimes, 1713–1867.* Vancouver: Univ. of British Columbia Press.

Wadden, Marie. 1996. *Nitassinan: The Innu Struggle to Reclaim Their Homeland.* Vancouver: Douglas & McIntyre.

Wallace, Bruce. 1999. "Move Over: A new generation of younger natives is coming into its own—and flexing its powerful muscles," *Maclean's,* Sept. 27, vol. 112, no. 39, pp.20–30.

Watkins, Mel, ed. 1977. *Dene Nation: The Colony Within.* Toronto: Univ. of Toronto Press.

Whitehead, Paul C., and Michael J. Hayes. 1998. *The Insanity of Alcohol: Social Problems in Canadian First Nations Communities.* Toronto: Canadian Scholars' Press.

Woodbury, Hanni, Reg Henry, and Harry Webster. 1992. *Concerning the League: The Iroquois League Tradition as Dictated in Onondaga by John Arthur Gibson.* Memoir 9. Winnipeg, Algonquian and Iroquoian Linguistics.

Wright, James V. 1995. *A History of the Native People of Canada, Volume 1 (10,000–1,000 B.C.)* Ottawa, Canadian Museum of Civilization.

Wright, Ronald. 1988. "Beyond Words." *Saturday Night,* April, vol. 103, no.4, pp.38–48.

York, Geoffrey. 1990. *The Dispossessed: Life and Death in Native Canada.* London: Vintage Books.

aci.mta.ca/projects/Courage_Remembered/native veterans.html ("Native Veterans." In *Courage Remembered: The world wars through Canadian Eyes.*)

http://kafka.uvic.ca/~vipirg/SISIS/Ipperwash/tapr2997.html ("OPP Officer Kenneth Deane Found Guilty in 1995 Murder of Dudley George." From *Anti-Racist Action Toronto.*)

www.aboriginalvoices.com/1999/06-03/robinson.html

www.escape.ca/~miko/articles/nativeamerican-soldiers ("In Honour of Our Aboriginal Veterans." From *Mesanagyun* [Indian and Métis Friendship Centre Newspaper] Winnipeg, November 1996.)

www.fvconnect.bc.ca/Chilliwack/fi...nations/Stolo%20Xolhmilh%20Reconnect.htm (Web site for the Xolmi:lh Family and Child Care Services of the Stó:lo Nation.)

www.inac.gc.ca/news/may98/1-9854.html ("Agreement-in-Principle Reached on Return of Former Camp Ipperwash Lands," DIAND news release, June 18, 1998.)

www.mala.bc.ca/www/discover/firstnat/elders.htm ("First Nations Studies: Malaspina University-College, Our Elders.")

www.nechi.com/hisover.html (Nechi Institute)

www.nnsl.com/nunavut99/2nun.html ("A role being defined." Includes quote from Jack Anawak.)

www.parl.gc.ca/english/senate/com-e/educ-e/06mn-e.htm (Proceedings of the Standing Senate Committee on Social Affairs, Science, Technology; Subcommittee on Post-Secondary Education February 11, 1997; Vivian Ayoungman and Don Fiddler quoted.)

www.sgc.gc.ca/epub/Abocor/eAPC11CA/eAPC11CA ("Healing, Spirit and Recovery: Factors Associated with Successful Integration," 1995, Solicitor General Canada.)

www.sgc.gc.ca/epub/Abocor/e199805/e199805.htm (Clairmont, Don and Rick Linden. 1998. "Developing & Evaluating Justice Projects in Aboriginal Communities: A Review of the Literature," APC 16 CA 1998, Solicitor General Canada.)

www.uccm.on.ca/Archive/April1999/web2.8.5.htm (Tribal Council News, April 1999, vol. 2, issue 8.)

www.uccm.on.ca/Archive/February1999/feature3.htm (Tribal Council News, February 1999, vol.2, issue 6.)

www.uccm.on.ca/Archive/June%201999/feature2.htm (Tribal Council News, June 1999, vol. 2, issue 10.)

www.usask.ca/nativelaw/jah_ross.html (Rupert Ross, "Aboriginal community healing in action: the Hollow Water approach.")

www.web.apc.org/~ara/spoint/sppr1.htm ("Stoney Point trials begin, 43 charges withdrawn by the Crown," Stoney Point press release, Oct. 22, 1996.)

www.web.net/~acaa/info-leaflets/04.html ("Justice for the Stoney Point People." *Anti-Colonial Action Alliance,* Info-Leaflet #4.)

www2.portage.net/~quill/philos.html (Web site for Yellowquill College.)

Index